THE
NEW ENTREPRENEURS
OF *EUROPE* AND *ASIA*

THE
NEW ENTREPRENEURS
OF EUROPE AND ASIA

*Patterns of Business Development
in Russia, Eastern Europe
and China*

Victoria E. Bonnell and Thomas B. Gold

Editors

M.E. Sharpe

Armonk, New York
London, England

Copyright © 2002 by M. E. Sharpe, Inc.

Library of Congress Cataloging-in-Publication Data

New entrepreneurs of Europe and Asia : patterns of business development in Russia,
Eastern Europe, and China / [edited] by Victoria E. Bonnell and Thomas B. Gold.
   p. cm.
     Includes bibliographical references and index.
   ISBN 0-7656-0775-1 (alk. paper); ISBN 0-7656-0776-x (pbk alk.)
       1. Entrepreneurship—Russia (Federation)—Congresses. 2. Entrepreneurship—
Europe, Eastern—Congresses. 3. Entrepreneurship—China—Congress. I. Bonnell,
Victoria E. II. Gold, Thomas B.

HB615.E458 2001
338′.04′094—dc21   2001032825

Printed in the United States of America

Contents

Part Two. Patterns of Entrepreneurialism

About the Editors and Contributors

Elżbieta W. Benson is a doctoral candidate in the department of sociology at the University of California, Berkeley. She is currently completing a dissertation on the emergence of a market for business information in contemporary Poland.

Victoria E. Bonnell is director of the Institute of Slavic, East European, and Eurasian Studies and professor of sociology at the University of California, Berkeley. Her recent books include *Russia in the New Century: Stability or Disorder?* (2000), coedited with George Breslauer; *Beyond the Cultural Turn: New Directions in the Study of Society and Culture* (1999), coedited with Lynn Hunt; and *Iconography of Power: Soviet Political Posters Under Lenin and Stalin* (1997). She is currently working on a study of the symbols, rituals, and mythologies of Russian national identity after communism.

Theodore P. Gerber is assistant professor of sociology at the University of Arizona. His research examines patterns of social stratification, migration, and political behavior in Soviet and post-Soviet Russia. He has published articles on these topics in *American Journal of Sociology, Social Forces, Sociology of Education, Social Science Research, International Journal of Sociology, Europe-Asia Studies, Post-Soviet Affairs,* and several edited volumes.

Bruce Gilley is a contributing editor at the *Far Eastern Economic Review* in Hong Kong and a visiting scholar at the Graduate School of Journalism, University of California, Berkeley. He has published two books on China, *Tiger on the Brink: Jiang Zemin and China's New Elite* (1998) and *Model Rebels: The Rise and Fall of China's Richest Village* (2001). His current research interests cover China's politics and economy.

Thomas B. Gold is associate professor of sociology at the University of California, Berkeley, where he has also served as the chair of the Center for Chinese Studies. He is executive director of the Inter-University Program for Chinese Language Studies at Tsinghua University in Beijing and coeditor of the forthcoming volume *Social Networks in China: Institutions, Culture, and The Changing Nature of Guanxi*. His current projects include books on China's private business sector and on Taiwan's political transformation.

Doug Guthrie is associate professor of sociology at New York University. He is author of *Dragon in a Three-Piece Suit: The Emergence of Capitalism in China* (1999) and coeditor of the forthcoming volume *Social Networks in China: Institutions, Culture, and the Changing Nature of Guanxi*. In addition to holding a faculty position at NYU, he is director of global activities, Office of the Provost, at NYU. He received his Ph.D. from the University of California, Berkeley.

Lyn Jeffery has a Ph.D. in cultural anthropology from the University of California, Santa Cruz and is currently at the Institute for the Future in Menlo Park. She is coeditor of the volume *China Urban: Ethnographies of Contemporary Culture* (2001).

György Lengyel is professor and chair of the Department of Sociology and Social Policy at the Budapest University of Economic Sciences and Public Administration (BUESPA). His main research interests are in economic sociology and in the sociology of elites. He has recently published a book, *Elites after State Socialism*, with John Higley (2000).

Gerald A. McDermott is assistant professor of multinational management in the Wharton School at the University of Pennsylvania. He received his Ph.D. in political science in 1998 from the Massachusetts Institute of Technology. His publications include *Embedded Politics: Industrial Networks and Institution Building in Post-Communism* (forthcoming); "Entrepreneurship and Privatization in Central Europe: The Tenuous Balance Between Destruction and Creation," *Academy of Management Review*, with Andrew Spicer and Bruce Kogut (July 2000); and "The Network Properties of Corporate Governance and Industrial Restructuring: A Post-Socialist Lesson," *Industrial and Corporate Change*, with Aydin Hayri (1998). His major areas of interest are political economy, institutional creation in emerging democracies, governance, and organizational learning, and he is currently analyzing the impact of domestic institutions and networks on attracting foreign investment in high value-added sectors in Latin America and East-Central Europe.

Margaret M. Pearson is associate professor of government and politics at the University of Maryland, College Park. She has written two books on China, *Joint Ventures in the People's Republic of China* (1991) and *China's New Business Elite* (1997). Most recently she has published several articles on China's entry into the World Trade Organization.

Vadim Radaev is vice-rector and chair of economic sociology at the State University–Higher School of Economics in Moscow. He received his Ph.D. in economics from Moscow State University. His publications include *Economic Sociology* (1997, in Russian), *Formation of New Russian Markets* (1998, in Russian), and articles in *International Sociology, Economic and Industrial Democracy, Problems of Economic Transition, International Journal of Sociology*, and elsewhere. His research focuses on economic sociology, the sociology of entrepreneurship, and the informal economy.

Ákos Róna-Tas is associate professor of sociology at the University of California, San Diego. His main research interest is the economic sociology of the post-communist transformation. He is the author of *Great Surprise of the Small Transformation: The Demise of Communism and the Rise of the Private Sector in Hungary* (1997) and articles in various journals, such as *American Journal of Sociology, Theory and Society*, and *East European Politics and Societies*, as well as chapters in edited volumes.

Vadim Volkov is associate professor of sociology, Department of Political Science and Sociology, The European University at St. Petersburg. He is a graduate of the Faculty of Economics of Leningrad State University and received the M.Phil. and Ph.D. in sociology from University of Cambridge, UK. Upon return to Russia in 1995, he became head of the department of political science and sociology at the European University at St. Petersburg. In 1998–2000 he was a Social Science Research Council-MacArthur Foundation postdoctoral fellow in the Program on Peace and International Security in a Changing World. Volkov has recently completed a book on the relationship between organized violence and market-building with a focus on post-Soviet Russia.

Alexei Yurchak is assistant professor of anthropology at University of California, Berkeley. His interests include linguistic anthropology, discourse analysis, theories of ideology, subjectivity, gender, socialism, and postsocialism. He has published articles in American, British, and Russian journals and collections, including "Privatize Your Name: Symbolic Work in a Post-Soviet Linguistic Market" (*Journal of Sociolinguistics*, 2000); "Gagarin and the Rave Kids: Transforming Power, Identity, and Aesthetics in the Post-Soviet Night Life" (1999, in *Consuming Russia: Popular Culture, Sex, and Society Since Gorbachev*, ed. Adele Barker); and "The Cynical Reason of Late Socialism: Power, Pretense and the Anekdot" (*Public Culture*, 1997). Currently he is completing a book that analyzes the cultural dynamic of late socialism through the lives of the "last Soviet generation," and he is working on a documentary film on the same topic.

Acknowledgments

This volume grew out of a Sawyer Seminar on Entrepreneurs, Entrepreneurialism, and Democracy in Communist and Post-Communist Societies. The seminar, which was funded by the Andrew W. Mellon Foundation, met biweekly at the University of California at Berkeley during the 1998–1999 academic year. In May 2000, we organized a follow-up international conference that brought together twelve scholars and a number of distinguished guests. All the papers from the conference are included in this volume.

Both the seminar and conference were stimulating and informative, and we are very grateful to all the participants. We were especially pleased to be able to bring together such a diverse group of scholars from so many different departments and professional schools in the United States, Europe, and Asia. Funding for the Sawyer Seminar made it possible to support two graduate students—Jay Dautcher and Jane Zavisca—and one postdoctoral scholar, Paula Gianoplus. We would especially like to thank Harriet Zuckerman, senior vice president of the Andrew W. Mellon Foundation, for her support and encouragement.

Jane Zavisca provided invaluable assistance during the entire project. Her editorial and formatting skills were indispensable when we prepared this manuscript for publication. We also appreciate the assistance we received from Laura Henry, Denise Monczewski, and Ken Foster in getting the chapters to press. As always, Dr. Edward Walker made many intellectual and practical contributions to the project. Finally, we would like to thank the Institute of Slavic, East European, and Eurasian Studies at the University of California at Berkeley and its executive director, Dr. Barbara Voytek, and the Center for Chinese Studies for facilitating the project in many ways, big and small.

Introduction

Victoria E. Bonnell and Thomas B. Gold

A command-administrative economy took form in the Soviet Union during the late 1920s and 1930s and was adopted by the communist countries in Europe and Asia after World War II. Its core features included a centralized plan, suppression of private business, and limited engagement with the global economy. This economic system began to undergo some fundamental changes in the 1970s and 1980s, first in the People's Republic of China (PRC) and Eastern Europe, then in the Soviet Union. Tentative moves in the direction of privatization and marketization rapidly gathered momentum, leading to a period of experimentation with economic models and methods of all types from around the world, a process that the Chinese Communists refer to as "crossing the river by feeling for the stones."

Although the timing and context varied from region to region and from country to country, the introduction of economic reforms in communist societies invariably took place at the initiative of party leaders and some segments of the party elites. Everywhere the process of reform involved official sanction for practices already under way in the second or informal sector.[1] As the reforms proceeded, states had to play a desperate game of catch-up, trying to create laws, regulations, and agencies to govern the new actors and behaviors in a dynamic and often unpredictable environment.

In each case, economic reforms had far-reaching repercussions. New social groups—including entrepreneurs—made an appearance, altering the social structure and stratification system of these societies. New forms of economic behavior—including entrepreneurialism—became more prevalent, partially or fully replacing the state planning system with decision making by individual firms or consortiums of firms operating in a global context and responsive to market factors. These developments, taken together, have had a profound impact on communist and postcommunist societies, reshaping institutions, ideologies, and patterns of collective behavior.

Within a few years, economic reforms, in combination with other factors, had destabilized the communist systems of Eastern Europe and the former Soviet Union. Between 1989 and 1991, communist regimes in these regions collapsed, culminating in the disintegration of the USSR in December 1991. China, the first country to introduce systemic reforms, took a different path. In the PRC, the Communist Party has remained hegemonic in the political sphere while continuing to promote private enterprise and a market economy.

This volume takes as its point of departure the remarkable constellation of changes in the transitional economies of Russia, Eastern Europe, and China during the last decades of the twentieth century. An international team of scholars from many disciplines focuses on two general themes: (1) Who are the new entrepreneurs of Europe and Asia? (2) What are their business practices? The twelve contributors have undertaken original research on a country or set of countries in an effort to analyze the profiles of entrepreneurs and the patterns of entrepreneurialism in communist and postcommunist societies.

Entrepreneurs and Entrepreneurialism

What do we mean by the term "entrepreneur"? As we discovered during a year-long Sawyer Seminar conducted at the University of California at Berkeley in 1998–1999, there is no consensus about the meaning of the term.[2] The concept of the "entrepreneur" was transformed after World War II, when America committed itself to fostering capitalist industrialization in less developed countries, and policy makers and scholars placed a great deal of importance on the role of individuals who could carry the burden of starting and managing new enterprises.[3] The "new states," as they were called, were charged with creating and maintaining—with American assistance—an environment conducive to the emergence and growth of entrepreneurs.

The post–World War II literature on development tried to explain why entrepreneurs flourished in some situations but not in others. One explanation emphasized the attributes of entrepreneurs. Accounts based on the work of Max Weber focused on the role of ideas and practices derived from "the Protestant ethic" or its functional equivalent. Others, influenced by the work of Joseph Schumpeter, conceived of the entrepreneur as a heroic individual, a pioneer, an innovator, a visionary, and a risk taker.[4] In the postwar era, many observers considered societies with "collective" orientations inhospitable to the development of entrepreneurs, who thrived in an environment that emphasized individualism and opportunity. The subsequent developmental success of several collective-oriented East Asian economies—Japan and the Four Tigers—prompted a reevaluation of these claims.

Beginning in the 1970s, the problem of identifying and profiling the entrepreneur again drew the attention of scholars. Doug Guthrie presents an overview of these studies in Chapter 7.[5] We can discern two major trends in this literature, which was generated, for the most part, by business schools. The first, focusing on the psychological characteristics of the entrepreneur, showed a good deal of continuity with earlier studies. A different body of literature, however, took a more structural approach, investigating the position of firms in relation to the state as well as to foreign investment, and the impact of this position on entrepreneurial activity.

Notwithstanding many innovative studies in recent years, the term "entrepreneur" remains highly contested. The contributors to this volume have worked with a broad definition that encompasses men and women (or collectivities) who organize and direct businesses, assuming risk for the sake of profit. Although the boundaries are sometimes murky, the term thus refers to individuals or groups who carry out certain necessary tasks, including perception of economic opportunities, assembling the financial and material resources and inputs for economic innovation, recruiting personnel, and dealing with suppliers, purchasers, and the government.[6] In their study of Korean entrepreneurs, Jones and Sakong call these the "lenticular" functions because the entrepreneur "is like a lens that focuses the energies of others."[7] Thus the "entrepreneur" may not be an individual—instead, it may be a family, group, or network. As chapters in this volume indicate, rather than hampering the entrepreneur, embeddedness in family and other types of networks frequently facilitates performance of entrepreneurial tasks.

Different typologies of entrepreneurs have arisen for various countries and regions. The most common categories include entrepreneurs in the private sector (including the self-employed, household, or small-scale entrepreneurs, and owners of medium-sized and large firms), entrepreneurs connected to enterprises currently or formerly under state auspices, and entrepreneurs who operate in the context of existing local institutions. Since the situation in Russia, Eastern Europe, and China is currently in flux and the transition from communist economic systems has taken many different forms, the chapters in this volume consider a range of entrepreneurs in all branches of the economy.

When entrepreneurs began to supplement or replace communist managers, they were faced with a novel set of issues and decisions. Operating with some form of private or state-owned assets, their very survival depended on their ability to master the skills of entrepreneurialism. The term "entrepreneurialism" refers to a broad range of business practices, including modes of capital accumulation, investment and marketing strategies, risk taking, innovation, business ethics, contracts and mutual trust, authority relations within firms, and the creation of networks. Entrepreneurialism is generally considered central to the vitality of market institutions, and it has been linked to the establishment of Western democracies.

Until the launching of marketizing reforms, open manifestations of profit-oriented business activity—particularly in the private sector—were effectively circumscribed in communist systems. Scholarly interest in business people and practices in market-oriented communist and postcommunist societies of the 1980s and 1990s is thus a relatively recent phenomenon. The chapters that follow explore an innovative field of inquiry: the impact of entrepreneurs and entrepreneurialism on the direction of social and political change in transitional economies.

Part One. Profiles of Entrepreneurs

Part One focuses on the attributes of entrepreneurs in Russia, Eastern Europe, and China with particular attention to their backgrounds (e.g., party-state apparatus, criminal underground, intellectual, technical, or scientific elite), demographic features, and the firms over which they preside. The authors pay close attention to the collective biographies of new entrepreneurs on the assumption that their past experiences, education, networks, and career trajectories (sometimes described as forms of capital) are powerful influences, among others, in shaping responses to market reform and the ability to succeed in the world of business.

The volume begins with Theodore P. Gerber's chapter, "Joining the Winners: Self-Employment and Stratification in Post-Soviet Russia." Gerber has assembled data to provide a systematic profile of people who joined the ranks of entrepreneurs (employing the labor of others) and those who have been engaged in individual labor activity (without employees) in Russia between 1991 and 1998. Both groups have benefited, albeit to different extents, from the transition to a market economy. Gerber's investigation of the attributes of the "winners"—their family background and regional context—yields some surprising results. Most importantly, he finds, "In Russia we observe only a weak and brief form of 'power conversion,' since Party membership proved an advantage only in entry to self-employment without employees, the less lucrative form of self-employment, and this effect was only temporary."

Ákos Róna-Tas takes up these issues in his chapter, "The Worm and the Caterpillar: The Small Private Sector in the Czech Republic, Hungary, and Slovakia." In these countries, small-scale private enterprises expanded rapidly in the wake of economic reforms, which raises the question of who these entrepreneurs are and what their role is in the new postcommunist economy. Rona-Tas's comparative research on the entrepreneurs of small businesses in the Czech Republic, Hungary, and Slovakia presents a contrast to Gerber's findings for the Russian case. In Eastern Europe, small-scale entrepreneurship functions, above all, as a type of self-employment undertaken by former employees who turn to individual labor activity as a type of defensive survival mechanism. Thus Róna-Tas argues that most of these small entrepreneurs should be viewed not as "winners" in the economic reform process but as extensions of the household economy (the "worms") with little prospect of becoming owners of medium- or large-size firms (the "caterpillars")." Indeed, Róna-Tas concludes that the proliferation of small private firms in these countries has ominous implications for economic growth, tax collection, labor conditions, environmental protection, and successful competition in a globalized market.

In the third chapter, "The Yu Zuomin Phenomenon: Entrepreneurs and Politics in Rural China," Bruce Gilley presents a detailed portrait of the rural cadre-turned-entrepreneur, Yu Zuomin, and the chaotic and unsettled business climate in Chinese villages that has offered boundless opportunities for a talented entrepreneur to exploit. Gilley provides an account of the ways Yu manipulated political ties in an attempt to set or interpret rules to benefit his own interests and those of his village. For a time, Yu achieved phenomenal success and became a model entrepreneur in the new economy. But eventually the rules changed, the climate changed, the officials changed, and Yu overstepped his bounds and crashed to earth.

Gilley's chapter explores the economic activities of political officials. As members of local village administrations, rural entrepreneurs have come to occupy an important position in the life of the community and perhaps even the nation, a development reminiscent of the 1920s in the USSR, when under the policies of the moderately market-friendly New Economic Program (NEP), prosperous peasants came to dominate many rural soviets. Like their NEP-era counterparts, politically active rural entrepreneurs in contemporary China have clashed with party bosses and central authorities who view their rise to power as a potential threat to communist hegemony.

In the early phases of the economic transitions in Europe and Asia, market-supporting laws have been rudimentary or nonexistent. Under these conditions, private entrepreneurs have been forced to do "business" without the elaborate set of market institutions found in developed capitalist societies. The explosion of market activity, both at home and increasingly through links to the global economy, has compelled communist and postcommunist states to elaborate laws to govern economic activity, which in turn has spawned a cadre of lawyers, law schools, and legal experts. Setting the rules to govern this activity is a social process. Since the unequal distribution of power is fundamental to such a process, it is also highly political.[8]

Of course, enforcing the new laws is another matter. As Vadim Volkov demonstrates in his chapter, "Security and Enforcement as Private Business: The Conversion of Russia's Power Ministries and Its Institutional Consequences," a new business sector arose in postcommunist Russia to provide services for businesses requiring law and rule enforcement, enforcement of contracts, protection of private property, and the collection and dissemination of information. An exodus of state security employees into the private sector was supplemented by recruits from criminal groups who stood ready to meet the demand for protection in a society where the state had lost its former authority, cadres, and coercive capacity. Indeed, during the Yeltsin era, private protection and enforcement replaced illegal activities as the primary source of revenue for criminal groups. Volkov argues that private protection companies have, on balance, been a positive force in the development of a fledgling market economy because they assume functions previously performed by the state.

Elżbieta W. Benson focuses on another new business sector in transitional economies: market research. Her chapter, "The Construction of a Professional Field: Resources, Skills, and Attributes of Founders of the Market Research Sector in Poland, 1989 to 1997," investigates the circumstances that generated Polish information entrepreneurs and a demand for their product. Nearly all of them came to the new business sector with backgrounds in social research, and they rapidly adopted a Western model of market research and professional standards. Market research in Poland (like private protection companies in Russia) has thus become a major new business sector that has privatized functions formerly carried out under government auspices.

In the final chapter of Part One, "Entrepreneurs and Democratization in China's Foreign Sector," Margaret M. Pearson turns our attention to entrepreneurial elites in the foreign sector of China's economy or, more specifically, to managerial elites in joint ventures and in foreign-owned enterprises, a group of not more than 100,000 at the end of 1999. These businesspeople are generally found in Western and Japanese firms, and they command the highest salaries, educational credentials, and status among their peers. Given their position in Chinese society, Pearson asks to what extent and in what ways do these elites embrace democratic political reform. She proceeds from the assumption that, as in earlier times and places, the bourgeoisie has provided strong support for democratization. But circumstances in contemporary China appear to have drawn elite entrepreneurs in the foreign sector in a different direction. Pearson's research points to widespread apoliticism and political passivity among this group, despite the fact that it is in the vanguard of the country's business class.

Part Two. Patterns of Entrepreneurialism

Part Two explores various aspects of entrepreneurial behavior and institutions in transitional societies. In the preexisting command-administrative economies, enterprise managers needed to behave in entrepreneurial ways in order to acquire financial resources and materials for their firms in conditions of chronic shortage and stifling bureaucratism. They also required skill in dealing with party and state officials. As marketization proceeded, state enterprise managers ("Red Directors") had to demonstrate exceptional entrepreneurialism to keep their firms afloat. With state firms subjected to the same hard budget constraints as private firms, their managers had to become risk takers comparable to capitalists in private sector businesses.

Doug Guthrie's chapter, "Entrepreneurial Action in the State Sector: The Economic Decisions of Chinese Managers," demonstrates how these managers must navigate in a complex world of state bureaucrats and foreign investors, and how their practices are, "in many ways, every bit as entrepreneurial as the individuals striking out in the private economy." Like Benson, Guthrie highlights the influence of foreign business practices on new entrepreneurs. He stresses the creativity and innovation of state managers dealing with the new structural conditions and how their actions are "creating the new economy in China."

In a study of Russian entrepreneurial strategies, Vadim Radaev also foregrounds the institutional context in which business is developing during the transition period. His chapter, "Entrepreneurial Strategies and the Structure of Transaction Costs in Russian Business," investigates business practices through the prism of transaction costs: the expenses a firm incurs (e.g., relating to property and resource acquisition, contracts, property rights, information, and advertising) that are not directly part of production. Radaev argues that the structure rather than the level of transaction costs has significant consequences for Russian entrepreneurs who must resort to a variety of tactics and strategies to contend with the shadow and virtual economies, obstacles created by state administrative and regulatory procedures, and the perils of dealing with other firms. To minimize transaction costs, entrepreneurs must rely heavily on a combination of informal networks and private resources (such as those analyzed by Volkov in Chapter 4).

The next two chapters (9 and 10) focus on a common set of questions: under what circumstances are firms created, and under what circumstances do they survive? Gerald A. McDermott's study, "The Embedded Politics of Entrepreneurship and Network Restructuring in East-Central Europe," compares and contrasts entrepreneurial performance in the Czech Republic, Poland, and Hungary. Over the past decade, the Czech Republic has been outpaced by Poland and Hungary in general economic development and specifically in the creation of small- and medium-sized enterprises (SMEs). McDermott's research discloses that the restructuring of sociopolitical networks is a key explanatory factor in the successful creation of SMEs. The restructuring of existing networks, he argues, "will depend largely on both the ability of public actors to become risk sharers and conflict mediators and the ability of the political system to allow public actors to experiment and learn to take on these new roles."

György Lengyel approaches these questions using a somewhat different analytical framework in his chapter, "Social Capital and Entrepreneurial Success: Hungarian Small Enterprises Between 1993 and 1996." Like McDermott, Lengyel emphasizes the importance of networks among entrepreneurs, but he frames his analysis in terms of various forms of capital: social, cultural, and economic. He estimates that two out of three enterprises with fewer than fifty employees survived between 1993 and 1996, and about one out of four expanded. Lengyel's study concludes that social capital and economic capital (market share and the legal form of the enterprise) have considerable influence over the capacity of a firm to survive and prosper, but cultural capital has a weak correlation with these outcomes.

Alexei Yurchak and Lyn Jeffery shift the focus in Chapters 11 and 12 to entrepreneurial techniques. Yurchak's chapter, "Entrepreneurial Governmentality in Postsocialist Russia: A Cultural Investigation of Business Practices," notes that in the 1980s and 1990s Russian entrepreneurs proved remarkably adept at acquiring the knowledge and skills required for private business—a situation Yurchak labels "entrepreneurial governmentality." How did they acquire this under Soviet conditions? Yurchak characterizes the late Soviet state as a hybrid with two distinct but related spheres: the officialized public sphere—with its institutions, laws, and ideologies—and the personalized public sphere. Soviet citizens needed to develop entrepreneurial skills to maneuver their way through the bureaucratic hurdles in their path. Paradoxically, while officially suppressing entrepreneurialism and stifling individual initiative except in the interest of the party-state, the Soviet system—by directing people's efforts into the personalized public sphere—fostered an environment in which entrepreneurial skills thrived. Marketization opened avenues to channel these talents into new directions.

In China, multilevel marketing (MLM), otherwise known as direct sales or network marketing, swept the country in the 1990s, making fortunes for some and engaging many thousands in a scheme that ultimately collapsed. In her chapter, "Marketing Civility, Civilizing the Market: Chinese Multilevel Marketing's Challenge to the State," Lyn Jeffery investigates the "meaning of entrepreneurship and entrepreneurial identity" in China as disclosed by this encounter with MLM. She argues that the entrepreneurial techniques of MLM centered around locally specific networks and involved the creation of new attitudes toward the self, the state, and morality. As a result, "the imperative to develop one's own network gave rise to a potent set of narratives that celebrated the free individual—running his or her own business and no longer dependent upon the state for his or her livelihood—such as 'being your own boss' (*zuo ziji de zhuren*) and 'relying on oneself to support oneself' (*kao ziji yang ziji*)." These appeals and the emphasis on a moral mission rather than mere commodity acquisition as the basis for entrepreneurialism —reminiscent of the ethical underpinnings of Weber's spirit of capitalism— mobilized many people in the scheme until the state moved in to suppress MLM in 1998.

The twelve chapters in this volume investigate a critically important phase in the transition to marketizing and privatizing economies in parts of the world that for many decades actively embraced quite different models for development. With its focus on three regions and six countries (Russia, Hungary, Poland, Slovakia, the Czech Republic, and China), this collection makes it possible to view the emergence of both entrepreneurs and entrepreneurialism in comparative perspective and from both macro and micro levels of analysis. What is most remarkable is that the appearance of new social groups and new business practices has taken place in societies where a powerful partystate attempted for many decades to suppress the impulse for private economic activity and to impose a centralized administration and scientific management. The accounts that follow tell a complex and amazing story of people who have refashioned themselves, often in difficult circumstances, and have begun to create institutions capable of meeting the challenges of the twenty-first century.

Notes

1. "Informal economy" refers to activities in capitalist and socialist economies that skirt the boundary of illegality, are not recorded in state accounts, and escape regulation. This would include what is sometimes referred to as the "underground," "black," or "shadow" economy. "Second economy" means the economy outside the "first" or socialized and planned economy in nonmarket systems. It includes legalized private activity, if it exists. See Thomas B. Gold, "Urban Private Business in China," *Studies in Comparative Communism* 22 (2/3), Summer/Autumn 1989, pp. 187–201; p. 188, and references therein.

2. The Sawyer Seminar, which was supported by the Mellon Foundation, took place between September 1998 and May 1999 under the title "Entrepreneurs, Entrepreneurialism, and Democracy in Communist and Postcommunist Societies."

3. For a literature review, see Mick Moore, "Societies, Polities and Capitalists in Developing Countries: A Literature Survey," *Journal of Development Studies* 33 (3), February 1997, pp. 287–363.

4. Max Weber, *The Protestant Ethic and the Spirit of Capitalism,* trans. Talcott Parsons (New York: Scribner's, 1930); Joseph A. Schumpeter, *The Theory of Economic Development: An Inquiry into Profits, Capital, Credit, Interest, and the Business Cycles,* trans. Redvers Opie (Cambridge: Harvard University Press, 1936).

5. See Chapter 7 below, pp. 162-5.

6. Leroy P. Jones and Il Sakong. *Government, Business, and Entrepreneurship: The Korean Case* (Cambridge: Harvard University Press, 1980), pp. 180–181; Peter Kilby, "Hunting the Heffalump," *Entrepreneurship and Economic Development,* ed. Peter Kilby (New York: Free Press, 1971), pp. 27–28.

7. Jones and Sakong, *Government, Business, and Entrepreneurship,* p. 181.

8. Neil Fligstein, "Markets as Politics: A Sociological View of Market Institutions," *American Sociological Review* 61, 1996, pp. 656–673.

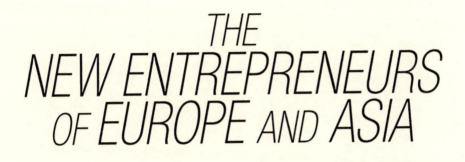

THE
NEW ENTREPRENEURS
OF EUROPE AND ASIA

Part One

Profiles of Entrepreneurs

1

Joining the Winners

Self-Employment and Stratification in Post-Soviet Russia

Theodore P. Gerber

Introduction

Scholars concerned with the social impact of market transition in postsocialist societies have often framed the issue in terms of "winners" and "losers" (e.g., Brainerd 1998; Titma, Tuma, and Silver 1998). This chapter demonstrates that the self-employed can be safely counted among the winners in Russia. Such status applies both to entrepreneurs who form businesses employing others and, more surprisingly, to those who engage in "individual work activity" (*individual'naia trudovaia deiatel'nost'*) without hiring employees. The chapter also shows that employment status, education, age, sex, affiliation with the Communist Party of the Soviet Union (CPSU), family background, and certain characteristics of place-of-residence all influence the chances Russians have of joining the ranks of the self-employed, at least for the period covered by our data, January 1991 to March 1998. While several of these factors operate in a similar way in Russia as they do in developed capitalist societies, others operate in a distinctive manner. This pattern most likely reflects the hybrid socioeconomic and cultural contexts of contemporary Russia and the relative novelty of self-employment as a route to material success.

For most of its history, the Soviet state prohibited private ownership of the means of production. The effective proscription of self-employment deprived the Soviet economy of the dynamism, spontaneity, flexibility, and innovation associated with entrepreneurialism in capitalist economies (Schumpeter 1942 [1975]; Moore 1954; Kornai 1992). In the final years before its collapse in late 1991, the Soviet regime permitted cooperatives to form, in an effort to improve the availability of services and provide a competitive spark to the economy (Jones and Moskoff 1991). But they faced

3

tight restrictions on their size, activities, and property arrangements. The Russian government introduced sweeping market reforms in January 1992, paving the way for self-employment to grow unimpeded in Russia for the first time since the early 1920s.

Russia's post-Soviet reformers have viewed private enterprise as the key to revitalizing the Russian economy (Boycko, Shleifer, and Vishny 1995). Some have argued that a market economy is best built from the ground up— that is, by encouraging the growth of small private enterprises which would compete with large, inefficient state enterprises (Kornai 1990). The burgeoning private sector would soak up the excess labor gradually shed by uncompetitive state enterprises. Small private firms would act as they do in American capitalism, as engines of job creation (Birch 1987).

However, Russian reform policies have focused on privatizing state enterprises rather than developing new private firms. Privatization does not appear to have produced the anticipated benefits, as privatized enterprises have been slow to restructure their workforces and product lines (Blasi, Kroumova, and Kruse 1997). Meanwhile, small entrepreneurship has grown more slowly in Russia compared to East European countries (Aslund 1995, p. 263). All the same, market reforms have brought a considerable number of new private firms to Russia. At the end of 1997, there were 861,100 officially registered "small enterprises" employing roughly 6.5 million workers in the Russian Federation (Goskomstat 1998, pp. 300, 302).[1]

In addition to the owners of these small businesses, we also count among the self-employed those whom the official statistics do not include: the many Russians who have taken up individual work activity without hiring employees. Thus, we define "self-employment" as working for oneself (as opposed to working as a hired or contractual employee), with or without hired employees, as one's *primary* occupation. We limit our attention to nonagricultural self-employment and exclude all workers in the agricultural sector from our data analyses, because employment and self-employment processes typically operate very differently in the agricultural sector (e.g., Loutfi 1991). The stipulation that individual work activity must be the primary work activity distinguishes full-time self-employment from individual work activity that supplements earnings from a main job as a hired employee. We base the distinction on the grounds that the latter type of activity is unlikely to bear the material advantages and levels of freedom and risk typically associated with self-employment.

The self-employed, defined in this fashion, may be not be conceptually identical to the ideal-typical image of "entrepreneurs," which often connotes a spirit of daring, adventure, and innovation. But the self-employed represent the concrete, identifiable social group most likely to approximate that ideal-typical image. Our data do not permit an assessment of how strongly the self-employed adhere to such an "entrepreneurial spirit." But they do permit us to determine whether the self-employed represent a distinct group in terms of their material standing and certain economic attitudes. If they are distinct in these ways, the mechanisms shaping who joins their ranks in contemporary Russia merit study whether or not the self-employed fully fit the bill of "entrepreneurs" by the somewhat intangible criterion of the "entrepreneurial spirit."

The issue of the distinctiveness of the self-employed is most heated in reference to the individually self-employed (those without hired employees).[2] Most would agree that small employers represent a distinctive class. But there has been some dispute over whether the individually self-employed are akin to small entrepreneurs, as our approach implies, or are closer to wage workers in their economic role, incomes, and attitudes. According to Form (1982), in the United States "manual proprietors" (most of whom have no employees) earn more than employees and may be somewhat more politically conservative. In contrast, Hanley (2000) concluded that in three post-communist East European countries, the individually self-employed barely differ from ordinary workers, while the self-employed *with* employees enjoy distinctively high economic status (see also Róna-Tas, Chapter 2 in this volume.)

Gerber and Hout (1998) reported that the self-employed had higher earnings than any other occupational class in Russia from 1991 to 1995, but that study combined those with and without employees into a single category. Those without employees surely constituted the lion's share of the aggregated category, which indirectly suggests that they too had higher earnings than the other classes. But it is also possible that high mean earnings of the aggregated self-employed stemmed entirely from extremely high incomes of employers. Evidently, the proper designation of the individually self-employed in contemporary Russia remains an unresolved empirical issue that must be addressed before proceeding to an analysis of the social factors that enhance or impede Russians' prospects for becoming self-employed.

In fact, the data analyses reported in the first part of this chapter confirm that in Russia the individually self-employed represent a distinct class, with higher levels of income, subjective material satisfaction, and support for market reforms than other Russians. Employers rank even higher on these criteria, though some of the gap between employers and the individually self-employed is attributable to differences in the composition of the two groups. In short, while there are differences in these two forms of self-employment, they both represent relative success in the struggle to adapt to the changed institutional environment of post-communist Russia. We thus gain insight into the emerging mechanisms of social stratification in post-communist Russia by analyzing the factors that increase access to both forms self-employment, considered together and separately—the second empirical task of the chapter.

Who Becomes Self-Employed? Some Orienting Hypotheses

Some studies have analyzed the political and social attitudes of Russian entrepreneurs (Radaev 1994; Wieviorka 1994; Vasilenko, Dulina, and Tokarev 1995). But no study has yet systematically examined the determinants of self-employment during the course of the post-Soviet era. This does not mean that the present analysis starts from scratch. Three bodies of literature suggest useful hypotheses to guide the data analysis: studies of the determinants of self-employment in the United States and other developed capitalist societies, the debate over changes in the stratification order resulting from market transition in current and former state socialist societies, and the growing literature on regional variations in economic conditions in post-Soviet Russia.

Determinants of Self-Employment in Developed Capitalist Countries: Age, Education, Labor Market Position, Sex, and Family Background

For the last decade or so, researchers have devoted considerable attention to the determinants of becoming self-employed in the United States and other developed capitalist societies (Evans and Leighton 1989; Steinmetz and Wright 1989; Loutfi 1991; Carr 1996; Arum 1997; Luber et al. 2000; Arum, Budig, and Grant 2000; Laferrere 2001; Shavit and Yuchtman-Yaar 2001). These studies have identified a number of individual characteristics that commonly promote entry to self-employment. I focus here on those attributes whose effects in contemporary Russia can be assessed using available data.[3]

Age and education increase the probability of being self-employed, though in both cases the effects may be curvilinear. Age is viewed as a proxy for workforce experience, which increases human capital, social capital, and other resources that facilitate success in self-employment, but at some point older workers become risk averse and thus increasingly less likely to enter self-employment. The effect of education, usually interpreted as a straightforward measure of human capital but also possibly a proxy for cultural capital (Robert and Bukodi 2000) or ambition, appears to vary across national contexts. Some studies of the United States indicate that the relationship is fairly linear (Evans and Leighton 1989; Carr 1996), at least for entry to professional self-employment (Arum 1997; Arum, Budig, and Grant 2000). But studies of Western European countries (see Luber et al. 2000), Hungary

(Robert and Bukodi 2000) and Israel (Shavit and Yuchtman-Yaar 2001) find curvilinear effects. In particular, those with intermediate or vocational levels of education are the most likely to be self-employed, presumably because tertiary degree holders are "pulled" away from self-employment by lucrative careers as employed professionals or managers in large organizations. The pull of professional employment offsets the enabling effect of human capital. The latter, along with blocked access to professional opportunities due to credential requirements, accounts for the greater propensity of those with intermediate levels of education to enter self-employment, relative to those with the lowest levels of education (Luber et al. 2000; Shavit and Yuchtman-Yaar 2001).

Another important, if controversial, finding is that weak labor market position, reflected in low wages or unemployment, "pushes" individuals into self-employment. This effect is reported at both individual and aggregate levels: the unemployed and low-wage workers are more likely to take up self-employment than well-paid employees (Evans and Leighton 1989), and aggregate levels of unemployment exhibit a counter-cyclical tendency (Steinmetz and Wright 1989). Finally, women have traditionally been less likely to become self-employed (Wharton 1989), but sex differences appear to have diminished since the 1970s (Carr 1996; Arum 1997).

To the extent that age, education, sex, and labor market position have roughly similar influences on becoming self-employed in post-Soviet Russia as in developed capitalist societies, we might conclude that certain generic traits favor and deter self-employment in a variety of institutional and cultural contexts. But the cultural and institutional legacies of the Soviet era, combined with the persistent economic crisis and chaos of the transition period, provide some basis for expecting the influence of these variables on self-employment to differ in post-Soviet Russia.

Younger Russians may be more favorably disposed to self-employment because they were educated and socialized during the post-Soviet era, invested less in skills that were specific to the Soviet-type economy, and have a longer time horizon in which to reap the benefits of a foray into self-employment. Thus, the effect of age may be negative in Russia. The same goes for education. Gerber and Hout (1998) argue that the particular type of market economy in Russia does not reward human capital. The same attributes that generate higher earnings in Russia—political connections, access to valuable social networks or goods inherited from the Soviet era, skill in providing various personal services—are likely to generate opportunities for self-employment. These traits are probably uncorrelated or negatively correlated with education: thus, education should have no effect or a negative effect on self-employment.

As for labor market position, Russians who are currently employed may have more access to financial resources, distribution chains, clients, and/or networks than the unemployed. Self-employment is especially risky in an atmosphere of great political and economic uncertainty and weak institutions. Thus, many Russians who wish to become self-employed might prefer to start with part-time self-employment concurrent with employment, which would then eventually lead to full-time self-employment. The Russian government has no programs to promote self-employment among the unemployed. Unemployed Russians and those out of the labor force probably lack the basic resources needed to become self-employed.

On the other hand, Russian women may be more likely than Russian men to become self-employed if "push" factors dominate the process of becoming self-employed. Russian women have faced greater wage declines and exposure to job loss than Russian men, at least during the outset of the market transition period (Standing 1994; Linz 1996; Gerber and Hout 1998). Faced with fewer opportunities in the realm of wage labor, women may find self-employment a more attractive alternative than men. However, there are some signs that women's disadvantages on the labor market were ambiguous or began to reverse by the mid-1990s (Gerber 1999a, 2000c). This would imply that women's rates of entry to self-employment may be slowing relative to men's, whereas in developed capitalist countries the opposite has been the case in recent years.

If those traits that contribute to self-employment in the West have different effects—or no effects—in Russia, we would conclude that the processes shaping who becomes self-employed vary substantially across institutional and cultural contexts. One effect that is almost certain to differ in the Russian context is family background. Parental self-employment has a strong positive effect on the likelihood of becoming self-employed (Laferrere 2001), an effect which holds even for communist-era Hungary, where the offspring of entrepreneurs were more likely to profit from opportunities in small-scale private farming (Szelenyi 1988). In contemporary Russia, however, virtually nobody has parents who were self-employed, due to the long duration of Soviet power there. But other aspects of parental background might be expected to increase the likelihood of becoming self-employed by transmitting necessary stocks of social capital, cultural capital, or financial resources. In particular, we might expect the offspring of professionals and managers and CPSU members—particularly CPSU cadres (paid members of the Party bureaucracy)—to be better endowed with such assets than those from other family situations, even controlling for other ascribed and attained characteristics. In essence, these family background characteristics may play the same role as parental self-employment in a social context where parental self-employment was not possible.

Market Transition or Power Conversion? CPSU Members and Self-Employment

In the literature on social stratification in postsocialist societies, much debate has focused on whether the demise of state socialist institutions reconfigures stratification along market lines (Nee 1989, 1991, 1996; Róna-Tas 1994; Bian and Logan 1996; Nee and Matthews 1996; Parish and Michelson 1996; Walder 1996; Xie and Hannum 1996; Gerber and Hout 1998; Nee and Cao 1999; Gerber 2000a, 2000c; Zhou 2000; Cao and Nee 2000). Analyzing the determinants of income in rural China, Nee and his associates argue that market transition increases the rewards to human capital, measured as the returns to education, and decreases the rewards to political position, that is, cadre status or Communist Party membership. This occurs because market institutions reward labor productivity, while redistributive institutions reward political power and authority.

Market transition theory implies that in Russia the effect of education on self-employment should be positive and linear, and that professionals should be more likely than other occupational classes to enter self-employment. The reverse should hold for former members of the CPSU, since presumably they owed their advantaged position under the Soviet system to their political connections rather than their human capital.[4]

The validity of market transition theory for Russia has been questioned. Gerber and Hout (1998) found that the income returns to education did not increase from 1991 to 1996. As noted above, they interpret this finding as evidence that Russian capitalism rewards entrepreneurial initiative and managerial authority, but not human capital as such.[5] This suggests, contrary to market transition theory, that education and professional expertise do not increase opportunities for becoming self-employed in Russia.[6]

Moreover, Gerber (2000a) showed that former CPSU members still enjoyed an earnings advantage in 1993, attributing this advantage to unobservable individual characteristics that influenced both selection into the Party and current earnings. Róna-Tas (1994) found in his study of Hungary that former party cadres were more likely to become small business owners and to succeed in these ventures than noncadres (see also Robert and Bukodi 2000). This confirms the "power conversion" thesis: former CPSU members—at least those who held paid positions in the Party and therefore probably qualify as "cadres"—are *more* likely to enter self-employment. Claims of widespread "*nomenklatura* privatization" or "*prikhvatizatsiia*" in Russia (Rutland 1994; Kryshtanovskaya and White 1996) suggest a strong component of power conversion. But these claims are based on anecdotal observation rather than systematic data on the backgrounds of self-employed Russians.

As the competing hypotheses pertaining to the effects of education, expertise (professional occupation), and CPSU affiliation show, we have much to learn about the emerging mechanisms of social stratification in post-Soviet Russia from the analysis of the determinants of self-employment entry and exit.

Regional Effects: Economic Policies, Economic Conditions, and Law Enforcement

State-level policies and economic conditions affect self-employment entry rates in the United States (Grant 1996; Arum, Budig, and Grant 2000). We would expect to find systematic regional variation in self-employment rates in post-Soviet Russia as well. During the Soviet period, regional differences in Russia were muted by the pervasive, centralized character of Soviet economic institutions and policies. But the post-Soviet era has witnessed a rapid diversification of regional economic policies and conditions.[7]

The collapse of the Soviet state freed regional leaders from central control. This led to a growing divergence of regional economic policies, as some regions avidly implemented market reforms, others slowed privatization and adopted price and trade restrictions, and others steered a course between radical and conservative strategies (Hanson 1996; Mau and Stupin 1997; Van Selm 1998). Meanwhile, regional differences in economic output, living standards, and labor market conditions have also grown, as the demise of the redistributive system has permitted some regions to capitalize on favorable resource endowments and/or industrial structures, while those without advantages in these areas face deteriorating economic conditions (Sutherland and Hanson 1996; Van Selm 1998; Mikheeva 1999; Popov 1999).[8]

Regional policies with respect to market reforms and regional economic conditions both might plausibly affect self-employment entry rates. Regions adopting more pro-market economic policies should, if anything, have higher rates of entry. We also expect that poorer regional economic conditions are associated with higher rates of entry. This somewhat counterintuitive hypothesis follows from the pattern in Western market economies where self-employment rates typically fluctuate counter to the capitalist business cycle—in a contracting labor market, self-employment becomes a more attractive option (see Steinmetz and Wright 1989).

Finally, we might expect the effectiveness of law enforcement institutions in a region to positively affect self-employment rates, as a reliable system to enforce contracts and protect property rights diminishes uncertainty. This hypothesis follows from the claim that the reason small businesses have developed exceptionally slowly in Russia compared to other former socialist countries is that in Russia they have been "far more suppressed by criminals and corrupt state officials" (Aslund 1995, p. 263).

Change Over Time

If regional variation in economic policies, economic conditions, and law enforcement affects individual-level entry to self-employment, we would expect temporal variation in these same variables to have similar effects. During the period covered in this study, January 1991 to March 1998, the Russian economy experienced price, exchange rate, and trade liberalization, mass privatization, hyperinflation, steep negative growth rates, burgeoning unemployment, wage arrears, capital flight, several political crises, and a general deterioration of state institutions. Any one of these developments could be expected to influence the self-employment rate. We anticipate that the rate of entry to self-employment increased over time, as the push factors associated with economic crisis intensified and the disappearance of Soviet-era restrictions became more certain.

However, this tendency could have been mitigated by dynamic selection (unobserved heterogeneity): as growing numbers enter self-employment, an ever smaller proportion of those not self-employed are prone to become self-employed. As the cross-sectional proportion of self-employed increases, the rate of entry to self-employment can correspondingly decrease. Thus, a useful working hypothesis suggests that the growing positive influence of push factors over time is eventually offset by the negative influence of dynamic selection. This would produce a curvilinear trend, shaped like an inverted U, in the baseline hazard of entering self-employment across the years under study.

A second aspect of change over time involves changes in the effects of other variables. As we have seen, patterns in developed capitalist countries suggest that the effect of sex should diminish over time. Market transition theory implies that effects of education, professional occupation, and CPSU affiliation will change as Russia's market transition proceeds (see Gerber and Hout 1998). Whether or not Russia meets one's criteria for a market economy, Russia has unquestionably become more marketlike since the collapse of the Soviet system.[9] The logic of the theory clearly mandates that with time the advantages of education and professional occupation will increase and those of CPSU affiliation will diminish.

Data and Methods

The data analyzed are from the Survey of Employment, Income, and Attitudes in Russia (SEIAR), which was given to a nationally representative sample of 4,818 in January and March of 1998.[10] A battery of questions was included to trace the labor market activities of respondents since 1990. The month and year of each change in employment status or job were recorded, as well as the characteristics of up to four new jobs held since 1990. Based on questions ascertaining the month, year, and nature of all changes of employment status and/or job since December 1990, continuous employment/ activity histories from January 1991 to January/March 1998 were prepared. The analysis sample for any given month is limited to 18–59-year-old respondents with completed (or almost complete) schooling who are either in school, voluntary nonparticipants in the labor force, unemployed, engaged in an "other" activity (excluding those on maternity leave, in the military, retired, or currently self-employed), or employed in a nonagricultural job. These restrictions produced a weighted sample size of 3,356 respondents, who were at risk of becoming self-employed for a total of 221,395 person-months.[11]

I assess the material and ideological positions of the individually self-employed and the self-employed with employees in two ways. First, I compare the mean levels of earnings, subjective material satisfaction, support for market reforms, and some demographic characteristics of both classes of the self-employed to those of the other occupational classes at the time the data were collected. Second, to rule out the possibility that the observed differences in the means stem from compositional differences rather than material or ideological effects of self-employment, I estimate regression models for earnings and logistic regression models for subjective material satisfaction and support for market reforms. In addition to dummy variables representing each form of self-employment, these models incorporate a set of other covariates that affect the respective dependent variables and that may be correlated with self-employment.

I analyze the determinants of entering self-employment using continuous-time hazard models for three outcomes: (1) entry to any form of self-employment; (2) entry to self-employment without hired employees; and (3) entry to self-employment with hired employees. For each outcome, the dependent variable is $\log(r_{it})$, the natural logarithm of the hazard rate of the outcome for individual i at time t, given that i was in the risk set at time t, where t refers to months elapsed since December 1990. Because there were only twenty-eight events of entry to self-employment with employees, I estimated a limited model omitting the regional and locality variables and did not test interactions.

For the first two outcomes, I started with a baseline model including the individual-level, regional, and locality characteristics corresponding to the above hypotheses and several control variables (described below), as well as dummy variables corresponding to each year of the period under study. Then

I expanded the baseline model in three ways. First, I determined whether the effect of age is linear or curvilinear by adding the appropriate quadratic term to the model and assessing whether the improvement in the model's fit to the data was statistically significant using a likelihood ratio test. Second, I incorporated a series of interaction terms (one by one) to test for changes in the effects of sex, professional occupation, education, and Communist Party affiliation over time. For each interaction tested, I considered three different patterns of change over time and determined which, if any, fit the data, again using a likelihood ratio test.[12] I excluded those interactions that were not statistically significant from the model. Third, I smoothed the trend in the baseline hazard across the years under study to conform to one of three theoretically plausible patterns.[13] The final models—which I discuss below—include only those quadratic terms and interactions that were statistically significant according to the likelihood ratio test, and the best-fitting expression of changes in the baseline hazard over time. The absence of a particular interaction in the final models means it was not statistically significant, and the particular patterns of the age effects, the significant interactions, and the change over time in the baseline hazard are the ones that best fit the data (among those considered).

Variables

Individual Characteristics

Current main activity is measured using dummy variables for four nonwork activities–in school, voluntarily out of the labor force, unemployed, and "other." The baseline category is "employed." Age is a time-varying covariate, centered at the minimum (18 years), which advances by one year each January. I tested for a curvilinear age effect by including an age-squared term and assessing the change in model fit with a likelihood ratio test. Sex is specified as a dummy variable for women. Education is entered as dummy variables for college degree, some college, specialized (technical) secondary education, and general secondary education. The baseline is less than secondary/lower vocational. This categorical specification is suitable for capturing any curvilinearity in the effect of education on entry to self-employment.

Although the data permit me to distinguish rank-and-file CPSU members from CPSU "cadres" (who held a paid post in a Party organ), preliminary analysis showed that this distinction was not significant and led to complications in the interpretation of the respective interaction effects. Accordingly, I combined the two categories into a single dummy variable indicating membership in the CPSU. Professional occupation is specified using a dummy variable based on the respondent's current occupation (ISCO88 codes 2000–2999), with zero values assigned to those who are not employed or have missing data on occupation. Parental background is measured using dummy variables indicating that the respondent had at least one parent who was, respectively, a rank-and-file member of the CPSU, a paid CPSU cadre, or a manager or professional (ISCO88 codes 1000–2999).

Regional Effects

I merged official data on regional characteristics (Goskomstat 1998) with the SEIAR data file to test the hypotheses regarding regional effects. I treat the following variables as measures of the degree to which regional authorities pursue pro-market policies:

1. *The (logged) annual cumulative percentage of apartments that have been privatized.* Regional authorities have had some discrepancy over the rate of apartment privatization. Presumably, authorities in those regions where the apartment privatization has proceeded more rapidly have been more committed to market reforms.
2. *The (logged) annual value of services sold per capita, in constant regionally adjusted prices.* The growth of the service sector has been an important by-product of market transition. This measure should capture the degree to which regional policies have stimulated this sector and, therefore, market processes.
3. *The proportion of registered businesses in the region that were "small" businesses at the start of 1998.* One would expect larger proportions of small private businesses in regions whose authorities have pursued reformist policies. Because this measure is available only for 1996–1998, I adopt the 1998 figure, so the variable is time-invariant.[14]
   I use two measures of regional economic conditions and one measure of the effectiveness of regional law enforcement:
4. *The annual regional unemployment rate.* Unfortunately, regional unemployment data are not available for 1991. I set the 1991 rate to 1.0 percent in all regions, imposing the unrealistic assumption that there was no regional variation in unemployment during the last year of the Soviet era. However, unemployment was low during this year and regional variation was probably negligible.
5. *The annual rate (per 10,000 habitants) of population change due to migration.* Gerber (2000b) showed that with or without controls for geography and quality of life measures, regions with (relatively) worse labor market conditions experience net out-migration, while

regions with (relatively) better labor market conditions experience net in-migration. Thus, more positive values on this measure indicate better regional economic conditions, and vice versa.

6. *The (logged) annual number of crimes registered per 100,000 population.* Of course, factors other than law enforcement affect regional crime rates, but in general we would expect higher crime rates in regions with less effective law enforcement.

These measures of regional policies, conditions, and law enforcement are imperfect, and the official data may not be entirely reliable. Furthermore, measurement error is built into them, since the survey data contain information only on the respondent's current place of residence, and some respondents undoubtedly changed regions between 1990 and 1998. But these measures are preferable to subjective classifications of regions, and, aside from the percentage of small businesses, they vary by year over the transition period.

Their variation by year complicates interpretation of the parameters that represent change over time in the baseline hazard rate, whether they are dummy variables or one of the three functions of year tested in the third step described above. Much of the change over time would be picked up by changes in the means of the regional measures—for example, the unemployment rate grew annually in almost all of the regions. In order to interpret parameters as measures of secular change due to the combined effects of macroeconomic and regional trends, the time-varying regional measures are centered at their annual sample means. As a result of this centering, which does not affect the parameter estimates associated with the regional effects, the intercept corresponds to the expected logged hazard rate in a region *with sample mean characteristics (for regions)* in a given year. The parameter(s) representing change across years measures variation in that rate.

Finally, I included a number of individual-level control variables to prevent omitted variable bias: dummy variables for managerial class (ISCO88 codes 1000–1999) and employment in the trade/catering and construction industries,[15] dummies for "missing occupation" and "missing industry" (so that person-spells lacking this information can be included without affecting the relevant parameter estimates), logged size of current locality of residence (initially coded in seven categories), and a dummy variable for Moscow residents (since the situation in Moscow might well be unique).

Descriptive Statistics

Descriptive statistics obtained by taking "snapshots" of the analysis sample at annual intervals from January 1991 through January 1997 capture some important changes of the transition era (Table 1.1).

Table 1.1

Descriptive Statistics, Weighted Analysis Sample from the SEIAR

	1991	1992	1993	1994	1995	1996	1997
Total weighted N	2,576	2,777	2,761	2,769	2,805	2,854	2,922
Current Activity (Analysis Sample Plus Currently Self-Employed (in percent):							
Employed	88.2	87.5	85.2	82.4	80.1	76.6	72.9
In school	5.1	4.6	4.9	5.4	6.5	7.9	10.2
Home/not in the labor force	4.1	4.3	4.8	5.3	5.5	6.2	6.7
Unemployed	1.1	1.2	2.0	2.4	3.3	3.5	4.4
Other	.4	.5	0.5	.6	.5	.6	.6
Self-employed, without employees	.5	.7	0.9	1.2	1.4	1.5	1.3
Self-employed, with employees	.6	1.2	1.7	2.7	2.7	3.8	4.0
Among Analysis Sample (in percent):							
Transitions to self-employment	.138	0.437	0.547	0.623	0.645	0.578	0.431
Transitions to self-employment without employees	.083	0.312	0.467	0.404	0.527	0.493	0.361
Transitions to Self-employment, with employees	.054	0.126	0.080	0.219	0.118	0.085	0.070
Age	37.1	36.8	36.9	37.1	37	36.7	36.4
Woman (in percent)	55.4	55.1	54.4	54.1	53.6	55.1	55.0
CPSU Members (in percent)	11.0	10.1	10.1	9.4	9.6	8.9	8.4
College degree (in percent)	17.3	17.6	18	17.6	17.8	17.3	16.1
Some college (in percent)	1.7	1.7	1.5	1.9	2.2	3.2	4.1
Specialized (technical) secondary (in percent)	29.2	29.5	29.3	29.4	29.6	29.4	28.5

General secondary (in percent)	20.2	20.5	21.2	20.8	21	21.3	23.4
Lower vocational/less than secondary (in percent)	31.6	30.8	30.0	30.3	29.5	28.8	27.8
Parents' characteristics							
(At least one parent (in percent)							
CPSU rank-and-file member	25.6	25.8	26.2	26	25.7	26.1	26.1
CPSU cadre	1.1	1.2	1.2	1.3	1.1	1.2	1.3
Manager or professional	24.3	25.0	25.0	25.3	25.7	26.9	28.3
Annual means, characteristics of of 41 oblasts represented in SEIAR*							
Log (crimes per 100,000)	7.24	7.5	7.52	7.47	7.5	7.480	7.41
Unemployment rate	1.0	4.96	5.75	8.16	9.88	10.310	12.23
Net migration, per 10,000 population	14.98	32.05	37.37	59.15	39.34	24.9	25.07
Services sold per capita (1991 rubles)	393	134	172	292	415	583	675
% Privatized apartments	5.6	10.7	25.2	33.5	37.1	39.6	42.4
% Small businesses in 1998	28.6	28.6	28.6	28.6	28.6	28.6	28.6

Source: Goskomstat 1998.

In January 1991 88.2% of the analysis sample was employed, falling to 72.9% in early 1997. Unemployment and nonparticipation grew steadily within the SEIAR sample as they did in the country as a whole. Self-employment grew as well—from 1.1% of the analysis sample in January 1991 to 5.3% in 1997. This is considerably below the figures in the United States, but nonetheless represents substantial growth.[16] Entry rates to self-employment increased from 1991 through 1994 or 1995, then tapered off. This suggests a curvilinear trend in the baseline hazard reflecting the combined effects of a secular increase in self-employment (due to market transition) and dynamic selection.

The means on the *oblast* characteristics reflect the growth in unemployment, apartment privatization, and services during the 1990s.[17] The average crime rates show no clear trend. On average, net migration rates were positive throughout, reflecting continuing in-migration of native Russians and Russian speakers from the "near abroad," which peaked in 1994.

Characteristics of the Self-Employed

Both the individually self-employed respondents and those with employees fit the bill of "entrepreneurs" in terms of their average earnings (Table 1.2).

Proprietors with employees earned 5.3 times the average monthly wage, while those without employees earned roughly 2.4 times the average wage, and these ratios are even higher using the geometric means (the antilog of the mean of logged earnings), which correct for positive skew in the distribution of earnings. Among other occupational classes, only managers come close in terms of earnings (and only when the arithmetic mean is used). Moreover, both classes of the self-employed enjoy the additional advantage that they are far less likely than other classes to have received no pay at all in the previous month, reflecting the exposure of employees to wage arrears.

The demographic characteristics also reveal several distinctive traits of the self-employed. First, the proportion of college-educated Russians among proprietors with employees is higher than the overall figure, but lower than the proportion of college-educated among professionals and managers. The proportion of college-educated among proprietors without employees is no higher than the overall proportion. Women are underrepresented among the self-employed, implying that they are either less likely to enter self-employment, more likely to exit self-employment, or both. Finally, in contrast to the situation elsewhere, the self-employed are on average younger than Russians in any other occupational class.

Turning to the subjective views of the self-employed (Table 1.3), we find more evidence of their material advantages: proprietors with employees are

Table 1.2

Earnings and Demographic Characteristics by Occupational Class, January–March 1998

Adapted Erikson-Goldthorpe class	N	Previous month's earnings (rubles)		No pay (%)	VUZ Degree (%)	Female (%)
		Arithmetic mean	Geometric mean			
Missing	77	715	112	7	12	71
IIa. Managers	89	1,174	274	19	50	38
IIb. Upper professionals	160	826	313	12	55	78
II. Lower professionals	234	617	128	22	60	69
IIIa. Upper routine nonmanual	143	774	203	18	20	55
IIIb. Lower routine nonmanual	426	525	167	16	8	80
IVa. Proprietors with employees	33	4,099	1,199	5	33	28
IVb. Proprietors without employees	91	1,846	1,044	1	21	33
V. Technicians	150	451	90	25	10	77
VI. Skilled manual	425	725	137	23	5	24
VIIa. Semi/unskilled manual	343	739	132	25	3	23
Total	2,168	780	171	19	19	52

Source: Weighted SEIAR sample, respondents 18–59 currently working outside agriculture.

5.3 times more likely and those without employees are 3.2 times more likely than the average to assess their material situation as good or very good. Both groups are correspondingly less likely to assess their material situation as bad or very bad. The self-employed—especially those with employees—are more likely to support continuing market reforms and less likely to oppose market reforms than any other occupational class. Even those without employees are more supportive of market reforms than professionals, despite the much higher proportion in the latter group with college education.[18] According to this indicator, reformers can count on the self-employed to provide political support for pro-market policies.

The descriptive data in Tables 1.2 and 1.3 suggest that both the individually self-employed and employers in contemporary Russia have distinctively high levels of earnings, subjective material satisfaction, and support for market reforms. Although employers rank higher on each of these dimensions, the individually self-employed also rank above all other classes, except perhaps in the area of support for market reforms. Thus, it appears that in Russia—in contrast to some Eastern European countries (Hanley 2000)—self-employment represents a path to relative material success, whether or not it involves starting a formal business with employees, and also is associated with a pro-market political outlook.

These apparent distinguishing characteristics of the self-employed could simply reflect their demographic makeup, since they are better educated, younger, and more likely to be male than other occupational classes. To assess this alternative explanation of the effects of (both forms of) self-employment, we turn to multivariate ordinary least square (OLS) and logistic regression models of (logged) earnings, subjective material situation (coded 1 for good or very good, 0 otherwise) and support for market reforms (coded 1 for pro-market, 0 otherwise).

The results from these models (Table 1.4) provide strong evidence that the material advantages and pro-market orientation of the self-employed are not attributable to compositional factors. Even controlling for the effects of age, sex, CPSU membership, education, locality of residence, private sector employment, and industry of employment, the dummy variables indicating self-employment of either form have statistically significant effects in the expected direction on each outcome.[19] The self-employed earn approximately 3.67 times more than employees with the exact same characteristics on all the other variables in the model.[20] The individually self-employed are 2.64 times more likely to positively assess their family's material situation than employees who are otherwise identical, even with respect to earnings, and 1.85 times more likely to say that market reforms should be continued. The latter two effects are even stronger for the self-employed who hire employees.

Table 1.3

Subjective Material Situation and Support for Market Reforms by Occupational Class, January–March 1998

Adapted Erikson-Boldthorpe class	N	Material situation of respondent's family			Should market reforms be continued?		
		Very good/good (%)	Average (%)	Very bad/bad (%)	Yes (%)	No (%)	Hard to say (%)
Missing	77	3	50	47	45	17	39
Ia./IIa. Managers	89	9	55	37	56	23	21
Ib. Upper professionals	160	6	51	42	53	13	34
IIb. Lower professionals	234	6	44	50	46	18	36
IIIa. Upper routine nonmanual	143	3	56	40	45	19	36
IIIb. Lower routine nonmanual	426	4	42	54	38	21	41
IVa. Proprietors with employees	33	27	60	13	77	9	14
IVb. Proprietors without employees	91	16	52	31	57	15	28
V. Technicians	150	2	45	53	38	21	41
VI. Skilled manual	425	3	45	52	38	23	39
VIIa. Semi/unskilled manual	343	4	39	57	38	20	42
Total	2,168	5	46	49	43	20	38

Source: Weighted SEIAR sample, respondents 18–59 currently working outside agriculture.

Table 1.4

OLS and Logit Regressions of Logged Earnings, Positive Assessment of Family Material Situation, and Support for Market Reforms, Nonagricultural SEIAR Sample Aged 18–59 (N = 2,245)

	Logged earnings		Good/very good material situation		Pro-market reforms	
	B	SE(B)	B	SE(B)	B	SE(B)
Self-employed, with employees	1.301**	0.528	1.282**	0.537	1.282**	0.476
Self-employed, no employees	1.295**	0.230	0.971**	0.460	0.613 *	0.342
Age (−18)	0.030**	0.015	−0.046	0.027	−0.036**	0.012
Age (−18) squared	−0.001**	0.001	0	0.001	0.001 *	0
Woman	−0.122	0.133	−0.292	0.233	−0.307**	0.106
CPSU member	0.163	0.206	0.433	0.314	−0.018	0.155
Education (General Secondary Diploma)						
College degree	0.476**	0.185	1.059**	0.363	0.655**	0.151
Some college	−0.080	0.343	0.002	0.678	0.279	0.270
Specialized secondary	0.156	0.176	0.236	0.377	0.223	0.141
PTU (Lower vocational)	−0.059	0.217	0.253	0.440	−0.286*	0.173
Less than secondary	0.320	0.268	1.045**	0.510	−0.550**	0.255
Log (city size)	0.086**	0.032	−0.058	0.060	0.072**	0.026
Moscow resident	1.150**	0.152	0.392	0.308	0.542**	0.142
Work in private sector	0.627**	0.174	0.235	0.328	0.358**	0.146
Industry (manufacturing)						
Missing	0.613	0.588	−0.027	0.808	−0.948	0.619
Extraction	0.142	0.760	0.410	0.825	0.588	0.541
Construction	−0.294	0.288	−0.650	0.574	−0.228	0.209
Transport/communications	0.393	0.255	0.173	0.409	0.064	0.182
Trade/catering/services	0.699**	0.189	0.156	0.371	0.130	0.168
Housing/communal services	−0.227	0.335	−0.306	0.754	−0.238	0.252
Health	0.514**	0.209	−0.840	0.580	−0.313	0.200

	Coef.	SE	Coef.	SE	Coef.	SE
Education/science	0.011	0.212	−0.443	0.418	0	0.167
Entertainment/culture/sport	−0.951	0.448	0.110	0.684	0.266	0.306
Finance/insurance	1.592**	0.266	0.116	0.574	0.541	0.381
Public administration	1.265**	0.235	−0.514	0.567	0.230	0.201
Other	0.456	0.505	−0.057	0.758	0.750**	0.357
Oblast mean wage	1.329**	0.560	−1.458	0.927	−0.749*	0.442
Logged earnings	—		0.207**	0.081	0.053**	0.019
Constant	4.075**	0.269	−3.940**	0.69	−.289	0.223
R^2/Pseudo-R^2	0.127		0.128		0.79	

Note: **p < .05, two-tailed; *p < .05, one-tailed.
Standard errors are heteroscedasticity-corrected ("robust").

The data show that the self-employed constitute two distinctive class positions in contemporary Russian society. Both of these positions are associated with higher economic status and greater support for market reforms. Employers appear to rank above the individually self-employed on both dimensions, but the self-employed clearly rank above other occupational classes. Thus, we observe two different grades or forms of self-employment, each of which represent "winners" in the process of market transition. The combined similarity and distinction between these two forms of self-employment call for considering them in tandem and separately, as we turn to analyzing the determinants of becoming self-employed.

Paths to Success: Statistical Models of Entry to Self-Employment

For the most part, the effects of the covariates of interest operate similarly, whether the dependent variable is entry to any form of self-employment, to individual self-employment, or to self-employment with employees (Table 1.5).

In contrast to patterns observed in most other countries, age has a negative effect on the probability that Russians become self-employed.[21] This confirms the view that socialization, longer time horizons, and, possibly, a worse labor market position make self-employment the province of younger Russians. This effect is a striking example of the continuing impact of the Soviet era and its aftermath on stratification mechanisms in Russia.

Turning to the effects of education, here Russia is not so distinct. Consistent with market transition theory, education increases the likelihood of becoming self-employed. This effect does not exhibit the curvilinear tendency found in some developed capitalist countries. Those with college degrees and technical secondary education are substantially more likely to become self-employed (with or without employees) than those with less than secondary, but general secondary degree holders do not differ significantly from the baseline. Most likely, this reflects the relatively limited opportunities for high earnings in professional occupations in transition-era Russia, reported by Gerber and Hout (1998) and evident in Table 1.2. Without lucrative professional positions to "pull" them away from self-employment, Russians with high levels of human capital seek to parlay this resource into rewards via self-employment. Also, the effects of education are especially pronounced for entry to self-employment with employees: college degree holders are 6.2 times ($e^{1.828}$) more likely than otherwise similar individuals with less than high school to become self-employed with employees, but only about twice as likely to take up individual work activity.

Russians currently engaged in work for hire are far less likely to become self-employed than those who are not, whether the latter be in school, voluntarily out of the labor force, or unemployed. These effects are consistent across types of self-employment and strong in magnitude: the unemployed are about 28.8 times more likely to become self-employed than otherwise similar hired workers.

Russian women are less likely to take up self-employment, net of other variables. The effect is somewhat weaker for entry to self-employment without employees, but still quite substantial, women's entry rate being 31.8% that of men with the same characteristics. None of the interaction effects involving sex were significant: women's disadvantage in access to self-employment has remained constant throughout the period 1991–1997, in contrast to the equalizing trends observed in many capitalist countries.

Parental service class occupation and CPSU affiliation both exert direct effects on entry to self-employment. As expected, respondents from more elite occupational class backgrounds are more likely to enter self-employment, even controlling for their human capital and other variables. This implies that in the absence of an entrepreneurial class, the professional-managerial class provides its offspring with motivation, social capital, and/or particular skills that facilitate becoming self-employed. However, this effect is not statistically significant for becoming self-employed with employees.

Contrary to our prediction, having a parent who was a cadre in the CPSU effectively prevents Russians from entering either form of self-employment: the negative direct effect is strong enough to outweigh any other variable. Perhaps Communist Party cadres remained convinced ideological opponents of capitalist institutions and socialized their children to disdain private enterprise. Given the widespread cynicism toward Soviet ideology during the final decades of Soviet power, however, another thesis is more plausible: the offspring of CPSU cadres were probably geared toward pursuing opportunities through organizational careers as professionals or managers. At any rate, this finding is quite dramatic and merits more serious analysis if it can be replicated with other data that include a larger number of offspring of cadres (the SEIAR analysis sample contains forty-four). Having a parent who was a CPSU member, but not a paid cadre, has no net effect on entry to self-employment.

As for respondents' membership in the CPSU, we find that the effects changed during the course of the transition period, as demonstrated by the significant interaction between CPSU membership and log ($y+1$) for overall self-employment and self-employment without employees. The trend in the multiplier effect of CPSU membership is shown in Table 1.6. During the final year of the Soviet era and the first year of transition, CPSU members

Table 1.5

Exponential Models for Entry to Self-Employment

	Any self-employment		Without employees		With employees	
	B	SE(B)	B	SE(B)	B	SE(B)
Activity (Employed)						
In school	1.722**	0.430	1.309**	0.462	1.932**	0.725
Home—not working	3.154**	0.343	3.010**	0.401	3.824**	0.587
Unemployed	3.359**	0.321	3.429**	0.357	3.311**	0.683
Other activity	2.464**	0.553	2.609**	0.559	−13.383**	0.506
Age (−18)	0.031	0.029	−0.022**	0.011	−0.049**	0.021
Age (−18) squared	−0.002**	0.001				
Woman	−1.160**	0.227	−1.147**	0.259	−1.445**	0.461
CPSU member	1.258*	0.674	1.289*	0.738	−0.171	0.679
Education (lower vocational/less than secondary)						
College degree	0.820**	0.343	0.693*	0.369	1.828**	0.697
Some college	0.160	0.545	−1.035	0.798	2.102**	0.906
Specialized secondary	0.680**	0.292	0.580*	0.313	1.461**	0.717
General secondary	0.313	0.329	0.269	0.352	0.514	0.866
Parent						
CPSU member	0.005	0.233	0.072	0.260	−0.278	0.446
CPSU cadre	−11.578**	0.308	−13.357**	0.381	−14.128**	0.403
Manager/professional	0.563**	0.265	0.556*	0.314	0.490	0.363
Industry (not trade/catering, Construction, or missing)						
Trade/catering	0.997**	0.414	1.119**	0.457	0.172	1.108
Construction	0.872**	0.434	0.724	0.545	1.305*	0.681
Missing	1.845**	0.760	2.008**	0.811	−10.511**	0.764

Occupational Class (not nanager, professional, or missing)						
Manager	0.083	0.568	−13.639**	0.263	1.918**	0.849
Professional	0.083	0.396	−0.121	0.478	0.776	0.691
Missing	−0.720	0.78	−0.710	0.840	−12.306**	0.695
Olbast characteristics						
Log (crimes per 100,000)	−0.923**	0.379	−1.439**	0.410	—	—
Unemployment rate	0.071*	0.041	0.055	0.046	—	—
Net migration rate	−0.003	0.002	−0.003*	0.002	—	—
Log (services sold)	0.717**	0.352	0.745*	0.390	—	—
% privatized apartments	−0.020*	0.011	−.015	0.011	—	—
% small businesses, 1998	−1.152	1.036	−1.108	1.078	—	—
Log (city size)	—	0.052	0.056	0.060	—	—
Moscow	−1.388**	0.582	−2.148**	0.660	—	—
Log (year)	0.916**	0.363	1.154**	0.437	0.919	0.614
Year-squared	−0.064**	0.015	−0.057**	0.017	−0.066**	0.033
CPSU member* log (year)	−1.346**	0.560	−1.457**	0.617	—	—
Constant	−9.008**	0.460	−9.128**	0.526	−10.751**	0.959
Number of events	143		115		28	
Log Likelihood	−507		−423		−139	
Number of cases: 3,356				Person-months at risk: 221,395		

Source: Weighted SEIAR data.
*Notes: **p< .05, two-tailed; *p<.05, one-tailed*
Standard errors are heteroscedasticity-corrected ("robust").

Table 1.6

Time-Varying Multiplier Effects in Models of Entry to Self-Employment
(computed from the relevant coefficients in Table 1.5)

	1991	1992	1993	1994	1995	1996	1997
A. Any self-employment							
CPSU membership	3.52	1.38	0.80	0.54	0.40	0.32	0.26
Baseline hazard (1991 = 1.00)	1.00	1.77	2.12	2.01	1.58	1.05	0.60
B. Self-employment without employees							
CPSU membership	3.63	1.32	0.73	0.48	0.35	0.27	0.21
Baseline hazard (1991 = 1.00)	1.00	2.10	2.82	2.96	2.56	1.89	1.20
C. Self-employment with employees							
Baseline hazard (1991 = 1.00)	1.00	1.77	2.11	1.97	1.52	0.99	0.55

were more likely to become self-employed than nonmembers with the same characteristics. But by 1993 this effect changed signs, and by 1997 CPSU members were only one-quarter as likely to enter self-employment as otherwise identical nonmembers.

In short, those CPSU members who missed the boat early on quickly found it more difficult to become self-employed than Russians with similar characteristics who had not been members of the CPSU. Although at the outset of market transition. Party members had some opportunity to "convert" their politically derived advantages into opportunities for self-employment, this possibility quickly evaporated as market transition progressed. Overall, then, the findings with respect to Party membership support an expanded version of market transition theory that incorporates processes of power conversion at the initial stages of the transition.

The findings do not support market transition theory's predictions for professionals. Neither the main effect of professional occupation nor any of the interactions between professional occupation or education and time were statistically significant. A majority of professionals have college education, so they are in fact more likely to become self-employed than nonprofessionals, consistent with market transition theory.[22] But this effect did not change magnitude as Russia became more marketlike. Although professional occupations do not apparently "pull" Russians away from any form of self-employment, *managerial* occupations apparently exert a strong pull away from self-employment without employees, even as they provide a favorable basis for entry to the more lucrative self-employment with employees. This is consistent with the finding of Gerber and Hout (1998) that the income returns to managerial authority and proprietorship have well outpaced the returns to professional expertise during the transition era. A similar "pull" mechanism operates in Russia as that identified with respect to college education in other countries, but in Russia it operates via managerial occupation.

Given the uncertain quality of the regional measures, it is quite striking that four of the six regional characteristics exerted statistically significant effects on the rate of entry to self-employment. Net migration barely misses statistical significance (t = -1.63); a more reliable measure (e.g., with data on the residential history of respondents) would probably render this effect significant. As expected, entry to self-employment is more common in regions with lower crime rates, higher unemployment, and, probably, net out-migration, controlling for the other variables in the model. The results are more ambiguous as regards the effects of pro-reform policies. While size of the service sector has the predicted positive effect, entry to self-employment is *less* common in regions with higher rates of apartment privatization, and the proportion of small businesses in 1998 has no significant effect. Most likely, the apartment privatization variable measures something other than regional authorities' level of commitment to market reforms, and the small business measure is simply inadequate because it is time invariant. Altogether, the results provide strong evidence that regional contexts influence entrepreneurship opportunities in Russia. Better data and measures would probably reveal even more pronounced effects.

Finally, curvilinear specifications of trends in the baseline hazard of entering self-employment provided the best fit to the data in each case. This means that the baseline hazard—the expected hazard for a Russian with "zero" values on all the variables in the model[23]—increased during the initial years of the transition, peaked in 1994 or 1995, and declined thereafter (Table 1.6). Most likely, a secular increase in self-employment due to expanding opportunities and spiraling macroeconomic push factors is eventually offset by dynamic selection on unobserved variables: as those who are prone to become self-employed do so, the remaining population who are still eligible to become self-employed is characterized by a lower average unobserved propensity. It is also worth noting that industry of hired employment has the expected effects on entry to self-employment, though employees in trade/catering are more likely to become self-employed without employees, while those in construction are more likely to start their own business with employees.

Discussion

Several factors identified as promoting self-employment in studies conducted in the United States and other developed capitalist countries operate in a similar fashion in post-Soviet Russia. Perhaps most importantly, human capital increases a Russian's chances of becoming a proprietor with employees and, to a slightly lesser extent, taking up individual work activity. This finding confirms the prediction of market transition theory that human capital is an important asset in transition-era Russia. But the linear effect of human capital—in contrast to the curvilinear pattern observed in developed capitalist societies—implies that employment as a hired professional is a less attractive alternative in contemporary Russia. If they can do so, college-educated Russians prefer to become self-employed—even individually self-employed —because professional employment does not offer lucrative rewards (Gerber and Hout 1998). Although the effect of human capital on entry to self-employment is significant, nontrivial in magnitude, and persistent throughout the post-Soviet period, this does not translate into an important role for human capital in the overall process of stratification, because self-employment remains relatively rare in Russia. In some sense, the finding that human capital increases the odds of pursuing material gains outside the labor market via self-employment confirms that, contrary to market transition theory, the Russian labor market does not reward human capital with higher earnings and better job mobility opportunities any more that it did during the Soviet era.

Rather than argue over whether market transition increases the returns to human capital, we might ask: in which fields of economic activity does human capital generate greater rewards as a result of market transition? Clearly, the strongest effects of human capital are observed in the process of becoming an entrepreneur with hired employees. The activities involved in this form of self-employment probably conform more closely to those of the classic capitalist: evaluating market opportunities, calculating ratios of risk and return, administering organizations, and allocating revenues to costs, consumption, and investment. It is not surprising that human capital would better prepare individuals to take on these tasks. Proprietors without employees are involved in smaller-scale, less durable operations. Most likely, they conform more closely to "merchant" capitalists (Burawoy 1997)—that is, they seek to benefit as quickly as possible from advantageous connections, particular assets, opportunities to profit from corruption or arbitrage situations, or service skills. We should not be surprised that human capital has a more muted effect on entry to this type of self-employment.

We also find in Russia that those who are currently employed are less likely to take up self-employment than those who are unemployed or out of the labor force. This may seem unusual, since we associate self-employment with high levels of initiative. But the same effects have been observed in Western countries, at both individual and aggregate levels. Women in Russia face greater obstacles to becoming self-employed than do men with similar traits, but, unlike in many Western countries, their disadvantage has remained stable. This is consistent with the view that the increase in women's self-employment in Western countries stems from their increased labor force participation, because women's labor force participation has decreased in Russia during the market transition—in the SEIAR data, women's voluntary nonparticipation grew from 5.2% to 11.0% between 1991 and 1997.

In Russia, family background influences entry to self-employment, even controlling for all the other traits that have effects and despite the virtual absence of entrepreneurs among the parents of contemporary Russians. Soviet-era managers and professionals appear to have passed on to their children motivation, social contacts, or unobservable skills that help them along the path to self-employment during the post-Soviet era. This unusual effect— not found, for example, in Hungary (Robert and Bukodi 2000)—may hold only in situations where there are practically no self-employed among parents, in which case parental professional/managerial status substitutes for parental proprietor status. If so, this effect will not obtain for those cohorts who grow up during the post-Soviet era. We also found a very strong negative effect on entry to self-employment of having a parent who was a paid cadre in the CPSU, which deserves further scrutiny in future studies with other data sets.

Russia has only recently emerged from seventy years of severe restrictions on self-employment and continues to have a hybrid cultural and institutional environment combining elements from the Soviet era with market institutions and practices. Many aspects of market economies have not translated well into the Russian context. Thus, there are striking similarities between Russia and countries where markets have been the norm for centuries in the *mechanisms* whereby individual characteristics such as human capital, labor market situation, sex, and family background affect entry to self-employment outcomes. There are indeed generic aspects to the process of becoming self-employed that are consistent across diverse institutional and cultural contexts.

Russia does have some distinctive characteristics, though. The effect of age is *negative* in Russia, at least starting at age 27. This is probably a cohort effect that will disappear as cohorts who socialized during the Soviet era leave the labor force. The effects of CPSU membership distinguish Russia not only from Western capitalist countries, where there is no equivalent variable, but also from Hungary, where Party members enjoyed advantages in gaining access to self-employment (Róna-Tas 1994; Robert and Bukodi 2000). In Russia we observe only a weak and brief form of "power conversion," since Party membership proved an advantage only in entry to self-employment without employees, the less lucrative form of self-employment, and this effect was only temporary. There are several possible explanations for this limited effect: former Party members might have been better placed in the labor market—for example, occupying managerial posts in relatively successful industries—at the outset of the transition and thus have lower incentives to take on the risks of self-employment. The noneffects in the data could result from left-censoring (i.e., the best placed CPSU members had already become self-employed by December 1990, leaving only those with fewer opportunities in the analysis sample). Or CPSU members may be disinclined to take up self-employment out of ideological convictions (though this seems least plausible). Whatever the explanation, the findings call for skepticism toward claims that the only "winners" in post-Soviet Russia are political elites from the Soviet era.

Another important finding is that regional characteristics have consequences for individual-level self-employment rates. The measures of regional policies, economic conditions, and legal environment employed herein are flawed and contain error. Despite these limitations, the significant regional effects identified in the statistical models confirm that self-employment opportunities represent yet another characteristic that has come to vary across regions in post-Soviet Russia. An important task for future research on regional variation and on the determinants of self-employment is to refine the regional measures, obtain data combining residential and employment histories, and further explore these effects.

As we have shown, both the individually self-employed and employers have been among the "winners" in Russia's transition from state socialism. The paths to both forms of self-employment thus merit continuing attention, as "victory" of this sort has eluded most Russians. This initial study has identified multiple paths, many of which are similar to paths found in other market societies, others of which are distinct to Russia. As Russia's socioeconomic institutions and culture continue to evolve, we might expect the mechanisms shaping who joins the self-employed ranks of the winners to change as well. One way to trace such changes will be to compare findings from future studies of the determinants of self-employment to those reported in this chapter.

Notes

A shorter version of this chapter appeared in the Summer 2001 issue of the *International Journal of Sociology* (volume 31, no. 2, pp. 3–37). The research reported herein was supported by a grant to the author from the National Science Foundation (SBR-9729225) and a Short-Term Travel Grant from IREX. I thank Walter Mueller, Peter Robert, and Thomas B. Gold for comments on an earlier draft, and Richard Arum for helpful discussions. Address correspondence to Professor T. Gerber, Department of Sociology, Social Science Building, Room 400, PO Box 210027, Tucson, AZ 85721–0027. E-mail: tgerber@email.arizona.edu.

1. "Small enterprises" are defined as commercial organizations in which government bodies and nongovernment institutions each hold less than a 25% ownership stake and the number of employees does not exceed specific limits: 100 for industrial firms, 60 for scientific concerns, 50 for wholesale trading concerns, 30 for retail trade, and 50 for other types of firms (Goskomstat 1998, p. 326).

2. In our survey, the response category identifying the self-employed who have employees explicitly excludes "family members working without pay." However, there is not a separate category identifying the use of such "voluntary" employees. Thus, self-employed respondents who make use of the unpaid labor of family members, but no paid employees, show up in the data as individually self-employed. We do not know how widespread the use of unpaid family members' labor is among the self-employed in Russia, nor whether these types of businesses differ fundamentally from those of the individually self-employed.

3. Four other factors are emphasized in studies of the determinants of self-employment in the West: (1) personality attributes such as a desire for autonomy, independence, and a personal locus of control may motivate individuals to become self-employed (Evans and Leighton 1989; Loutfi 1991); (2) family structure appears to influence women's self-employment (Carr 1996); (3) certain ethnic and immigrant communities exhibit higher levels of self-employment in the United States (Light 1972; Borjas 1986); and 4) family financial resources help some overcome liquidity barriers to self-employment (Laferrere 2001). These factors may also be relevant in Russia. Unfortunately, the data do not contain the information necessary to examine their influence.

4. In more recent formulations, Nee argues that persisting cadre advantages in earnings and access to self-employment are consistent with market transition theory (Nee and Cao 1999; Cao and Nee 2000), so long as the advantages accruing to education grow more rapidly than those accruing to political position. This logic might be appropriate for the initial phase of the transition, when Party affiliation (cadre status) remains an institutionalized advantage. However, following the absolute demise of the institutions which politically privilege Party members, any remaining advantages they have net of human capital and other measured variables must stem from unmeasured traits (i.e., other dimensions of human capital) that distinguish them from non-Party members or from the superior social networks they inherit from the Communist era (see Gerber 2000a). In either case, the logic of market transition theory—which attributes cadres' advantages under state socialism to their political capital—would seem to be undermined.

5. Brainerd (1998) reached somewhat different conclusions using different specifications.

6. Gerber and Hout (1998) did not explicitly model the effects of human capital on self-employment, but their reduced form models (which do not include occupational controls) also reveal no increasing returns to education. If entrepreneurship indirectly magnified the returns to education, it would be evident in their reduced form models.

7. By "regions" I refer to the eighty-nine territorial subjects of the Russian Federation—of which forty-one are represented in the data at hand—including autonomous republics, *krais*, *oblasts*, *okrugs*, and the cities of St. Petersburg and Moscow.

8. To be more precise, all regions experienced steep declines in output, wages, and employments, but the declines were more precipitous in regions with unfavorable resource endowments and industrial structures.

9. In recent rejoinders to Gerber and Hout (1998) and other critics of market transition theory, Nee and his coauthor assert that Russia is not a market economy and that therefore the theory is not relevant to the Russian context (Nee and Cao 1999; Cao and Nee 2000). However, market *transition* theory is manifestly a theory about change. Nee and Cao do not challenge the claims of Gerber and Hout (1998) that, according to market transition theory, returns to education should increase as Russia becomes more marketlike and should be higher in the private sector, neither of which is confirmed empirically.

10. Details about the data, including sampling procedures, refusal rates, quality control, and the exact questions used to construct the employment histories, are available in Gerber (1999b).

11. I calculated postsampling weights to reproduce within the sample the gender*age*urban residence*education distribution in the population. I dropped thirty-two respondents whose histories could not be reliably prepared due to incongruities or missing data.

12. For each independent variable whose effects were hypothesized to change over time, the interaction terms consisted of the product of the independent variable and a function of calendar years elapsed since December 1990, $f(y)$. Three patterns of temporal change in the effects of a variable x on the logged hazard rate are plausible, each corresponding to a different $f(y)$: (1) The effect could change dramatically as a result of the introduction of market reforms in January 1992, remaining stable thereafter, that is, $f(y) = 0$ for $y = 0$ (i.e., calendar year 1991) and $f(y) = 1$ for all other years (i.e., 1992–1997); (2) The effect could change rapidly in the initial years of the reform era, then more gradually, corresponding to $f(y) = \log(y + 1)$. We add 1 to y so that the interaction term equals zero in 1991 and a positive number in subsequent years; (3) The relationship between time and the magnitude of the effect could be curvilinear—for example, the effect could increase in strength over the first few years following the onset of market reforms, then decrease. This pattern can be captured using the log-quadratic function of y: $f(y) = \log(y + 1) + y^2$. For this specification, two parameters must be estimated: one for $x*\log(y + 1)$ and one for $x*y^2$.

13. The patterns are the same as those described in the previous note. This step must be saved for last because the tests of interactions in the second step are more reliable when change across years in the baseline hazard is not constrained to follow any particular functional form, which is what the dummy-variable specification in the baseline model accomplishes.

14. This information is not provided separately for the cities of Moscow and St. Petersburg, so I assigned the respective values for Moscow and Leningrad *oblasts*.

15. Self-employment, in Russia as elsewhere (e.g., Luber et al. 2000), is most widespread in trade/catering and construction. Therefore, employees in these industries should have greater opportunities to become self-employed than employees in other industries.

16. According to data from the Panel Study of Income Dynamics, in 1992 self-employment accounted for 15.0% of nonfarm employment among American men, 9.0% among women (Arum 1997, p. 219). It is also worth noting, as further demonstration of the credibility of the SEIAR data, that the analysis sample reflects the decline of the manufacturing sector (from 38.2% to 25.7% of the employed sample) and the growth of trade/catering (9.4% to 15.8%) and public administration (2.5% to 4.6%) that have marked the post-Soviet era in Russia.

17. The measure of services drops in 1992 because the measure is price adjusted

and regional inflation rates peaked in 1992. In other words, the volume of services provided increased in 1992 but their nominal value did not increase rapidly enough to keep up with inflation.

18. College education is a very strong predictor of promarket views in Russia. See Gerber (2000d) for an analysis of the effects of education on ideology and voting in the 1995 Duma election.

19. Because this chapter focuses on self-employment, I do not discuss the other effects in the models reported in Table 1.4. They generally conform to expectations, with one important exception: the effect of sex on earnings is not statistically significant. This probably reflects the greater exposure of Russian men to wage arrears (Gerber 1999a).

20. The logged dependent variables in all the multivariate models reported in this chapter mean that the exponential of a covariate's coefficient corresponds to the multiplicative effect on the raw dependent variable of a one-unit increase in the covariate. For dummy variables, the exponential thus provides the multiplicative effect of being in the group coded 1. Thus, we take the exponential of 1.3, the coefficient for "self-employed with employees," to obtain the multiplicative effect of being in this group ($e^{1.3} = 3.67$).

21. At first glance, the effect of age is curvilinear for entry to any form of self-employment. Age-squared is retained in the model based on the likelihood ratio test, which found it significantly improves the model's fit to the data. However, the effect reverses direction at 27 years of age and is linear and negative in the separate models for entry to different forms of self-employment. The age at which the effect changes direction is given by the formula: $-\frac{1}{2}*(\beta_{age}/\beta_{age\text{-}squared})$. Since age is centered at the minimum value (18 years), we must add 18 to the solution of this formula.

22. The magnitude of the nonsignificant professional effect is sufficiently small to rule out any suppression of the college effect due to its inclusion. But to be sure, I estimated the models without the dummy variable for professionals and found only trivial differences in effect sizes.

23. Because all the variables are either centered or dummy variables, this corresponds to an 18-year-old, employed, male, non-CPSU member with less than secondary education, neither of whose parents were managers or professionals or CPSU cadres, who is not himself a professional or manager, does not work in trade/catering or construction, and lives in an average-sized locality outside Moscow in a region with average values on all the regional characteristics in a given year.

Bibliography

Arum, Richard. 1997. "Trends in Male and Female Self-Employment: Growth in a New Middle Class or Increasing Marginalization of the Labor Force?" *Research in Social Stratification and Mobility* 15, pp. 209–238.

Arum, Richard, Michelle Budig, and Don Sherman Grant II. 2000. "Labor Market Regulation and the Growth of Self-Employment." *International Journal of Sociology* 30, pp. 3–27.

Aslund, Anders. 1995. *How Russia Became a Market Economy.* Washington, DC: The Brookings Institution.

Bian, Yanjie, and John W. Logan. 1996. "Market Transition and the Persistence of Power: The Changing Stratification System in Urban China." *American Sociological Review* 61, pp. 739–758.

Birch, David L. 1987. *Job Creation in America: How Our Smallest Companies Put the Most People to Work.* New York: Free Press.

Blasi, Joseph R., Maya Kroumova, and Douglas Kruse. 1997. *Kremlin Capitalism: Privatizing the Russian Economy.* Ithaca and London: Cornell University Press.

Borjas, George. 1986. "The Self-Employment Experience of Immigrants." *Journal of Human Resources* 21, pp. 485–506.

Boycko, Maxim, Andrei Shleifer, and Robert Vishny. 1995. *Privatizing Russia.* Cambridge: MIT Press.

Brainerd, Elizabeth. 1998. "Winners and Losers in Russia's Economic Transition." *American Economic Review* 88, pp. 1094–1116.

Burawoy, Michael. 1997. "The Soviet Descent into Capitalism." *American Journal of Sociology* 102, pp. 1430–1444.

Cao, Yang, and Victor G. Nee. 2000. "Comment: Controversies and Evidence in the Market Transition Debate." *American Journal of Sociology* 105, pp. 1175–1188.

Carr, Deborah. 1996. "Two Paths to Self-Employment? Women's and Men's Self-Employment in the United States, 1980." *Work and Occupations* 23, pp. 26–53.

Evans, David S., and Linda S. Leighton. 1989. "Some Empirical Aspects of Entrepreneurship." *American Economic Review* 79, pp. 519–535.

Form, William. 1982. "Self-Employed Manual Workers: Petty Bourgeois or Working Class?" *Social Forces* 60, pp. 1050–1069.

Gerber, Theodore P. 1999a. "When Earnings Are Not Enough: Post-Socialist Forms of Stratification." Paper presented at the semiannual meeting of the Research Committee on Social Stratification (RC 28) of the International Sociological Association, Warsaw, Poland, May 1999.

———. 1999b. *Survey of Employment, Income, and Attitudes in Russia.* Codebook, Technical Report, and Machine-Readable Data File. Inter-University Consortium for Political and Social Research. The University of Michigan, Institute for Social Research, Ann Arbor, MI.

———. 2000a. "Membership Benefits or Selection Effects? Why Former Communist Party Members Do Better in Post-Soviet Russia." *Social Science Research* 29, pp. 25–50.

———. 2000b. "Regional Migration Dynamics in Russia Since the Collapse of Communism." Paper presented at the annual meetings of the Population Association of America, Los Angeles, CA, March 2000.

———. 2000c. "Labor Markets, Transition, and Labor Market Transitions in Contemporary Russia." Paper presented at the Annual Meetings of the American Sociological Association, Washington, DC, August 2000.

———. 2000d. "Market, State, or Don't Know? Education, Ideology, and Voting in Contemporary Russia." *Social Forces* 79, pp. 477–521.

Gerber, Theodore P., and Michael Hout. 1998. "More Shock Than Therapy: Employment and Income in Russia, 1991–1995." *American Journal of Sociology* 104, pp. 1–50.

Goskomstat Rossii. 1998. *Regiony Rossii, 1998.* Moskva: Goskomstat.

Grant, Don Sherman II. 1996. "The Political Economy of New Business Formation Across the American States, 1970–1985." *Social Science Quarterly* 77, pp. 28–42.

Hanley, Eric. 2000. "Self-employment in Post-Communist Eastern Europe: A Refuge from Poverty or Road to Riches?" *Communist and Post-Communist Studies* 33, pp. 379–402.

Hanson, Philip. 1996. "Regions, Local Power and Economic Change in Russia."

Pp. 21–78 in Alan Smith, ed., *Challenges for Russian Economic Reform*. Washington, DC: Brookings Institution.

Jones, Anthony, and William Moskoff. 1991. *Ko-ops: The Rebirth of Entrepreneurship in the Soviet Union*. Bloomington: Indiana University Press.

Kornai, Janos. 1990. *The Road to a Free Economy: Shifting from a Socialist System—The Example of Hungary*. New York: W.W. Norton.

———. 1992. *The Socialist System: The Political Economy of Socialism*. Princeton, NJ: Princeton University Press.

Kryshtanovskaya, Olga, and Stephen White. 1996. "From Soviet *Nomenklatura* to Russian Elite." *Europe-Asia Studies* 48, pp. 711–733.

Laferrere, Anne. 2001. "Self-employment and Intergenerational Transfers: Liquidity Constraints and Family Environment." *International Journal of Sociology*. In press.

Light, Ivan. 1972. *Ethnic Enterprises: Business and Welfare Among Chinese, Japanese, and Blacks*. Berkeley: University of California Press.

Linz, Susan J. 1996. "Gender Differences in the Russian Labor Market." *Journal of Economic Studies* 30, pp. 161–185.

Loutfi, Martha F. 1991. "Self-Employment Patterns and Policy Issues in Europe." *International Labour Review* 130, pp. 1–20.

Luber, Silvia, Henning Lohmann, Walter Müller, and Paolo Barbieri. 2000. "Male Self-employment in Four European Countries: The Relevance of Education and Experience Across Industries." *International Journal of Sociology* 30, pp. 5–44.

Mau, Vladimir, and Vadim Stupin. 1997. "The Political Economy of Russian Regionalism." *Communist Economies and Economic Transformation* 9, pp. 5–25.

Mikheeva, Nadezhda. 1999. "Differentiation of Social and Economic Situation in the Russian Regions and Problems of Regional Policy." Working Paper 99/09. Economic Education and Research Consortium, Moscow.

Moore, Barrington, Jr. 1954. *Terror and Progress USSR: Some Sources of Change and Stability in the Soviet Dictatorship*. Cambridge, MA: Harvard University Press.

Nee, Victor. 1989. "A Theory of Market Transition: From Redistribution to Markets in State Socialism." *American Sociological Review* 54, pp. 663–681.

———. 1991. "Social Inequalities in Reforming State Socialism: Between Redistribution and Markets in China." *American Sociological Review* 56, pp. 267–282.

———. 1996. "The Emergence of a Market Society: Changing Mechanisms of Stratification in China." *American Journal of Sociology* 101, pp. 908–949.

Nee, Victor, and Yang Cao. 1999. "Path Dependent Societal Transformation: Stratification in Mixed Hybrid Economies." *Theory and Society* 28, pp. 799–834.

Nee, Victor, and Rebecca Matthews. 1996. "Market Transition and Societal Transformation in Reforming State Socialism." *Annual Review of Sociology* 22, pp. 401–435.

Parish, William L., and Ethan Michelson. 1996. "Politics and Markets: Dual Transformations." *American Journal of Sociology* 101, pp. 1042–1059.

Popov, Vladimir. 1999. "Reform Strategies and Economic Performance of Russia's Regions." Paper presented at the conference "Economic Growth and Institutional Development: Lessons from Economic Reform in Russia." Moscow, December 1999.

Radaev, Vadim. 1994. "On Some Features of the Normative Behavior of the New Russian Entrepreneurs." *Problems of Economic Transition* 37, pp. 17–28.

Robert, Peter and Erszebet Bukodi. 2000. "Who Are the Entrepreneurs and Where Do They Come From? Transition to Self-employment Before, Under and After Communism in Hungary." *International Review of Sociology* 10, pp. 147–171.

Róna-Tas, Akos. 1994. "The First Shall Be Last? Entrepreneurship and Communist Cadres in the Transition from Socialism." *American Journal of Sociology* 100, pp. 40–69.

Rutland, Peter. 1994. "Privatisation in Russia: One Step Forward, Two Steps Back?" *Europe-Asia Studies* 46, pp. 1109–1132.

Schumpeter, Joseph A. 1942 [1975]. *Capitalism, Socialism and Democracy.* New York: Harper and Row.

Shavit, Yossi, and Ephraim Yuchtman-Yaar. 2001. "Ethnicity, Education, and Other Determinants of Self-Employment in Israel." *International Journal of Sociology.* In press.

Standing, Guy. 1994. "The Changing Position of Women in Russian Industry: Prospects of Marginalization." *World Development* 22, pp. 271–283.

Steinmetz, George, and Erik Olin Wright. 1989. "The Fall and Rise of the Petty Bourgeoisie: Changing Patterns of Self-Employment in the Postwar United States." *American Journal of Sociology* 94, pp. 973–1018.

Sutherland, Douglas, and Philip Hanson. 1996. "Structural Change in the Economies of Russia's Regions." *Europe-Asia Studies* 48, pp. 367–392.

Szelenyi, Ivan. 1988. *Socialist Entrepreneurs: Embourgeoisement in Rural Hungary.* Madison: University of Wisconsin Press.

Titma, Mikk, Nancy Brandon Tuma, and Brian D. Silver. 1998. "Winners and Losers in the Post-communist Transition: New Evidence from Estonia." *Post-Soviet Affairs* 14, pp. 114–136.

Van Selm, Bert. 1998. "Economic Performance in Russia's Regions." *Europe-Asia Studies* 50, pp. 603–618.

Vasilenko, I., N. Dulina, and V. Tokarev. 1995. "Sotsial'nye ustanovki molodykh predprinimatelei." [Social orientations of young entrepreneurs]. *Sotsiologicheskie Issledovaniia,* no. 3, pp. 170–174.

Walder, Andrew. 1996. "Markets and Inequality in Transitional Economies: Toward Testable Theories." *American Journal of Sociology* 101, pp. 1060–1073.

Wharton, Amy S. 1989. "Gender Segregation in Private-Sector, Public-Sector, and Self-Employed Occupations, 1950–1981." *Social Science Quarterly* 70, pp. 923–940.

Wieviorka, Michel. 1994. "Les Nouveaux Entrepreneurs et les Directeurs d'Entreprises en Russie." [The new entrepreneurs and enterprise directors in Russia]. *Revue d'Etudes Comparatives Est-Ouest* 25, pp. 65–78.

Xie, Yu, and Emily Hannum. 1996. "Regional Variation in Earnings Inequality in Reform-Era Urban China." *American Journal of Sociology* 101, pp. 950–992.

Zhou, Xueguang. 2000. "Economic Transformation and Income Inequality in Urban China: Evidence From Panel Data." *American Journal of Sociology* 105, pp. 1135–1174.

2

The Worm and the Caterpillar

The Small Private Sector in the Czech Republic, Hungary, and Slovakia

Ákos Róna-Tas

Introduction

Eleven years after the collapse of communism, Central Europe can boast of a large and lively private sector. The success has been spectacular. Small private enterprises have been mushrooming all over the region. By 1998, for every 1,000 inhabitants there were 196 registered enterprises in the Czech Republic, 109 in Hungary, and 71.5 in Slovakia, compared to 51.8 in the European Union. This is especially stunning if one recalls the extreme concentration of state socialist economies, where a few thousand state-owned big companies produced almost the entire GDP. The explosion in the number of mostly small enterprises happened at a time when the economically active population was shrinking and the economies were going through a major recession.

Along with foreign investment, the small private sector is often touted as the bright hope of postcommunist economies. From the popular press to international financial institutions, everyone seems to pin their hopes on the vibrant small private sector. During the early days of the economic transition, opponents of radical policies contended that shock therapy was bound to fail because the existing industrial structure was essentially unreformable. Even privatization was thought to be unlikely to mend it. Instead, the future of a new, capitalist economy would lie with the organic growth of new private enterprises, unfettered by the organizational inertia of the socialist giants. This bottom-up capitalism foresaw the proliferation of small companies, the best of which would grow and eventually edge out the dinosaurs.

Of the three countries under investigation, Hungary started with a decided advantage. Before 1990, Hungary developed a small private sector that was very modest compared to its current one, but that was large compared to that of any other state socialist country, with the exception of Poland (Róna-Tas 1997). Czechoslovakia, on the other hand, toed an orthodox

communist line and tolerated no private enterprise until its communist leaders were deposed by the Velvet Revolution of 1989 (Árvay 1994; Benáček
1994). Yet quite unexpectedly, the Czech Republic claims the largest small
private sector in the region. In this chapter I will argue that the optimism
surrounding the small private sector in Central Europe is largely misplaced
and is a consequence of a conceptual misunderstanding. A large number of
small businesses are for the most part not manifestations of entrepreneurship
but forms of self-employment. While entrepreneurs with capacity to grow
do exist in Central Europe, they are vastly outnumbered by the self-employed.
I will first sketch two theoretical positions, the entrepreneurial paradigm vs.
the labor market approach. I draw upon Max Weber's distinction between
enterprise and household to point out crucial differences between the two
approaches. Then I will present empirical evidence that there are many more
worms—self-employed who will never grow out of the boundaries of their
households—than caterpillars—small entrepreneurs, who initially may look
very much like the self-employed, but who then metamorphose into full-
fledged businesses.

The Small Sector as the Sector of Entrepreneurs

The dominant approach to the small private sector in Eastern Europe per-
ceives its expansion as an upsurge in entrepreneurialism (e.g., Róna-Tas and
Lengyel 1997–1998; United Nations 1997; Ivy 1996; Acs and Audretsch
1993). This paradigm, shared by analysts, governments, and international
organizations alike, is illustrated by the following statement in 1997 by Milan
Cagala, then the minister of the economy of the Slovak Republic:

> Small and medium enterprises play a significant and irreplaceable role in
> all countries with a market economy. Their dynamic development is one of
> the basic presumptions of healthy economic development. Small and me-
> dium enterprises with their high adaptability to market requirements and
> their innovative and creative approach are able to respond immediately to
> the newest demand trends and to satisfy the requirements of the most ex-
> acting customers. A no less important role is played by SMEs in the area of
> creating new job opportunities, and with their healthy diffusion they posi-
> tively affect employment growth. (Národná 1997)

An Organization for Economic Cooperation and Development (OECD)
report on the SMEs in transition economies agrees:

> SMEs are playing a key role in the restructuring of former centralized econo-
> mies. For example, small enterprises increase the dynamism of the market

and thereby help to maintain the momentum of adjustment to new economic and political conditions. (OECD 1996, p. 7)

The fuel of small private-sector growth is entrepreneurial initiative. Entrepreneurialism is key in making these small enterprises innovative, adaptable, flexible, and able to adopt new technologies. The protagonist is the entrepreneur, Schumpeter's creative genius, whose brilliance in linking the factors of production (capital, technology, personnel, etc.) in a novel way is rewarded by profit for him or her and economic development for all (Schumpeter 1936, 1947/1989, 1949/1989; Kirzner 1973; Kirzner et al. 1980).[1]

The main unit framing entrepreneurial decisions and activity is the enterprise, which is separated from the household and follows its own logic (Weber 1921/1978, pp. 161–164, 375–380). The enterprise keeps accounts separate from the household budget. The enterprise with its own interests guides entrepreneurial action. Through the success of the enterprise, the entrepreneur will achieve his or her own economic success. The entrepreneur, therefore, will follow the logic of profit maximization, market expansion, and accumulation. To achieve these goals, the entrepreneur must calculate rationally and try to find the most profitable combination of production factors. Profit is reinvested into the enterprise but credit is also constantly sought as the enterprise grows.

The small enterprise is both horizontally and vertically networked. It interacts with both small and large companies as supplier or subcontractor and purchaser. Its market is limited only by the opportunities available and can reach beyond the boundaries of the locality, the region, and even the nation-state when profitable.

The entrepreneurial approach sees economic units in the private sector on a continuum from the smallest, single-person business to the largest company. Each size is a station in the process of entrepreneurial expansion. Of course, not all of the caterpillars will grow into butterflies, but all have the potential to do so. Growth has its limits, but not before the business reaches at least medium size. The very expression "small- and medium-sized enterprises" (SME) suggests that small and medium-sized enterprises are similar in principle and there is a smooth progression from one to the other.

In the creation of new enterprises, the entrepreneurial approach emphasizes opportunities and pull factors. People start small enterprises because they see new opportunities opening up in the market. Entrepreneurship is an active choice and not a forced, defensive move. Enterprise growth follows the business cycle. During bad times, the number and size of small entrepreneurs contracts, while during good times there is entrepreneurial expansion. During periods of growth, small enterprises employ greater numbers and hire new people from the open labor market.

Adopting the entrepreneurial paradigm results in important policy biases. Policy makers view small enterprises as a major source of taxes, even given awareness that tax collection is not always easy. From this perspective, the main policy instrument to stimulate small enterprises is credit. To make credit available to small businesses, policy makers must set up special funds that give loans to small enterprises, guarantee funds that entrepreneurs borrow from banks, or persuade banks through regulation or various financial incentives to offer loans on favorable terms. Stimulating the small sector thus can be an instrument for cutting unemployment through the expansion of existing businesses that need to hire more employees.

The causes of the upsurge of the small private sector, the entrepreneurial paradigm argues, are new opportunities, some of which are the long-term legacies of the socialist economy. Small businesses thrive because they fill the holes created by the weakness of the service sector, the poor supply of consumer goods, the deficiencies of socialist trade, and the inefficiencies of a concentrated, overcentralized economy. Coupled with the information revolution and the process of globalization, these factors create new possibilities upon which entrepreneurs seize.

The Small Sector as the Sector of Self-Employment

Drawing on the works of Teréz Laky (1994, 1998), Mihály Laki (1998), and István R. Gábor (1997), one can develop an alternative paradigm, called the labor market approach. This second paradigm results in a very different appraisal of what has happened in Eastern Europe in the last decade and leads to contrasting policy recommendations. It also offers a contrasting explanation for the sudden burst of the small private sector (Table 2.1).

The point of departure of the labor market approach is not the adventurous entrepreneur, but rather the risk-averse worker, who can choose between various options for deploying his or her labor. Other factors of production are either incidental or serve the sole purpose of increasing the value of labor. The small private sector is first and foremost a form of self-employment. While the self-employed have more autonomy than most employees do and must show some initiative compared to those who work for others, this newly gained freedom is not the freedom to create but the freedom to adapt. Far from being innovative, the self-employed are imitative and reactive.

In many instances, small entrepreneurs are simply employees who lost their benefits and security and now as contractors do very much the same as they did before. The employer is better off because he does not have to absorb fluctuations in demand, which are now pushed onto the contractor. Moreover, the employer does not have to pay payroll taxes (Azudová 1998).

Table 2.1

Contrasting the Two Approaches

	Entrepreneurial Caterpillar	Labor market Worm
Main actor	Entrepreneur	Self-employed
Main unit	Enterprise with its own accounting and space	Household
Main goal	Accumulation	Consumption
Main asset	Smart combination of factors of production	Labor
Size	Continuum from small to large	Segmented
Genesis	Pull	Push
Entrepreneurship	Innovation, initiative	Defensive, reactive, imitative
Calculation	Rational, accounts well-kept	Traditional, poor bookkeeping
Commitment to enterprise	High, full-time	Low or intermittent, part-time
Contracts	Formal, legal	Informal
Employment	Employs others	Employs only self, family, and people with strong ties
Legal form	Incorporated Limited liability	Sole proprietorship Unlimited liability
Market	Anywhere, potentially even outside the country	Local, geographically bounded
Relationship to large companies	Supplier, subcontractor	None or buyer
Source of profit	Market opportunities	Self-exploitation
Business cycle	Expansion in up cycle	Expansion in down cycle
Taxes	Major source of tax revenue	Tax evasion (even when business is legal)
Solution to unemployment	Business expansion	New business creation
Policy intervention	Credit	Training
Growth	Likely to grow when successful	Keeps its small size even when successful

Some of these savings may be passed onto the contractors, who now must fend for themselves when they get sick or grow old.

To receive social security benefits, a large segment of the self-employed run their businesses part-time, merely complementing their salaries and benefit packages from regular employment. Unlike the medium-sized enterprises that function continuously until they go bankrupt, the small enterprise often goes through periods of dormancy, existing only on paper, to resume activity whenever new opportunities emerge. During this time, the entrepreneur lives off wages.

The genesis of small enterprises is driven by push factors. People start those enterprises because they have few other choices. They are forced into self-employment precisely when other market opportunities are withering. The expansion of the small private sector, therefore, runs counter to the business cycle. During bad times, the number of small entrepreneurs expands; during good times, the entrepreneurial sector contracts (Róna-Tas 2000).

The labor market approach sees radical differences between small- and medium-sized units. Small, and especially micro, businesses are not medium-sized enterprises in waiting (Kuczi 2000). They are different not only in size but also in kind. The difference between small and larger enterprises can be traced back to the essential point of the relationship between enterprise and household. In small businesses, the household and the enterprise are not separated. Small business is just one part of a portfolio of strategies aiming not at profit maximization but at the maximization of household consumption. This is reflected in the legal form most small businesses take. They are not incorporated companies with limited liability, but sole proprietorships, where a single individual and his or her household carries all the responsibility for the business.

Accumulation is social. What the self-employed save, they accumulate as resources in housing and other goods that enhance social status. They also invest in the human capital of their children. Because expansion is not the main goal, they rarely seek credit. Whatever extra money is needed is borrowed from family and friends. The main assets of the self-employed are their labor and skills. As a result, the two most obvious ways to increase income are to work more and to upgrade skills.

The labor market approach argues that the small enterprise will not grow because it is not separated from the household. Its budget is a subordinate part of the household budget. The enterprise is not interested in growth. Its natural limits are set by the (extended) household. When small enterprises hire new workers, they hire from a limited pool of relatives, friends, and acquaintances and not from the anonymous labor market. Small entrepreneurs do not have the organizational skill to command a staff, and they are reluctant to take on the responsibilities of an employer, because that means that they would lose flexibility, including the possibility of temporarily suspending their operation. As a result, the size of small enterprises is inelastic. This approach would agree that the small sector can alleviate unemployment—its counter-cyclicality makes it even more useful in mitigating the effects of recessions. But it would also argue that small enterprises help the unemployed not by hiring more people but by giving the unemployed a chance to start their own businesses.

While a real entrepreneur would find business wherever opportunity emerges, the self-employed, tied to their households, are geographically locked into local markets near their residences. And they are most unlikely to step outside the confines of the domestic market. Their share in exports is meager. Their spatial inertia is reinforced by the important role of family and close friends in the operation of the enterprise.

The main policy instrument, the labor market approach contends, is not making credit available, but helping to upgrade skills. Since the single most important asset these small businesses have is labor, improving skills helps them the most.

The self-employment paradigm explains the upsurge of small businesses with a set of factors different from those proposed by its rival. It points to the collapse of universal state employment, the transformational recession (Kornai 1994), the weak postcommunist state that can enforce tax discipline only for larger companies, and precommunist traditions of artisanry and petty trade.

The Worm and the Caterpillar

Having sketched the ideal types[2] characterizing each approach, I do not pretend that supporters of either paradigm are so foolish as to believe that only their type of small business exists. Those subscribing to the entrepreneurial paradigm will readily admit that there are self-employed people who may never rise above their current solitary state. Those in the opposite camp also acknowledge that there are true entrepreneurs in the small private sector. The point of empirical disagreement between the two camps is twofold. On the one hand, they disagree over the relative weight of the two types in the economy. This is a disagreement over the distribution of the types at a given point in time. On the other hand, the two approaches differ in how they expect small businesses to behave over time. The self-employment thesis believes that the small private sector has little growth potential, so that the small will stay small. The entrepreneurial thesis posits that while certainly not all enterprises will grow, many will. This second disagreement is the central bone of contention. Had we found that the vast majority of small enterprises show the characteristics of self-employment, the entrepreneurial approach would still argue that the form of the enterprise is endogenous, changing as soon as business success requires it to change. The caterpillar may look like a worm, but when the time comes, it turns into a butterfly.

In the next part of the chapter, I will review the legacies of the precommunist and communist past for the small private sector. I will then survey the main institutional developments since 1990. These will be followed by a discussion of the measurement problems one faces in studying the small private sector and what the problem of bad business registers can tell us about the nature of the private sector. Then I will present data from a multinational SME panel survey from 1995 and 1997 directed by Eurostat, the statistical office of the European Union.[3] While the two years between the two waves is rather short, there is substantial evidence that the vast majority of the small businesses in the three countries are indeed primarily a form of self-employment.

Legacies

Precommunist Legacies

Before 1948, the small private sector had been a main pillar of the Czechoslovak and Hungarian economies. Being less urbanized, developed, and industrial, Hungary's small businesses were somewhat more backward and had stronger linkages to agriculture than their Czechoslovak counterparts in the Czech lands (Róna-Tas 1997). Nevertheless, in both countries, the small sector was populated primarily by artisans and craftsmen in industry and services, small tradesmen in commerce, and small farmers in agriculture. These people, while self-employed and dependent on their own initiative, were nevertheless traditional. Their line of activities was fairly inflexible. Shoemakers made shoes, textile traders traded textiles, and apple growers grew apples for their entire lives, and they were more likely to give up their independence and find employment in their specialization than to switch to another line of business. In the more agricultural regions, artisans also kept household farms where they raised food staples for their own consumption and to a limited extent for sale.

The household played a major role in the small sector, providing labor and other resources for the enterprise. Employing family members was a goal of the enterprise, and apprentices and non-kin employees were often treated as family members. The home was often the workshop or the store, and when the business needed extra financial resources, those were taken from household consumption; when the business produced extra profit, the surplus was gobbled up by the household.

These small businesses were risk averse and rarely grew, but bankruptcy was also uncommon except in times of economic recession. Small businessmen sought to move their sons and daughters into the higher classes through education.

While the bulk of the small private sector in the precommunist era had little to do with Schumpeterian images of entrepreneurship, this sector nevertheless fostered personal attributes often found in entrepreneurs. It promoted independence, rational calculation, diligence, and even a measure of creativity.

Communist Legacies

After 1948, small producers were almost completely erased by communist economic policies. The Czechoslovak and Hungarian economies, just like the others in the Soviet bloc, went through a rapid and extreme concentration and became dominated by a few large companies. By the mid-1960s, the entire Czechoslovak economy was consolidated into approximately 1,400 companies, 400 of which were in industry (McDermott and Mejstrik 1993; Bohatá and Mládek 1998; Zemplinerová and Stíbal 1994). In Hungary, the concentration was less extreme; nevertheless, it was still staggering. About one-third of the workers employed in the 1,400 Hungarian industrial firms worked with more than 1,000 fellow employees (Róna-Tas 1997). The size distribution of companies in state socialist economies can be depicted as an upside-down pyramid: Most of the workforce worked in large companies, a much smaller proportion in medium-sized enterprises, and even fewer workers found employment with any of the small firms.

Concentration of production dovetailed with the concentration of property rights in the hands of the state. As a result, the overwhelming majority of the economically active population were state employees in large establishments working set hours in ill-paid but secure jobs, receiving benefits ranging from free or subsidized child care to home loans and vacations. This system of universal state employment was the major paradigm that integrated the population into the economy. In Hungary, universal state employment started to disintegrate gradually after its peak in the early 1960s, once the insatiable manpower needs of the socialist industrialization began to run up against the physical limits of available labor.

In the last decade of Hungarian communism, small entrepreneurship and self-employment began to gain ground, although mostly in the interstices of the state sector. Most private activities were part-time and on the side, with people keeping one foot firmly in the state sector for security, using their state job to gain access to resources, clients, information, and so on, which then could be used in the private business. Moreover, given the shortages constantly regenerated by the state sector, the small private sector had no worries about demand for its products and services. There was little or no competition, because demand always outstripped supply. Productive accumulation was out of the question, because the ever vigilant communist state until the very end wanted to keep small businesses small. By the late 1980s, there was a vigorous private sector in Hungary, comprised of small units in the form of self-employment and various business partnerships, though the entire sector had a strong socialist stamp on it. In its waning days, the Hungarian Socialist Worker's Party embraced entrepreneurs and developed an ideology waxing poetic about the initiative and resourcefulness of the small entrepreneur. The small entrepreneur was seen as a welcome complement to socialist large-scale production. When communism collapsed, Hungary already possessed a sizable protoprivate sector of small units producing around an estimated 20% of the country's GDP.

In Czechoslovakia, the private sector was more thoroughly eliminated. By 1961, only 12,000 artisans were left, a fifth of the figure in Hungary around that time. The system of universal state employment survived until the very end, and entrepreneurship and private enterprise had been demonized and criminalized longer than they were in Hungary. The private sector was negligible until 1989, contributing only 4% of the GDP (Árvay 1994). In the 1990s, the Czech and Slovak small private sector had to be built from scratch (Benáček 1994).

Although socialist economies made a heroic attempt to eliminate all markets, they were never completely successful. With some exceptions, consumer goods were almost always distributed through markets, as distorted as they were. The alternative, centralized rationing, has never played an important role in allocating consumer goods. Households, bound by "hard budget constraints" (Kornai 1980), had to make choices about how to spend their incomes. As labor shortages became endemic from the 1960s, a limited (and later, in Hungary, a more liberal) labor market began to emerge. By the late 1980s, in some ways, households were more attuned to the ways of the market than most state companies were.

Yet another communist legacy was the disproportionate emphasis put on industry and the neglect of services. By 1989, this was again more true for Czechoslovakia than for Hungary, which boasted one of the strongest tourist industries in Europe at the end of the 1980s.

The communist era thus left a highly centralized economy, more so in Czechoslovakia than in Hungary, a budding private sector in Hungary but virtually none in Czechoslovakia, and certain elements of the market in the sphere of household consumption, which socialist economies were never able to completely eliminate.

Institutions

Small Privatization

The entrepreneurial paradigm lays heavy emphasis on the importance of the creation of private property rights and the privatization of the economy. Small privatization was carried out both in Hungary and in Czechoslovakia with great success. In Hungary, over 10,000 small businesses were auctioned off. Most of them were restaurants, bars, motels, and shops. About 23,000 small businesses in the Czech Republic and around 10,000 in Slovakia were privatized mostly through auctions, but also through direct sale. Another 20,000 units were returned as restitution to their pre-1948 owners in the two countries, which separated in 1993. Apart from small privatization, a few people were able to obtain small stand-alone pieces of larger state companies, most often involving only the machinery or the premises but not the workforce.

While small privatization was a necessary and useful step, it ran its course by 1994. Moreover, the return of a few tens of thousands of units to private hands hardly explains the creation of the hundreds of thousands of new small businesses. In fact, most small businessmen not only never participated in privatization, but they also often felt contemptuous about the privatization process, which they considered corrupt and criminal.

Laws on Competition

A series of laws and regulations lifted entry barriers in all but a few areas in the three countries. Laws were created to guard competition and an Office of Economic Competition was set up in Hungary and Slovakia, while a Ministry of Economic Competition is guarding against cartels and monopolies in the Czech Republic. In all three countries, a market share of over 30% triggers intervention. The laws on competition are useful and can protect small businesses from encroaching monopolies, but most small businesses are in market segments where no company threatens to achieve such a large market share. Laws on competition primarily benefit medium and large companies against other even larger businesses.

Tax Laws

Tax laws are almost impenetrable in these countries. In Slovakia, for instance, between 1992 and 1998 the main eleven laws were modified seventy-seven times (Lampl 1998). In 1998, over three-quarters of Hungarian entrepreneurs in a survey claimed "that tax legislation is so complicated that even professional accountants find it difficult to handle," and 95% agree that tax rules change too frequently (Tóth and Semjén 1998). Tax laws and their fickle nature are one of the main complaints of small-business people.

Two elements of the tax system tremendously stimulated small enterprise formation. The first is high payroll taxes. In Hungary, the employer pays 49% of the wage in social security taxes, one of the highest figures in Europe. Czech and Slovak employers pay less, 33% and 35%, respectively (OECD 1996, p. 72). This creates an incentive for employers to contract their workers and pay for the job as an expense and not a wage. This also allows them to save on other overhead costs.

The very same rules that contribute to the *increase in the number* of small enterprises also *retard the growth* of each small enterprise. Hiring anyone as an employee is expensive for small businesses, too.

The second element is the opportunity for fudging the dividing line between personal consumption and business cost. For Americans or West Europeans, there is nothing new in writing off personal expenditures as business expenses. In Eastern Europe, high income taxes and value added tax (VAT) create a powerful inducement to set up small businesses as tax shelters.[4]

Enterprise Funds

A series of funds was set up to help small businesses. These enterprise funds not only serve just their usual function but also must compensate for a poor banking system. Commercial banking has emerged fairly recently in these countries. In Hungary, bank reform started earliest, in 1987 (Bartlett 1997), while Czechoslovakia created its two-tier banking system in 1990. The banking sector in the region has been notoriously trouble-prone. Bad loans and poor services drove several banks to the verge of (or into) bankruptcy. Several bail-out packages were dispatched to rescue various banks.[5] In Hungary and Slovakia, small enterprises rarely borrow money from banks. Interest rates are high, the collateral required is prohibitive, and banks are not very interested in small lending because of the high transaction cost relative to the return. In the Czech Republic in the first part of the 1990s, bank credit was more available, but it has become tighter since 1997. Some of the enterprise funds were created by foreign organizations (European Union, European Bank for Reconstruction and Development, World Bank, etc.), but each government has its own set of programs as well. At the end of the decade, there were eight small enterprise funds in the Czech Republic and seven in Hungary and Slovakia. Some of these programs are narrowly targeted, while others address more general needs. These programs can be very helpful, but they are often an inefficient way of creating new employment, because the self-employed are reluctant to employ others, especially strangers. By 1997, the largest Slovak SME support program had created only 820 jobs at a cost of almost half a billion SK (Národná 1997).

The Legal Forms

Private business can take various legal forms, and the choice already indicates the nature of the enterprise. There is a key distinction between individual (physical/natural) and legal persons, and full and limited liability businesses. The sole proprietor (*egyéni vállalkozó, fyzické osoby*) is a natural person and is fully liable for his business. This means that he is solely and fully responsible for his business, its debts, and any liabilities. Unlimited liability links the finances of the business with those of the household. If the sole proprietor goes into bankruptcy, his home, his car, his furniture, and his savings can all be seized.

In all three countries, sole proprietors register not at the business registry but in an office of the local government. Sole proprietors need no capital and are allowed to follow a simplified form of bookkeeping (unless the value of their sales becomes very high). They pay no corporate taxes, but rather are taxed through the income they derive from their business. Sole proprietors can employ others, but only a small minority do. The vast majority of private businesses in all three countries consist of unincorporated individual businesspersons (Table 2.2).

One or more persons can form a company (*társaság, spoločnost*, or *společnost*). Companies are registered at the business registries. In limited-liability companies, owners are responsible only to the extent of the assets of the company. Each company must have base capital at the time of registration. The company pays corporate taxes and must follow double-entry bookkeeping and undertake rigorous reporting responsibilities. The majority of incorporated companies are limited liability companies. The rest are mostly joint-stock companies and cooperatives.

Finally, there are companies that stand halfway between sole proprietorships and limited liability companies. These are partnerships and they do not limit liability of all owners. At least one is fully responsible for the company's liabilities. Confusingly, these are called legal persons in Slovakia and the Czech Republic and nonlegal persons in Hungary. Members in general or unlimited partnerships (*közkereseti társaság, verejná obchodná spoločnost*) are all liable financially. Limited partnerships (*betéti társaság, komanditná spoločnost*) have at least one member who is fully liable and can have others

Table 2.2

The Distribution of Businesses in Hungary, the Czech Republic, and Slovakia in 1999

Hungary		Czech Republic		Slovakia	
Individual businesses		Individual businesses		Individual businesses	
Sole proprietors	660,139	Sole proprietors	1,528,151	Sole proprietors	295,750
Full liability partnerships					
Partnerships	211,835				
Limited liability businesses		Legal entities		Legal entities	
Limited liability companies	160,647	Limited liability companies and partnerships	167,064	Limited liability companies	45,277
Joint-stock companies	4,350	Joint-stock companies	13,009	Joint-stock companies	4,060
Cooperatives	8,191	Cooperatives	10,236	Cooperatives	1,802
Other corporations	3,938			Other legal entities including partnerships and nonbusiness organizations	32,136
Total incorporated units	177,436	Total legal business entities	190,309	Total legal entities	83,275
		Other legal entities including nonbusiness organizations	244,859		
Total	1,049,410	Total	1,963,319	Total	379,025

Source: For Hungary, KSH 2000; for the Czech Republic and Slovakia, CESTAT 1999.

who are not. These are business partnerships and are popular in Hungary, but very rare in the other two countries.

Importantly, the legal form of the business imposes different modes of operation. Full personal financial responsibility sets limits to growth. While there are plenty of small limited liability companies with a single proprietor, only a handful of large companies are sole proprietorships. Hiring others and investing in capital are much riskier for sole proprietors than for corporate companies. Differences in tax policy for different legal forms assume that sole proprietors maximize personal (or family) income only, while owners of companies are driven by business success. The more rigorous bookkeeping and reporting requirements put pressure on corporate companies to keep better records and organize information more rationally than individual entrepreneurs.

Overregistration and Underreporting

Data on the small private sector are of much worse quality than data for the rest of the economy. In all three countries, several agencies gather information about businesses. The main source of public information is the Central Statistical Office, but economic units must submit information to a host of other institutions, such as the tax authorities, the National Labor Office, the Social Security Administration, and the business chambers.[6] When businesses register themselves, they receive their tax identification number, and they must update their registry entry as their condition changes. The business registry is in various states of disarray in the three countries. Eurostat estimated that about 64% of registered Czech enterprises were active in 1995.[7] In Hungary and Slovakia, the figure is somewhat higher, but that still leaves over one in five businesses registered but not functioning (Table 2.3 and Marková 1998).

The rate of overregistration is a function of size: the smaller the business, the more likely it is to be registered but inactive. Overregistration is a subtle and interesting phenomenon. It turns the usual problem of the underground economy, that is, production without registration, on its head: registration without production. The phenomenon exists for several reasons, some of which are relevant to our understanding of the nature of the small private sector. Overregistration exists partly because some companies are in the purgatory of bankruptcy or in the process of winding up. This applies to only a small percentage and explains mostly the registration discrepancy for the larger companies. (The Hungarian figures do not include these firms on the way out.) There are also costs for deregistering. More importantly, to deregister, the company must give a final accounting. This costs money, and some companies may have debts they would rather not face. But the most significant

Table 2.3

The Extent of Overregistration in Hungary and the Czech Republic
(percent active by size and legal form in Hungary and by economic branch in the Czech Republic)

Number of employees	% Active
Hungary 1999	
0	72.7
1–9	95.1
10–19	73.6
20–49	86.3
50–249	99.7
250–499	99.8
500+	99.5
Legal form	
Sole proprietorships	70.8
Partnerships	91.9
Limited liability companies	95.1
Total	79.2
Czech Republic 1999	
Selected Economic Branches	
Industry	60.3
Construction	39.4
Wholesale and retail	33.4
Hotels and restaurants	35.2
Transportation	45.3
Financial intermediation	19.0
Agriculture	34.5

Source: CESTAT 1999; Czech Ministry of Industry estimates.

reason for overregistration is the desire of many to increase their options to make and save money. Their purpose is not to create and develop a company, but to have a tool to save on taxes and use it when it is to their advantage in formal contracts. As registered entrepreneurs, they can write off a long list of things as cost of business and also avoid the sales tax. In its most blatant form, the enterprise is simply a way of cutting the costs of household purchases. From computers to cars, from cell phones to book purchases, anything and everything can be written off. If in a given year using the business is not worth the hassle of doing the necessary paperwork, the business lies dormant, only to come back to life whenever it benefits the owner.

Almost all of the registered but inactive businesses belong to people who have jobs elsewhere or are receiving pensions. In Hungary, in 1998 only 59% of all sole proprietors worked full-time in their enterprises. Twenty-nine percent worked part-time and the rest were pensioners (Laky 1999, p. 134).

Overregistration is therefore a sign of the owner's casual commitment to the business enterprise.

The poor state of business registration, however, raises a series of questions about any data on the small private sector. While all larger companies must submit statistical reports monthly, quarterly, and annually, statistical offices obtain their data for small enterprises through annual sample surveys. The samples are drawn from the registries. Since nonresponse is high, the office can only guess which small enterprises exist but refuse to answer, and which should not be in the registry at all. The surveys are short, covering only a few, basic topics out of fear of losing even more potential respondents. The tax authorities do get financial data from most businesses, but for the smallest ones the data are so distorted that no one believes them. The average income of Hungarian sole proprietors, for instance, is reported to be minimum wage, although the Central Statistical Office estimates that this is one-fifth of what they actually earn.

Results of the Eurostat Panel Survey

In this last section, I turn to the Eurostat panel of small- and medium-sized enterprises, entitled Demography of Small and Medium-sized Enterprises (DOSME). The survey has been carried out in eleven countries in East and Central Europe.[8] These data allow us to investigate some of the contrasting claims of the two theoretical approaches. The survey started in 1995 and has gathered information annually ever since. Each year, interviews are conducted with companies formed that year, except during the first wave, when the sample was drawn from all existing companies. In 1997, the 1995 sample was reinterviewed, providing a two-year window on the development of small businesses. This means that the data on change are "censored." The companies that went bankrupt provided no data in 1997, and therefore the sample in that year is more successful than the average. This biases the data against the self-employment thesis, because obviously the proportion of growing companies will be higher among survivors than among survivors and failures together.[9] The DOSME panel seems to be representative of the businesses by legal form in the Czech Republic, Hungary, and Slovakia (Table 2.4). For the other countries, the quality of the sample varies.

Table 2.5 includes data from all eleven countries and shows the distribution of two variables by legal form, size, and method of establishment. The variables were measured in 1995 and refer to the practice of the enterprises the year before. The first column shows the percentage of companies that invested in 1994. The lowest figure is for sole proprietors. Only 27.5% made any investments. On the other end of the scale, 56.8% of public limited liability (joint-

Table 2.4

The Distribution of Businesses in the Eurostat Sample by Legal Form
(in percent)

	Czech Republic	Hungary	Slovakia
Sole proprietorship	89.7	64.7	87.9
Partnership	0.0	15.1	0.4
Cooperative	0.4	0.6	0.4
Limited liability company	8.4	13.8	10.1
Public limited liability company	0.7	0.5	1.0
Others (joint venture, etc.)	0.8	5.3	0.3
Total	100.0	100.0	100.0

Source: DOSME.

Table 2.5

Investment and Record Keeping of Businesses for All Eleven Countries in the Eurostat Sample by Legal Form, Size, and Method of Establishment
(in percent)

	Invested in 1994	Compiled a complete set of accounts
Legal form		
Sole proprietorships	27.5	14.4
Partnerships	37.6	36.7
Cooperatives	40.8	95.3
Limited-liability companies	43.9	97.6
Public limited companies		
(joint-stock companies)	56.8	98.6
Number of employees		
0	20.1	9.7
1	21.9	14.6
2	24.2	25.1
3–4	39.1	42.6
5–9	45.4	51.9
10–19	56.6	64.5
20–49	65.2	79.2
50+	72.4	91.2
Method of establishment		
Privatization	49.6	40.3
Newly created	29.6	28.9
All enterprises	31.0	30.1

Source: DOSME.

stock) companies made investments. The numbers grow consistently from individual entrepreneurs with unlimited liability, to legal entities with limited liability. The same monotonic increase can be observed as we move from small to larger businesses. The second column informs us that sole

Table 2.6

Investment and Record Keeping of Businesses in the Czech Republic, Hungary, and Slovakia (in percent)

Country	Invested in 1994	Invested more than 10% of turnover in 1994	Compilation of complete set of accounts
Czech Republic	39.8	21.4	15.7
Hungary	42.1	21.2	23.2
Slovakia	39.0	20.1	16.1

Source: DOSME.

proprietors and small businesses are less likely to keep complete accounts than limited liability and larger businesses. Since small companies tend to be new start-ups, and privatized firms are larger and incorporated, we see that new businesses both invest less and keep worse records.

It we focus on the Czech, Hungarian, and Slovak data, we find that in all three countries businesses invested in excess of the region's average (Table 2.6). Hungarian businesses are the most likely to invest, 42.1%, followed closely by the Czechs and the Slovaks. This means that three in five businesses made no investment. If we consider serious investors, those who invested at least 10% of their turnover, only one in five made substantial investment. Even in these three countries, the vast majority of the companies show no interest in expansion.

Keeping complete accounts, an indicator of the extent to which businesses are engaged in rational calculation, shows a similar picture. In 1994, Hungarian firms kept the best records, but less than a fourth kept complete accounts, and in the other two countries this figure was around 16%. Accounts are not business but tax instruments, as most businesses keep records not for strategic planning or to gauge the success of the enterprise, but simply to comply with the tax authorities.

After looking at the snapshot of businesses, we can turn to their moving image. The DOSME panel allows us to investigate the actual changes that happened between 1995 and 1997. In the Czech Republic and Slovakia, about two-thirds of the businesses that survived did not even have their own independent office, operating out of the owner's home in 1995 (Table 2.7). In those two countries, the spatial mixing of the household and business was considerable. Hungary was different. There, just over one-third worked at home. By 1997, only a small proportion of firms had moved out of the home, and of those who had a separate office in 1995 about the same proportion gave up their independent workplace and moved back into their residence.

Table 2.7

The Physical Separation of Business and Home of Surviving Enterprises Between 1995 and 1997 in the Czech Republic, Hungary, and Slovakia (in percent)

	Czech Republic	Hungary	Slovakia
Independent place in 1995 as principal place of business activity			
Independent place in 1997	73.8	82.0	73.4
Manager's home in 1997	26.2	18.0	26.6
Total with independent place in 1995 as principal place of business activity	36.7	62.5	36.8
Manager's home in 1995 as principal place of business activity			
Independent place in 1997	17.7	27.5	29.4
Manager's home in 1997	82.3	72.5	70.6
Total with manager's home in 1995 as principal place of business activity	63.3	37.5	63.2

Source: DOSME.

Table 2.8

The Change in Number of Local Units of Surviving Enterprises Between 1995 and 1997 in the Czech Republic and Slovakia (in percent)

	Czech Republic	Slovakia
One local unit in 1995		
One local unit in 1997	95.9	96.2
More than one local unit in 1997	4.1	3.8
Total with one local unit in 1995	93.8	93.2
More than one local unit in 1995		
One local unit in 1997	58.1	58.2
More than one local unit in 1997	41.9	41.8
Total with more than one local unit in 1995	6.2	5.5

Source: Národná . . . 1998, Czech Ministry of Industry data.

On balance, in all three countries there is a slight trend away from working at home, as somewhat more businesses moved out of the home than into it. This trend was strongest in Slovakia and weakest in the Czech Republic. But by and large, if a company started at home, it is likely to remain at home.

The small private sector is local and stays local. We can see that the vast majority of Czech and Slovak enterprises have a single local operation (Table 2.8). Less than 7% had more than one in 1995, but by 1997 over half of those lost all but one of their units. (These figures are not available for Hungary.) Business people operate if not out of their homes, then in the vicinity. Other data sources indicate that their customers are also predominantly local or at least domestic. In Slovakia, the share of sole proprietorships of the total output is eighty times larger and in the Czech Republic fifty times larger than their share of the total export, which is under one-half percent in both countries. Small businesses sell domestically.

If low investment, lax record keeping, using the home as an office, and lack of geographical expansion are all signs that businesses are unlikely to grow, it comes as no surprise that the vast majority of even those firms that survive stay small. Of those enterprises that had no employees in 1995, only a few had some by 1997 (Table 2.9). The vast majority, 94.2% of the Czech, 91.4% of the Hungarian, and 83.7% of the Slovak businesses, remained in this category. Most of those who moved up hired no more than 1 or 2 employees. Companies with 1 to 49 employees either lost all of their workers (17.7% in the Czech Republic, 52.5% in Hungary, and 21.9% in Slovakia) or remained within this size category. Only a minuscule portion was able to climb over the 49-employee benchmark. The small stay small; the medium either shrink or stay that way. When asked in 1997, only 11 and 10 percent of the Czech and Hungarian companies respectively planned to increase their

Table 2.9

Enterprise Growth in Terms of the Number of Employees of Surviving Businesses Between 1995 and 1997 in the Czech Republic, Hungary, and Slovakia (in percent)

	Czech Republic	Hungary	Slovakia
0 employees in 1995			
0 employees in 1997	94.2	91.4	83.7
1–49 employees in 1997	5.8	8.6	16.3
50+ employees in 1997	0.0	0.0	0.0
Total with 0 employees in 1995	78.7	63.1	55.7
1–49 employees in 1995			
0 employees in 1997	17.7	52.5	21.9
1–49 employees in 1997	81.2	47.2	77.1
50+ employees in 1997	1.1	0.3	1.0
Total with 1–49 employees in 1995	20.5	36.4	42.9

Source: DOSME.

Table 2.10

Employment Expectations of Businesses in 1997 in the Czech Republic, Hungary, and Slovakia (in percent)

	Czech Republic	Hungary	Slovakia
Increase	10.8	10.0	12.9
Same	86.7	72.1	83.4
Decrease	2.5	17.9	3.7
Total	100.0	100.0	100.0

Source: DOSME.

Table 2.11

Size Structure of the Slovak, Hungarian, and Czech Registered Enterprises Compared to the Average of the 15 EU Countries (in percent)

Number of employees	Slovakia 1999	Hungary 1999	Czech Republic 1999	EU 1996
0–9	94.3	96.5	96.9	92.7
10–49	4.2	2.8	2.5	6.2
50–249	1.2	0.4	0.5	0.9
250–499	0.1	0.05	0.06	0.1
500+	0.1	0.05	0.04	0.1
Total	100*	100	100	100

Source: For Slovakia and the Czech Republic, CESTAT 1999; for Hungary, KSH 2000; for the EU the European Observatory 1997.
  *The discrepancy is due to rounding.

staff (Table 2.10). In Slovakia, 13% were optimistic in this regard. Most enterprises did not grow and had no such plans.

The DOSME panel strongly suggests that the small private sector in the three countries is predominantly the sector of self-employment rather than dynamic entrepreneurship. The three countries are similar, but Hungary's small businesses seem somewhat more entrepreneurial, probably a reflection of its history of small enterprise in the final years of communism.

Conclusion

The fecundity of the small private sector actually threatens the health of the economy. Never growing up to become medium-sized companies, the "too small and too many" (Gábor 1997) microbusinesses create a distorted size structure in the economy (Table 2.11).

The comparison with the average of the fifteen members of the European Union shows that all three countries are bottom heavy in the size structure of their economy, although the EU countries have a smaller industrial sector, where units tend to be larger than average, and a bigger service sector, where the reverse is true. Much of the imbalance in the 0–9 category comes from the companies employing 0, 1, or 2 people. In the upper end of this size category, EU countries enjoy a big lead.

The oversized small private sector is replacing the socialist economy of giants with its equally undesirable mirror image: an economy of dwarfs that cannot take advantage of real economies of scale, cannot improve productivity by substantial investment in fixed capital, and cannot successfully compete in a globalizing world market.

Because small businesses rarely expand in Central Europe, most medium-sized companies are either created from larger ones, spun off by big companies in the process of privatization, or must start out as medium-sized. This increases the threshold to entry in this segment of the economy.

The ocean of small businesses is a nightmare for the tax-collecting state. With payroll taxes unpaid, its systems of health care and unemployment compensation are underfinanced. Its pay-as-you-go pension system is especially starved for revenue because of the rapidly growing proportion of retirees. The proliferation of microbusinesses also hamstrings the state's efforts to act as regulator: to protect the environment, uphold work safety, and defend consumers from fraud and shoddy products and services.

There *are* caterpillars in Central European economies. Some of them are successful and others can be made successful with the kind of policies the entrepreneurial paradigm proposes. And there is a need for worms, as well: Not all businesses in the small private sector have to have the potential to grow beyond self-employment. But the balance is now tilted in the wrong direction. That some of these countries are heading out of the transformational recession is not the doing of the microbusinesses. It is mainly the result of foreign investment and improving performance of the medium- and larger-sized enterprises. It remains to be seen how improving economic conditions will change the size structure of postcommunist economies.

Notes

I would like to thank Teréz Laky, Mihály Laki, Helmut Wiesenthal, Herbert Kitschelt, Zsuzsanna Lampl, and the participants of the Mellon-Sawyer conference for helpful suggestions, and Karen Buerkle for research assistance.

1. There is an element of the reductionist fallacy behind the boundless enthusiasm of this approach. Arguing that innovation and success at the entrepreneurial level automatically translate into economic development at the level of the national economy is an unwarranted logical jump, as Baumol pointed out with his famous distinction between good and bad entrepreneurship (Baumol 1990). Nevertheless, few would argue that economic dynamism can come about without entrepreneurial forces.

2. The distinction between the entrepreneur and the self-employed is similar to the difference between the *qiye jia* and the *geti hu* in China. The first refers to the enterprise, the second to the household.

3. I would like to thank Peter Meszaros of Infostat, Katalin Ambrus, and Ferenc Takács of the Hungarian Statistical Office for giving me partial access to the Demography of Small and Medium-sized Enterprises (DOSME) project.

4. In spite of all that, in Hungary, small businesses are net payers; large companies, which are mostly foreign owned, are net recipients of state funds, because large companies receive a host of subsidies for which small businesses are ineligible (Csaba 1998).

5. Banks in the Czech Republic looked relatively solid (Komerční Banka was the highest rated financial institution in the region) until recently, when it was revealed that nonperforming loans were vastly underestimated in their portfolios.

6. In none of the three countries are the data from these various institutions pooled.

7. In the Czech Republic, the Ministry of Industry estimated that in 1999 only about 38% of all companies registered are active.

8. Those countries are Albania, Bulgaria, Czech Republic, Estonia, Hungary, Latvia, Lithuania, Poland, Romania, Slovakia, and Slovenia.

9. Any retrospective data have this same problem. Asking businesses about practices last year will miss those units that went under last year. But going back two years, as the panel does, makes the selection problem even worse.

Bibliography

Acs, Zoltan, and David B. Audretsch, eds. 1993. *Small Firms and Entrepreneurship: An East-West Perspective.* Cambridge: Cambridge University Press.

Árvay, János. 1994. "A magán szektor terjedelme." (The extent of the private sector.) In *A magánszektor fejlodése Magyarországon 1990–1993* (The development of the private sector in Hungary 1990–1993), pp. 96–111. Research Report for the State Privatization Agency. Budapest: TÁRKI.

Azudová, L'ubica. 1998. "Význam a podpora malopodnikatel'ského sektora v Európskej únii a v Slovenskej republike z pohl'adu zamestnanosti." (The meaning and support of the small entrepreneurial sector in the European Union and in the Slovak Republic from the standpoint of employment.) *Práca a sociálna politika* 6/4: 6–11.

Bartlett, David L. 1997. *The Political Economy of Dual Transformations: Market Reform and Democratization in Hungary.* Ann Arbor: University of Michigan Press.

Baumol, William J. 1990. "Entrepreneurship—Productive, Unproductive, and Destructive." *Journal of Political Economy* 98/5: 893–921.

Benáček, Vladimír. 1994. "Small Business and Private Entrepreneurship During the Transition: The Case of the Czech Republic." Prague: CERGE-EI Series No. 53.

Bohatá, Marie, and Jan Mládek. 1998. "Development of the SME Sector in the Czech Republic." In *The Hungarian SME Sector Development in Comparative Perspective*, ed., László Csaba, pp. 145–168. Budapest: Kopint-Datorg.

Csaba, László. 1998. "Introduction." In *The Hungarian SME Sector Development in Comparative Perspective*, ed. László Csaba, pp. 5–18. Budapest: Kopint-Datorg.

CESTAT. 1999. *CESTAT Statistical Bulletin.* 1999/4. Budapest.

The European Observatory. 1997. *Fifth Annual Report.* Web site, http://www.eim.nl/eim_net_in/facts/Summary/summary.htm.

Gábor, István R. 1997. "Too Many, Too Small: Small Entrepreneurship in Hungary—Ailing or Prospering?" In *Restructuring Networks in Post-Socialism: Legacies, Linkages, and Localities*, eds. G. Grabher and D. Stark, pp. 158–175. Oxford: Oxford University Press.
Ivy, R.L. 1996. "Small-Scale Entrepreneurship and Private Sector Development in the Slovak Republic." *Journal of Small Business Management* 34/4: 77–83.
Kirzner, Israel M. 1973. *Competition and Entrepreneurship*. Chicago: University of Chicago Press.
Kirzner, Israel, et al. 1980: *The Prime Mover of Progress: The Entrepreneur in Capitalism and Socialism*. London: Institute of Economic Affairs.
Kornai, János. 1980. *Economics of Shortage*. Amsterdam: North-Holland.
———. 1994. "Transformational Recession: The Main Causes." *Journal of Comparative Economics* 19/1: 39–65.
KSH. 2000. *A müködo gazdasági szervezetek száma*. (The number of active economic organizations.) Budapest: Központi Statisztikai Hivatal (Central Statistical Office)
Kuczi, Tibor. 2000. *Kisvállakozás és társadalmi környezet*. (Small enterprise and social environment.) Budapest: Replika Kör.
Laki, Mihály. 1998. *Kisvállalkozás a szocializmus után*. (Small enterprise after socialism.) Budapest: Közgazdasági Szemle Alapitvány.
Laky, Teréz. 1994. *Vállalkozások a Start-hitel segitségével*. (Enterprises with START credit.) Budapest: Magyar Vállalkozásfejlesztési Alap.
———. 1998. "A kisvállalkozások növekedésének korlátai." (Limits of growth for small enterprises.) *Szociológia* 1: 23–40.
———. 1999. *Main Trends in Labour Demand and Supply*. Budapest: Labour Research Institute.
Lampl, Zsuzsanna. 1998. *Vállalkozások és vállalkozók 1989 után*. (Enterprises and entrepreneurs after 1989.) Dunaszerdahely, Slovakia: Lilium Aurum.
Marková, Viera. 1998. *Faktory ovplyvòujúce rozvoj malých a stredných podnikov*. (Factors influencing the development of small and medium-sized enterprises.) Banská Bystrica: Univerzita Mateja Bela.
McDermott, Gerald, and Michal Mejstrik. 1993. "The Role of Small Firms in Czechoslovak Manufacturing." In *Small Firms and Entrepreneurship: An East-West Perspective*, eds., Zoltan Acs and David B. Audretsch, pp. 155–181. Cambridge: Cambridge University Press.
Národná Agentúrav Pre Rozvoj Malèho a Strednèho Podnikania. (National Agency for Development of Small and Medium Enterprises) 1997. *Stav Malèho a Strednèho Podnikania 1997*. (The state of small and medium sized enterprises 1997.) Bratislava.
———. 1998. *Stav Malèho a Strednèho Podnikania 1998*. (The state of small and medium sized enterprises 1998.) Bratislava.
OECD. 1996. "Small Business in Transition Economies." OECD Working Papers No. 4. Paris.
Róna-Tas, Ákos. 1997. *The Great Surprise of the Small Transformation: The Demise of Communism and the Rise of the Private Sector in Hungary*. Ann Arbor: University of Michigan Press.
———. 2000. "Legacies, Institutions and Markets: Small Entrepreneurship in Hungary, Slovakia and the Czech Republic." In *Successful Transitions: Political Factors of Socio-Economic Progress in Post-Socialist Countries*, eds. Jürgen Beyer, Jan Wielgohs, Helmut Wiesenthal. Baden-Baden: Nomos Verlag.

Róna-Tas, Ákos, and György Lengyel, eds. 1997–1998. "Entrepreneurship in Eastern Europe I-II." *International Journal of Sociology* Special Double Issue 27/3–4.

Schumpeter, Joseph A. 1936. *The Theory of Economic Development: An Inquiry into Profits, Capital, Credit, Interest, and the Business Cycle.* Trans. Redvers Opie. Cambridge: Harvard University Press.

———. 1947/1989. "The Creative Response in Economic History." In *Essays,* ed. Richard V. Clemence, pp. 221–231. New Brunswick: Transaction.

———. 1949/1989. "Economic Theory and Entrepreneurial History." In *Essays,* ed. Richard V. Clemence, pp. 253–271. New Brunswick: Transaction.

Tóth, István János, and András Semjén. 1998. "Tax Behaviour and Financial Discipline of Hungarian Enterprises." In *The Hungarian SME Sector Development in Comparative Perspective,* ed. L. Csaba, pp. 103–134. Budapest: Kopint-Datorg.

United Nations. 1997. *Enterprise Management in Countries with Economies in Transition with a Special Reference to Small and Medium-sized Enterprises.* New York: United Nations Department for Development Support and Management Services, Division for Governance, Public Administration and Finance.

Weber, Max. 1921/1978. *Economy and Society,* eds. Guenther Roth and Claus Wittich. Berkeley: University of California Press.

Zemplinerová, Alena, and Josef Stíbal. 1994. "Evolution and Efficiency of Concentration: Manufacturing in the Czech Economy 1989–1992." Prague: CERGE-EI Series No. 52.

3

The Yu Zuomin Phenomenon

Entrepreneurs and Politics in Rural China

Bruce Gilley

Introduction

Economic reform in China's countryside since the early 1970s has been aimed at dismantling the power of the former commune (collective) structure and returning more economic power to individuals, households, and villages. The pace, direction, and scale of such reforms have differed across the country. But a common element has been the emergence of entrepreneurs to lead the reform movement in place of the commune cadres who ran the old system.

Often, these new entrepreneurs held positions in the old commune system. Sometimes they are the former commune leaders themselves. But in their new personas, they act and think as entrepreneurs serving local and private interests rather than as cadres serving state interests.

The economic role played by these entrepreneurs is primarily to provide the broad framework in which subordinates can operate private or village-owned enterprises. This includes lobbying for political support for the enterprises from upper-level officials, securing inputs (both materials and finance), opening up markets, and ensuring a consensus in support of the running of the enterprises within villages. Thus, much of what these entrepreneurs do is to provide "safe passage" for the enterprises under their leadership.

While extensive study has been done on the economic impact of these entrepreneurs, their political role is less studied. Yet the nature of their entrepreneurship means that their political role is significant, indeed that it is inseparable from the entrepreneurship itself.

As rural China's post commune economy has expanded, a whole new range of conflictual issues has arisen between various levels of the party and government on the one side and rural residents on the other. The handling of many of these political issues—like taxation, finances, bank lending, and investment—puts added requirements on the skills of entrepreneurs. Lacking a well-developed democratic system in which their views can be heard by government, the entrepreneurs must resort to a variety of methods to advance the economic causes of their villages or enterprises, from subtle efforts like bribing and lobbying local officials to extreme ones like organizing mass protests.

Besides this "external" politics of rural entrepreneurs vis-à-vis the outside state, there is an "internal" dimension of their politics vis-à-vis their own villages or towns. Here, the entrepreneurs struggle to achieve and then maintain political power, which can be used for both personal and community purposes. The skills of the entrepreneurs in representing their constituencies are a key resource that allows them to obtain and hold political power. So too is the creation of political structures by the central government through which entrepreneurs can gain power.

While we can fairly confidently see the seeds of democratization in the external politics of rural entrepreneurs, the evidence is more varied with respect to their internal politics. Many are starkly undemocratic at home even as they agitate for greater transparency and accountability from the top.

The tentative conclusion here is that while some rural entrepreneurs are subverting the cause of democracy, for the most part they exert a positive influence on this process. First, they almost all gain power through the open and clear consent of their villagers, which is to say they are, at least initially, legitimate. Second, the goals they pursue in their external politics are the goals of livelihood and justice rather than pure power, which is to say they represent the interests of their constituents. And third, while they may stifle dissent in their own villages, the evidence is that this is not possible for any length of time. Soon the same search for legitimate and representative rulers throws them from power.

Thus, rural entrepreneurs can be seen as laying the groundwork for democracy in China. In the absence of moves by Beijing to expand direct, popular elections beyond the village or township level, the political activities of entrepreneurs in rural China could provide the necessary bottom-up pressure. In that sense, the rural entrepreneurs are one of many forces that could advance the democratic transition in China.

In the following sections, we consider one of the best-known cases of a rural entrepreneur of the reform era who was also a political leader, Yu Zuomin. We then consider such cases more generally and conclude by looking at the implications for democracy in China.

The Case of Yu Zuomin

Yu Zuomin was the Communist Party secretary of the village of Daqiuzhuang (or Daqiu), a hamlet in the largely rural county of Jinghai in the south of the municipality of Tianjin, a port city in north China. Throughout the 1980s and 1990s, Daqiu was celebrated as "the richest village in China." It had achieved wealth mainly through steel factories but by the early 1990s was home to five major business groups, all owned by a village holding company engaged in diverse industrial and consumer production.[1]

Yu was born in 1929. He joined the Chinese Communist Party in 1954 and became an accountant in the village's agricultural cooperative. After the cooperative was reorganized into a communal production brigade in the late 1950s, Yu became the brigade's party secretary. In the next twenty years, he witnessed first-hand the disasters of state planning in rural China—and was outspoken in his criticism of the era in later years.

In 1977, Yu proposed to villagers that they pool their money to build a small steel-processing factory. The plan was approved and, within five years, Daqiu had four factories making steel, electrical goods, and paper products. Yu remained at the helm of the village, whose industrial activities remained collectively owned by a village holding company. Under his leadership, Daqiu's move into industry was a great success. The village's 3,000-odd natives by the early 1980s had a per capita annual income of Rmb4,100 ($720) in 1984. By 1990, when the native population of the village reached 4,000 people, per capita income reached Rmb20,000. Daqiu was toasted as "the richest village in China."

The role of Yu Zuomin as entrepreneur was critical in the success of Daqiu village. In this context, entrepreneurship was primarily a matter of pooling and organizing resources as well as providing the necessary political leadership both within the village and vis-à-vis upper-level officials to ensure that the factory-building program succeeded. Others in the village with specific skills in accountancy, factory management, or steelmaking were delegated with these tasks. Yu's role as chief entrepreneur was mainly to provide the secure political environment and forge the social consensus in the village for the development of the factories.

The creation of the village's first factory, a cold-rolled steel strip factory, in 1978 was the brainchild of Yu, who at that time was under pressure to step down as Daqiu's party secretary in favor of a younger cadre. Yu hired a village member who had worked in a similar factory in a nearby city to set up the plant and deceived the county government into lending the village money, saying it was for irrigation works. With the village's own savings, the factory was built and was easily able to sell its output, given severe steel shortages.

In the following four years, three more factories were set up, making pipes, printed goods, and electrical components. A decade later, in the early 1990s, all four original companies had become conglomerates, with dozens of sub-

Table 3.1

Evolution of Village Corporate Structure

1978: Daqiu Village Cold-Rolled Steel Strip Factory
1979: Daqiu Village Pipes Factory
1980: Daqiu Village Printing Plant
1982: Jinhai Electrical Equipment Factory
1983: Daqiu Village Agriculture, Industry, and Commerce United Co.
　　　Daqiu Village Cold-Rolled Steel Strip General Factory
　　　Daqiu Village Pipes General Factory
　　　Daqiu Village General Printing Plant
　　　Daqiu Village Electrical Equipment Factory
1992: Daqiu Village Enterprise Group Corp.
　　　Wanquan Group
　　　Yaoshun Group
　　　Jinmei Group
　　　Jinhai Group
　　　Huada Group (agriculture)

Table 3.2

Total Number of Enterprises and Joint Ventures Under All Groups

Year	Enterprises	JVs
1987	107	NA
1990	195	21
1992	262	33
1995	335	40

sidiaries producing a broad range of consumer and industrial products. The rapid growth of the village economy under the four enterprises can be seen in Tables 3.1–3.4.

The success of Yu Zuomin as entrepreneur is inseparable from his political activities. It was those activities that provided the political security and later the political support for the village to thrive. Not only were jealous county officials kept at bay by Yu's politicking, but state banks lent the village money, other state enterprises bought its goods or sold it materials, and central government leaders provided high-level publicity by visiting the village, all as a result of Yu's skillful politicking.

We can roughly divide Yu's "external" political activities into three distinct periods: the beginning of the village's factory push from 1977 to 1983; the major expansion of its industry from 1984 to 1989; and the zenith of its economic achievements from 1990 to 1992. In each of these periods, the issues, goals, methods, and means of Yu Zuomin's political struggles against the outside state on behalf of his village changed.

Table 3.3

Cumulative Profits and Taxes of the Four Groups to 1990

Company	Net profits (Rmb mil)	Taxes paid (Rmb mil)
Wanquan Industrial	90	43
Daqiu Village Industrial	130	25
Jinmei Industrial	56	34
Jinhai Industrial	75	NA

Table 3.4

Revenues and Staff of the Four Companies in 1990

Company	Revenues* (Rmb mil)	Staff
Wanquan Industrial	165	1,538
Daqiu Village Industrial	286	1,500
Jinmei Industrial	117	1,685
Jinhai Industrial	156	1,359

Note: US$1 = Rmb5.81
*Includes intercompany sales.

Given the appearance of this tiny industrial powerhouse on the rural plains of northern China, it is no surprise that conflicts arose between Daqiu and the government and party organs of Jinghai county, the Tianjin municipality, and the central authority in Beijing. Even though the county was a major beneficiary of Daqiu's success through tax revenues, and even though Daqiu's rise was applauded in Beijing as a confirmation of the wisdom of the party's post-1978 economic reform policies, many issues arose that brought Daqiu into confrontation with the state.

In the initial period 1977 to 1983, the issues of Yu's politicking were very closely related to the village's factory program. Although village enterprises were gradually accepted by Beijing in this decade, the county government officials responsible for Daqiu did not fully endorse the moves until 1984. In the six years to then, Yu spent much of his time dealing with their disapproval. Sometimes he bribed them to keep quiet. Other times he outright rejected their criticisms by appealing to central directives that sanctioned village factories. Still other times, he simply lied about the village's use of funds from the county, saying they were for irrigation works when in fact they were ploughed into factory construction.

The village also learned in this period how to end-run central and local regulations on the payment of taxes through the constant creation from within existing companies of new companies that enjoyed an automatic two-year tax holiday on all their business. The period is also marked by the county's sending of a twenty-person inspection team to the village in 1982 to investigate alleged corruption. The standoff saw villagers treating the inspectors badly and refusing to divulge anything that might incriminate the village.

The second period, 1984 to 1989, is marked by the appearance of a fictional account of Daqiu's rags-to-riches story in the high-level official magazine *People's Literature* in early 1984. The story, called "Yanzhao Elegy," brought national fame to Daqiu and thereby sanctioned its factory strategy. In this period, Daqiu's growing national fame and continued economic expansion provided much greater leverage to Yu Zuomin to push his agenda. Yet the issues of that agenda also changed. In this period, Yu began to articulate a universal (i.e., not just specific to Daqiu) ideology of freedom and justice for China's long-suffering peasants that often rubbed ideologues in Beijing the wrong way. In 1986, for example, he coined a slogan urging peasants to "concentrate on money" rather than on communist ideology. Yu also took on state policies that discriminated against rural factories in favor of urban state factories and that defined socialism in terms of state ownership of the means of production rather than the creation of common prosperity. He was also one of the earliest public critics of what he called the "conservative faction" of leaders in the country, while painting himself as a member of the "reformist faction"—an indication of his awareness of the larger political game he was playing.

While Yu was clearly being motivated for the first time by personal goals of seeking recognition and of venting his anger at upper-level officials, these issues also served Daqiu well and thus continued to be seen by villagers as part of Yu's representations on their behalf. In essence, Yu placed the village politically on the ultraliberal side of the spectrum of views on economic policy and ideology in 1980s China. As a result, not only was the village able to manage itself in these ways (by introducing steep incentive pay scales for factory managers, for example, or by virtually abandoning political indoctrination classes for workers), but it also attracted investments and government grants from supporters as well.

The final period of 1990 to 1992 is marked by a sharp acceleration of both the economic riches and political fame of Daqiu and of Yu Zuomin's political campaign as leader of the village. While an economic austerity program was launched in the wake of the 1989 Tiananmen Massacre in Beijing, Daqiu's industrial expansion continued apace—partly because its excellent political reputation allowed it access to bank loans. When patriarch Deng Xiaoping set off a national economic boom with a trip to southern China in early 1992, Daqiu was already ramping up production, and the impact of Deng's trip took it to higher levels. By the end of that year, the village's 4,500 native residents had a per capita annual income of Rmb23,000 ($4,000) and were employing nearly three times their own number in the village's factories.

In this period, Yu articulated more fully a discourse of political, economic, and social equality for China's peasants—a comprehensive critique of communist China's rural policies. Politically, this discourse called for the promotion of capable rather than ideologically sound village leaders and for the removal as far as possible of party organs from village government. Economically, it called for complete equality between rural factories and state enterprises. And socially, it called for peasants to get rich and to flaunt their wealth through conspicuous consumption, thereby winning equal treatment and respect from city folk. As in the previous period, much of the motivation for this discourse was Yu's personal quest for recognition. But again, it was also seen as directly relevant to Daqiu's own development needs, and the village benefited immensely as long as Yu's discourse won favor in Beijing.

However, the politicking of Yu Zuomin came to a sudden end in early 1993 as a result of his attempts to block an investigation by police of a murder in the village in which Yu had been complicit. The reports of lawlessness in the village gave opponents of Yu's discourse just the excuse they needed to crack down on the village. The end result was a startling siege of the village by paramilitary troops in February 1993, followed by the arrest and sentencing of Yu to twenty years in prison alongside a raft of other village officials. Released on medical parole in early 1999, Yu died in the hospital in October 1999, apparently by suicide.

Since 1993, Daqiu Village has come under the direct control of upper-level authorities. It was elevated from a village to a town in late 1993, which stripped it of the right to elect its own village leaders and control many of its own internal affairs (including policing). County and city leaders are now prevalent in the village's leadership. It continues to enjoy modest official support as an economic model. But its life as a political pathbreaker died with Yu Zuomin. As the official Xinhua News Agency put it: "Following the storm, the people of Daqiu are marching forward with a new posture in the direction pointed by the Party."[2]

While by no means unique, the Yu Zuomin story is the most stark example of the relationship between rural entrepreneurs and democracy in China. It shows a typical rural entrepreneur, namely one who emerged from the old commune system as a strong leader in the market era because of his ability to rally others and perceive market needs. It also shows how such entrepreneurs become involved in politics and how their politicking can be seen as laying the groundwork for democracy in China. While Yu himself was a stern ruler within his own village, his calls for social and economic equality for China's peasants, and his arguments in favor of allowing villages such as Daqiu to run themselves, are the very stuff of representative politics. Moreover, Yu's case is important because his village was extremely wealthy and thus his ability to promote this agenda was greater. As one Chinese scholar said after Yu was purged: "We had people like Yu Zuomin in the past too, but under the planned economy they lacked any economic base or power. They could fight for power but they could only deploy so much resources. Yu Zuomin on the other hand had huge economic power."[3]

Thus, what is now called "the Yu Zuomin phenomenon" in China refers to rural entrepreneurs who are emboldened by their success to engage in political actions that the state considers illegal or subversive or both.

Rural Entrepreneurs and Political Power

The link between entrepreneurs and democratization (as distinct from an already established democracy) is much debated in social sciences. While there are good reasons to believe in theory and much evidence in practice that entrepreneurs have a positive effect on the transition to democracy, such a link is not always assured. In order to establish such a link, we have to be as specific as possible about which entrepreneurs we are talking about, how and why their actions promote democracy, and whether they could be promoting some other political outcome.

In the case of rural China, the entrepreneurs of interest are those who achieve formal political power, because in China's highly centralized and hermetic Leninist political system, it is difficult to influence the system from the outside. A great deal of evidence suggests that leading entrepreneurs in rural China are indeed increasingly taking over formal political positions, and this must be the starting point for a discussion of their potential impact on democratization.

Formal political positions can be obtained in four main bodies: the village Communist Party branch committee (*cun dang zhibu weiyuanhui*); the villager committee (*cunmin weiyuanhui*); the villager representative assembly (*cunmin daibiao huiyi*); and the village conglomerate (*cun jituan, cun zong gongsi*). Although on paper there are distinct differences in the powers and roles of these four positions, in practice they have all been used as the basis for political leadership roles by rural entrepreneurs.

Macrolevel figures suggest a growing role of rural entrepreneurs in these formal political structures. In elections to 1,500 villager committees in Sichuan's Bazhong district in 1997, for example, 1,100 of the 2,600 newly elected committee members (6,300 incumbents were returned as well) were classified as either "get rich experts" or "private merchants."[4] In the rural

Shanghai county of Qinghui, 36 of 52 party branches were headed by private businessmen as of mid-2000.[5]

Anecdotal evidence also abounds that suggests a wave of entrepreneurs taking over political posts:

1. In Liaoning's Zhangshabu village, a former party chief of seventeen years lost the race for village chief in 1995 to a forty-six-year-old, Su Fenghua, a successful entrepreneur who does not belong to the Party and who originally had not wanted the job.[6]

2. Wang Bingqiang of Zhaili village in Shandong province's Changcheng town (under Zhucheng city) became party secretary of his village in 1992 after developing a successful private business in water-heating equipment. In an article, the party secretary of Changcheng town (who appointed Wang) cited Wang as a good example of the need "to push rural party cadres into the market so that the peasants can rely on their outstanding economic initiatives to themselves be pushed into the market and towards wealth."[7]

3. In Datong village in Guangdong province, a successful local brickmaker named Tan Fuhua defeated a party cadre from the district government in a 1998 election to head the villager committee after villagers accused the latter of being arrogant. Tan, who won the election with a 68 percent mandate, promised a government "every bit of which will closely accord with the interests of the people."[8]

The movement of rural entrepreneurs into politics (or the regaining or maintenance of political power by former cadres under the commune system who have proven their entrepreneurial mettle) has spawned a whole new terminology to describe them. They are variously called "capable people" (*nengren*), "take the lead people" (*daitouren*), "show the way people" (*lingluren*), "train engines" (*huochetou*), and "get rich experts" (*zhifu nengshou*). Scholars in China have even coined the phrase "capable people politics" (*nengren zhengzhi*) to describe the emergence of these rural entrepreneurs into political power. As the official Xinhua News Agency noted in 1999: "In these elections, many farmers have given their trust to a number of warmhearted entrepreneurs, who, they believe, can lead them to an even richer life."[9]

Indeed, entrepreneurs are increasingly seen as the *only* people qualified to take over political positions in rural areas. The ability to hold power is coming to depend wholly on one's economic performance in many areas. One example is Song Zhiqiang, who is both villager committee head and village party secretary of Anli village in Henan province's Wenan county. Song helped found the village's earliest commune enterprises in 1973. After the communes were dismantled in the late 1970s, he and his brothers set up their own enterprises making building materials. He put his private interests under the village holding company when he gained power in 1990, and the village has since set up plastics and wire factories. Song promised he would foot any losses from the factories, telling one official magazine: "If they lose money, it's a clear indication that I am not rural official material. If so, then I will step down." In the event, the factories have been a success, producing an output of Rmb20 million in 1995 and lifting per capita income in the village in that year to Rmb2,500—high by the standards of inland China.[10]

All these cases, along with the Yu Zuomin case, illustrate a phenomenon in rural China in which successful entrepreneurs are being viewed as necessarily suited to political office because of their economic success. By the same token, party-appointed village party secretaries who manage to enrich their villages by becoming entrepreneurs are seen as having succeeded, and those who fail to do so are seen as having failed.

Socially and culturally, the examples above, and many more, suggest that the rural entrepreneurs who attain political power are almost always native to the village, usually with strong connections to its leading families through clan ties or relatives. Song Zhiqiang of Anli, for example, was the son of one of the village's senior cadres from the early years of communist China. Their self-presentation, however, rarely draws attention to their legacy in the old villager elite. Nor does their self-presentation draw on their adherence to central party policies or ideology. Rather they usually appear as non-ideological, practical-minded workers who promise to make their constituents better off—a claim usually substantiated with welfare projects such as schools, roads, houses, and hospitals.

At both the theoretical and practical levels, the entry of large numbers of entrepreneurs into positions of power comes as a shock in a communist state. Worried ideologues talk of such leaders as having a "communist hat, capitalist head" *(gongchan maozi, ziben naozi).*[11] The fact that these rural leaders do not rely much on central patronage to remain in power is a more practical concern. But in general, Beijing has sanctioned their rise to power, believing that as with all experiments in representative government at the local level, it will ensure a better-ruled and less discontented countryside. As the Xinhua News Agency in 1998 quoted Minister of Civil Affairs Doje Cering as saying: "Farmers need someone capable of leading them to prosperity and the election of entrepreneurs is fully justified so long as said individuals refrain from illegal activities during the election process."[12]

Rural Entrepreneurs and External Politics

During the 1989 prodemocracy protests in China, the privately owned electronics and computer company Stone Group, based in Beijing, played a large role in financially supporting student groups and research into political reforms.[13] This was a very direct and stark connection between entrepreneurs and democracy in China. It seemed to signal the belated involvement of the country's entrepreneurial class in the country's transition towards democracy. Yet in the decade since then, urban entrepreneurs who agitate for political change have been conspicuously absent.

Rather, it is in rural areas where entrepreneurs have become more politically active in the decade since Tiananmen. There are two possible reasons for this. The greater number of elected or strongly representative political institutions in rural areas gives entrepreneurs a system—a "political opportunity structure," as it often called—in which to act. Secondly, the greater overlap of the interests of rural entrepreneurs with those of other villagers, especially when economic activities remain partly controlled by a village collective, also makes it easier to gain support.

In addition, urban entrepreneurs often "work the system" in ways that reinforce a closed, undemocratic political process. Rural entrepreneurs, by contrast, are often working from the outside, which requires them to engage in more adversarial and open politicking. Rural entrepreneurs depend less on *guanxi* (personal relationships) in their relationships with the outside state than urban ones—although it must be stated that they are far from being what we would call truly "independent" of state support so far as that is possible in a communist state like China.

While rural entrepreneurs have rarely been so directly involved in prodemocracy activities as Stone Group executives were, we can see in their behavior the emergence of many of the antecedents of democracy: a concern for the rule of law and property rights; a concern for individual rights vis-à-vis the state; an emphasis on representative government, however constituted; and the politics of livelihood rather than ideology. The politicking of rural entrepreneurs is thus laying the groundwork for democracy in China far more than the occasional dabbling in democracy debates by urban entrepreneurs.

Besides Yu Zuomin, there are now many well-known rural entrepreneurs who, having attained political power within a system designed to bolster the Chinese Communist Party's rule, go on to challenge its rule on many fronts. One of the best known was Pei Anjun, "the cement-eating cadre with an iron heart," as he was known during his time as party secretary of Shanxi province's Qiancun village. Pei led the 630-household village to modest wealth by developing factories and making deals in the early 1990s. But he began to anger local officials by ignoring state policies on land title transfers and grain procurement. "Although he had just the minor position of a village cadre, he threw his weight around beyond his status," the provincial party newspaper,

Shanxi Daily, said in a charge reminiscent of those made against Yu Zuomin.[14] In early 1996, Pei was finally ousted by the provincial government along with seven of the village's fifteen-member party committee.

Another example was Chen Yiner, the party secretary of Qiuer village in Zhejiang province, a village often referred to as the southern counterpart of Daqiu because of its enormous wealth. Chen was similar to Yu Zuomin: a former commune cadre who had taken the lead in the early 1980s by opening up a metals factory in the village that by the mid-1990s had expanded into a forty-four-factory village conglomerate called the Yinfa Group. In addition to being a National Model Worker, Chen was named a delegate to the party's fourteenth national congress in 1992, an honor that Yu Zuomin had tried but failed to achieve. Like Yu, Chen alarmed Beijing by throwing his weight around as his village's wealth and fame grew. His favored way of building political capital was to hand out shares in village companies to local officials. He even built a resort in the United States where he sent political allies on vacations in return for their support. After fleeing first to the United States and then to the Philippines, he was arrested and sent back to China in early 1997, where he was sentenced to six years in jail on bribery charges.[15]

The common pattern that emerges from these cases is that rural entrepreneurs, having attained some form of political power, begin to use that power to set policies and deploy resources for collective welfare and to struggle against the state. On the "demand" side of this phenomenon is the growing number of complex issues that arise in the relations between rural communities and the communist state as those communities grow richer, more free, and more aspiring of fair and equitable treatment. On the "supply" side, those same issues can empower their ability to struggle against the state. In this scheme, rural entrepreneurs in political positions become a crucial resource for such struggles and in turn mobilize other resources. While often the entrepreneurs have mixed personal motives for pursuing this course—including personal incentives of fame and wealth—they nonetheless are seen by their constituents as true representatives of village interests since they spurn top-down ideology and policies that do not accord with the constituents' wishes. The doyen of party sociologists in China, Dang Guoyin, warned in an internal report in 1998 of "a new power class" that was forming "independent interest groups" in rural areas that openly challenged central policies.[16] While the central government would like to portray many of these new rural politicians as nothing better than warlords or criminal gang bosses, more often than not they are simply bold enough to articulate the interests of the new rural moneyed classes in ways that challenge Beijing's right to rule them. Yu and other village leaders like him are populists who act in the interests of their villagers—that is, they represent them, an important democratic principle and a key difference between the village politicians and the often hated warlords. Second, the politics of a place like Daqiu or Qiuer was the politics of livelihood and economics, not the politics of power. As in nine-teenth-century Japan and medieval Europe, it was an organization and ar-ticulation of common demands from a growing class of merchants whose aim was to push back and control the predatory state, not overthrow it. This also is an important foundation of democracy, and a stark difference from warlordism.

Rural Entrepreneurs and Internal Politics

While the politics of rural entrepreneurs vis-à-vis the external political envi-ronment may hold the seeds of democracy, it is important to note the much less optimistic situation with respect to their politics vis-à-vis the internal political environment in their villages. While entrepreneurs usually come into power as truly representative leaders, the politics they practice after-wards are often calculated to reduce democratic participation.

In the case of Yu Zuomin, it is clear that while support for Yu remained high at most times because he was delivering the economic goods, he was also extremely intolerant of the occasional signs of dissent. In 1990, his in-tolerance led to the beating death of a villager. Yu was able to command the huge resources of the village to stifle dissent. As far as can be ascertained, there were never any elections held in Daqiu for the would-be government, the villager committee. It did not exist or function in Daqiu in anything but name. Yu held all power as the county-appointed party secretary and self-appointed holding company president of the village. While he himself re-mained popular and would likely have won a villager committee election, it is far from clear that the people he appointed to run the various government and business functions in the village would have done likewise. Indeed, in a recent article on the village by a mainland China scholar, Yu is quoted as saying: "Not a single one of the people I use has been elected by the people. Elections would probably bring into power a bunch of nice old guys, but they would not necessarily produce benefits. Many capable people would never be elected."[17]

Evidence from elsewhere in China suggests that indeed rural entrepre-neurs are often authoritarian in their rule. In a detailed survey of politics within villages across China, Oi and Rozelle find that in villages with a fac-tory manager as leader, villager representative assemblies meet less often and villager committee elections are contested less often.[18] "Village leaders who are involved in running factories will try to resist calls for greater politi-cal participation," Oi and Rozelle report, because "a leader of an industrial-

ized village generally has more to lose than his counterpart in a purely agricultural village. As a result these leaders should be expected to minimize the
development of . . . representative institutions."[19]

This disincentive to develop democratic politics within the villages is of
course greatly reinforced by the fact that such leaders have the resources of
the village's wealth at their disposal, which can be used to bolster their own
political standing and stymie rivals. In Daqiu, for example, Yu Zuomin introduced a robust welfare system in which villagers were given free housing, electricity, and other benefits. He also used his position to head off the
only serious challenge to his leadership.

Oi and Rozelle believe that their results provide evidence that is "at odds
with the commonly held perception that political participation increases with
rising wealth."[20] Beijing too has sought to characterize many of the politically engaged rural entrepreneurs as bullies, criminals, and warlords, whose
behavior is contrary to the interests of the people they purport to represent.

Yet we need not be led to such pessimistic conclusions. For it may be that
the period of rising incomes and falling political participation is a transitory
one. Oi and Rozelle note that at early stages of income growth, contested
elections become more common because villagers begin to take a greater
interest in local politics in order to protect their new interests. However,
beyond a certain income level, such political participation falls when the
incumbent leaders stifle democracy.[21] But this period itself can be expected
to reverse beyond a certain point when incomes continue to grow. That is,
the period of antidemocratic behavior in wealthy villages may be just an
intermediate phase between periods of economic development. The growing
complexity of the village economy means that the normal positive relationship between income and participation will reassert itself since other powerful entrepreneurs begin to contest the elections.

Put another way, in the anomalous antidemocratic period, the relative power
accumulated by the leader is greater than that accumulated by the society at
large. As a result, we see participation falling as the leader buys off villagers
with TVs or uses his resources to employ propaganda against opponents.
But beyond a certain point, this relative position changes because powerful
new entrepreneurs emerge who can challenge the leader with their own resources. This is exactly what happened in Daqiu village after the fall of Yu
Zuomin. The villager committee and the village conglomerate leadership
posts are now held by several different people from different families and
companies. As one commentary said: "While this system of rule by one man's
diktat helped unite people's strength and attitudes at the beginning . . . it
increasingly constrained the village's advance as the scale of enterprises grew
and markets became more complex."[22] Across China, it may be that few

Figure 3.1

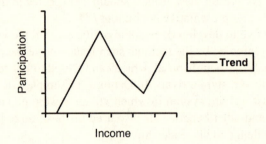

villages have yet reached this highest income stage at which representative forces reassert themselves.

This three-phase relationship between economic development and political participation can be represented by Figure 3.1.

Conclusion

Entrepreneurs in rural China have emerged in response to the dismantling of the former collectives and the more general withdrawal of the central state from economic life in the countryside. Yet in sharp contrast to entrepreneurs in countries with developed market economies and democratic polities, political activities have been a critical part of the role played by these entrepreneurs.

These entrepreneurs attain political power in a variety of ways. Much depends on local political conditions. In a village whose supervising township or county is run by a party committee that is supportive of a political role for the entrepreneurs, an entrepreneur may find himself appointed village party secretary (as Song Zhiqiang was, above). Where there is a more hostile reception to the entrepreneurs from above, they may pursue power via the villager committee or even through a self-constituted body like a trade association.

Once in power, rural entrepreneurs play the politics of livelihood, practicality, and fairness—the same issues that affect their own businesses. This kind of "bourgeois politics" may have been unrepresentative of rural aspirations in the pre-1949 era. But in today's increasingly bourgeois Chinese countryside, it is often aligned with wider interests. As a result, rural entrepreneurs find themselves accumulating broad support. The result is a kind of protodemocratic revolution in China's countryside that as yet remains little studied.

The implications for the rule of the Chinese Communist Party are clear enough. It is caught in a dilemma of political reform: allow the rural entrepreneurs to seize power and see its own ability to enforce unpopular policies weakened; or struggle against the tide and see popular resentment grow. "Nowadays, the consciousness of the peasants with regard to democracy and the rule of law is much stronger. They will no longer accept the appointment or sending of village cadres they do not like," one county cadre told an official journal.[23] Given the speed with which protodemocratic entrepreneurs have come into political power in village China, it is no wonder that Beijing is reluctant to allow entrepreneurs to contest for power at higher levels of rural government (at township and county levels). For the farther these entrepreneurs climb up the political ladder, the more pressure will increase for representative government at all levels.

Notes

1. I have detailed this story in my *Model Rebels: The Rise and Fall of China's Richest Village* (Berkeley: University of California Press, 2001). One useful book on the Daqiu story is Yu Hongfeng, *Huihuangzhongde yinying: Zhongguo "shou fu cun" Daqiuzhuang jiemi* (The shadow amidst splendour: Revealing the secret of China's "first rich village" Daqiuzhuang) (Beijing: Jingguan jiaoyu chubanshe [Police officer education press], 1993).

There are also several major newspaper stories on the village, including: Fang Ling, "'Zhongguo diyi cun' Daqiuzhuang jianwen" (Sights and sounds of "China's richest village" Daqiuzhuang), seven part series, *Dagong bao* (Ta kung pao newspaper, Hong Kong), 11–17 November 1992; Gao Xiufeng and Liu Linshan, "Fengkuang 'zhuangzhu': Yu Zuomin zuixing lu" (Crazy "village boss": Yu Zuomin's crimes), *Fazhi ribao* (Legal Daily), 28 August 1993, pp. 2–4; Qi Lin, and Du Jichang, "Daqiuzhuang xunli" (Daqiuzhuang pilgrimage), four parts, *Guangming ribao* (Guangming daily), 9–12 June 1992; and Zhang Jianwei, "Zhongguo diyi cun jiemi" (Revealing the secrets of China's richest village), seven-part series, Zhongguo qingnian bao (China youth daily), 15–22 January 1993. The Jinghai county annals are also useful: Jinghai xianzhi bianxiu weiyuanhui (Jinghai county annals editorial committee), *Jinghai xian zhi* (Jinghai county annals) (Tianjin: Tianjin shehui kexue yuan [Tianjian Academy of Social Sciences], 1995), "Daqiuzhuang," ch. 24, pp. 813–838.

The only scholarly works on the village in English are by Lin Nan, including: Lin Nan, "Local Market Socialism: Local Corporatism in Action in Rural China," *Theory and Society* 24 (1995), pp. 301–354; Lin Nan and Chen Chih-Jou, "Local Elites as Officials and Owners: Shareholding and Property Rights in Daqiuzhuang industry," paper presented at conference on property rights in China, Hong Kong University of Science and Technology, 12–15 June 1996; and Lin Nan and Ye Xiaolan, "Chinese Rural Enterprises in Transformation: The End of the Beginning," *Issues and Studies* 34 (November/December), 1998.

Important general references on rural industry in China include: William A. Byrd and Lin Qingsong (eds.), *China's Rural Industry: Structure, Development and Reform* (Washington, DC: World Bank, 1990); Daniel Kelliher, *Peasant Power in China:*

The Era of Rural Reform, 1979–1989 (New Haven: Yale University Press, 1992); Edward B. Vermeer, Frank N. Pieke, and Woei Lien Chong (eds.), *Cooperative and Collective in China's Rural Development: Between State and Private Interests* (Armonk, NY: M.E. Sharpe, 1998); David Zweig, *Freeing China's Farmers: Rural Restructuring in the Reform Era* (Armonk, NY: M.E. Sharpe, 1997); and Kate Xiao Zhou, *How the Farmers Changed China: Power of the People* (Boulder: Westview Press, 1996).

2. Xinhua, 27 August 1993.

3. Zhang Xiaoshan, Head of the Chinese Academy of Social Sciences Rural Development Institute quoted in "Yu Zuomin an xuanpan zhi hou" (After the verdict in the Yu Zuomin case), *Zhongguo nongmin* (China Peasant magazine), October–November 1993, pp. 6–9.

4. *Nongcun gongzuo tongxun* (Rural work bulletin), July 1998, pp. 16–17.

5. Liu Changfa, "Ye tan wuzhi liyi yuanze" (On the principle of material interests), *Zhongliu* (Mainstream) 3, July 2000, pp. 16–17.

6. *Asian Wall Street Journal*, 18 May 1995.

7. Dong Hongxiang, "Ba nongmin dangyuan tuixiang shichang" (Push peasant party members into the market) in *Nongcun gongzuo tongxun* (Rural work bulletin), June 1993, pp. 36–37.

8. *Dagong bao* (Ta Kung Pao newspaper, Hong Kong), 18 January 1999, p. 4.

9. Xinhua, 22 February 1999.

10. "Anli cun de daitouren" (Anli village's leader), *Nongcun gongzuo tongxun* (Rural work bulletin), November 1998, pp. 32–33.

11. Liu Changfa, "Ye tan wuzhi liyi yuanze," pp. 16–17.

12. Xinhua, 25 June 1998.

13. See Scott Kennedy, "The Stone Group: State Client or Market Pathbreaker," *China Quarterly*, December 1997, 746–777.

14. *Shanxi ribao* (Shanxi daily), 13 June 1996, pp. 1, 3.

15. Shenyang ribao wanbao zhoumouban (Shenyang daily evening paper, weekend section), 20 March 1999, p. 5.

16. *Guangjiaojing yuekan* (Wide Angle Monthly), January 1999, pp. 23–25.

17. Fan Yinhuai, "Daqiuzhuang zhuangzhu Yu Zuomin xingshuai mi" (The enigma of the rise and fall of Daqiuzhuang boss Yu Zuomin), in *Shenghuo shibao* (Lifestyle times), 11–12 January 2000.

18. Jean Oi and Scott Rozelle, "Elections and Power: The Locus of Decision-Making in Chinese Villages," *China Quarterly*, June 2000, No. 162, pp. 513–539, Table 6, and Yu's views were cited in several prominent media outlets in China, including China Central Television, Hebei Province Television, the *Guangming Daily*, the *Ta Kung Pao* newspaper in Hong Kong, the *China Youth Daily*, and the *Township and Village Enterprise Daily*.

19. Ibid., pp. 529, 539.

20. Ibid., p. 539.

21. Ibid., p. 537.

22. Xinhua News Agency, 17 December 1998.

23. *Nongcun gongzuo tongxun* (Rural work bulletin), August 1998, p. 14.

4

Security and Enforcement as Private Business

The Conversion of Russia's Power Ministries and Its Institutional Consequences

Vadim Volkov

The institutional analysis of economic markets differentiates the rules from the players and focuses on organizations that have developed as a consequence of rule-structure (North 1990: 4). Following this approach, I suggest that entrepreneurs can also be differentiated into those actively concerned with rule-structure and conventional players affected by that rule-structure. This article examines how entrepreneurs concerned with rule-structure emerge and evolve. The research focuses on former Soviet state security and enforcement employees who have over a very short period of time created a new business sector that deals in rule enforcement and property protection, that is, in particular institutional services.

The major players in this new sector are private protection agencies—legal commercial entities whose business is the management of organized force and information. Like other economic subjects, they operate in pursuit of profit. Yet the commodities they deal in are of a different nature: they concern certain key elements of the business environment rather than any particular business. Private protection agencies have turned the maintenance of the institutional environment into a particular form of private business. These agencies produce and sell services such as protection, informational support, dispute settlement, and contract enforcement. The success of their business is conditioned on their superior ability to use and manage organized force and information.[1]

The privatization of security and law enforcement organs is a major structural change resulting from Russia's liberal reforms. Comparable in significance to the rapid privatization of the economy from 1992 to 1995,[2] this shift has gone largely unexamined by scholars.[3] Economic historians have long established that in the past the formation of the market economy was accompanied, if not conditioned, by the proliferation of specific institutions that protect private property and ensure orderly transactions. This process took decades if not centuries (North and Thomas 1973; North 1979). In Russia, a new cycle of institution building was triggered by political and economic reforms that shattered the formal institutions of state socialism. The outcomes are still far from clear, but some contours are already discernible. Throughout the 1990s, private protection and enforcement agencies have created a hybrid sector between the economy and the state. This creation did not figure on the agenda of those who designed Russian reforms. Rather, it resulted from a combination of short-term political decisions aimed at reducing the power and capacity of the old Soviet state security institutions, adaptive responses of state security personnel to these policies, and the institutional demands of emerging markets that led to the quick formation of this entirely new business sector. So in contrast to the creation of the private economy, which was the primary reform target from the start, the privatization of protection and enforcement came as an unintended and ambiguous development.

Reform of the State Security Organs

On August 22, 1991, a huge statue of Felix Dzerzhinsky, the founder of the Soviet security service, was triumphantly toppled by a crowd of people in front of the KGB headquarters in Moscow in the aftermath of the failed coup d'etat. This event was the culmination of spontaneous popular protest against the communist system. The act was deeply symbolic: the KGB embodied the coercive power of the state, and the conspicuous popular violence toward it signified defiance and liberation. In the mass consciousness, the communist state and its coercive organs represented a major obstacle to liberal reforms that was symbolically removed.

Reforms of the state security organs followed. Their aim, as Vadim Bakatin, Yeltsin's appointee to the post of the head of the KGB, overtly admitted, was to fragment and decentralize state security organs in order to diminish their power (Bakatin 1992: 77). From 1991 to 1993, several former KGB directorates were transformed into separate agencies under federal or direct presidential jurisdiction. Thus the formerly united organization was split into five separate agencies: the External Intelligence Service (SVR), the Federal Agency for Government Communications and Information (FAPSI), the Federal Counter Intelligence Service (FSK), the Chief Guard Directorate including the Presidential Security Service, and the Border Guard Service. In 1995, FSK was renamed the Federal Security Service (FSB) (Korovin 1998: 80–86). Under the new Federal Law of August 12, 1995, all of these agencies, plus the Interior Ministry (MVD), the Tax Police, and the Federal

Custom Service, were designated to carry out detective and operative work and to keep their own paramilitary units. In comparison to the Soviet period, the number of agencies entitled to this capacity grew from three to seven. By mid-1995, Russia had fourteen state internal intelligence, security, and law enforcement agencies (Waller and Yasmann 1997: 198). The new division of spheres of competence and jurisdiction was ill-defined, and the agencies competed with and duplicated one another, weakening their overall coordination. Both FSB and MVD, for example, have directorates in charge of fighting against organized crime as well as directorates concerned with economic crime, and all four target the same range of criminal phenomena. Consequently, the efficiency of state security and law enforcement organs has decreased significantly.

The restructuring of state security was accompanied by personnel reductions. Negative public attitudes created moral pressure that devalued the status of this profession, while inflation and the shrinking of the state budget devalued wages. All this strongly induced security officers to seek alternative employment. Over 20,000 officers left or were discharged between September 1991 and June 1992. A significant number left after the crisis of October 1993, including members of the special elite antiterrorist units Alpha and Vympel. In 1992 President Yeltsin ordered that the 137,000-strong central apparatus of the former KGB be reduced to 75,000 (a 46 percent reduction) during the process of restructuring. While a substantial proportion of the former staff of the central apparatus was transferred in 1992–1993 to the newly established bodies (SVR, FAPSI, etc.) and to regional FSB directorates, 11,000 had to leave state security permanently.[4]

According to expert sources, besides these obvious factors that caused an exodus of state security employees into the private sector, there were more subtle considerations that operated in the same direction. The new tasks before the state security organs included the struggle against organized crime and the promotion of state interests in the rapidly privatized economy. One method for acquiring information needed to fulfill these tasks became the direct infiltration of private businesses. Thus, while it is possible to distinguish analytically between the search for a new job by ex–state security employees and their new operative assignments, an empirical distinction between the two phenomena has become virtually impossible.

Organizational Solutions

The first organizational solution—a counter-move—that enabled FSB to address its new problems—personnel reduction, decline in material welfare, and the need for infiltration—was the creation of the institution of the so-called assigned staff (*prikomandirovannye sotrudniki*). Article Fifteen of the Federal Law "On the Organs of the Federal Security Service" maintains that "in order to carry out security tasks the military personnel of the organs of FSB, while remaining in service, can be assigned to work at enterprises and organizations at the consent of their directors irrespective of their form of property."[5] This provision allowed thousands of acting security officers to hold positions in private companies and banks as "legal consultants," as this position was modestly called. Using their ties with the state organs and information resources of FSB, they perform what became known as "roof" functions—protecting against extortion and cheating by criminal groups and facilitating relations with the state bureaucracy. Expert estimates suggest that up to 20 percent of FSB officers are engaged in informal "roof" business as *prikomandirovannye*.[6] I will return to this subject later.

A long-term solution for the commercial utilization of the personnel, informational, and technical resources of the state coercive organs was found in the legalization of informal security and rule enforcement business. The legal framework for such activities was provided by the Federal Law "On Private Detective and Protection Activity," adopted on March 11, 1992, and the special Government Decree of August 14, 1992, that specified some aspects of its application. Now private agencies were entitled to "protect legal rights and interests of their clients" on a commercial basis. The law permitted private agencies a broad range of activities: to physically protect citizens and property, engage in security consulting, collect data on lawsuits, conduct market research and collect information about unreliable business partners, protect commercial secrets and trademarks, search for people claimed disappeared, recover lost property, and conduct investigations into the biographies of potential employees of client companies.

Getting a license to set up a private security agency is relatively easy: the Commission for Licenses and Permissions, set up at every regional MVD directorate, requires from a prospective head of a security agency a higher education degree and evidence of special qualifications or of three or more years of professional experience in state law enforcement or security organs. The procedure was designed to facilitate registration for former security and police employees.

The most widely cited data on the service origin of the heads of private security agencies were provided by the executive director in charge of security of the Association of Russian Banks Vitalii Sidorov (former deputy minister of interior) in 1995. According to Sidorov, half of the chiefs of private security are former KGB officers, another quarter are from MVD, and the rest come from GRU (Army intelligence) and other organizations.[7] These rough proportions are likely to relate to the Moscow banking sector. Exact figures for the entire private security sector as of July 1, 1998, are the following: out of a total of 156,169 licensed private security employees in Russia, 35,351 (22.6%) came from MVD, 12,414 (7.9%) from KGB-FSB, and 1,223 (0.8%) from other security and law enforcement organizations. On the whole, private security agencies have absorbed nearly 50,000 former officers of the state security and law enforcement organs, most of whom, especially the ex-KGB, occupy key managerial positions.[8] The reemployment of state security officers has been partly managed by the professional association Business and Personal Security, created by former FSB employees in 1992. From 1992 to 1994, the association helped to retrain and employ over 4,000 former state security servicemen, half of whom became heads of private security agencies.[9]

Private Security Agencies

The law defined the licensing procedures for three types of security agencies and their personnel: *chastnye detektivnye agenstva*, private detective agencies (PDA), *chastnye sluzhby bezopasnosti*, private (company) security services (PSS), and *chastnye okhrannye predpriyatiia*, private protection companies (PPC). PDAs normally execute narrow and specific tasks requested chiefly by private individuals regarding their private matters. Consequently, autonomous detective agencies are few (just over a hundred for the whole country), and their services expensive. They will not concern us in this paper.[10]

All enterprises, independent of their size and form of ownership, were permitted to establish a special security subdivision, the private security service. These were set up in large numbers by private and state enterprises and financial institutions for physical and economic protection, information gathering, and analysis. Large banks and companies, especially those entrusted to deal with state financial assets or strategic resources, were organized and staffed by former high-ranking state security officers. To give just a few examples, V. Zaitsev, one of the former commanders of Alpha, the special unit of the KGB, became the head of security of Stolichnyi bank; M. Gorbunov, who used to serve in the Chief Directorate of Intelligence of the Soviet Army (GRU), became head of security of Inkombank; the former KGB deputy chief Philip Bobkov heads the corporate security service of Most financial group (Kryshtanovskaia 1995: 96). Security for the largest PSS, 13,000-strong Gazprom, the natural gas monopoly, is headed by the former KGB colonel Victor Marushchenko and consists of forty-one subdivisions at the company's installations across the country.[11] The majority of PSSs, however, are much smaller. Many were created to secure a one-time deal or simply to legalize armed bodyguards for the company's boss and continue to exist mainly on paper.

In contrast to PSSs, private protection companies are autonomous from their clients and act as independent market agents supplying services on a contractual basis. Originally, even before the adoption of the law on private protection, many future PPCs started as private guards or informal security services for concrete business projects. For example, a St. Petersburg PPC Severnaya Pal'mira, headed by the former colonel of military counterintelligence Evgenii Kostin, was initially set up as a security service for Muraveinik, the city market of construction materials. Later it became an independent supplier of security to a number of construction companies, such as Business Link Development, Com & Com, and the official Peugeot dealer in St. Petersburg, Auto-France.[12] This case represents a typical evolution pattern of a PPC from being tied to particular clients to becoming an autonomous supplier of services on the market.

The corporate principle that sustains the identity of employees of the state security ministries is also closely observed in the private security sphere. Many successful PPCs were founded by tightly knit communities of former officers of special task units who sought to convert their skills and reputations into a marketable asset. Not least, attempts by the central government to use special antiterrorist units as an instrument of internal political struggle during the crises of August 1991 and October 1993 frustrated officers and led many to quit the service and consider new employment. Thus the former commanders of the KGB special antiterrorist unit Alpha, I. Orekhov and M. Golovatov, left the unit to set up a family of protection companies whose name openly points to the original affiliation of its staff: Alpha-A, Alpha-B, Alpha-7, and Alpha-Tverd'.[13]

After the KGB antiterrorist unit Vympel had refused to participate in the storming of the Parliament during the October 1993 crisis, it was transferred to the jurisdiction of MVD. Of the 350 Vympel officers, only five decided to continue under MVD; 215 found new employment in FSB and other state security organs; and 135 left to work in the sphere of private security.[14] Many of them were employed by the PPC Argus, set up by one of the former senior commanders of Vympel, Yurii Levitsky. Now Argus is one of the largest private security operators in the Moscow region. In St. Petersburg, the largest PPC, Zashchita, was set up by former MVD special unit employees and is known to actively recruit former officers of the Regional Anti-Organized Crime Directorate (RUOP). A group of former officers of the Soviet Army paratroop units, who shared combat experience in Afghanistan, stood at the origin of Aleks-Zapad, another large private security operator in northwestern Russia. In an interview with the author, Boris Markarov, the chief of Aleks, mentioned the corporate principle of recruitment, admitting that he personally trusts "the army caste much stronger than the militia or the KGB."[15]

Hence, most large PPCs tend to preserve their corporate identity and resemble privatized segments of the state defense and security ministries. The chiefs of PPCs openly admit what they call mutually beneficial cooperation with state organs, meaning an exchange of operative information for money or equipment.

The Structural Dynamic

Soon after the adoption of the law on private security, the new business sector began to expand at unprecedented rates, especially in Moscow and St. Petersburg. By the end of 1999, the number of private security agencies reached 11,652, including 6,775 PPCs and 4,612 PSSs, while the number of licensed security personnel reached 196,266 (the total number of employees exceeds 850,000). In 1998 the city of Moscow had a total of 3,125 and St. Petersburg 816 private security agencies, which amounted to 29 and 7.6 percent of the total number of agencies in Russia for that same year respectively. Between 1993 and 1996, the growth was especially dramatic; the number of private security agencies almost doubled, reaching nearly 8,000. After 1996, growth continued, but the rate slowed down (see Table 4.1).

Several factors were responsible for the leveling of growth after 1996. First, the reshuffling of the state security, which had generated the supply of jobless specialists, receded. Second, the initial market demand for protection services was met, and the possibilities for extensive growth were exhausted. Third, MVD supervising organs tightened control and inspection measures, closing down more than 600 agencies each year since 1995 for violating regulations. In May 1995 the government of Moscow issued a decree that urged the regional MVD to intensify control over the activity of private security agencies on its territory and to introduce an electronic accounting and identification system.

Table 4.1 also shows a structural trend: over the last three years, the growth of the private security industry has been caused by the growth of PPCs, while the number of PSSs decreased progressively. Ivan Mayatsky, the head of the Committee for Licensing and Permissions of MVD, explained this trend by two basic factors. First, many PSSs were created by banks during the period of their multiplication in the early 1990s. As some banks subsequently went bankrupt, their security services disappeared too. Second, for a bank or a company to maintain a PSS proved more expensive than to contract an independent PPC, and gradually many turned to the latter, more efficient option.[16]

This second factor seems to point to an important trend toward the externalization of protection. If in the beginning companies tended to inter-

Table 4.1

The Development of the Private Security Sector in Russia, 1992–1999

	1992	1993	1994	1995	1996	1997	1998	1999
Total number of agencies	0	4,540	6,605	7,987	9,863	10,487	10,804	11,652
Private protection companies	0	1,237	1,586	3,247	4,434	5,280	5,995	6,775
Private security services	0	2,356	2,931	4,591	5,247	5,005	4,580	4,612
Agencies closed down by authorities			73	640	622	978	1,364	1,277

Source: Mir Bezopasnosti, 2, 1997; 3, 2000; Biznes i bezopasnost', 2, 1999.

nalize protection by creating their own security service, later many turned to external protection. Because of the economy of scale and allegedly better technical equipment, large PPCs are more cost-efficient. A PSS has a different advantage. Being a subdivision of a private company or bank, it operates under two different authorities, public regulations for this kind of activity and private orders of the company's general director. The latter authority is naturally stronger, and in case the two authorities clash, the PSS is likely to circumvent formal regulations of external (state) authorities. In contrast, autonomous suppliers tend to be less constrained by their customers (unless they are created by the latter). But because they produce services for sale rather than for internal consumption, they are constrained by the rules of the market. According to the public claims of their managers, PPCs prefer to conduct their business on the basis of the formal contract and respect for the law. This, however, may be just a successful marketing strategy. Whatever the actual practice, the degree of autonomy of PPC vis-à-vis PSS is greater by definition. The growth of the former and the decline of the latter after 1996 may indicate that, for customers, considerations of economy are becoming more important than the ability to exercise direct management of force. If this is correct, then the outcome would be a growing differentiation whereby economic and security enterprises are more clearly separated.

Functions

To be sure, the downsizing of the army and security sectors of the Russian state could not alone have caused the rapid growth of the private security industry. No less important factors lie in the realm of the nascent market economy. What generated the increasing demand for security and enforcement services? How did private violence-managing agencies integrate into the economy, and what institutional functions do they perform?

Elsewhere I defined the activity of private agencies that manage organized force as violent entrepreneurship—a set of organizational solutions and action strategies enabling the conversion of organized force (or organized violence) into money or other market resources on a permanent basis (Volkov 1999). PPCs were not the first to discover this entrepreneurial niche. Since the late 1980s, as the first cooperative and private enterprises started to emerge, organized criminal groups moved in to extract tribute from private business, as the latter received virtually no protection from the state. As extortion became regular, it turned into a protection racket—an institutionalized practice whereby tribute is collected on behalf of a criminal group that, in exchange, claims to offer physical protection from other such groups. But as the private sector expanded and the intensity of business transactions grew, criminal groups got engaged in more sophisticated activities such as debt recovery, contract enforcement, dispute settlement, and negotiations with the state authorities concerning registration, export licenses, tax exemptions, and the like. I have distinguished these activities from the protection racket and defined them as "enforcement partnership"—the function performed by a criminal group or other violence-managing agency deriving from the skillful use of force on a commercial basis and facilitating the maintenance of certain institutional conditions of business.[17]

On the one hand, criminal groups by their very methods created a dangerous business environment and proceeded to extract payments from economic subjects for reducing the danger. As a matter of fact, any wielder of force is able to provide protection only insofar as it itself is capable of creating dangers. Its activities, therefore, inevitably contain at least some elements of a protection racket. As Charles Tilly notes, "which image the word *protection* brings to mind depends mainly upon our assessment of the reality and externality of the threat. Someone who produces both the danger and, at a price, the shield against it is a racketeer. Someone who provides a needed shield but has little control over the danger's appearance qualifies as a legitimate protector, especially if his price is no higher than his competitors'" (Tilly 1985: 173).

On the other hand, there was a range of factors that generated independent demand for a variety of enforcement services. Insufficient business experience and the propensity of some businessmen toward dishonest conduct increased business risk and lowered the level of trust.[18] The resulting disputes and tensions could not be resolved by the official institutions due to poor definition of property rights, inefficiency of the state courts of justice (*gosarbitrazh*), and their incapacity to enforce decisions (Varese 1996).

Having accumulated considerable force (physical as well as firepower) and perfected intimidation methods, multiple criminal groups, composed mainly of former sportsmen, came to be best suited to act as private enforcers and mediators of disorganized and unpredictable markets. Private protection and enforcement rather than traditional forms of illegal (drugs, arms, illicit services, etc.) trade or theft became the major engagement and the source of regular revenue of criminal groups in the period of market reform. Illegal and in most cases compelled enforcement partnerships are a new type of criminal business in Russia, brought to life by a combination of economic liberalization and the weakening of the state. Such activities should be distinguished from Soviet-era organized crime inasmuch as the market for private protection and enforcement can be distinguished from the market for stolen or illicit goods. Already by the beginning of the 1990s, virtually no firm in the small business sector could get by long without engaging or being engaged by a private enforcement partner. In 1993–1994 about 70 percent of contracts (that were not self-enforcing) were enforced without recourse to the state, that is, by private enforcers (Tambovtsev 1999: 198).

Of course, entrepreneurs of violence do not think in terms of the institutional functions that they perform, although generally they have a very positive image of themselves as people who exercise justice and maintain order as they understand it. In their language, they "solve questions" for or "work" with a certain businessman or a company. The outcome of their joint effort is the reproduction of a particular set of constraints that affect the behavior of private economic actors. Entrepreneurs of violence, then, may be said to perform the function of enforcement partnerships, maintaining the institutional structure that enables the development (not necessarily the most efficient) of certain segments of the private economy which, in turn, feed them.

From 1992 to 1995, the rapid privatization and the rise of private financial institutions brought new, large segments of the economy, including medium and large enterprises, into the sphere of free-market relations. The legal and institutional problems mentioned above were still far from being resolved by the state powers, and the level of business risk remained very high. According to rough estimates presented at the seminar of the chiefs of security services of Russian banks in January 1995, in the beginning of 1994 the amount of unrepaid credits in Russia equaled 3 trillion 609 billion rubles (US$1.64 billion) and reached 8 trillion (US$1.75 billion) in 1995.[19] Criminal groups, so it seemed, were moving toward attaining full control over the privatized economy. However, it is precisely at this stage that criminal syndicates encountered a powerful commercial rival in the form of private protection and security agencies set up by former police and security employees. This is not to say that the law on private protection was designed as an anticriminal measure (later we shall discuss its negative influence as well). At that time, the state authorities had neither a strategy for institution-building nor an anticriminal program, and it is more likely that the legal provision for the business of private protection was adopted merely as a tactical solution for the reemployment of the former staff of the "power ministries." But it produced consequences that went beyond initial pragmatic considerations.

By the mid-1990s, the business of private security became firmly integrated into the new market economy. The demand for private enforcers increasingly came from the milieu of enterprise directors who, as a recent study revealed, tend to avoid dealing with official justice organs out of the fear that they would lose their personal influence if they relied on the impersonal legal institutions of the state (Hendley 1997). Understandably, the large, established PPCs operate in those sectors that managed to survive and are capable of generating profits, such as the oil and gas industry, banking, communications, high-technology, export-oriented production, and the like, including the majority of foreign companies. Among the clients of the holding of security enterprises Al'ternativa-M, for instance, are the large chemical consortium Rosagrokhim and Gromov aerospace research and test center.[20] In St. Petersburg, the PPC *Staf*, headed by M. Timofeev, the former major of the KGB, got started by collecting debts from the clients of the telephone company Peterstar. Then it became the security and enforcement partner of PTS, the major state-owned telephone network, as well as of Delta Telecom, a major cellular phone operator in the northwestern region. As a result, the PPC, which, as its chief has admitted, maintains close relations with FSB, now supervises a vast regional communication network.[21]

With the entry of the KGB and MVD cadres into the market as private agents, the age of the "roofs" came into full fledge. "Roof" (*krysha*) is a key term in the contemporary business lexicon, referring to an enforcement partner, criminal or legal, and signifying a complex of services provided by the latter to its clients in order to protect them physically and minimize their business risks. Unlike some other business terms that have gained currency in recent years, *krysha* did not belong to the criminal jargon but came from the professional vocabulary of the intelligence service, where it signified an official cover-up—diplomatic, journalistic, etc.—of a spy. Yet the term was quickly adopted by racketeers and acquired a criminal flavor.

An enforcement partnership ("roof") should be distinguished from mere physical protection. Physical protection and security, which PPCs provide by supplying private guards and security equipment on a contractual basis, is not the primary mission of PPCs. The actual practice of a successful PPC first of all includes the acquisition and analysis of information about prospective business partners, the supervision of business transactions, and, most importantly, the ability to engage in informal negotiations with other enterprises and their enforcement partners in case of a breach of contract or failure to repay a debt. This informal practice of problem solving through negotiation between enforcement partners is most valued in business circles and is the basis for the reputation of the violence-managing agency, be it a PPC or a criminal group. So the enforcement partnership is not just protection of individual clients but an activity and a function that relates to the institutional structure of the economy as a whole. The extension of the activity of private protection agencies beyond mere physical or informational security and into the sphere of business transactions and civic property relations distinguishes the security industry in Russia of the 1990s from its similar counterparts in other countries.

Private Protection Companies and Criminal Groups

To achieve success, private protection agencies have to steer between the legal regulations increasingly tightened by the state authorities and the actual practice of private enforcement that rests on informal dealings and frequent use of semicriminal methods. This situation derives from the highly informal character of business relations in Russia and the heavy presence of criminal groups. The latter also strove to use the law on private protection to their advantage, creating their own PPCs in order to obtain licenses to carry concealed weapons and legalize their protection services. Thus, in St. Petersburg one of the oldest protection companies, Scorpion, was set up and headed by Alexander Efimov (nickname "Efim"), one of the leaders of *tambovskaya* criminal group, and actively recruited police officers to perform "roof" functions. Scorpion was closed down by the authorities at the end of 1996; its director managed to escape but was tracked down in Ukraine and arrested a year later.[22] The PPC Adris, providing protection to over a dozen companies, including the chain of ice-cream shops Baskin Robbins, is known to belong to the *malyshevskaya* criminal group.[23]

The use of force and intimidation in order to recover debts and settle disputes among businessmen is one of the major activities of criminal groups. Many PPCs are also involved in this business, using purely criminal methods. For example, in September 1996 the police arrested the director general of the PPC Barrs Protection, the former KGB major V. Zhukov, and his driver. They were accused of beating up and threatening the director of Petrotrade, the PPC's client company, and demanding 35 percent of the company's shares and US$20,000 as payment for an alleged debt. The case, however, was settled informally and the PPC staff were released without criminal charges.[24] In the last two years, the MVD authorities have intensified their control, trying to eradicate the informal practice of debt recovery. They issued warnings and published a list of companies known to practice debt recovery, but these measures so far have not had any tangible effect.[25]

Yet, on the whole, despite many cases of PPCs' involvement in criminal affairs, the overall effect of their activity was more positive than negative. While not being manifestly anticriminal agencies, they nonetheless managed to weaken the economic basis of organized crime and limit its expansion. "To save a company from being taken under the 'roof' by a criminal gang is very hard," asserts Levitsky, the head of the PPC Argus. "That is why we are proud that none of our clients ended up 'under the mafiya.' If the establishment of a [criminal] 'roof' is already under way, we get in contact with the leaders of the criminal group and talk to them in language they understand."[26] On another occasion, Levitsky summed up the overall effect of the private security industry: "Several years ago all Russian business was criminalized. We could have become a 'bandit' state. Now, five years later 'roofs' are [legal] security structures. We accomplished the task quietly, without revolutions and shooting."[27] Overall, the anticriminal effects were achieved through the higher quality of services offered by PPCs at lower prices and through their active interaction with the state police organs.

Already in 1991, in pursuit of a supplement to their devaluing salaries, informal groups of police and state security officers offered private business an alternative protection and enforcement solution, thus entering into direct competition with criminal groups. Those companies that managed to contract a police officer or a KGB "roof" could cease fearing a visit by gang members offering their protection. The informal rule that "every businessman has to have a roof," well known to all entrepreneurs operating on the Russian market, was a peculiar way to acknowledge the burden of transaction costs, but it also presupposed multiple options and hence a competition between those who claimed these costs. While a separate study would be required to assess the impact of private enforcers upon economic growth and to say which option is best for which type of business, it is possible to describe the basic noncriminal options, the logic of choice, and the consequences.

The cheapest solution is to have or make a friend among police officers, in particular in the special anti–organized crime unit (RUOP). This gives the entrepreneur the opportunity to claim RUOP as his "roof" and to ask the friend to help out in case of an attempt by a criminal gang to demand protection fees. The owner of a small network of pharmacy shops in St. Petersburg would be a typical client of such an informal, "friendly" police "roof." His payment for protection may consist of occasional provision of medicine for the policeman's parents.[28] This solution pertains mainly to small business and gives advantages to those who happen to have the right kind of friends. Its reliability, however, is low, matching the low cost.

The hiring of an acting or retired FSB officer as a "manager" or "law consultant" is another widespread "roof" arrangement that enables a company to avoid paying protection money to a criminal group. This "law consultant" acts as a kind of multipurpose fixer, shielding the company from criminal and bureaucratic extortion and mediating relations between the private business and the state authorities. Interview sources indicate that hiring (formally as well as informally) an FSB officer became a widespread practice in medium-sized companies, especially in Moscow. Such a "lawyer" would normally cost the company an equivalent of US$1,000 or higher per month. Thus, a Moscow-based company producing silicon medical supplies was approached by a criminal group from the city of Kazan, where the company's production site was located. Unwilling to end up under criminal protection, the director had to urgently find an alternative solution. First he hired a retired KGB colonel and later an acting FSB officer (*prikomandirovannyi*, see above) as his company's "roof." Unfortunately, the officer was later killed in Chechnya performing his state service duties. Subsequently, the company signed a contract with a PPC.[29]

A client company and a PPC normally sign a formal contract that specifies the range of services and their price. If the company requires armed guards, the price is calculated on the basis of the standard US$4–6 per guard per hour or up to US$2,000 per month for an alarm system including a hotline connection with a fast-reaction team normally kept by a PPC. To obtain regular information about another company costs US$100–300 per month.[30] Alternatively, the contract may resemble medical insurance, where a monthly fee of US$250 or higher, depending upon the size and nature of business, is paid to a PPC whose help is requested only in case a problem arises. If the problem is serious enough, such as the need to recover a debt or to resolve a dispute, especially if the adversary is a criminal group, the deal is likely to be negotiated on a noncontractual basis, and the fee, normally quite high, would be adjusted to the value of the disputed property, the level of risk, and the amount of operative work. But not all PPCs provide such services. An alternative protection strategy, then, is to assist the client in engaging the state organs of justice to resolve the problem in a legal manner. In this case, the role of the PPC is to ensure efficient treatment of its client by state justice organs and to help enforce the decision. Many PPCs have a legal subdivision that provides legal support to its clients and interacts with the state organs of justice. According to the codirector of the St. Petersburg PPC Avanpost, "Now one can make the state organs of justice work more efficiently. In case we need to help our client recover a debt, we have a legal option to make them seize the accounts of the debtor, which carries a potential damage incomparable with the amount of the debt. This is how we compel debtors to start peaceful negotiations."[31]

Notwithstanding that the realm of private security and enforcement approximates a "market," some serious limitations of choice remain—in particular, the freedom of choice of enforcement partner. Once a company gets caught unprepared for a visit by representatives of a criminal group, yields to intimidation, and starts paying protection money, it is likely to develop path dependency. Likewise, once a company appeals to a criminal group to resolve a problem, it will most probably continue under protection of this group, and any attempt to break free would provoke severe sanctions. Understandably, a company is likely to engage or be engaged by illegal enforcers if it operates in the shadow sector of the economy, not to mention illicit trade. Criminal groups are known to lure clients by offering cheap start-up credits and loans, which subsequently allow the group to hold sway over this enterprise as a shareholder. The most prominent example of this kind is the fate of the Ekaterinburg machine-building giant Uralmash, which suffered a severe cash shortage at the end of 1991 and was on the verge of closure. A local criminal group, now known as *uralmashevskaya*, supplied the badly needed cash and thus established its control over several premises belonging to the enterprise.[32]

As interview sources indicate, the contractual nature of the relationship, higher degree of predictability of behavior, and higher quality of services make a PPC a more competitive security solution compared to the criminal one, given that the constraining factors mentioned above do not interfere. Unlike criminal groups, PPCs normally do not interfere in the business of their clients, but they also would not provide loans. Experts have estimated that clients of criminal groups are forced to pay up to 30 percent of profits, while the cost of debt recovery is normally 50 percent of its value. The price of security and enforcement charged by noncriminal PPCs is negotiable and varies depending upon the size and the nature of the client business. But it takes the form of a fixed monthly payment rather than a tax on profits or turnover as in the case of criminal protection. The charge for debt recovery varies between 15 and 40 percent of the sum of the debt.[33]

Managers of large PPCs claim to provide better quality services due to the professional experience of their personnel. While maintaining formidable firepower, large companies rely on informational and analytic methods acquired during their managers' career in state service. The major emphasis lies not on direct physical protection or intimidation, but on the preventive neutralization of potential conflicts and threats. The vice chairman of the security service of the Association of Russian Banks, A. Krylov, thus described the methods of legal enforcement partners: "To recover debt one does not need recourse to violent means—it is sufficient just to demonstrate that you have information that compromises the debtor and the channels for its dissemination."[34] The director of Aleks North-West claims his company has a database on all business enterprises in the region, allowing it to assess the reliability of its clients' potential partners before entering into business relationships.

More directly related to anticriminal activity are those PPCs that provide a rare but increasingly demanded service, the so-called "removal of the roof" (*sniatie kryshi*). Involving great risk, this task consists in forcing the criminal group that controls an enterprise to leave it. The PPC would then naturally provide alternative protection. As was earlier mentioned, it is very hard for a company to break free from a criminal group; the costs of such an action would normally exceed the benefits. Yet, if the client company wishing to do so is not itself engaged in illegal business and has high commercial potential, and if the PPC is powerful enough and well connected to police organs, it can decide to take the risk and force the criminal group out of business. This practice represents a truly extraordinary profit-motivated, private form of anticriminal activity, whereby manifest commercial interest that drives the struggle for the client has the latent outcome of relative decriminalization of business. Baltik-Escort, the first PPC in St. Petersburg, was set up in April 1993 by former MVD employee R. Tsepov and former FSB officer I. Koreshkov. The core of the staff of Baltik-Eskort was recruited from the ranks of the former special task police unit (OMON) stationed in Vilnus and Riga, the capitals of the ex-Soviet republics. The PPC started by clashing with the Chechen gang over a car maintenance company, Inavtoservis, whose management was seeking an alternative protection arrangement. Far from peaceful, the competition ended in favor of the PPC, which thus acquired its first permanent client. Then the company began to escort trucks that carried imported goods from the West to St. Petersburg through Ukraine— the route controlled by criminal gangs and considered one of the most dangerous for drivers. This, maintains Tsepov, was key to the company's subsequent commercial success as it earned Baltik-Escort the reputation of a tough and reliable security partner. Now the PPC provides protection to over twenty companies, including a Volvo dealer, the electric equipment plant Energomashstroi, and the computer firm Cityline, as well as to VIP visitors to St. Petersburg, including business magnate Boris Berezovsky and fashion model Claudia Schiffer.[35]

Conclusion

The trajectory of the Soviet security organs in post-communist Russia reveals an important aspect of the complicated transition from state socialism, with a transition from an emphasis on the coercive role of the state to a different model whereby owners of means of coercion enter into commercial relations with private economic agents. It also enables us to conceive of social change in a nonteleological manner. The reform of state security was devised and executed out of short-term political considerations when Yeltsin and his team sought to strengthen political authority and neutralize possible threats to the new regime. The radical liberalism and anticommunism of the early 1990s made this policy fully legitimate. Blind to longer-term structural consequences, the government did little to strengthen security and law enforcement while launching economic liberalization. In this context, the downsizing of state security quickly led to the proliferation of informal institutions of security and enforcement, as both discharged and acting security officers discovered a way to convert their skills into a marketable asset. Destroying the old Soviet system of coercion, the government did not undertake to create new institutions for the protection of private property. But former state police and security employees had no idea of institution-building in their minds either: most of them were just adapting to the new economic conditions. Violent entrepreneurship, the methods of which had already been perfected by criminal gang members, was their major adaptive response. Looking back at the chaotic forces unleashed by the rapid collapse of the old order and their violent struggle in the early 1990s, it is important not to miss the structural consequence of the formation of a set of informal institutions that shaped the emerging markets. Organized force became a major market resource convertible into profits irrespective of the origin and legal status of the group that managed this resource. Hence various armed formations such as criminal groups, private guards, paramilitary units attached to fragmented state security and police organs, and the like rapidly proliferated. Once the state failed to control the process of institution-building, it also lost the monopoly of force and the fiscal monopoly vital to its very existence.

The law on private protection, adopted in 1992, can be seen as a successful example of a legal development whereby informal practices, in this case the private use of force and coercion, acquired legal status and became subject to state regulation. This was a rare instance when the adoption of a law reflected the effort to acknowledge, codify, and regulate an already existing practice rather that to create something from above, although one may add that the state was simply incapable of the "from above" strategy. The growth rates of the new, now legal business of private protection and enforcement testify to the success of this legal initiative and to its meeting of a huge demand. The context of the conception and adoption of this law requires additional exploration. Based on research conducted to date, it appears to have been pushed through by a narrow group of former security employees seeking to expand and legalize their business. But subsequently, it enabled the state authorities to achieve at least some degree of control over the private use of force and coercion.

The most controversial consequence of the privatization of state security and law enforcement and of the legalization of the business of private protection was the indirect anticriminal effect achieved by the growing competition in this domain. One is left wondering only at the dialectical nature of the legalization of private protection and enforcement in Russia. On the one hand, it can be seen as a juridical acknowledgement of the de facto fragmentation of the state monopoly of violence and justice. On the other hand, it may be seen as a step toward the restoration of public control over the use of force and thus toward the reconstruction of the state, as licensed protection agencies were increasingly made accountable to state authorities and compelled to play by the rules set by the latter. Being itself incapable of efficient protection and enforcement in the economic realm and facing the challenge of the criminal sector, the state was led to delegate these vital functions to its former employees on a private basis. The "soft" monopoly of violence and justice that thus emerged—a condition whereby the state has selective and indirect control over the use of force in the civic domain—is likely to undergo further evolution. To restore public control over the use of force and dispute settlement (adjudication), the government does not necessarily need to ban private security agencies, but rather to establish and enforce a clear division of competence, limiting the activity of these agencies to physical and informational security while strengthening state arbitration and justice.

Notes

An earlier version of this paper was published as "Between Economy and the State: Private Security and Rule Enforcement in Russia." *Politics and Society* 28, no. 4 (December 2000): 483–501.

1. The main data comes from interviews with experts, heads of private protection companies, entrepreneurs, police officers, and informal private enforcers (nineteen focused interviews altogether), as well as from specialized periodicals on private security.

2. On privatization see Blasi et al. 1997; Boycko et al. 1995.

3. With the exception of Frye 1996.

4. *Izvestiya*, 2 March 1994.

5. *FSB Rossii* (Moscow, 1995), 18.

6. *Novaya Gazeta* 27, 13–19 July 1998.

7. *Bdi*, no. 4 (1995): 4.

8. *Biznes i bezopasnost′ v Rossii*, no. 2 (1999): 34.

9. *Sekiuriti*, no. 2 (1995): 5.

10. Several private detective agencies are subdivisions of large PPCs. This reduces costs and gives the companies additional legal rights to conduct surveillance.

11. *Biznes i bezopasnost′ v Rossii*, no. 2 (1997): 6.

12. *Lichnosti Peterburga. Bezopasnost,′* no. 1 (1998): 36.

13. *Biznes i bezopasnost′ v Rossii*, no. 9–10 (1998): 28–29.

14. *Izvestiya*, 3 March 1994.

15. Author's interview with Boris Markarov, 14 April 1999.

16. *Mir bezopasnosti*, no. 1 (1999): 2.

17. Ibid., 741.

18. For the assessment of risks and the role of business culture, see Radaev 1998.

19. *Bdi*, no. 2 (1995):15.

20. *Mir bezopasnosti*, no. 9 (1997): 10.

21. *Lichnosti Peterburga*, no. 1 (1998): 54–55.

22. *Operativnoe prikrytie*, no. 1 (1997): 8–9.

23. Author's interview with "Amir," a member of the Chechen gang, 25 April 1999.

24. "Chastnye okhrannye predpriyatiya Sankt-Peterburga," *Analiticheskaya zapiska Tsentra zhurnalistskikh rassledovanii* (St. Petersburg, 1998): 4–5.
25. *Biznes i bezopasnost'v Rossii*, no. 2 (1999): 18.
26. *Chastnyi sysk, okhrana, bezopasnost'*, no. 9 (1995): 12.
27. *Operativnoe prikrytie*, no. 3 (1999): 29.
28. Author's interview with Vadim, the owner of a pharmacy retail trade network, 16 January 1999.
29. Author's interview with Vladimir, a company director, 20 February 1999.
30. *Den'gi*, no. 24 (23 June 1999): 28.
31. Author's interview with Dmitrii Moshkov and Dmitrii Tiutiaev, codirectors of *Avanpost*, 6 June 2000.
32. For more details, see Zhitenev 1993.
33. *Ekspert*, no. 2 (1996): 20.
34. Ibid.
35. Author's interview with Roman Tsepov, 10 June 1999. Also see published interview in *Lichnosti Peterburga*, no. 1 (1998): 56.

Bibliography

Bakatin, Vadim. *Izbavlenie ot KGB*. Moscow: Novosti, 1992.
Blasi, Joseph, Maya Kroumova, and Douglas Kruse. *Kremlin Capitalism: Privatizing the Russian Economy*. Ithaca: Cornell University Press, 1997.
Boycko, Maxim, Andrei Shleifer, and Robert Vishny. *Privatizing Russia*. Cambridge, MA: MIT Press, 1995.
Diego, Gambetta. *The Sicilian Mafia: The Business of Private Protection*. Cambridge, MA: Harvard University Press, 1996.
Frye, Timothy. "Contracting in the Shadow of the State: Private Arbitration Commissions in Russia." In Katharina Pistor and Jeffrey Sachs, eds. *The Rule of Law and Economic Reform in Russia* (Boulder: Westview Press, 1997)
Hendley, Kathryn. "Legal Development in Post-Soviet Russia." *Post-Soviet Affairs* 13, no. 3 (1997): 228–251.
Konstantinov, Andrei. *Banditskii Peterburg*. St. Petersburg: Folio-press, 1997.
Korovin, Vladimir. *Istoriya otechestvennyx organov bezopasnosti*. Moscow: Norma, 1998.
Kryshtanovskaia, Olga. "Nelegal'nye struktury v Rossii." *Sotsiologicheskie issledovaniya*, no. 8 (1995).
North, Douglass. *Structure and Change in Economic History*. New York: Norton, 1979.
North, Douglass. *Institutions, Institutional Change, and Economic Performance*. Cambridge: Cambridge University Press, 1990.
North, Douglass, and Robert Thomas. *The Rise of the Western World*. Cambridge: Cambridge University Press, 1973.
Radaev, Vadim. *Formirovanie novykh rossiiskikh rynkov: transaktsionnye izderzhki, formy controlia i delovaia etika*. Moscow: Tsentr politicheskikh tekhnologii, 1998.
Sachs, J., and K. Pistor, eds. *The Rule of Law and Economic Reform in Russia*. New York: Westview Press, 1997.
Tambovtsev, Vladimir. "Ekonomicheskie instituty rossiiskogo kapitalizma." In T. Zaslavskaya, ed., *Kuda idet Rossiya?* Moscow: Logos, 1999.

Tilly, Charles. "War Making and State Making as Organized Crime." In P. Evans, D. Rueschemeyer, and T. Skocpol, eds., *Bringing the State Back In.* Cambridge: Cambridge University Press, 1985.

Varese, Federico. *The Emergence of the Russian Mafia: Dispute Settlement and Protection in a New Market Economy.* D.Phil. thesis, Faculty of Social Studies, University of Oxford, 1996.

Volkov, Vadim. "Violent Entrepreneurship in Post-Communist Russia." *Europe-Asia Studies* 51, no. 5 (1999): 741–754.

Waller, Michael, and Victor Yasmann. "Russia's Great Criminal Revolution: The Role of the Security Services." In P. Ryan and G. Rush, eds., *Understanding Organized Crime in Global Perspective: A Reader.* London: Sage, 1997.

Zhitenev, Viacheslav, ed. *Mafiya v Ekaterinburge.* Ekaterinburg: Novaya Gil'diya, 1993.

5

The Construction
of a Professional Field

Resources, Skills, and Attributes of Founders of the Market Research Sector in Poland, 1989 to 1997

Elżbieta W. Benson

Information is a valuable resource. Shortages and uneven distribution of information hinder the chances of individuals and societies to succeed. Scholars of the Polish postsocialist transition have observed, for example, that exclusion from information networks prevented many individuals from participating fully in the privatization of Polish state assets (Staniszkis 1991). Despite the promise of beneficial outcomes, however, every reorganization of information flows naturally generates discontent among those whose informational advantages it challenges. In Poland, the state and the newly independent National Chamber of Commerce clashed when the latter attempted to seize control of business registers in the 1990s (*Życie Gospodarcze* 1996, no. 4, p. 40; Benson 1997). Concurrently, the business community accused both institutions of trying to revive monopolistic control over information. New arrangements for organizing information flows can also fail because they are either too difficult or expensive to use, or because they lack cultural legitimacy. Particularistic interests, institutional inertia, shortages of resources, and cultural or cognitive dissonance, in sum, may delay or prevent innovation in the information domain.

For these reasons, the emergence and growth of the market research sector in Poland between 1989 and 1997 constituted an extraordinary achievement.[1] How was it possible that the sector came to flourish in a country where "for many years almost nobody thought of market research as a commodity" (Kulikiewicz 1990) and where very few people understood its techniques and purpose?

In this chapter I will argue that the market research sector accomplished this goal first by adopting well-established professional strategies to "construct, communicate [and legitimate] . . . expertise, consistency, fungibility, and contractual relations" (Nelsen and Barley 1997). Yet professionalization of market research in Poland did not evolve in an institutional vacuum, free of Western influence. In the early 1990s, the arrival in Poland of international corporations with a voracious appetite for market research provided the initial impetus for older social research firms and newly emerging market research firms to seek the institutional backing of venerable Western professional associations. The proliferation of contacts with foreign clients and competitors also provided emerging local market research firms with ample opportunities to acquire new skills and master new technologies. And finally, by working for wealthy Western clients, Polish firms acquired the funds necessary for organizational expansion and modernization.

Over time, however, the proliferation of powerful Western corporations and research firms began to threaten the local research sector, which had less control over external sources of legitimacy than its Western competition. In response, Polish firms created local sources of professional legitimacy in order to diminish the distance separating local, inexperienced clients from the market research profession. To successfully communicate with these clients, leaders of the market research sector began to offer training seminars and literature. Furthermore, a new local association of market researchers emerged to set standards and scrutinize the conduct of individuals and firms involved in market research. Finally, professionalization offered a platform for pooling of scarce organizational resources, which were then spent on improving the public image of the market research sector.

New Fashion—The Power of Professions

Structural Change

Political and legal changes of the late 1980s and early 1990s opened new opportunities for entrepreneurship in Poland. In particular, the Statute on Economic Activity (December 23, 1988) extended the freedom to engage in economic activities to private enterprises (Banasiński and Przybysz 1997, pp. 93–104; Biernat and Wasilewski 1997; Kosikowski 1995), and new laws introduced in the late 1980s and early 1990s opened the Polish market to foreign firms and liberalized international trade (Włodyka 1996, chapter 14). How did these changes affect market research in Poland?

Functional Response

A typical answer to this question combines functional causal logic with elements of classic economics and an allowance for historically specific contingencies. According to this approach, legal and political changes produced market competition in its "classic understanding" (Kall and Sojkin 1996, p. 2). Proliferation of competitive enterprises, including international companies, increased the demand for information. And finally, information entrepreneurs recognized the emergence of demand and formed organizations to satisfy it (Kall and Sojkin 1996; Siemieniuk 1995, pp. 5–6).[2]

Empirical evidence, however, challenges this causal argument. First, the demand for information services remained confined to a small group of enterprises during the formative period of the market research sector. As late as 1995, researchers reported, for example, that almost 60 percent of 270 trade and trade-production enterprises never ordered any kind of external market research from professional providers (Kłosiewicz and Słomińska 1996).[3] Between 1992 and 1995, however, as Kall and Sojkin themselves observe, the share of Polish managers who proclaimed the necessity of conducting market research grew from 25 to 75 percent (Kall and Sojkin 1996, p. 5). Kall and Sojkin dismiss this development as a passing "fashion" induced by the arrival of Western firms in Poland. Another observer, however, proposes an interesting explanation for the so-called fashion in the following statement: "Research mania from 1992 to 1995 saw firms contracting market research more as a status symbol, rather than viewing it as a tool for making better strategic decisions" (*Warsaw Business Journal*, June 16–22, 1997, p. 17).

The Fashion for Market Research—Social Legitimation

For a fashion for market research or any other business practice to emerge, social actors must perceive such a practice as available to them and advantageous for obtaining desired outcomes. In other words, such a practice must gain cognitive and sociopolitical legitimacy (Hannan et al. 1995; Baum and Powell 1995). Market research became one among many new business practices that became available early in the 1990s. The prominence of market research increased when it was appropriated by those social actors—suppliers and consumers of information—who enjoyed a central position in their respective economic networks. The most common pattern of sociopolitical legitimation involves the introduction of endorsements and sanctions by the state and/or other supervisory entities. In Poland in the early 1990s, however, dissemination of organizational and institutional innovations typically preceded legal regulations. Thus the positive valuation of market research evolved through the pluralist process of advancing compelling narratives that associated this practice with achieving desirable outcomes or traits. In other words, social actors transformed market research into an "approved means" for obtaining desired ends, which themselves had been socially defined (DiMaggio and Powell 1991b). This functional explanation, for example, invoked a powerful economic narrative that equates the use of market research with a capacity to reach rational and informed strategic decisions. What were the sources and the content of these legitimating narratives, and what mechanisms facilitated their dissemination?

Professional Resources in Institutionalization

Professions have traditionally served as an important source of new institutional narratives (DiMaggio and Powell 1991a, pp. 70–71; DiMaggio 1991, p. 282). Whether professions aimed "to define the conditions of their work, to control 'the production of producers' and to establish a cognitive base and legitimacy for their occupational autonomy" (DiMaggio and Powell 1991a, p. 70; Larson 1977), or to claim "jurisdictional vacancies" from others (Abbott 1988), they always sought to capture and define social ills and to offer compelling solutions for them. Scholars have typically focused on the emergence of organizational structures—including professional associations, university-based education, self-policing, licensing, examinations, ethics code, and professional journals—as a measure of the progress of professionalization (for a literature review, see Abbott 1988, pp. 1–31; Nelsen and Barley 1997). This chapter views these structures as a form and locus of resource consolidation in the hands of professional entrepreneurs, whose goal is to present their firms as legitimate providers of a legitimate solution to the problem of information transparency and, by doing so, secure their organizational survival. Such key resources facilitated internal cohesion of the market research sector and improved communication among market researchers and potential consumers of market information (DiMaggio 1991, pp. 275–276). Within the profession, increased cohesion disseminated and reinforced ethical and technical standards. In relations with the public, such cohesion exuded authority and confidence. Finally, access to effective means of communication was indispensable for capturing public attention.

Because the profession of market research in Poland emerged in the organizational context of market research firms, at times it becomes virtually impossible to empirically desegregate the process of the emergence of the field from professionalization processes within the field. Both processes shared common features and, in fact, informed each other. Like professions, organizational fields "only exist to the extent that they are institutionally defined." Like professionalization, institutional definition of the field, or "structuration," involves "an increase of the extent of interactions (. . .); the emergence of sharply defined inter-organizational structures of domination and patterns of coalition ["center-periphery structure"]; an increase in the information load with which organizations in the field must contend; and the development of a mutual awareness among participants in a set of organizations that they are involved in a common enterprise" (DiMaggio 1991, pp. 277–278; DiMaggio and Powell 1991a, p. 65).

For these reasons, I frequently find it impossible to discern whether, for example, central professional figures derived their position from the strength of their respective firms, or whether their firms achieved central positions in the field on the basis of the professional prominence of their founders and/or managers. I believe, however, that this lack of clear causal sequencing leaves intact the basic premise of this paper that the fashion for market research in Poland owes its origins to the power of collective persuasion of market researchers.

The commercialization of information gathering and disseminating was one of several institutional solutions proposed to improve information transparency in Poland in the early 1990s. The state actively promoted the creation of the central register of business enterprises. The National Chamber of Commerce (Krajowa Izba Gospodarcza) also supported the central register, but recommended that it be anchored within its organizational structures (Benson 1997). Finally, business insiders continued to swap information, but such clandestine information networks faced increased social and legal restrictions.[4] In sum, the institutional battle over information in Poland in the 1990s centered on two interrelated questions: who could be trusted to provide fair access to reliable information, and what broad logic should inform and guide information exchange? I argue that the emerging consensus in Poland favors information flows built on the basis of specialized knowledge, contractual relations, and transparency, in which experts serve as impartial brokers.[5]

Data and Methods

This paper draws on in-depth interviews with managers and/or owners of twenty-four market research firms in Poland, which I conducted in 1997. I selected the respondents by cross-referencing a directory of Polish members of the European Society of Opinion and Marketing Research (ESOMAR) with rankings of market research firms in Poland produced by two national dailies, *Rzeczpospolita* and *Gazeta Wyborcza* (both publications are discussed later in the paper). I requested interviews with twenty-six firms, and I completed twenty-four of them. One firm refused to grant me an interview, and a date for meeting with the other firm could not be scheduled before I left Poland. Considering that the entire population of market research firms in Poland at that time was estimated at either twenty-seven or thirty firms, with a majority of publications citing even lower numbers, I reached about 80 percent of members of this population.

Interviews lasted between two and eight hours, with longer interviews conducted over several separate meetings. To make the data comparable, I used a questionnaire. I also encouraged respondents to offer their own insights whenever they felt that my questionnaire overlooked any important matters, and I adjusted the questionnaire accordingly. Furthermore, upon completing the first several interviews, I developed a list of events, such as particular altercations between companies in the field, which I introduced in subsequent interviews. Respondents' opinions about those specific events illuminate the chemistry among firms.

Foundations of Market Research in Poland

Founding Ethos

A sense of adventure accompanied the inception of market research in Poland. Young founders marveled over new opportunities and pondered ways to ensure that early successes continued beyond the initial, euphoric stage. Firm A emerged at the forefront of a wave of such firms, which sprouted like "mushrooms after the rain" in the early 1990s and played an important role in shaping market research in Poland.[6] Its founders, twenty-something classmates at the Sociology Institute of Warsaw University, viewed it all as an "adventure."[7] "We [and many like us] were in such a comfortable situation that we could afford to fail, [and even if we did], we still would have been better off than others, because we at least did something." A lighthearted tone concealed the pride with which my respondent remembered those early years. Somewhat bashfully he recalled how, from the beginning, their adventure "had a meaning and a kind of ethos, a pioneering ethos— without exaggeration—but [such an ethos] is something that one can consider as our firm's philosophy, something that gives the firm energy to act" (4/9/97, 10 AM). Despite these enthusiastic beginnings, founders were fully aware that their survival rested on their ability to transform market research into a household name. Some were even doubtful about whether it could be done, and, to hedge their risks, they maintained their day jobs at universities (4/29/97, 10 AM).

Immediate financial rewards were not the primary motive for founding market research firms. Profits were often consumed by mounting business expenses, including property leases, equipment, taxes, salaries, and the like. Unruffled, founders listed "being on one's own" and seeing their firms grow as the most satisfying aspects of their first business endeavor (4/9/97, 10 AM, and 4/17/97, 4 PM). This is not to say that theirs was an overtly idealistic philosophy. They had good reasons to believe that the economic prosperity of the early 1990s offered ample opportunities for people who were willing to "take matters into their own hands." The arrival of Western concerns in Poland further expanded opportunities, even to inexperienced market researchers. The beginning of "1992 . . . was a moment in the [development of] the market for market research, and, more broadly, in the sphere of economic information in Poland . . . , when one could count on serious companies—Polish and international—to . . . order research from firms without much of a history, brand new ones, [which were] completely unknown" (4/9/97, 10 AM).

Since so few market research firms existed, opportunities abounded. "There were no other firms with such a narrow specialization in research, . . . and *some professions* and some specializations were so new then, that it could not have been said that somebody was more or less experienced in those areas. There were no opportunities to gain such an experience [prior to 1992]" (4/9/97, 10 AM; my emphasis).[8] Such a comfortable situation did not last long, since new market research firms emerged every day. Low capital requirements stimulated this rapid proliferation. The majority of early firms started in one room of a private apartment, "invaded" office space at universities and other institutions, or even used P.O. boxes as their first address (4/9/97, 10 AM; 4/29/97, 10 AM; 4/17/97, 1 PM; 6/4/97, 10 AM; 6/27/97, 3 PM). Very few early firms had more than one computer or a typewriter, and some clandestinely "borrowed" computing power from their day jobs. The relatively high remuneration rates of market research, as compared to the costs of running a business, also attracted many young entrepreneurs to this line of business. But, as I said earlier, founders quickly reinvested their profits into expanding their firms (4/29/97, 10 AM).[9] "During the first two years, one piece of research (one questionnaire), could bring in enough money to open a [leased] office and buy equipment for it" (4/9/97, 10 AM).

Challenges—Structural Disturbances

With a rapidly increasing number of firms competing for the same few orders, the realization began to settle in that the survival of local market research firms directly depended on making them attractive to Polish information consumers. Furthermore, older market research firms could no longer assume that a Western corporation would choose them to serve its research needs over a cheaper newcomer. Many firms attempted to beat this trend on their own by intensifying their search for new clients. The founders of firm A, for example, who prided themselves on making it on their own without any special breaks and without having anybody "clear the way" for them, adopted inventive ways to identify new clients. The founders daily perused newspapers in search of ideas and opportunities for research. Once they found an inspiration, such as an advertisement about a new product or service, they called the producers to convince them that with some market research their chances for successful sales on the Polish market would greatly improve (4/17/97, 4 PM).

Yet all these efforts did not suffice. Between 1992 and 1995, the entry of large and wealthy international research firms into the sector heightened and redefined competition.[10] The subsequent fall in prices for research produced diminished returns among local firms and forced some new firms to seek partners with capital or to borrow money from friends (4/16/97, 10:30 AM).[11] The accompanying increase in salience of Western technical standards marginalized some less sophisticated market research firms in Poland and their potential clients, who became wary of the technical language of the field. New barriers to entry—money, technical expertise, and international connections—emerged outside of the control of local firms.

Two contradictory strategies were adopted in response to these developments. On the one hand, local market researchers challenged the Western legitimizing ethos by stressing their own superior familiarity with—and embeddedness in—the local environment. On the other hand, they attempted to appropriate Western professional models. The embeddedness strategy aimed to distinguish local firms from international newcomers and to appeal to domestic sensitivities. In the short term, this approach worked quite well. Firm A, for example, secured a large research order from a Polish bank because it "did not really know how to find [anybody else], and because it believed that the Polish market was better known to Polish research firms" (4/9/97, 10 AM). Emphasis on local knowledge, however, proved insufficient to stem the rising trend toward legitimation based on Western technical criteria. "Three years ago it was customary to stress familiarity with the Polish market," but not so much any longer (4/11/97, 12 N). The main, but not the sole, reason for this development was the increased prominence of international market research firms in Poland. As a founder of A remarked, "It is we who try to meet Western standards and not the other way around" (4/9/97, 10 AM).

An additional push for Westernization resulted from the contradictory nature of the embeddedness strategy and from its unintended consequences. The strategy, in fact, produced more problems than it solved. As a criterion for adjudicating among competing claims to expertise in handling information, it was excessively imprecise and thus too difficult to measure. Consequently, every market research firm, including international firms with predominantly Polish personnel, claimed it was well prepared to handle local problems. In sum, the advantage that the strategy promised for distinguishing local market research firms from their international competitors quickly evaporated.

The strategy also failed in its second role as a tool to ease the misgivings about market research among local information consumers, who often did not comprehend the technical intricacies of the research apparatus. To approach such novice clients, local market research firms used the claim of local expertise as a surrogate beacon of legitimation. While such an approach, indeed, sometimes produced a more intimate bond between an individual research firm and its client, it did little to establish market research as a taken-for-granted business practice. To accomplish the latter goal, market research entrepreneurs had to find ways to develop and promote a set of measurable and compelling criteria by which the social utility of market research could be assessed and on the basis of which clients could adjudicate among competing claims of expertise. In sum, it became increasingly obvious that the survival of individual market firms depended on the ability of the sector as a whole to develop and disseminate a cohesive and compelling institutional definition of its goals, practices, and functions.

Agency

There is no doubt that the transformation of the institutional makeup of market research in Poland constitutes an example of competitive isomorphism (Nohria and Gulati 1994, p. 540). However, as Westney shows in her analysis of Meiji reforms in Japan, foreign models undergo permutations as they are adapted to new environments (Westney 1987). Some models are discarded along the way because they are ill equipped to fit the local structures and culture. Other models lose their original supporters or attract considerable opposition. In sum, successful transplantation between distinct environments is a creative process led by active agents grounded in specific social relations.

The founders of market research in Poland in the 1990s strove to secure the survival of their firms at the same time as they sought to preserve their occupational autonomy. Through trial and error, Polish information entrepreneurs identified the Western professional model of market research as the most promising vehicle for unifying the field and signaling their legitimacy to relevant audiences. In many ways it was a match made in heaven. Social research backgrounds, shared by almost all founders of market research firms, equipped information entrepreneurs with considerable theoretical and practical knowledge (4/16/97, 10:30 AM).[12] Social research also shared with market research a commitment to principles of fairness in relations with information consumers, research participants, and the research profession (key "provisions of the *ICC/ESOMAR International Code of Marketing and Social Research Practice"*—4/29/97, 10 AM). Finally, social research awarded information entrepreneurs with opportunities to gain social recognition, when the results of their work on election returns, voting preferences, and other expressions of public opinion appeared in the domestic and foreign press and at international conferences in the early 1990s.

Internal Consolidation of Market Research

As I have already indicated, dissemination of institutions is embedded in relational networks, which serve as a means to consolidate and transmit institutional resources and filter out undesirable traits. In other words, links among social actors facilitate dissemination of professional standards and innovations. Through these networks, proponents of different institutional solutions encounter and debate each other, ultimately arriving at acceptable compromises. To be sure, not all actors enjoy equal leverage in these debates, and as structuration of the field progresses, a select group of central actors acquires growing influence over final institutional outcomes.

Such relational networks evolved in the market research sector in part through historical personnel ties among individual firms. Early firms like A, F, and C over time became incubators for other firms (4/8/97, 9:30 AM). In fact, all but one original firm experienced periodic exits of cadres who left to create their own firms, such as newer firms B and E (4/9/97 5:30 PM). Such transfers of cadres facilitated dissemination of institutional standards.

Founders of market research firms also frequently shared educational and professional backgrounds.[13] A majority of the founders and/or managers of market research firms in Poland were originally students and professors of sociology, psychology, political science, and business at Warsaw University and the Central School of Trade (Wyższa Szkoła Handlowa) in Warsaw. According to a respondent from firm A, "among [local private] firms in Warsaw, several [at least 6] . . . were created by people from 18 Karowa Street, i.e., by [faculty and students] from the Sociology Institute of Warsaw University" (4/9/97, 10 AM). One large firm, formerly the state public opinion research center, was entirely staffed by people associated with the Sociology Institute, and another such firm hired many people with this background. These former state centers also served as incubators for private firms, and at least four such firms were founded or managed by former employees of CBOS (Centrum Badania Opinii Społecznej—Center for Social Opinion Research), a so-called foundation for social research supported by both state funding and also market research for commercial clients (4/11/97, 12 N; 5/26/97,

3:30 PM). Thus sociologists, psychologists, and political scientists directly from academia and via state research centers populated the field of market research (4/9/97, 5:30 PM). Finally, the Sociology Institute supplied core cadres for many international market research firms with branches in Poland and for mixed-ownership firms.

Over time, the Institute and the Central School remained the main sources of new recruits. Polish market research firms deemed "direct searches"—a form of head-hunting without a recruiting agency—more reliable, cheaper, and faster than other methods of hiring new employees.[14] "We knew [all] the advanced students in social sciences, [and] we observed people who hung around the firm. . . . We [also] have people who have friends in college, working for us, and we tell them to look for somebody who has certain knowledge and who fits into our team" (4/9/97, 10 AM; almost identical statements on 4/9/97, 5:30 PM; 4/8/97, 9:30 AM; 4/18/97, 1 PM; 5/20/97, 12 N; 6/17/97, 10 AM; 7/10/97, 3 PM). Some Western firms attempted to transplant head-hunting through agencies to Poland, but after a few failed searches they realized that personal recommendations worked much better (4/11/97, 12 N). Some of them also used advertising (7/14/97, 9 AM). Generally, Western firms experienced a much greater rotation of cadres, and they were thought to "lack a good hand in selecting local cadres" (4/16/97, 10:30 AM). In sum, avenues to entry into the profession of market researcher and the field of market research became increasingly associated with training at select schools, even though those schools rarely offered market research oriented curricula, or, as one respondent put it: "there are no ready-made market researchers at universities" in Poland (4/16/97, 10:30 AM).[15] The emergence of such curricula will likely become the next step in the professionalization of market research in Poland, as many founders continue to teach in academia (4/9/97, 5:30 PM).

The common educational background fostered communication among competing firms, whose managers met at dinners, award ceremonies, and professional events like the festival of advertising films in Cracow (mentioned by several respondents), and who shared lecture halls and students. On such occasions, comments were exchanged about results of recent contract competitions, clients' opinions, and so on (4/9/97, 5:30 PM; 4/14/97, 8:30 AM). Firms, however, "watch their backs" when it comes to clients' secrets, particularly those having to do with recent products or innovations (4/9/97, 5:30 PM). In sum, social networks and hiring practices reinforced the centrality of professional market researchers who, in turn, expanded their considerable influence to reinforce institutional and professional standards in the sector.

Not everyone, however, was ready to submit to increasing professional pressures, and some firms resisted the coalescing of the field. Challengers, however, had to contend with increasingly powerful informal and formal networks of individuals and firms that wanted to scrutinize the conduct of other firms in the field to uphold professional standards. Behaviors deemed harmful to the image of the sector, that is, unprofessional, met with disapproval. For example, firm A asserted, "[O]ne cannot accuse us of [the sort of] showmanship" exercised by some firms, whose colorful and voluminous research reports contain very little "solid information." Firm A also complained about clients who failed to distinguish between a showman, that is, a person in fashionable attire with a tendency to abuse English vocabulary, and a genuine expert (4/9/97, 10 AM).

The growing reliance on a system of mutual referrals, a form of a utilitarian network, rewarded those who played by the rules and punished dissenters. In 1997, "[I]f a client calls me to ask about data which I do not have, I no longer tell him that I do not know where to find it, but [instead] I say, you should call AMER Nielsen or some other company" (4/9/97, 10 AM). Firms which could not or would not offer such advice risked being perceived as ignorant or marginal and thus experienced further isolation and mistrust. Conversely, firms that demonstrated familiarity with the field were viewed as insiders, who could be consulted on important matters. Similarly, firms that never received referrals not only missed business opportunities, but also risked falling into oblivion. In sum, referrals both reflected and induced an increasing interconnectedness among firms, and between firms and their clients. They also affected relations of domination in the field. And finally, as the referral system was based not only on personal friendships, but also on an objective assessment of firms' qualifications, it helped define the criteria by which firms were judged.

In sum, the shared educational and professional experiences of the original founders of market research firms in Poland fostered the emergence of close communication networks whose members used their considerable power to promote and reinforce Western professional standards. As I already mentioned, however, the development of internal cohesion within the market research sector was a necessary but not sufficient condition for winning a cultural mandate. The latter required that the institutional goals and practices of market research be accepted by the public.

External Signaling

Communication between market research professionals and consumers of information happened at several levels. At the most intimate level, individuals simply exchanged opinions and ideas. During the early years of market research in Poland, market researchers more often listened than talked. Typically, international firms (both as clients and as researchers seeking local subcontractors) approached Polish market research firms with well-defined and articulated expectations (4/9/97, 10 AM; 4/9/97, 5:30 PM). They often instructed local research firms about specific research techniques and forms of data reporting, and, on some occasions, simply presented them with a ready-made research design to replicate. International market research firms also hired and trained their local employees, who often later left to create their own firms or to join the existing local firms (5/27/97, 2:30 PM; 6/4/97, 10 AM). Polish information purveyors subsequently introduced this newly acquired expertise to their clients as their own, representing themselves as legitimate guardians of professional standards.

To reach the largest possible audience, market research entrepreneurs engaged in an educational crusade that aimed to explain how and why to use market research. "We believe that it is in our best interest and in the interest of the market for economic information in Poland, that our clients are well educated and know what they want," said a founder of firm A (4/9/97, 10 AM). To this end, they organized training seminars for potential clients, both free of charge and for a fee (5/22/97, 2 PM). Firms A, H, and D, for example, offered seminars to disseminate technical know-how and attract potential clients through face-to-face interactions.[16] During seminars, local firms presented reference lists of their domestic and international clients and introduced the firms' founders and/or managers (4/24/97, 10 AM). Slick promotional brochures portrayed the founders in fine suits over starched shirts adorned with ties or bow ties, traditionally worn in Poland by academics or artists. Picture captions stressed the founders' educational credentials—increasingly linked to Poland's most prestigious academic institutions—and their Western experience. Attendees also had a chance to hear company managers and/or founders as seminar leaders, that is, legitimate bearers of professional expertise.

Local firms also tested their images during seminars and other trade and professional gatherings. Firm A, for example, distributed promotional materials that linked the firm's legitimacy to the professionalism and individual achievements of its founders, and firm D issued newsletters popularizing various market research techniques. In light of a shortage of market research literature in Polish, one firm also translated and published a book by a Western scholar of market research, but failed to make any profit on this venture (4/22/97, 10 AM). Promotional brochures evoked the founders' membership in ESOMAR, the professional association of individual market researchers, as a marker of organizational legitimacy.

The truly groundbreaking step was taken when firms like A began to offer certificates to participants of training seminars. This reflected a new emphasis on indigenous claims to professional status among market researchers in Poland. Professionalization was traditionally associated with the emergence of specialized formal training institutions and certification systems, and local firms attempted to make up for the absence of these constitutive ingredients in Poland by offering both the training and certificates. In other words, firms, at first independently of each other, engaged in erecting the institutional architecture of the field—the boundaries of the field and its internal rules, standards, and norms. Furthermore, certification became a means of connecting information consumers to the larger project of the institutionalization of market research.

Market researchers also used media to expand the public visibility of the field and of individual firms within it (5/22/97, 2 PM; 6/27/97, 3 PM). Because, however, not all firms enjoyed equal media access, this strategy also increased the interorganizational stratification of the field (4/29/97, 10 AM). Firm A, for example, lamented its limited presence in the media, explaining that firms that conducted research for media outlets, such as *Gazeta Stołeczna* or *Gazeta Wyborcza*, were most frequently cited in these popular dailies (4/17/1997, 4 PM). Newspapers sometimes—ever so rarely—reviewed research by Polish and international firms, improving the standing of select firms (4/29/97, 10 AM).

Newspapers and magazines also published catalogues/directories and rankings of market research firms and offered space for paid advertisements. Catalogues, which usually listed firms in exchange for a fee, exercised less influence than rankings, which rated firms on the basis of financial data and supplied interesting details about firms' history, specialty, and so on. Both rankings and catalogues, however, helped establish market research as an economic sector in Poland and introduced its members. For example, the *1996–1997 Book of Lists*, a ranking published annually by *Warsaw Business Journal (WBJ)*, positioned the category of market research within a larger category of professional services, which also included consulting and law firms, film studios, public relations, advertising, security, and recruitment agencies.[17] This issue ranked twenty-three market research firms in Poland by their 1995 revenue from market research. An additional four market research firms appeared unranked at the bottom of the list, because they were either too new to have a 1995 revenue report (two firms founded in 1995) or refused to disclose such data (two). The list also included three paid advertisements for market research firms, offering to send additional information about these three firms to readers who filled out a request form at the end of the publication. My interviews and visits to various public venues indicate that the publisher's goal "to provide transparency and structure to an emerging market that has few windows into its inner workings" met with broad interest and approval (*WBJ, 1996–1997 Book of Lists*, 1996, p. 4).

Gazeta Wyborcza, in turn, devoted each of its *Special Reports* to a different sector of the economy. The report from March/April 1997 was entirely dedicated to market research and included a ranking list prepared by the Polskie Towarzystwo Badaczy Rynku i Opinii (PTBRiO—The Polish Society of Market and Opinion Researchers) on the basis of firms' response to a mail questionnaire. The list included thirty firms, of which twenty-three were ranked on the basis of a self-reported 1995 turnover, and seven were not ranked (p. 4). Those seven firms, for whom the publisher lacked turnover data, again appeared at the bottom of the list. The report also featured seventeen paid advertisements, a score of articles on market research ethics and techniques, like CATI (Computer Assisted Telephone Interviewing) and focus groups, and remarks by founders and/or managers of leading market research firms. The report advanced the institutional cause of the field of market research by prominently publishing an article by the president of the PTBRiO, Andrzej Ludek, and advice to potential clients based on the Ethical Code of ESOMAR.

The report also advertised upcoming professional seminars, such as Mercator '97, second in the series of seminars devoted to market research in Poland, and promised to issue, together with a Cracow firm, ESKADRA, a special supplement about the seminar (mentioned by several firms, for example, on 4/18/97, 1 PM; 6/4/97, 10 AM; 6/17/97, 10 AM). Among "scientific" partners of the seminar, the article listed, in alphabetical order, the following market research firms and institutes: Amer Nielsen, ARC, BBM, Demoskop, GfK Polonia, and OBOP. The presenters included lecturers from SMG/KRC, Almares, CEM, Pentor, Unilever, IQS & Quant Group, Codes, GETAS IRWiK, Pasad, and Economic Academy in Cracow. Combined, these two lists covered almost all key market research firms in Poland, both domestic and international. Through financial sponsorship of Poczta Polska (the Polish Post), Motorola, ERA GSM, Coca-Cola, Philips, Optimus, Easy Call, Opus, PPA Bank, Międzynarodowe Targi Poznańskie (International Trade Show in Poznań), Cezex, Confactor, and Kompass, the seminars drew in a whole new group of economic actors, which thus became involved in structuration of market research in Poland. Last but not least, several advertising agencies, which were frequent clients of research firms, such as Ammirati Puris Lintas, BBDO Warszawa, Codes, Corporate Profiles DDB, DMB & B Warsaw, Grey Warszawa, Leo Burnett, Optimum Media, and J. Walter Thompson, provided "substantive aid" to the seminar (the role of ad agencies was stressed, for example, in interviews on 4/17/97, 4 PM; 4/16/97, 5 PM; 4/18/97, 1 PM; 6/4/97, 10 AM; 6/23/97, 9:30 AM). The official patrons of the seminar included RFM. FM (a popular commercial radio station broadcasting for all of Poland), *Gazeta Wyborcza* (arguably the most popular Polish daily), and Polish monthlies like *Businessman Magazine*, *PRESS*, *Aida Media*, *Marketing Serwis*, and *Sekretariat* (*Gazeta Wyborczo. Special Report.* March/April 1997, p. 13). By reproducing these lists, I hope to show the breadth of organizations and institutions that constituted the structural underpinning of the project of legitimizing the field of market research in Poland. In fact, this relation was mutual, because market research firms endorsed catalogs by using their mostly computerized databases in their research.

Television also publicized market research firms, but usually in their social and public opinion research capacity. For example, an evening show called *Polaków Portret Własny* (Poles' Self-Portrait) routinely invited managers from leading firms to discuss both methods and results of national surveys (4/17/97, 4 PM). The news service on a commercial TV network, POLSAT, on June 12, 1997, discussed research by a Warsaw market research firm, Demoskop. *Forum*, a show on channel 1 of state television (TVP), on June 16, 1997, cited research by CBOS. Television brought new clients to market research firms through such citations (4/17/97, 4 PM).

In comparison with the media, the state had little to say about the existence or shape of market research in Poland. For example, *Statistical Yearbook* for 1996, published by the Central Statistical Office (GUS), altogether omitted this category. To be sure, it also overlooked most other professional services. *Polski Almanach Gospodarczy* (Polish Economic Almanac), commercially published in 1997 by CompAlmanach Polski, a limited liability company, in cooperation with the Ministry of Industry and Trade and the National Chamber of Commerce, which "included 20,000 enterprises selected from among a million active Polish firms" on the basis of their "leading position in general rankings and research of their branches or regions, and in experts' opinion," recorded ten firms under the category of market research (Volume II).[18] *Business Foundation Book: General Trade Index & Business Guide: Poland*, published by the Business Foundation independently of the state but endorsed by Lech Wałęsa and the ambassadors of France, Germany, Italy, Russia, the United Kingdom, and the United States of America, used the Central Product Classification system developed by the UN to categorize entries submitted by companies in different sectors. The book included two market research firms under the category of "technical and other commercial services."[19]

Relations between the state and the market research profession and firms were peculiar in the 1990s. As a source of economic statistics, GUS, the state's statistical arm, was criticized for producing outdated data riddled with errors (4/16/97, 5 PM; 7/9/97, 12:30 PM). This was in part because, as a gatherer of such data, GUS, armed with the Law on Statistical Reporting, placed undue demands on Polish firms, including market research firms, to fill out lengthy questionnaires and calculate complex economic indicators, which they resisted (4/17/97, 4 PM). Market research firms, domestic and international, however, purchased statistical samples from Centralny Bank Danych Powszechny Elektroniczny System Ewidencji Ludności (CBD PESEL— Central Data Bank [of the] Universal Electronic System of the Population Census), the PESEL registry of all holders of Polish internal IDs, which included their names, birth dates, gender, and addresses, to use in surveys (7/9/97, 12:30 PM; 6/17/97, 10 AM). As personal data were protected in Poland by the law, firms had to provide written explanations of the purpose and significance of a planned survey (for example, 6/27/97, 3 PM). By the end of the decade, the state restricted access to the PESEL and GUS databases to those firms that employ members of ESOMAR (*Rzeczpospolita*, 6/17/1998).

As the source of laws, the state affected market research through the 1994 Law on Public Orders, which defined procedures for entering the bidding process for contracts from budget institutions. But the effects of this law on market research firms were minimal, as it covered projects of high magnitude, and the state often used CBOS for its own research (4/17/97, 4 PM).[20] Firms were aware, however, that if some new changes to the regulation of access to information were introduced, their business would change (4/9/97, 5:30 PM). Finally, market research firms, like most private firms in Poland, complained about high taxes. Some also objected, although not ardently, to preferential treatment received by CBOS in this respect (4/9/97, 5:30 PM).

Formal Representation of the Profession

Professional associations served as an ultimate display of professional unity. ESOMAR most certainly provided legitimacy to Polish market researchers and their firms (6/4/97, 1 PM). It served as a sort of "older brother," providing psychological comfort and a promise of help in times of trouble (4/9/97, 5:30 PM). ESOMAR acquired a more tangible role when it selected its own local representative from among Polish researchers and offered training seminars in Poland (4/14/97, 8:30 AM; 4/11/97, 12 N). According to almost all respondents, the ESOMAR *Directory of Members*, grouped by country and available both in paper and on-line, provided the first and, arguably, still the most important resource for many clients looking for market research firms (4/17/97, 4 PM; 4/9/97, 5:30 PM; 4/14/97, 8:30 AM; 7/14/97, 9 AM).

PTBRiO, the local association, however, was created only in 1995, and by 1997, it still struggled to gain broad approval in the field (4/9/97, 5:30 PM;

4/28/97, 12 N; 6/4/97, 10 AM; 6/17/97, 10 AM). According to some respondents, it aroused suspicion by admitting some firms with a questionable reputation for data reliability, that is, firms whose professionalism was in question (4/9/97, 5:30 PM). Another possible reason was that its president, Andrzej Ludek, formerly an employee of an international market research firm and, in 1997, an owner of a small and new firm, did not enjoy a sufficiently prominent position in the field (4/14/97, 8:30 AM).

In 1996, however, PTBRiO somewhat improved its standing, or at least gained more recognition, when it attempted to lead an effort toward an agreement among market research firms against using dumping prices to win contracts. The effort failed because "the firms which initiated these talks, large firms, themselves practiced dumping" (4/9/97, 10 AM). The threat of price undercutting came mainly from existing firms, because newcomers could no longer enter the field without substantial founding capital. Among the existing firms, foreign and mixed-capital firms, for example, could afford to forgo profits for many years in order to secure their share of the market. Despite these difficulties, PTBRiO began to make a name for itself, and some respondents even hoped that the society would manage to "somehow civilize the market [for market research]" (5/22/97, 2 PM). It issued a monthly, *Marketing in Practice*, which included several paid advertisements, brief bios of market research firms, and brief articles.

Self-Definition

By 1997, all of these efforts paid off. Consumers of market research became not only familiar with individual firms and the sector as a whole, but also with the basic professional underpinnings of market research. By the same token, individual researchers and firms became aware of each other and fully cognizant of the shared responsibility to maintain high professional standards as the best guarantee of institutional and organizational survival. In 1997, "[O]ne can say . . . that the sector, if I were to consider serious firms, [and] there are some fifteen to twenty of them in the country, or maybe fifteen, [experienced] a considerable isomorphism of methods, techniques, and procedures. One can say that they are compatible," they share the same professional language, and the sector increasingly "professionalizes" itself. The standards became so well established that "now, nobody would trust a start-up company" (4/9/97, 10 AM; 4/9/97, 5:30 PM). Through training and media campaigns, market researchers overcame apprehension and ignorance. They also defined information transparency as an important social goal and offered their services to reach it.

Definition of the professional traits of individual researchers constituted an integral part of this process. To be a professional, that is, legitimate, market researcher, one was expected to display *rzetelnośc merytoryczną* (substantive integrity) by acting in "agreement with the principles of the art [of market research], which means . . . in agreement with the ESOMAR Code, which regulated various aspects of ethical and methodological conduct, and in agreement with knowledge learned in college and acquired from specialized literature." The statute of the PTBRiO reiterated almost identical formulas (4/28/97, 12 N).

One was also expected to give priority to clients' interests over the firms' desire for "coconut deals" (a roaring trade) and to strive to develop long-term commitments to clients and other firms in the field (4/9/97, 10 AM). And finally, the professional work environment was to foster individual self-realization, creativity, freedom, and authorship, particularly among qualitative researchers (4/9/97, 5:30 PM).

Professionalism had to be maintained at the levels of the firm and the individual. Both research reports and the personnel testified to the quality of a firm. "I am interested in who works for these firms, in the sense of their qualifications, maybe not so much their qualifications as proved by their diplomas, but rather, qualifications in the sense of communicational competence" (4/9/97, 10 AM). Individual traits and qualifications came into focus during the hiring of new employees. "If a person is completely unknown to me, and nobody among [our] acquaintances would be able to recommend her—as you know, in this circle we all know each other very well—so if nobody can say anything about her, then we have to check if she has a statistical package . . . and at least a passing comprehension of English under her belt" (4/9/97, 5:30 PM).

Market researchers also built their identity by emphasizing connections between social and market research. Former and current academics translated expertise in social research into an advantageous attribute in market research, because academia gave them "a sort of professional background" (4/29/97, 10 AM). Some people working as market researchers directly combined their two hats and used market research data to complete their doctoral dissertations on the side (4/17/97, 4 PM).

Conclusion

Market research emerged as an unwanted and largely misunderstood child of the Polish postsocialist transition. A typical Polish enterprise director in the early 1990s viewed market research as a sort of curiosity, which for some inexplicable reasons worked for Western companies, but had very little relevance for the local environment and its problems. Early experiences with market research only added to this general confusion. Some local enterprises, which reached for market research in hopes of solving all their ills, felt disappointed with the results. They wanted to find answers to all their questions and to do it cheaply. The vast majority of local firms lacked the expertise to interpret research results, so they also questioned the utility of conducting market research. In sum, market research was a hard sell in Poland in the early 1990s.

Local market researchers ventured to reverse these negative perceptions. They concluded that the main task at hand was to familiarize Polish information consumers with the purpose and techniques of market research. To this end, they organized training seminars and publicity campaigns. Some researchers worried, however, that the trained consumers might no longer need external experts to satisfy their information needs. Yet others hoped to reap the benefits of the legitimation of market research without bearing their share of the work. In sum, efforts to mobilize individual entrepreneurs and firms in the name of the collective good of legitimation met with considerable obstacles. Extraordinary pressures had to be employed to minimize dissent, freeloading, and inertia.

Professional networks became the most important tool for exerting these pressures on the members of the profession, as well as an abundant source of organizational and cultural resources. Professionalization evolved on the basis of preexisting and shared educational and professional experiences. A combination of these multiple relational ties allowed market researchers to set standards governing business and professional conduct in the sector. It also offered tangible means, such as formal exclusion and social ostracism, to enforce these standards. Finally, by becoming a collective actor, the market research profession fortified its jurisdiction over the information domain.

Notes

I thank Victoria Bonnell, Ann Swidler, Neil Fligstein, and the participants in the Mellon conference, *Entrepreneurs, Entrepreneurialism and Democracy in Communist and Post-Communist Societies*, at the University of California at Berkeley for comments and encouragement. I also thank my respondents in Poland. Funding for this project has been provided by the Berkeley Program in Soviet and Post-Soviet Studies, the American Council of Learned Societies (Fellowship in East European Studies), and the University of California Regents Fellowship.

1. Expenditures on market research grew from near zero in the early 1990s to $35 million in 1996 (*Warsaw Business Journal*, 6/16–22/97, p. 17). Furthermore, the ranking of market research firms prepared by *Warsaw Business Journal* shows that several market research firms almost doubled their revenues between 1995 and 1996. According to the data compiled by a daily, *Rzeczpospolita*, and Polskie Towarzystwo Badania Rynku i Opinii (The Polish Society of Market and Opinion

Research), returns of the entire market research sector in Poland increased by about 78 percent between 1993 and 1994; by 68 percent between 1994 and 1995; by 43 percent between 1995 and 1996; and by 74 percent between 1996 and 1997 (*Rzeczpospolita*, 6/17/1998). Interestingly, in 1997, for the first time, revenues of a local market research firm, SMG/KRC (22.9 million *złoty*), exceeded those of any of its foreign competitors on the local market (*Rzeczpospolita*, 6/17/1998).

2. This argument about the priority of the independent variable of demand closely resembles those advanced by the marginalist school of economics (see Frenzen, Hirsch, and Zerrillo 1994).

3. Scholars of the British market research industry also argued against attributing the proliferation of market research firms to the growth in the demand for information. For example, between 1974 and 1976, when orders for the British market research industry declined rapidly, not only did a few market research firms disappear, but also many new small firms emerged (Simmons 1978, p. 157).

4. Like Western investors (n. 1), Polish shareholders enjoyed the most effective means of voicing their displeasure with inside information swapping. For example, the news about the withholding of information by Elektrim SA sent its stock down by 28.2 percent in November 1998 (*Rzeczpospolita*, 1/9/99). Importantly, foreign shareholders, acting through Merrill Lynch, played the pivotal role in ousting the old management of Elektrim (*Rzeczpospolita*, 7/26/99). Investors acted not only with their wallets, but also through the Securities and Exchange Commission, which, in this case, requested an investigation of Elektrim SA by the Regional Prosecutor's Office in Warsaw.

5. A similar shift toward rational principles of legitimation took place in Western societies in earlier historical periods. Between the nineteenth century and the end of the twentieth century, "the principle of rationalization . . . embodied in the scientific ethos and in rational authority of technical expertise" became a leading legitimizing component of most "ideological structures" (Larson 1977, pp. 56–63). On the distinction between institutional (including ideological) and technical sources of legitimacy for professions and organizations, see DiMaggio 1991, p. 288.

6. Sometimes I am forced to omit specific factual details in order to protect the identity of my respondents.

7. Other founders told similar stories (5/26/97, 3:30 PM).

8. The term "our profession" pops up throughout the entire interview with this respondent, a manager and founder of one of the five oldest private market research firms in Poland.

9. Capital markets were underdeveloped at that time, and business loans were practically unavailable for small enterprises.

10. According to my respondents, some international companies had permanent contracts with research firms. Polish researchers entered such relations only as local subcontractors.

11. Prices of research conducted on representative samples (1,000–1,200 sample) of the general population remained very high. Respondents attributed it to monopolistic positions of firms dominating such labor-intensive research (4/9/97, 10 AM).

12. Early orders for social research came from international newspapers, universities, polling agencies, and the Polish state (4/29/97, 10 AM).

13. Current owners and/or managers of fourteen market research firms held degrees in either sociology or psychology, or both. Seven firms were managed or owned by people with degrees from the Central School of Trade. Managers of some firms

combined both degrees. Managers of only six firms received their education in fields other than sociology, psychology, political science, or business.

14. Head-hunting agencies already existed in Poland at that time. As for classified ads, a supplement to *Gazeta Wyborcza*, called *Gazeta Pracy* (Employment Newspaper), made the Monday issue of the paper the best-selling one. Firms also received unsolicited applications and sometimes used them to hire people for positions of research assistants and administrative staff (4/9/97, 5:30 PM).

15. Similar complaints about the absence of such curricula were printed in *Badania Rynku* (March-April 1997), *Special Report* by *Gazeta Wyborcza* (p. 3). In another section of the *Report*, academic curricula were described as having a "retirement-like" air about them (p. 13).

16. Firm A considered fairs, conferences, seminars, and trade meetings to be the best grounds for finding new clients (4/9/97, 10 AM).

17. Business services, such as catering, office supplies, exhibition organizing, and printing ventures, constituted a separate category.

18. Some market firms used databases prepared by CompAlmanach Polski and Kompass for their research.

19. These firms, however, did not appear in the subject index under the heading of "market research," which listed several firms that were not in other ranking or cataloging publications.

20. The Law on Public Orders [Ustawa o Zamówieniach Publicznych] was approved by the parliament on June 10, 1994, and entered into life on January 1, 1995 (Izdebski 1996, p. 313).

Bibliography

Periodicals

Gazeta Wyborczo [Electoral Daily]
The New York Times
Przegląd Organizacji [Review of Organizations]
Rzeczpospolita [The Republic]
The Wall Street Journal
The Warsaw Business Journal
Wiadomości Statystyczne [Statistical News]—published by the Central Statistical Office
Życie Gospodarcze [Economic Life]

Books and Articles

1996–1997 Book of Lists. The W.B.J. Guide to Polish Business Services. Supplement of the *Warsaw Business Journal*. 1996. Warsaw.

Abbott, Andrew. 1988. *The System of Professions: An Essay on the Division of Expert Labor*. Chicago: University of Chicago Press.

Balcerowicz, Ewa. 1990. *Przetarg Planistyczny: Mechanizm i Skutki Społeczno-Gospodarcze* [Plan bargaining: Mechanism and socioeconomic consequences]. Warszawa: Państwowe Wydawnictwo Ekonomiczne.

Banasiński, Cezary, and Piotr Przybysz. 1997. *Wybór Aktów Prawnych do nauki prawa gospodarczego* [Selection of legal documents for the study of economic law]. Warszawa: Liber.

Baum, Joel A.C., and Walter W. Powell. 1995. Cultivating an Institutional Ecology of Organizations: Comment on Hannan, Carroll, Dundon, and Torres. *American Sociological Review* 60: 529–538.

Ben-David, Joseph. 1984. *The Scientist's Role in Society.* Chicago: University of Chicago Press.

Beniger, James R. 1986. *The Control Revolution: Technological and Economic Origins of the Information Society.* Cambridge, MA: Harvard University Press.

Benson, Elżbieta W. 1997. Public Servant or "Superspy"? State Control of Economic Information in Post-Communist Poland. *Center for Slavic and East European Studies Newsletter* 14: 8–10.

Bieniek, Gerard. 1997. *Przedsiębiorstwa państwowe: Przypisy i komentarze* [State enterprises: Regulations and commentaries]. Warsaw: Wydawnictwo Prawnicze.

Biernat, Stanisław, and Andrzej Wasilewski. 1997. *Ustawa o działalności gospodarczej—komentarz* [The statute on economic activity—commentary]. Kraków: Kantor.

Buchner-Jezierska, Anna, and Julia Evetts. 1997. "Regulating Professionals: The Polish Example." *International Sociology* 12: 61–72.

Coe, T.L., and B.J. Coe. 1976. "Marketing Research: The Search for Professionalism." In *Educator's Proceedings*, ed. K.L. Bernhardt, 257–259. American Marketing Association No. 39.

DiMaggio, Paul J. 1983. "State Expansion and Organizational Fields." In *Organizational Theory and Public Policy*, ed. R.H. Hall and R.E. Quinn, 147–161. Beverly Hills, CA: Sage.

———. 1991. Constructing an Organizational Field as a Professional Project: U.S. Art Museums, 1920–1940. In *The New Institutionalism in Organizational Analysis*, ed. W.W. Powell and P.J. DiMaggio, 267–292. Chicago and London: University of Chicago Press.

DiMaggio, Paul J., and Walter W. Powell. 1991a. The Iron Cage Revisited: Institutional Isomorphism and Collective Rationality of Organizational Fields. In *The New Institutionalism in Organizational Analysis*, ed. W.W. Powell and P.J. DiMaggio, 63–82. Chicago and London: University of Chicago Press.

———. 1991b. Introduction. In *The New Institutionalism in Organizational Analysis*, ed. W.W. Powell and P.J. DiMaggio, 1–38. Chicago and London: University of Chicago Press.

Dingwall, Robert, and Philip Lewis, eds. 1983. *The Sociology of the Professions.* New York: St. Martin's.

Fligstein, Neil. 1996. Markets as Politics: A Political-Cultural Approach to Market Institutions. *American Sociological Review* 61(4): 656–673.

Forsyth, Patrick B., and Thomas J. Danisiewicz. 1985. Toward a Theory of Professionalization. *Work and Occupations* 12(1): 59–76.

Freidson, Eliot. 1986. *Professional Powers: A Study of the Institutionalization of Formal Knowledge.* Chicago: University of Chicago Press.

Frenzen, Jonathan, Paul M. Hirsch, and Philip C. Zerrillo. 1994. Consumption, Preferences, and Changing Lifestyles. In *Handbook of Economic Sociology*, ed. Neil J. Smelser and Richard Swedberg, 403–425. Princeton, NJ: Princeton University Press.

Geison, Gerald L., ed. 1983. *Professions and Professional Ideologies in America.* Chapel Hill: University of North Carolina Press.

Górzyńska, Teresa. 1999. *Prawo do informacji i zasada jawności administracyjnej* [The right to information and the principle of administrative disclosure]. Kraków: Kantor Wydawniczy Zakamycze.

Haber, Samuel. 1991. *The Quest for Authority and Honor in the American Professions, 1750–1900.* Chicago: University of Chicago Press.

Halliday, Terence C. 1983. *Professions, Class, and Capitalism. Archives Européennes de Sociologie* 24 (2): 321–346.

———. 1987. *Beyond Monopoly: Lawyers, State Crises, and Professional Empowerment.* Chicago: University of Chicago Press.

Halliday, Terence C., Michael J. Powell, and Mark Granfors. 1993. After Minimalism: Transformation of State Bar Associations, 1918–1950. *American Sociological Review* 58(4): 515–535.

Halpern, Sydney A. 1992. Dynamics of Professional Control: Internal Coalitions and Crossprofessional Boundaries. *American Journal of Sociology* 97(4): 994–1022.

Hannan, Michael T., Glenn R. Carroll, Elizabeth A. Dundon, and John Charles Torres. 1995. Organizational Evolution in a Multinational Context. *American Sociological Review* 60: 509–528.

Higley, John, and György Lengyel, ed. Forthcoming. *Elites After State Socialism: Theories and Analysis.* Rowman and Littlefield.

Hodson, Randy, and Teresa A. Sullivan. 1995. *The Social Organization of Work.* Belmont, CA: Wadsworth.

Izdebski, Hubert. 1996. *Historia Administracji* [History of administration]. Warsaw: Liber.

Kall, Jacek, and Bogdan Sojkin. 1996. Badania marketingowe w Polsce [Marketing research in Poland]. *Marketing and Rynek* 2: 2–5.

Kłosiewicz, Urszula, and Bożena Słomińska. 1996. Niematerialne zasoby firmy zródłem sukcesu na rynku [Nonmaterial resources of a firm as a source of (its) market success]. *Marketing and Rynek* 10: 17–20.

Kornai, János. 1992. *The Socialist System: The Political Economy of Communism.* Princeton: Princeton University Press.

Kosikowski, Cezary. 1995. *Wolnośc gospodarcza w prawie polskim* [Economic freedom in the Polish law]. Warszawa: Państwowe Wydawnictwo Ekonomiczne.

Kufel, Jan, and Wojciech Studa. 1996. *Prawo gospodarcze dla ekonomistów* [Business law for economists]. Poznań: Scriptus.

Kulikiewicz, Paweł. 1990. Badania Rynku—zapomniany towar (?) [Market research— A forgotten commodity (?)]. *Przegląd organizacji* 11: 16–18.

Larson, Magali Sarfatti. 1977. *The Rise of Professionalization: A Sociological Analysis.* Berkeley: University of California Press.

Meyer, John W., and Brian Rowan. 1977. Institutionalized Organizations: Formal Structure as Myth and Ceremony. *American Sociological Review* 83: 340–363.

Nee, Victor, and David Stark, ed. 1989. *Remaking the Economic Institutions of Socialism: China and Eastern Europe.* Stanford: Stanford University Press.

Nelsen, Bonalyn J., and Stephen R. Barley. 1997. For Love or Money? Commodification and the Construction of an Occupational Mandate. *Administrative Science Quarterly* 42: 619–653.

Nelson, Elizabeth, and Tony Cowling. 1982. The Challenge of Change. *Journal of the Market Research Association* 24(3): 200–238.

NIK. 1994. *Raport Najwyższej Izby Kontroli: Informacja o wynikach kontroli realizacji zasad jawności i aktualności rejestrów i ewidencji podmiotów prowadzących działalnośc gospodarczą oraz ustawowego obowiązku przekazywania informacji w nich zawartych organom administracji publicznej* [The Report by the Supreme Control Chamber: Information about results of the control of the implementation of principles of full-disclosure and timeliness of the registers and records of the entities engaging in economic activity, and [of the control of the implementation] of a legal obligation to forward information contained in [such registers and records] to the agencies of public administration]. Warsaw: December 1994.

Nohria, Nitin, and Ranjay Gulati. 1994. Firms and Their Environments. In *The Handbook of Economic Sociology*, ed. Neil J. Smelser and Richard Swedberg, 529–555. Princeton, NJ: Princeton University Press.

Nowak, Krzysztof. 1998. *Polski rynek kapitałowy: Instrumenty, uczestnicy, inwestycje* [The Polish capital market: Instruments, participants, [and] investments]. Poznań: Wydawnictwo Wyższej Szkoły Bankowej.

Powell, Michael J. 1989. *From Patrician to Professional Elite: The Transformation of the New York City Bar Association*. New York: Russell Sage Foundation.

Robinson, Daniel J. 1999. *The Measure of Democracy: Polling, Market Research, and Public Life, 1930–1945*. Toronto: University of Toronto Press.

Róna-Tas, Ákos. 1994. The First Shall Be Last? Entrepreneurship and Communist Cadres in the Transition from Socialism. *American Journal of Sociology* 100: 40–69.

———. 1997. *The Great Surprise of the Small Transformation: The Demise of Communism and the Rise of the Private Sector in Hungary*. Ann Arbor: University of Michigan Press.

Siemieniuk, Nina. 1995. *Koncepcje budowy banku informacji o otoczeniu przedsiębiorstwa* [Framework for constructing a bank of information about an enterprise's environment]. Białystok: Dział Wydawniczy Filii UW w Białymstoku.

Simmons, Martin. 1978. The British Market Research Industry. *Journal of the Market Research Society* 20: 135–165.

Staniszkis, Jadwiga. 1991. *The Dynamics of Breakthrough in Eastern Europe: The Polish Experience*. Berkeley: University of California Press.

Suski, Paweł. 1994. *Rejestry sądowe spółek handlowych, spółdzielni, przedsiębiorstw państwowych* [Court registers of commercial partnerships, cooperatives, [and] state enterprises]. Warszawa: Wydawnictwo Prawnicze.

Swedberg, Richard. 1994. Markets as Social Structures. In *The Handbook of Economic Sociology*, ed. Neil J. Smelser and Richard Swedberg, 255–282. Princeton, NJ: Princeton University Press.

Torstendahl, Rolf, and Michael Burrage, ed. 1990. *The Formation of Professions: Knowledge, State, and Strategy*. Newbury Park, CA: Sage.

Weber, Max. [1922] 1978. *Economy and Society: An Outline of Interpretive Sociology*. Berkeley: University of California Press.

Westney, Eleanor D. 1987. *Imitation and Innovation: The Transfer of Western Organizational Patterns to Meiji Japan*. Cambridge: Harvard University Press.

Wilensky, Harold L. 1964. The Professionalization of Everyone. *American Journal of Sociology* 70: 137–58.

Włodyka, Stanisław, ed. 1996. *Prawo gospodarcze prywatne: Prawo spółek* [Private economic law: Commercial company law]. Kraków: OPSIZ.

Zhou, Xueguang. 1993. Occupational Power, State Capacities, and the Diffusion of Licensing in the American States, 1890 to 1950. *American Sociological Review* 58(4): 536–552.

Appendix I—Schedule of Interviews

1. April 9, 1997, 10:00 AM, with a continuation on April 17, 1997—market research firm in Warsaw, Poland—Firm A
2. April 9, 1997, 5:30 PM—market research firm in Warsaw—Firm B
3. April 29, 1997, 10:00 AM, with a continuation on May 9, 1997, 3:00 PM —market research firm in Warsaw—Firm C
4. May 22, 1997, 2:00 PM—market research firm in Warsaw—Firm D
5. April 8, 1997, 9:30 AM, with a continuation on April 14, 1997, 8:30 AM—market research firm in Warsaw—Firm E
6. April 17, 1997, 1:00 PM, with a continuation on April 25, 1997, 10:00 AM—market research firm in Warsaw—Firm F
7. April 11, 1997, 12:00 N—market research firm in Warsaw—Firm G
8. April 16, 1997, 10:30 AM, with a continuation on May 21, 1997, plus participation in two training seminars on April 24, 1997, 10:00 AM, and May 8, 1997, 1:00 PM—market research firm in Warsaw—Firm H
9. April 16, 1997, 5:00 PM, with continuation on April 23, 1997, 4:00 PM—market research firm in Warsaw—Firm I
10. April 18, 1997, 1:00 PM—market research firm outside Warsaw (I do not identify the city because only four to six substantial firms existed outside of Warsaw, and by providing this piece of information, I would effectively reveal the identity of the respondent)—Firm J
11. April 22, 1997, 10:00 AM—market research firm in Warsaw—Firm K
12. April 28, 1997, 12:00 N (interviews with two different respondents)—market research firm in Warsaw—Firm L
13. May 20, 1997 12:00 N—market research firm in Warsaw (two additional interviews were conducted with former heads of this firm)—Firm M
14. May 26, 1997, 3:30 PM—market research firm in Warsaw—Firm N
15. May 27, 1997, 2:30 PM—market research firm in Warsaw—Firm O
16. June 4, 1997, 10:00 PM—market research firm in Warsaw—Firm P
17. June 4, 1997, 1:00 PM—market research firm in Warsaw—Firm R
18. June 17, 1997, 10:00 PM—market research firm in Warsaw—Firm S
19. June 23, 1997, 9:30 AM—market research firm in Warsaw—Firm T
20. June 27, 1997, 3:00 PM—market research firm in Warsaw—Firm U
21. July 9, 1997, 12:30 PM—market research firm in Warsaw—Firm V
22. July 10, 1997, 3:00 PM—market research firm in Warsaw—Firm W
23. July 14, 1997, 6:00 AM—market research firm in Warsaw—Firm X
24. July 14, 1997, 12 N—market research firm in Warsaw—Firm Y

6

Entrepreneurs and Democratization in China's Foreign Sector

Margaret M. Pearson

The economic reforms initiated in China by Deng Xiaoping beginning in the late 1970s will be remembered as having unleashed one of the most rapid transformations of a society in history. In the current era, when market ideology is king and American economic power appears unrivaled, it is often assumed that countries such as China that have tried to bring about a convergence of their economies with global markets are also on a path to political convergence with democratic values. Facile assumptions of a link between economic reform and democratization are particularly potent among U.S. policy makers. (Witness repeated assertions by President Clinton that admission of China into the World Trade Organization will promote democratization [Clinton 2000].) This assumption is also made by many citizens and scholars, and not just in the United States. The prime group to shoulder this burden of a transformation to democracy is usually considered to be not dissident intellectuals or reform elements in the government (both prime candidates for this role), but the country's newest economic group: economic entrepreneurs. Often, moreover, it is assumed that those entrepreneurs with extensive contacts with the outside world will be at the forefront of democratization.

This chapter seeks to dissect the assumption that creation of a class of Chinese entrepreneurs will lead easily and automatically to democratization in China. It lays out the logic underlying this assertion and attempts to show where that logic has theoretical and empirical support and where it does not. The empirical focus of the chapter is on entrepreneurs in the foreign sector of China's economy, that is, those who are managerial elites in joint ventures, wholly foreign-owned enterprises, and representative offices (ROs) of foreign firms.

The chapter is organized as follows. The first section lays out a simple heuristic for thinking about the logical link between entrepreneurs and democratization, one that suggests where the common thinking about this linkage is weakest. The second section profiles the new business elite in the foreign sector. The third section shows where new "market-oriented" and "liberal" behaviors and beliefs have emerged within this group and notes evidence from other sectors showing new behaviors and ideologies that have resulted from China's economic reforms. The final section of the chapter considers the degree to which we see evidence that the rise of an entrepreneurial elite, with new economic and social behaviors and beliefs, has led to—or, more realistically, laid the groundwork for—democratization during the first two decades of reforms. This section begins by looking more specifically at theories of democratization and civil society, emphasizing where they are flawed. It then goes on to argue that, concluding from the case of China's foreign sector, evidence simply does not yet support confident assertions of a direct linkage between entrepreneurialism and democratization.

The Logic Path Underlying Assumptions of an Entrepreneurialism-Democratization Link

What are the processes by which the rise of a class of entrepreneurs might promote democratization? Unfortunately, such processes are not usually specified by those who assert they exist. The underlying assumption is that since markets and democracy work well together,[1] and since they share the requirement of certain (albeit different sets of) liberties,[2] they are inextricably linked, and one must follow from the other.

But if, indeed, the rise of entrepreneurial groups and democratization are causally linked, what is the process by which the former leads to the latter? Michael Santoro (2000, 41–43) suggests a straightforward logic that can be used to clarify where problems exist in the entrepreneurialism-democratization linkage. In Santoro's framework, which he applies to the question whether foreign businesses promote human rights in China, change is conceived of as a two-step process. In the first step, the increased presence of foreign business leads to new behaviors and beliefs among entrepreneurs in the foreign sector—beliefs such as the value of meritocratic hiring. (See Figure 6.1.) The link between the presence of foreign business and new behaviors is causal and direct. In the second step, the relationship between the new behaviors and a more positive human rights situation is not causative, but there nonetheless is an "elective affinity" (in the Weberian sense) by which A (new behaviors and values) may not *inevitably* lead to B (improved human rights), and yet A may create conditions *favorable* to B. Applied to the question raised in this chapter, Santoro's framework suggests the following logic: the

Figure 6.1 **The Logic of an Entrepreneurialism-Democratization Linkage**

step 1   step 2

Rise of entrepreneurialiam———→ **new behaviors** --------→ **democratization**

   (causal)   (creates
                                         favorable
                                         environment)

Source: Adapted from Santoro (2000).

rise of an entrepreneurial class will lead to new behaviors on the part of this group, which creates an environment favorable to democratization. In other words, new entrepreneurial behaviors and beliefs are intervening variables between the rise of entrepreneurs and democratization. This formulation is attractive because it does not eliminate the possibility of a linkage in the second stage, but suggests a high degree of complexity, path dependence, and even serendipity.

Unfortunately, many observers of political change in China have confused the possibility of an "elective affinity" relationship with a causal one. (Examples of such problematic reasoning are provided later in this chapter.) While there is plenty of evidence to support the first-step linkage, there is little evidence at this point to support the second step or even to show how the behavior changes might be mediated into political change.

A Profile of China's Foreign Sector Business Elite

China's new business elite in the foreign sector of the economy is part of a broader modern, business class, a portion of which is supported by foreign capital but which also includes private entrepreneurs. The term "business elite" refers to a group defined primarily according to its position in the economy, and its members' income, education, and prestige.[3] Other segments of the business elite, not employed in the foreign sector, include entrepreneurial managers of state-owned enterprises and township and village enterprises (TVEs); managers in quasi-governmental investment organs such as the China International Trade and Investment Corporation and its provincial equivalents; former government officials (who have resigned their posts to take jobs in private business); and children of high-level government or Communist Party cadres (so-called "princelings," or *taizidang*) who work in the private sector. Many in these groups are able to use contacts gained through official channels to their advantage in making business deals.

Building on this general definition of China's new business elite, what are the specific attributes of this group in the foreign sector?[4] China's foreign business sector appeared first during the late 1970s and became established as a significant force in the economy in the mid-1980s. Whereas the Maoist government had long rejected the idea that foreign businesses should be allowed to operate on Chinese soil, the post-Mao reformers actively encouraged such activities, hoping that foreign businesses would bring in not only capital but also technology and managerial skills. Since the late 1970s, foreign-backed companies have been established across a wide range of industries in China, including computers, chemicals, pharmaceuticals, automobiles, consumer goods (textiles, shoes, toys, foodstuffs, etc.), trading companies, and, beginning in the early 1990s, financial services and real estate.

Members of China's foreign sector business elite work in the most advanced sectors of the reform economy. Departing from a rather simplistic Leninist definition, members of the foreign business elite are not primarily owners but, rather, professional and technocratic managers of modern companies. They have gained their position by managing assets that belong in large part to foreign companies. These managers have "property rights" in the sense of having latitude to acquire, use, and dispose of assets, and hence have authority on a par with or near to that of owners.[5]

While the growth of foreign investment in China was slow in the early 1980s and erratic in the mid- and late 1980s, dramatic growth began in the first half of the 1990s. Total pledged foreign investment exceeded $300 billion (in more than 217,000 enterprises) by the end of 1994 (Pearson 1991, 69–78; Lardy 1992).[6] The astronomical inflow of incoming foreign capital made China the second largest recipient of foreign direct investment in the world, after the United States, for a number of years. The pace of foreign investment slowed dramatically with the advent of the Asian financial crisis in 1997, yet the absolute volumes have remained significant—exceeding $40 billion per year in 1998 and 1999 (www.moftec.gov.cn).

Foreign sector businesses in China take several forms, the three most common of which house the elite of foreign sector managers discussed here. First, Sino-foreign joint ventures (JVs), both equity and contractual, represented approximately 85 percent of the total number of foreign direct investments (and 75 percent of the total pledged value) during the 1990s.[7] Second, wholly foreign-owned enterprises (WFOEs), which involve no Chinese investment, often are preferred by foreign investors because they can maintain a greater degree of control over their operations and technology. The third type of foreign sector businesses studied are ROs. These are not technically direct investments but, rather, serve as agents for large foreign companies, and they tend to be located in Beijing and Shanghai.

Members of China's business elite who work in the foreign sector are

People's Republic of China (PRC) nationals who work alongside expatriates. A shortage of trained Chinese managers has capped the ability of foreign companies to employ Chinese managers. Indeed, surveys (e.g., EIU 1997) consistently suggest that difficulty hiring skilled Chinese managers is one of the greatest impediments to operations of foreign-funded enterprises. Nevertheless, both Chinese and foreign participants have preferred to promote high-quality PRC nationals to middle- and senior-management levels wherever possible, for reasons of both cost and image. The recent rapid growth in numbers of foreign-backed enterprises has intensified the demand for talented indigenous managers.

Not all foreign sector managers can be considered part of the business "elite." In particular, the elite group excludes old-line managers who have been transferred to JVs from the Chinese state-owned parent company. They often have many years of on-the-job experience (and hence seniority) and tend to be in their late forties or fifties. Generally, however, they have not received either university degrees or schooling in Western managerial methods. Rather, they have obtained their position in the foreign sector enterprise because of their status in the parent company, through personal ties with others involved in the venture. They tend to be risk averse in business and to avoid responsibilities that might contravene standard practice in state-owned enterprises. These characteristics also are common to managers in state-owned enterprises (Child 1994). A second type of manager, also not part of the "elite," is found in Hong Kong– and Taiwan-funded investments. Most of these investments are small factories involved in value-added manufacturing or processing, or in producing goods using fairly low-level technologies. Their managers tend to be recruited through family or clan networks rather than through experience- or education-based procedures (Redding 1995). Anecdotal evidence suggests that their salaries are lower than salaries in Western- and Japanese-funded enterprises and that their status is not as high. Hong Kong- and Taiwan-funded enterprises have been important in China's economic development; nevertheless, they are not the major source of the foreign sector's new business elite.

The core of the foreign sector business elite is quite small—not more than an estimated 100,000 as of the end of 1999.[8] Members of the foreign sector business elite are disproportionately concentrated in Western and Japanese firms, which tend to offer managers the highest salaries and status, and to hire managers with the highest educational credentials at their middle and upper tiers.

The business elite is defined in part by its members' relatively high income; foreign sector managers are compensated at a level many times the average wage in the PRC. Managers surveyed in joint ventures and wholly foreign enterprises earned about 850 yuan ($160) per month (including pay, bonuses, and subsidies) in 1992 (Frisbie and Brecher 1992). Chinese managers in ROs earned even more, generally making between 1,000 and 3,500 yuan ($190 to $670) per month, plus benefits, in the early 1990s (McGregor 1991). These salaries had risen significantly by 1996 (Rosen 1999, 101): in Shanghai the average managerial salary had risen several-fold to about 9,600 yuan (including benefits), though it was somewhat lower in other major cities located near Shanghai, Nanjing, Hangzhou, and Wuxi (8600 yuan).[9] By the end of the decade, the salary of a top-level operations manager in an American corporation could average 20,000 yuan ($2,400) per month (Santoro 2000, 45). These salaries compare favorably with other typical salaries, including those of managers in state-owned companies. The salaries of some RO managers have been astronomical by Chinese standards; in Shanghai, Chinese JV managers were ranked fourth among categories of the "richest people," after private entrepreneurs, entertainers (actors and singers), and government bond traders ("Shanghai's Richest" 1993).[10] This higher income translates directly into a better standard of living, as measured by owning modern conveniences, purchasing luxury consumer items, dining out, and sometimes living in more spacious surroundings or even owning an apartment.

The educational level of members of the business elite is similarly high. As education and expertise once again have become valued in postrevolutionary China, these attributes have become conduits for business opportunities, especially for members of the generation in their twenties and thirties (Davis 1992, 1075–76). Although, as a whole, members of the business elite tend to be extremely well educated, there are exceptions of those who have succeeded by virtue of their business acumen. The prime exception stems from the disruption of education during the Cultural Revolution, which meant that the portion of the population who would have entered a university between 1967 and 1969 could not do so. Many in this cohort, who in the mid-1990s were in their mid-40s, did not return to school after they were sent to work in villages and factories, yet have risen to the top on the basis of their intelligence and determination.

Because investments by Western and Japanese firms are likely to incorporate advanced technology and appropriate management skills compared to Hong Kong and Taiwan businesses, these firms tend to be interested in hiring managers of high intelligence and with some advanced education—meaning college level or beyond. Such training occurs in a variety of venues. The most advanced management training is in Western-style MBA programs located in China or abroad.[11] The number of Chinese students enrolled in MBA programs located overseas is increasing. Yet the number overall remains small, and the number of those who return to work in

China even smaller. Management training for most elite foreign sector managers is provided in Chinese government-run universities or in special training centers (such as those established in Shekou and Wuxi) that are financed by foreign governments, universities, or the World Bank. Alternatively, many foreign sector entrepreneurs are graduates of China's premier universities, who then receive in-house management training from their firms either in or outside of China. In part as a result of their training, members of the business elite tend to have less cautious managerial styles compared to their old-line counterparts.

Their position, education, and income level have translated into considerable prestige for the new business elite in urban society. Employees of Western and Japanese businesses are the highest tier of foreign sector managers in terms of status as well as income and education. Yet the high regard in which many Chinese hold members of the business elite, including but not limited to those in the foreign sector, is not universal. Association with foreign companies can evoke the taint of "compradorism," especially in times of heightened nationalism. More generally, disapproval from older people and those who are politically conservative reflects in part the historically low status of merchants in Chinese culture, a view accentuated by Marxist-Leninist and Maoist disdain for market-related activities and consumerism. The fact that many of the post-Mao era's first entrepreneurs were from groups not generally respected (notably the unemployed and ex-convicts) and operated on the fringes of "socialist legality" also hurt the image of business. In the reform era, corruption scandals involving members of the business elite, particularly former government officials, have had a spillover effect on all portions of the business elite. To counter this image, the government initiated a campaign in the official press in the early 1990s emphasizing the contributions and good behavior of entrepreneurs (Sabin 1994, 961). Perhaps in part because of such campaigns, but most directly as a result of their financial success, the business elite has continued to gain considerable status and prestige in post-Mao society, especially among young people.

The foreign sector's elite managers are a self-selecting and ambitious group. They have applied for highly competitive schools, often located far from their families. They are attracted to jobs in the foreign sector because these positions allow them to use their skills and to have more responsibility at a younger age. Indeed, in a system that privileges age, seniority, and connections, talented young people often have difficulty finding jobs in state enterprises commensurate with their skills and ambition. Foreign companies offer young managers more chance for upward mobility. Many are attracted, moreover, by the opportunity to gain international experience and travel abroad. Working for a foreign company may enhance their chances for emigration, although this does not appear to be a primary motive for taking a job in the foreign sector. As we shall see, the risk-taking nature of members of this group has tended to accompany a more independent attitude about the state and a willingness to sever (or loosen) the bonds that tie them to it.

A New Relationship with the State

Structural Autonomy from the State

In considering a possible linkage between the rise of an entrepreneurial elite and democratization in China, it is necessary to examine the relationship of entrepreneurs to the state. As we shall see later, the view in the civil society literature, as well as in the popular perception and political discourse, that entrepreneurs will act as an agent for democratization against an authoritarian state assumes that entrepreneurs are not captured by the state. In other words, creation of a sphere outside of and separate from the state is crucial for acting against the state. Consideration of entrepreneurial autonomy is especially crucial in post-1949 China, where penetration of the economy by the state consistently has been deep and at times nearly total.

Members of China's new business elite have not only taken on new economic roles, they have carved out a new relationship with the socialist state. Their situation contrasts significantly to that in which managers in state-owned enterprises operated during most of post-1949 history. Under the "iron rice bowl" system of lifetime employment in one work unit, members of the business elite could not be entrepreneurs; they were tied to and dependent—politically, economically, and personally—on the party-state. Their work was overseen by party cadres within the enterprise. Their economic well-being, especially housing, medical care, pensions, and bonuses, was dependent upon a system in which the party cadres who distributed these benefits tended to reward political loyalty and personal connections as much as or more than managerial capacity. Dossiers (*dangan*) of the state enterprise managers' activities, including any political activity by the managers or their families, were kept in the enterprise. In the absence of labor, housing, and other markets, the contents of these dossiers could influence job promotions or job transfers. These political, socioeconomic, and personal dependencies of state-sector managers bound them tightly to the enterprise and, through it, to the state (Walder 1986).

This system has been changing throughout China in the reform era, including in the state-owned sector (Walder 1995). In the state sector, change is particularly evident in enterprises with significant contact with foreign firms (Guthrie 1999). Still, changes there have lagged behind those in foreign-funded enterprises, where dependence on the Communist party-state has largely been severed (Pearson 1997). The comparatively deep market orientation of this sector, and the presence of foreign firms as an alternative source of authority for managers in foreign firms, have translated into a significant degree of autonomy, especially in southern China and Shanghai. Hence, in foreign-funded enterprises, party presence is minimal and ineffectual. Labor mobility is great; people switch jobs frequently in search of higher pay and more responsibility. Personnel dossiers still must be maintained, but are kept outside of the enterprise in fee-for-service centers, where they are essentially ignored by foreign employers. Welfare benefits are provided, if at all, by enterprises outside of the state system. For example, managers in foreign-funded enterprises must frequently use their higher salaries to purchase or rent housing. This, of course, removes some of the security that most Chinese have seen as a birthright, but to members of the business elite the rewards are usually worth the risk.

Business Practices

There is some solid, if incomplete, evidence that elite managers in both the foreign and state sectors have adopted (and believe in) business practices that are part and parcel of the practices of their foreign firms. Their behavior and business values are being influenced strongly by their work environment. Santoro's study with regard to the business values and business behaviors of foreign sector managers is especially instructive (2000, ch. 4).[12] Santoro finds significant changes in three dimensions. First, consistent with the information presented previously on the attributes of this group, Santoro found that managers in China's foreign sector placed a great value on the practice of hiring by merit. They were grateful to be able to use their skills and be promoted on the basis of skills rather than political acumen or personal connection, a practice they claimed remains rampant in the state sector. Significantly, Santoro argues that managers who learned these skills in foreign businesses applied them to state sector jobs to which they moved. Second, Santoro posits that subordinates in foreign-backed enterprises learn that they can exercise initiative and take responsibility. They come to value a much flatter organizational style, a value that complements some visions of democratization. Finally, he finds that the common business practices of "team-building" and of cross-functional information sharing fostered in competitive foreign-funded companies have affected the business practices of the managerial elite. These practices require Chinese managers to break down the walls and hierarchies that exist across units within the company, to value a free exchange of information, and to cooperate in new ways.   ·

Three additional scholars make supportive arguments about changes in business practices as a result of the foreign business presence in China. Scott Kennedy argues, based on his study of business associations, that lobbying by foreign business associations has created a demonstration effect for PRC companies (personal communication, April 5, 2000). Daniel Rosen argues that foreign-funded enterprises "influence Chinese society by bringing a dif- ferent workplace culture—one characterized by initiative taking, career development, and quality control" (1999, 242). Though less sanguine than Rosen, Kennedy, or Santoro about the immediate beneficial impact of foreign business on behavior, Doug Guthrie (1999) also suggests in his research on state-owned enterprises that the rationalization of business practices fueled by foreign business contacts affects the managerial mindset of people exposed to these practices. He finds, for example, that companies with close contacts with a foreign firm or in a JV are more likely to apply the Company Law (which helps foster a rule of law), though not necessarily for "rational" or profit-maximizing reasons.[13]

Ideology

In addition to engaging in new business practices, members of China's new business elite hold *views* of both business and politics that are decidedly more liberal than the dominant views expressed in official policy.[14] Business entrepreneurs consider near total use of markets to drive the economy, and extensive privatization, to be necessary for China's development. They see competition among enterprises, people, and national economies to be beneficial. They prefer to have the economy run according to rational relationships and institutions rather than personal connections. They believe steps in this direction should be swift, but at the same time must be carefully crafted so as not to produce social unrest. (For many, the example of the rapid privatization that occurred in the former Soviet Union is extremely negative.) These managers are highly internationalist, moreover; they see virtually nothing in the workings of the international economy that they judge to be inappropriate to China. Perhaps the most passionate case for reforms is made concerning narrower changes, that is, practices and policies that cause difficulties for these businesses. For example, the inability of these managers to freely and quickly obtain visas to travel abroad is perhaps the complaint voiced most often. Restrictions on hiring qualified employees also generate considerable criticism.

In their views of politics in China, the most notable sentiments are, at best, indifference and, at worst, hostility and disgust. Going well beyond the very standard (and official) opinion in China that the state should be absent from operational decisions about business, members of this group betray a strong distaste for communism. Indeed, an important reason for choosing jobs in these two leading sectors is to escape from the politics—campaigns and so forth—that have been thrust upon them. Antipathy to party politics is often present despite a strong nationalism and feeling of obligation to aid the country's development. Managers frequently take pride in their ability to express a dislike of the party or in telling stories about how they ignore party directives to have political considerations influence their operations.

As for what sorts of political systems these managers prefer, opinions vary. Location and time spent abroad appear to be the major factors in the variance. Foreign sector managers from the south (particularly the Special Economic Zones) are most likely to say they favor "democratization." Their views of what constitutes "democracy" often are quite vague, however. Competition among candidates for local office and rule of law are sometimes mentioned. These are important factors in democratization, of course, but are already sanctioned by the Chinese state and so less risky to advocate. Outside the south, managers are more reluctant to discuss political change or have less strong opinions about it. Nevertheless, they report that they tend to favor political liberalization that would promote their freedom to run their life and work as they see fit. It is important to note that the freedoms they claim to value most are small ones—again, the ability to travel freely is often mentioned—rather than democracy writ large. On the other hand, members of this group, despite a strong concern for social stability, do not advocate "neoauthoritarianism," a school of thought popular in some intellectual and government circles during the 1980s and 1990s (Sautman 1992).[15]

These findings on the economic and political views of members of the foreign-sector business elite are consistent with expectations raised by the theory of "postimperialism." This theory contends that the foreign sector managers—members of an international, modern, technocratic, and educated managerial bourgeoisie—have been strongly influenced by the norms of international capitalism and are not opposed to the ideas of democratization (Sklar 1976; Becker 1983; Payne 1994). Moreover, quite a lot of "learning" of ideas exogenous to China has occurred among the foreign sector business elite (Levy 1994; Johnston 1996). Members of the foreign sector elite have been strongly influenced by their work experiences in foreign-backed companies, by contacts with foreigners, and often by their experiences abroad. (This finding is consistent with those of Guthrie [1999] and Santoro [2000].) Many of the ideas expressed by members of the business elite are already floating around in China. But because of the self-selecting nature of the group, and due to the relative autonomy of the foreign sector from the state, these ideas at least *appear* to be held more deeply by this group.

China's new business elite has thus created a new relationship with the state that diverges substantially from what existed under Maoism and even from what exists for most of the urban population even today. Members of the business elite in the foreign and private sectors have structured lives for themselves largely outside the purview of the state. This independence, plus the higher level of income, provides them with greater resources that potentially could be used to mobilize against the state if they should so choose. They have strong, cosmopolitan opinions about the need for China to move away from the status quo—farther away than is officially accepted even by reformers in the government.

This profile is perhaps unsurprising, given the nature of people attracted to this sector in the first place. But can these features be expected to lead to political activism on behalf of democratization (or against the state) in the way that is often assumed? A negative answer to this question, focusing on the limits of business elites' strength vis-à-vis the state, and on the absence of a desire to mobilize, is offered in the next section.

But Toward Democratization?

From the previous discussion, it is clear that the presence of foreign corporations and, indeed, of economic reforms, has generated changes in how elite managers in the foreign sector behave and think. There is considerable preliminary evidence to support the left half of Santoro's framework (see Figure 6.1, step 1, p. 132), which posits a causal link between the growth of an entrepreneurial elite and concrete behavioral and ideological change. Yet the right half of the logic chain (step 2), which purports to show a linkage between those intermediate changes created by the growth of a foreign sector and democratization, is considerably less robust.

Before proceeding with the discussion, a caveat is necessary. The conclusion to be drawn is not that democratization in China is impossible. Indeed, there is substantial comparative evidence that the rise of a new entrepreneurial class as a result of economic reform has contributed to democratization in other places, including Taiwan and South Korea (Moore 1996, 53). Moreover, there is a long-term statistical correlation between wealth creation (often as a result of deliberate economic reform) and democratization (Moore 1996). The main contention to be made here, however, is that the assumption that the growth of a foreign-backed business elite will lead willy-nilly and inevitably to democratization is simplistic and often wrong. Rather, a multitude of variables may be involved in such a transition, including not only the growth of new wealthier classes but also the particular mode and distribution of power among new classes, their interests, and—and this last element is too often overlooked—the relative weight and interests of the state.

To show the weakness of the linkage between democratization and the behavioral and ideological changes arising from the growth of a foreign sector, it is necessary first to discuss the theories that make assumptions about how such change occurs, particularly the literatures on civil society and "transitions" to democracy.

The Problem with Theory: Suppositions About Democratic Change

Literature on civil society (not just as applied to China) has a deep and specific history (Keane 1988; Pelczynski 1988).[16] The term is commonly understood to describe a society "comprising a complex of autonomous institutions—economic, religious, intellectual and political—distinguishable from the family, the clan, the locality and the state." It is, moreover, a society that possesses "a distinctive set of institutions that safeguard the separation of the state and civil society and maintain effective ties between them." In the economic arena, civil society guarantees "the rights of individuals and particularly the right of property" and forms "a constellation of many autonomous economic units or business firms, acting independently of the state and competing with each other" (Shils 1991, 7).[17] For most scholars in this genre, an important source of civil society is *non*economic actors, particularly intellectuals, who are especially active in erecting institutionalized limits on the state. Such constraints include the pillars of liberal democracy: competing political parties, an independent judiciary, and a free press. At base, the term "civil society," broadly conceived, refers to bourgeois society of the sort that emerged onto the scene in seventeenth- and eighteenth-century Western Europe, in which social forces, economic and noneconomic, act separately from and often against the state.

With regard to the transition of communist regimes in the late twentieth century, the civil society model has taken on a somewhat revised format. It borrows heavily from the precepts of modernization (Lipset 1959; Moore 1996) and emphasizes the role of *economic* classes and elites. (The emphasis on classes is reminiscent of Barrington Moore's [1966] influential formulation, "No bourgeoisie, no democracy.") The post-communist civil society formulation tends to argue that economic reform invariably gives rise to pressures for, and eventually the realization of, political liberalization. Often, those at the leading edge of economic reform will also lead political reform. Such a model starts with the observation that economic development and a middle class are highly correlated with democracy (Lipset 1959). It assumes that a middle class (including business interests) will arise that has an interest in pressing for greater freedom from state control and, ultimately, democratization—or, at the very least, that freedoms won to protect markets will provide defenses against the state's curtailment of political freedoms (Burks 1983; Glassman 1991).[18]

This modernization-influenced, economistically oriented civil society literature views the linkage between economic reform and democratization as proceeding through two interrelated sets of steps. (These steps hark back to the logic chain proposed by Santoro.) The first set of steps involves the devolution of economic power away from the state and the creation among economic actors of greater space in which to press for political change. Successful economic reform, it is suggested, requires that both resources and decision-making be put in the hands of nongovernmental actors, especially owners and managers outside the state sector, thereby weakening the power of the central bureaucracy. Economic reforms further foster autonomy from the state in that markets create an alternative source for goods (such as housing) that previously have been guaranteed by the state. These processes provide economic actors with greater autonomy to express their diverse interests in the marketplace. Once freed from dependence upon the state, economic actors have greater opportunity to develop horizontal relationships with their counterparts in society and to strengthen intrasocietal bonds (McCormick and Kelly 1994).

If these structural changes are to translate into actual political change initiated from below, a second set of steps involving consciousness and political behavior must occur. Strengthened horizontal relationships will lead to a greater consciousness on the part of societal actors that they can determine their own economic fate. This realization, it is posited, will in turn stimulate involvement in political activity at the same time that the reform's emphasis on economic values undermines the legitimacy of the unifying ideology. Not only will new economic groups act readily, they will act toward certain ends. New economic groups, civil society theories predict, will be motivated to act by mistrust that the existing state will protect these groups' emerging interests in free markets. Ultimately, these new groups will press for extensive liberalization and democratization of the polity, since political freedoms will be seen as necessary to protect economic freedoms.

The position that civil society arises as a direct result of economic marketization and the rise of an entrepreneurial class is fraught with problems. The major difficulty is that the concepts of democratization and civil society in the context of socialist systems, and the processes by which they emerge, are too vague. While the civil society model describes the general trend toward societal autonomy from the state, upon closer reflection the details of how this occurs are not specified clearly enough to offer much guidance as to the details of the evolution of state-society relations or of the process of democratization. To the extent that democratization models suppose that the rise of a middle class is a precondition for liberalization, they fail to see that the emergence of a middle class may not be a sufficient condition for the emergence of democracy. In other words, the linkage between the intermediate changes that have in fact occurred as a result of the rise of entrepreneurialism, on the one hand, and moves toward democratization, on the other hand (the second set of steps posited here, and the right half of Santoro's logic stream), is very poorly defined.

To see that such vague notions are too easily tolerated by even serious researchers, we need only look at the suppositions of some of those scholars who have made perfectly reasonable and well-supported claims about the behavioral and ideological changes made by new entrepreneurs (the first half of Santoro's logic chain). Writing of the new "meritocratic" cadre working in foreign businesses, for example, Santoro (2000, 48) writes that this "well-heeled and highly educated social class in China with the power and interests separate and distinct from those of the state . . . could someday pose a threat to the authoritarian rule of the Communist Party."[19] This is the end of the reasoning; an explanation for this translation from interests and ideology into political action is absent.

Researchers who assume processes leading to civil society to be operative too often do not consider the complexity of forces at work in reforming societies. Or, writers in this genre (e.g., Robinson 1996) may say that marketization creates "conditions" for the rise of democratization, but subsequently cite all sorts of other factors—particularly the role of other groups, the state, and international factors—as necessary for an actual transition to occur. Hence, although economic reform may indeed set forth certain underlying conditions conducive to democratization, the processes leading to political liberalization are multifaceted. To quote Mick Moore on the role of material prosperity in supporting democratization, "A wealth of recent literature emphasizes the role of short-term and intangible factors in such processes, above all the tactical and strategic calculations of various political actors and groups, and the important roles played by political elites and international influences" (1996, 39). (See also Diamond et al. 1989.) Even where economic reform succeeds in generating pressures on the state from below, the will to act and the goals of societal actors are heavily influenced by *noneconomic* factors.

Sometimes, of course, these other factors may support democratization, as in the case of student protests in China in the 1970s and 1980s, when economic reform bolstered protesters' confidence in the gains to be had from political action. But factors unrelated to economic reform, particularly the greater tolerance by the state for a plurality of views, were more important for opening up political space and motivating students to protest than was economic reform. At other times, noneconomic variables may hinder any prodemocracy tendencies arising from economic reforms. In particular, the *interests* of new economic actors cannot be assumed to support democratization. Such a dynamic is present in Korea, for example, where business interests have long colluded with the authoritarian regime to protect themselves against unruly protests (Cheng and Haggard 1992). In Taiwan, the business elite has promoted its own interests and gained more influence as a result of democratization, but it has not been at the forefront of democratization the way middle-class intellectuals have (Chu 1994).

The more specified theory of democratic "transitions" brings into focus the importance of assuming that any link between economic reform, entrepreneurialism, and political change is complex (e.g., Przeworski 1991; O'Donnell and Schmitter 1986; Haggard and Kaufman 1992). The transitions literature addresses broader dynamics of political change than those considered here and does not focus empirically on the business elite. It nevertheless is useful for considering the linkage between entrepreneurialism and democratization because it supports the suggestion that the outcomes of moves toward democracy in any particular case are far from determinate but, rather, are path dependent and will be much influenced by noneconomic variables.[20]

Although not a unified literature, the core "transitions" works find two major factors to be most important for successful democratization. Success requires, first, substantial organization on the part of societal actors. Such organization is not automatic and depends much upon the context. Positive examples of such organization do exist. For example, the well-organized Solidarity movement in Poland benefited from its links with the leadership of the Catholic Church in its ability to press for democratization (Friedheim 1993). A fragmented business elite in Brazil was able to organize enough to support democratization in that country in 1988 (after having supported military governments in the 1960s and 1970s) (Friedheim 1993; Payne 1994). In contrast, East Germany provides a negative example, where newly emergent business or middle-class interests that might be deemed favorable for democratization have been rendered ineffectual by poor organization.

Transitions theory emphasizes, second, the actions of the state. This variable, which sits in direct contrast to the idea of autonomy posited by civil society theories, can influence the potential for democratization (including that arising from pressures from new economic actors) in a variety of directions (Robinson 1996; Moore 1996). Successful transitions to democracy, in the view of this literature, tend to result from negotiated pacts between reformers in an authoritarian government and the societal forces of opposition. In particular, leaders of both the state and opposing forces must be able to make correct strategy choices and to negotiate pacts (Friedheim 1993).

Transitions theory therefore suggests the importance of focusing on these two conditions, societal organization and state strategy. As to the latter, we can say fairly certainly that, although a reformist leadership faction certainly exists in China, it is unprepared to engage in serious negotiation with business entrepreneurs. This circumstance further suggests the necessity to consider other possible strategies on the part of the state, including co-optation (Przeworski 1991, 58). In particular, it leads our inquiry to the role of the state in designing institutions to preempt the growth of organized pressure from new economic actors, even while the state is encouraging these actors in other areas.[21]

If it is so flawed, why do scholars even need to take seriously civil society theory as applied to China? Why would they not simply engage the superior "transitions" literature instead? The main reason is that "civil society," particularly as a new cloak for "modernization" theory, has captured the popular imagination, and the hearts of policy makers, at least in the United States. The idea that the creation of a middle class will push China toward democratization is the centerpiece of the political push for economic "engagement" and expanded trade with China. Such ideas, moreover, pervade journalistic treatments of China, as well as popular discourse (e.g., Maibach 1995).

In sum, there are two central conclusions to be drawn from the above ruminations. First, civil society–based theories of democratization that are dominant in the study of China fail to provide a detailed picture of how the rise of an entrepreneurial group will lead to democratization. Yet the grand assumptions that lurk behind them have a tenacious hold on the popular mindset and influence policy makers and, most recently in the 1990s, international aid donors (Robinson 1996, 69). The power of this mindset means it cannot be ignored, no matter how naive its application may be. Second, transitions theories illuminate the fact that the process of democratization is highly complex and, specifically, that a linkage between entrepreneurialism and democratization cannot ignore the role of societal organization and state power.

The Problem of Evidence: Absence of Empirical Support for Civil Society–Based Theories of Democratization

It is useful to look once again at the empirical record on whether China's foreign sector business elite has translated its privileged position in society, its relatively greater autonomy from the state, and its liberal ideology into political action. The simple answer is that it has not, at least as yet.

Most entrepreneurs in the foreign sector wish to be free of politics, wish for the freedom to be apolitical. This translates not into activism but, rather, into passivity. They do not seek out horizontal ties of the sort identified as necessary for societal organization in transitions theory, nor have these ties simply popped up spontaneously. These are the same horizontal ties that advocates of civil society have in mind when they posit collective action by entrepreneurs against the state. Nor have foreign sector entrepreneurs shown much inclination to seek out opportunities to engage in organized lobbying with the state to bring about changes in business policy.

Furthermore, they do not feel that they can express their views to state officials about the need for change or that, if they were to do so, they would be influential. Specifically, when foreign sector managers were asked in the mid-1990s whether they could and did express to the government their suggestions for changing business policies of concern to them, they almost uniformly gave negative answers. One typical respondent said, "There is no way to express the need for change to the government. I don't know what channel a person could use" (quoted in Pearson 1997, 102). Others opined that even if they had a channel to complain, their efforts would be ineffectual because officials either do not wish to help or mistrust entrepreneurs in the foreign sector.

Even these kinds of pressure on the state—suggestions for policy change made through institutional channels—are a far cry from active opposition to the state or even attempts to democratize it. On these latter dimensions, there is virtually no activity whatsoever. An intriguing exception is the interest, expressed by a tiny fraction of these foreign sector entrepreneurs, in joining the party to try to change the party (rather than to further their business goals). But, as mentioned, this is exceptional.

State-Entwined Alternatives for Influence by Entrepreneurs

It is not as though entrepreneurs in the foreign sector fail to communicate with state officials. Indeed, their businesses depend heavily upon such communication, in order to obtain permissions, licenses, and the like—means that are especially crucial to import/export and foreign investments. Despite the growth of markets, the state remains involved in administering many aspects of the economy, and entrepreneurs need good relations with state officials. They therefore foster informal personal relationships (*guanxi*) with central and, more often, local officials. Entrepreneurs may try to work through official bureaus, such as the local customs agency. Yet the basis of their ability to proceed through these channels is their cultivation of connections with selected officials with whom they build relationships over time, rather than a regularized and impersonal venture into the bureaucracy. Such behavior is also found in studies of China's new private entrepreneurs (e.g., Wank 1999; Dickson 2000–01).[22]

Thus, for example, a foreign sector entrepreneur will invite officials for a visit to the factory, provide a nice banquet, and/or send them gifts at Chinese New Year. (The entrepreneur often must *seek* to develop the personal relationship with officials, since it is unusual for an official with direct authority over an issue relevant to the entrepreneur to be tied through school, familial, or other connections.) Having built the basis for a relationship, an entrepreneur may then try to leverage the relationship into narrow types of influence, such as evading a rule or fee, gaining a favorable interpretation of a rule, or shortcutting an onerous process for permits or licenses. Bribery and other corrupt practices certainly are used for influence too.

The goal in using personal, clientelist connections, then, is to more easily navigate an existing bureaucratic setup, or to avoid it, rather than to change the structure itself. It is an attempt by entrepreneurs to create some stability for themselves in an uncertain administrative world.[23] Use of *guanxi* is, ultimately, an individualist strategy rather than a collectivist one, and it works precisely because of (and is wholly dependent on) tight vertical links between state officials and entrepreneurs, not because of a separation between them. Ironically, then, entrepreneurial managers in the foreign sector strive to rebuild connections with the state.

One organized channel does exist through which entrepreneurs can interact with and presumably lobby the state, and that is through business associations. In the foreign sector, the business association is the China Association for Enterprises with Foreign Investment (CAEFI). This association was formally set up as a "nongovernmental" (*minjian*) organization, a way for entrepreneurs to channel information and suggestions up to the government and for the government to send information back to enterprises under the association's jurisdiction. As even this brief description implies, however, there is much about the association that keeps it from being truly independent and effective—and from signaling an emergent civil society. It is largely the result of the state's efforts to co-opt foreign sector businesses, and part of a larger scheme by the government to avoid the growth of independent trade associations. Despite the formal moniker of "*minjian*," the associations are usually described as serving as a functional "bridge" between business and government, and as an aid of the party and government in the economic reform effort.

Thus, leaders of this and other like associations in different sectors are retired officials, the association must be registered with the state and affiliated with state organizations, and there can be only one association per sector. At the same time, the association does sanction the idea that they have legitimate interests that they wish to pursue—hence the effort to make associations appear independent. This is a classic state corporatist strategy (Schmitter 1974). Yet the association falls short in a crucial dimension, and that is in making members of the sector it represents feel as though the association is an effective advocate. Those foreign sector managers who have heard of CAEFI feel that it is useless and ineffectual for accomplishing their goals, unless of course an association official has strong personal connections with key state officials!

Conclusions

The major conclusion of this chapter is that an economic group that is often assumed—in civil society literature and in public and policy discourses—to be a harbinger of democratization has as yet shown few signs that it can play such a role, despite an extensive degree of autonomy from the state. Nevertheless, this study is far from the final word on the complex problem of an entrepreneurialism-democratization link. Three limitations are particularly notable. First, other economic and noneconomic groups need to be considered. Other economic groups may have at their disposal processes for converting their economic or social position into political change and may conceivably be more interested in taking political risks that might hurt their businesses—though such a willingness to risk instability is difficult to envision for any fledging entrepreneurial group, not just those in the foreign sector. A broad middle class that arises as a result of the "wealth factor" would be an obvious such group, as would be urban and rural workers, and, especially, members of the domestic private sector. The potential for entrepreneurs or the middle class to ally with noneconomic groups, such as intellectuals, dissidents, students, and rural villagers, also should be addressed. Moves by the state itself (or, more realistically, reform-oriented portions of it) toward some elements of democratization also warrant consideration. (A propos of state-initiated democratization, it is common among state bureaucrats to say that China can achieve democracy in the future—perhaps in twenty years—though the country is not now ready for it. If these statements can be believed, such state-initiated processes are obviously an important *noneconomic* source of democratization.)

A second, obvious, reason for caution is the time period under consideration—just slightly over two decades since economic reform was initiated and even less since the foreign sector (and private sector) have taken off. Institutional and other changes necessary for democratization, if they occur at all, can be expected to take much longer (Wright 2000).[24]

Third, following Santoro's heuristic framework presented in Figure 6.1, it *may* very well be that new behaviors and beliefs that arise from entrepreneurialism can create a favorable environment for democratization (the second step in the framework). (See also Robinson 1996.) The way they might actually lead to change is exceedingly complex and unclear, but it is not, in my view, impossible. Thus, this study stops short of saying that democratization will not happen in China. But I do suggest that the direct link between the rise of entrepreneurs and democratization that is often assumed is facile and probably flawed. There is insufficient support for the assumption of a clear causal link between economic reform of a socialist economy and democratization from below. My complaints are both theoretical and empirical. Theoretically, civil society viewpoints—which are centered on what happens in the right-hand stage of Figure 6.1—are too vague about the concrete mechanisms by which a linkage may work. They are not well defined enough to be predictive. More thorough transitions theories point to other variables that would seem to trump the likelihood of an "entrepreneurial uprising." Indeed, the factors that are likely to break, or to weaken, this linkage, particularly the efforts of a still powerful state, must be taken seriously.

Empirically, it is true that market reforms have produced a business elite with substantial autonomy, and with opportunities for and even possibly interest in political change. In this sense, the left stage of Santoro's logic stream has solid evidence backing it. The importance of these sorts of changes should not be underestimated, given the implications they have for the workings of the market economy and for people's everyday livelihood. It is true, further, that the economic and political reforms have greatly narrowed the scope of political authority and therefore allowed greater autonomy for the individual. Yet these changes have not yet dictated the emergence of a politicized civil society within the business class in China's foreign sector. It is this crucial link, between behavioral and ideological changes at the individual level and democratization at the societal level, that remains uncertain.

Notes

1. On the fact that all democracies are market systems, but also the argument that the two systems do not *of necessity* go together, see Lindblom (1977).

2. There are exceptional "illiberal democracies," that is, countries where democratic rights exist without political liberties; for example, Peru under Fujimori. See Zakaria (1997).

3. This definition based on socioeconomic variables is consistent with the term "elite" used in Ding Xueliang's study of China's "political elite" and "counterelite" (1995, 10–13). It is also consistent with views of members of the Chinese business elite, as expressed in a survey of 1,100 employees of Shanghai joint ventures, banks, trading companies, hospitals, news media, and universities. The respondents "regard significant incomes, solid academic backgrounds and high positions as musts for white-collar status. Some consider 'good taste' an essential qualification as well" (United Press International, 1993).

4. Much of this section is derived from Pearson (1997, 5–8). Many of the empirical conclusions in this chapter are based on a sample of interviews with fifty-one members of the foreign sector business elite conducted in the mid-1990s.

5. Management as a basis for significant authority has long been recognized in mainstream literature on business organization. See Berle and Means (1932). More recent class-based theories have adopted a "control of resources" definition, most notably the theory of postimperialism (Sklar 1976; Becker 1983). On property and management rights in China, see Granick (1990). Some of the earliest arguments that the bourgeoisie was constituted by managers as well as property owners were from Djilas' famous critique of the "new class" (1959).

6. This figure is inflated in that it includes funds from the People's Republic of China channeled through Hong Kong and back into China in order to gain the privileges accorded foreign investors. The true figure is probably about 60% of this.

7. Equity JVs are separate limited liability companies owned by a new legal entity. Contractual JVs are similar to partnerships in which no separate legal entity is formed. In both forms, the foreign partner usually contributes capital, technology, and perhaps some equipment, and the Chinese partner generally contributes land, facilities, and some equipment. Equity JVs constitute approximately 70% of the number of all JVs.

8. I estimate this figure as follows: there were an estimated three PRC managers at senior- and middle-management levels in each of the approximately 136,000 equity and contractual JVs and WFOEs with actual investment by the end of 1999, and in the estimated 20,000 ROs. This totals 468,000 PRC managers in all three segments. (Of the 340,000 foreign direct investment projects (FDI) contracted for, approximately 40% are operational.) (These figures are derived from Pearson [1999] and www.moftec.gov.cn.) Members of the foreign sector business elite tend to be found in Western and Japanese enterprises, which historically have comprised about 20% of the overall number of foreign sector firms, implying that there are about 94,000 such managers. Although the fact that a portion of managers in Western and Japanese firms are old-line would reduce this figure, this gap is compensated for by the fact that there may be more than three foreign sector managers in the largest Western and Japanese investments.

9. In JVs, some of the salary goes to the Chinese JV partner or to the government, or is fed into special welfare funds in the JV. Still, the take-home pay remains higher than in a comparable Chinese enterprise. Interview data from 1995 suggests that RO managers were paid approximately 4,000 yuan per month ($475).

10. The categories following JV managers were: managers of township and village TVEs, managers of new companies, managers of profitable state-owned enterprises, tour guides for foreigners, and taxi drivers.

11. Reflecting the educational bias of the system, even those trained in "modern management" tend to be more oriented toward "hard" knowledge (e.g., quantitative techniques based on engineering approaches) rather than "soft" concepts (e.g., marketing and organizational behavior). Recently, "soft" subjects have gained greater acceptance.

12. As will become clear below, however, I disagree with Santoro's conclusions about the political behavior of foreign sector managers.

13. A key point of Guthrie's is that contact with foreign firms does not always trigger the "rationalization" that economic rationalists would expect; rather, many managers—such as when adopting the Company Law—"have little sense as to what the changes will mean substantively. Others recognize the process. . . as purely symbolic" (p. 149).

14. These comments on ideology are based on the interviews described in note 4, above. Because of the inherent difficulty of discerning "ideology," the sensitivity of the issue, and the fact that the information is from a moderate number of interviewees rather than large-scale survey data, these findings on ideology are meant to be suggestive and to encourage further research.

15. Neoauthoritarianism took different forms at different times during this period, but generally it advocated the rule of a strong leader to bring reform to China. For some advocates, this means eventual democratization, but it also often means simply the use of a strong, beneficent leader to carry out radical economic reform.

16. Hegel, Kant, Voltaire, Paine, Tocqueville, Marx, and Habermas are most associated with theories of civil society as applied to Western society. A major contribution of Hegel was to include the market economy as a crucial component and guarantor of the autonomy from the state. Marx subsequently narrowed the definition of "civil society" to include almost exclusively the capitalist market economy.

17. The concept of civil society is distinct from that of pluralism, though, for it avoids the latter's nearly singular emphasis on the group as the sole valid unit of analysis and encompasses a notion (albeit vague) of transition.

18. Although ultimately skeptical of these arguments, Brus (1983, 122–129) states a version of them elegantly. The absence of a middle class is considered a key structural reason for the failure of democratizing reforms in the former Soviet Union (Bova 1991, 113–138).

19. Other instances of this sort of unexplored conclusion are sprinkled throughout Santoro's book.

20. It should be noted that much of the "transitions" literature is not directly relevant to the issue of the link between economic and political change that is the major consideration here, for the literature focuses on either economic reform or political reform, not the causal linkage between them. On political transitions see, for example, Huntington (1992). On economic reform, see the debates over "shock therapy" versus gradualism summarized in Adams and Brock (1993). Those writings that do discuss the link between economic and political reform tend to assume that the state explicitly intends democratizing reform at the same time as it carries out economic reform, which has not been the case in China (Moore 1996). Another major impetus for democratic transition is regime collapse, but this leads to a more insecure and often short-lived democracy. As with the civil society model, early entries into this literature drew vague depictions of the emergence of civil society (Levine 1988).

21. The explicit strategy of the Guomindang in Taiwan in the 1970s was to form state-controlled peak business associations, for example (Cheng, Haggard, and Kang 1995).

22. These findings contrast with those of Guthrie for state sector managers during approximately the same time period; Guthrie's conclusion is that the growing importance of market relations are "rendering *guanxi* unimportant" (1999, 194). The difference in these two findings may be attributable to the difference in sectors examined (state vs. private and foreign sector) or in the fact that Guthrie inquired as to a trend (declining influence over time), rather than absolute level of importance in the context of a range of strategies.

23. This is consistent with Guthrie's conclusion that efforts to cope with uncertainty are central to the strategies of entrepreneurial state sector managers (1999, 203).

24. Wright's is a thoughtful essay about the length of time it takes for market forces to translate to political freedoms, and the ability of the state to thwart such change, sometimes over centuries.

Bibliography

Adams, Walter, and James Brock, *Adam Smith Goes to Moscow: A Dialogue on Radical Reform* (Princeton: Princeton University Press, 1993).

Becker, David G., *The New Bourgeoisie and the Limits of Dependency: Mining, Class, and Power in "Revolutionary" Peru* (Princeton: Princeton University Press, 1983).

Berle, Adolf Augustus, and Gardiner C. Means, *The Modern Corporation and Private Property* (New York: Macmillan, 1932).

Bova, Russell, "Political Dynamics of the Post-Communist Transition," *World Politics*, 44 (October, 1991), pp. 113–138.

Brus, Wlodzimierz, "Political Pluralism and Markets in Communist Systems," in *Pluralism in the Soviet Union: Essays in Honor of H. Gordon Skilling*, edited by Susan Gross Solomon (New York: St. Martin's Press, 1983), pp. 122–129.

Burks, R. V., "The Political Implications of Economic Reform," in *Plan and Market: Economic Reform in Eastern Europe*, edited by Morris Bornstein (New Haven: Yale University Press, 1983), pp. 373–402.

Cheng, Tun-jen, and Stephan Haggard (eds.), *Political Change in Taiwan* (Boulder, CO: Lynne Rienner Publishers, 1992).

Cheng, Tun-jen, Stephan Haggard, and David Kang, "Institutions, Economic Policy and Growth in Korea and Taiwan," paper prepared for the United Nations Commission on Trade and Development Project on Economic Development in East Asia (unpublished manuscript, 1995).

Child, John, *Management in China During the Age of Reform* (Cambridge: Cambridge University Press, 1994).

Chu Yun-han, "The Realignment of Business-Government Relations and Regime Transition in Taiwan," in *Business and Government in Industrializing Asia*, edited by Andrew MacIntyre (Ithaca: Cornell University Press, 1994).

Clinton, William Jefferson, "China's Opportunities, and Ours," *New York Times*, September 24, 2000.

Davis, Deborah, "Job Mobility in Post-Mao Cities: Increases on the Margins," *China Quarterly*, No. 132 (December 1992), pp. 1075–1076.

Diamond, Larry, Juan J. Linz, and Seymour M. Lipset (eds.), *Democracy in Developing Countries: Vol. 3: Asia* (London: Adamantine Press Limited, 1989).

Ding, Xueliang, *The Decline of Communism in China: Legitimacy Crisis, 1977–1989* (Cambridge: Cambridge University Press, 1995).

Dickson, Bruce, "Cooptation and Corporatism in China: The Logic of Party Adaptation," *Political Science Quarterly*, 15 (2000–01), pp. 517–540.

Djilas, Milovan, *The New Class: An Analysis of the Communist System* (New York: Praeger Press, 1959).

Economist Intelligence Unit, *Multinational Companies in China: Winners and Losers* (Wanchai, Hong Kong: EIU, 1997).

Friedheim, Daniel V., "Bringing Society Back into Democratic Transition Theory after 1989: Pact Making and Regime Collapse," *East European Politics and Societies* 7, No. 3, (1993), p. 505.

Frisbie, John, and Richard Brecher, "FIE Labor Practices," *China Business Review* 19, No. 5 (1992), p. 25.

Glassman, Ronald M., *China in Transition: Communism, Capitalism, and Democracy* (New York: Praeger, 1991).

Granick, David, *Chinese State Enterprises: A Regional Property Rights Analysis* (Chicago: University of Chicago Press, 1990).

Guthrie, Doug, *Dragon in a Three-Piece Suit: The Emergence of Capitalism in China* (Princeton: Princeton University Press, 1999).

Haggard, Stephan, and R. Kaufman, *The Politics of Economic Adjustment: International Constraints, Distributive Conflicts, and the State* (Princeton: Princeton University Press, 1992).

Huntington, Samuel, "How Countries Democratize," *Political Science Quarterly* 106, No. 4 (1992), pp. 579–616.

Johnston, Alastair Iain, "Learning Versus Adaptation: Explaining Change in Chinese Arms Control Policy in the 1980s and 1990s," *The China Journal* 35 (January 1996), pp. 27–62.

Keane, John, "Despotism and Democracy: The Origins and Development of the Distinction Between Civil Society and the State 1750–1850," in *Civil Society and the State*, edited by John Keane (London: Verso, 1988), pp. 35–77.

Lardy, Nicholas, *Foreign Trade and Economic Reform in China, 1978–1990* (New York: Cambridge University Press, 1992).

Levine, Daniel H., "Paradigm Lost: Dependence to Democracy," *World Politics* 25, No. 3 (1988), pp. 377–394.

Levy, Jack S., "Learning and Foreign Policy: Sweeping a Conceptual Minefield," *International Organization* 48 (Spring 1994), pp. 279–312.

Lindblom, Charles L., *Politics and Markets* (New York: Basic Books, 1977).

Lipset, Seymour Martin, "Some Social Requisites of Democracy: Economic Development and Political Legitimacy," *American Political Science Review* 53 (1959), pp. 69–105.

McCormick, Barrett, and David Kelly, "The Limits of Anti-Liberalism," *Journal of Asian Studies* 53, No. 3 (October 1994), pp. 813–814.

McGregor, James, "Foreign Firms in China Upset by Added Tax," *Wall Street Journal*, April 15, 1991.

Maibach, Michael, "Hi-Tech Tradeoffs with China," *Asia-Pacific Economic Review* 3, No. 3 (1995), p. 10.

Moore, Barrington, *Social Origins of Dictatorship and Democracy* (Boston: Beacon Press, 1966).

Moore, Mick, "Is Democracy Rooted in Material Prosperity?" in *Democratization in the South: The Jagged Wave*, edited by Robin Luckham and Gordon White (Manchester: Manchester University Press, 1996), pp. 37–68.

O'Donnell, Guillermo, and Philippe C. Schmitter, *Transitions from Authoritarian Rule: Tentative Conclusions About Uncertain Democracy* (Baltimore: Johns Hopkins University Press, 1986).

Payne, Leigh A., *Brazilian Industrialists and Democratic Change* (Baltimore: Johns Hopkins University Press, 1994).

Pearson, Margaret M., "China's Integration into the International Trade and Investment Regime," in *China Joins the World: Progress and Prospects*, edited by Elizabeth Economy and Michel Oksenberg (New York: Council on Foreign Relations Press, 1999), pp. 161–205.

————, *China's New Business Elite: The Political Consequences of Economic Reform* (Berkeley: University of California Press, 1997).

————, *Joint Ventures in the People's Republic of China* (Princeton: Princeton University Press, 1991).

Pelczynski, Z. A., "Solidarity and 'The Rebirth of Civil Society' in Poland, 1976–81," in *Civil Society and the State*, edited by John Keane (London: Verso Publishers, 1988), pp. 363–364.

Przeworski, Adam, *Democracy and Markets: Political and Economic Reforms in Eastern Europe and Latin America* (New York: Cambridge University Press, 1991).

Redding, Gordon, "Overseas Chinese Networks: Understanding the Enigma," *Long Range Planning*, 28, No. 1 (1995), pp. 61–69.

Robinson, Mark, "Economic Reform and the Transition to Democracy," in *Democratization in the South: The Jagged Wave*, edited by Robin Luckham and Gordon White (Manchester: Manchester University Press, 1996), pp. 69–118.

Rosen, Daniel H., *Behind the Open Door: Foreign Enterprises in the Chinese Marketplace* (Washington, DC: Institute for International Economics, 1999).

Sabin, Lora, "The Growth of Non-State Sector Employment," *China Quarterly*, No. 140 (December 1994), pp. 944–999.

Santoro, Michael A., *Profits and Principles: Global Capitalism and Human Rights in China* (Ithaca: Cornell University Press, 2000).

Sautman, Barry, "Sirens of the Strong Men: Neo-Authoritarianism in Recent Chinese Political Theory," *China Quarterly*, No. 129 (March 1992), pp. 72–102.

Schmitter, Philippe C., "Still the Century of Corporatism?" in *The New Corporatism: Social-Political Structures in the Iberian World*, edited by Frederick B. Pike and Thomas Stritch (Notre Dame, IN: University of Notre Dame Press, 1974), pp. 90–110.

"Shanghai's Richest." *China Focus*, 1, No. 4 (1993), p. 7.

Shils, Edward, "The Virtue of Civil Society" *Government and Opposition*, 26, No. 1 (1991), pp. 3–20.

Sklar, Richard, "Postimperialism," *Comparative Politics* 9, no. 1 (1976), pp. 75–92.

United Press International, "Government to Ease on Job Moves, Tighten on Transients" (July 13, 1993), reported in *China News Digest* (online), July 15, 1993.

Walder, Andrew G., "The Quiet Revolution from Within: Economic Reform as a Source of Political Decline," in *The Waning of the Communist State*, edited by Andrew G. Walder (Berkeley: University of California Press, 1995).

————, *Communist Neo-Traditionalism: Work and Authority in Chinese Industry* (Berkeley: University of California Press, 1986).

Wank, David, *Commodifying Communism: Business, Trust, and Politics in a Chinese City* (New York: Cambridge University Press, 1999).

Wright, Robert, "Gaining Freedom by Modem," *New York Times*, January 28, 2000, p. A27.

www.moftec.gov.cn. (web site of the Ministry of Foreign Trade and Economic Cooperation, PRC).

Zakaria, Fareed, "The Rise of Illiberal Democracy," *Foreign Affairs* 76, No. 6 (1997), pp. 22–43.

Part Two

Patterns of Entrepreneurialism

7

Entrepreneurial Action in the State Sector

The Economic Decisions of Chinese Managers

Doug Guthrie

The last two decades have seen dramatic economic and social changes sweeping across the transforming command economies of the former communist bloc. In all of these transforming economies, the emergence of a viable private sector has played a central role in the transition from plan to market. Even in the case of China, which has chosen a gradual path to the reforms over the rapid privatization of "shock therapy," the emergence of a private economy has played a crucial role in the evolution of a competitive marketplace (Naughton 1995).

Entrepreneurs are often associated with the emergence of private economies; accordingly, architects and observers of these transitions have been interested in this category of economic action. From questions of the extent to which elite positions translate into entrepreneurial advantages (Szelenyi 1988; Nee 1989, 1991; Róna-Tas 1994) to the ways that the private economy is reshaping social life (Gold 1989a, 1989b), the role of entrepreneurs in transforming socialist economies has been a crucial area of inspection. However, while the growing literature on the role of entrepreneurs in transforming socialist economies has shed light on the economic outcomes of entrepreneurs, the discussion has remained tied to a narrow definition of entrepreneurs—the individuals striking out on new business ventures in the private economy. In recent years, a growing literature has focused less on the economic outcomes of entrepreneurs and more on defining and understanding the central characteristics of entrepreneurship itself. As such, this literature focuses more on the behavior of individuals than it does on the position of these individuals in the economy. Central to this literature is a consideration of the extent to which managers themselves act as entrepreneurs. It is this literature that I will engage with in the pages that follow.

In China's economic reforms, managers of state-owned enterprises (SOEs) share attributes with entrepreneurs on a number of levels. Based on data gathered through in-depth interviews with general managers in industrial Shanghai, I will show that managers in industrial China are the innovators of the reforms, at economic, technical, and social levels. They are also often risk takers, strategic actors, and the creators of new institutional forms— they are, in many ways, the "institutional entrepreneurs" (DiMaggio 1988) creating the new economy in China. The entrepreneurial behavior that this group of individuals brings to China's economic reforms is one of the major sources of economic change in China. However, contrary to economistic assumptions about entrepreneurial behavior in free markets, which broadly assume that, given the freedom to do so, individuals will strive to maximize profits and personal income, I will advance a structural analysis of entrepreneurial action in China. Embedded in the industrial hierarchy of the former command economy and surrounded by the foreign models of joint venture companies, managers, bureaucrats, and the organizations they run are shaped by these institutional constraints (and opportunities) in fundamental ways. And profit maximization is only one part of this story. More often, managers in China are striving to create stability in the turbulent markets of the economic reforms. They take their cues for entrepreneurial action from the state bureaucracy and the foreign investors that make up their social worlds, as well as their own educational backgrounds, which increasingly emphasize economics and business knowledge over technical knowledge.

Theoretical Issues

Studies of Entrepreneurs in Transforming Socialist Economies

Research on transforming socialist economies has taken great interest in the private sector and entrepreneurs. Victor Nee's market transition theory has generated a debate that has placed entrepreneurship and the private economy at the center of transforming socialist economies. Nee (1996, p. 945) views "the pursuit of power and plenty by economic actors in society" as the central force driving transitions from socialism to capitalism, and he sees the structural changes that follow the dismantling of the command economy as primarily creating opportunities and incentives for entrepreneurial activity. In Nee's words, "The growth of markets expands the range of opportunities outside the boundaries of the redistributive economy, changing the structures of opportunity and incentives and stimulating entrepreneurship" (1991, p. 267). According to Nee's theory, with the rise of entrepreneurship and the organizational power of the market and private economy comes a decline in the positional power of cadres; in other words, as entrepreneurs gain, those employed in the state sector ("redistributors") lose. Other scholars have also contributed to this debate, arguing that, while entrepreneurs gain power, Nee's prediction of the declining positional power of cadres and other individuals within the transforming state sector has not been borne out empirically (Róna-Tas 1994; Walder 1996). While the data and arguments I present here cannot adjudicate between the poles of this debate, I would like to note that the basic focus in this line of research is on the outcomes (usually defined in terms of income) of entrepreneurs relative to other economic actors in these transforming socialist economies.[1]

Other scholars of entrepreneurship and the private sector in transforming socialist economies have moved beyond the focus on income and relative social and economic status to think more generally about what the private economy means for these rapidly changing societies. Researchers in this area have examined the connection between entrepreneurship and social/political autonomy (Gold 1989a, 1989b, 1990, 1991), the ways that entrepreneurship has helped create an elite business class in China's private sector (Pearson 1997), and the ways that entrepreneurs have aligned themselves with state agents to create a political economic coalition between the private economy and officials in the transforming economy (Wank 1999; Hsing 1998). All of these studies have been useful for exploring and illuminating the impact of entrepreneurship on changing social, political, and economic arrangements in China and other transforming socialist economies. However, like research that focuses on the economic gains of those in the private economy, this line of research takes as a given the very notion of what being an entrepreneur means: An entrepreneur is anyone who is part of the private economy. The problem here is that in the turbulent and uncertain markets of China's transforming economy, many economic actors are "entrepreneurial" in their behavior and are, for all intents and purposes, entrepreneurs, although they are technically not part of the private economy. Understanding the actions of managers and officials as falling under the rubric of entrepreneurial action will illuminate the decisions and practices of individuals in these other economic categories.[2] It is useful, then, to think about what an entrepreneur actually is and whether the attributes of entrepreneurship extend beyond those individuals who are striking out in the private economy.

What Is an Entrepreneur? (And Are Entrepreneurs Different from Managers?)

In all of the research on entrepreneurship in transforming socialist economies, few scholars have considered the question of what an entrepreneur is or what the relationship between entrepreneurialism and management is. It is unfortunate that these questions have been largely elided in the research on transforming socialist economies, because these turbulent economies, where institutional and social space are up for grabs—where economic practices are anything but standard—serve as wonderful testing grounds for such issues. In literatures coming mostly out of business schools, however, the question of what attributes lead to entrepreneurial decisions is a very common one.[3] Here the focus is not on the outcomes of entrepreneurship (for example, income or social status) or the implications of participation in this social category. Rather, the focus is on what type of person becomes an entrepreneur and whether these individuals are fundamentally different from those individuals who become managers in large organizations.[4] The interest here is in understanding the underpinnings of the "entrepreneurial spirit" and what types of individuals make the decision to become an entrepreneur (Sexton and Bowman 1985; Carland et al. 1984).

This literature can be broken down into two categories. The first comprises research that probes the psychological attributes of the entrepreneurial personality. In this body of literature, entrepreneurs are viewed as being fundamentally different—a "breed apart" (Ginsberg and Buchholtz 1989)—from other economic actors (such as managers). Entrepreneurs simply have a different psychological makeup, and this "economic psychology" defines the economic decisions they undertake (Begly and Boyd 1987a; Brockhaus 1982; Kaish and Gilad 1991; Low and MacMillan 1988). Entrepreneurs are seen as being risk-taking, "rugged" individuals (Begley and Boyd 1987a; McGarth et al. 1992; Stevenson and Gumpert 1985) and even, in an extreme view of behavioral differences, prone to engage in socially deviant behavior (Shapero 1985). Much of the research in this literature is based on psychological assessment tests that compare entrepreneurs to managers. For example, based on the results of one such study, Fagenson (1993, pp. 409–10) has argued, "Entrepreneurs [give] significantly more weight than managers to the following terminal values: self respect, freedom, a sense of accomplishment, and an exciting life. . . being honest, ambitious, capable, independent, courageous, imaginative, and logical. In contrast, managers [give] greater weight than entrepreneurs to. . . true friendship, wisdom, salvation, and pleasure. . . being loving, compassionate, forgiving, helpful, and self-controlled." In another study comparing the psychological makeup of entrepreneurs to managers in large corporations, Ohe et al. (1990) found that entrepreneurs prefer an "entrepreneurial" (read: autocratic) as opposed to a consensus decisions style, "extrinsic" over intrinsic rewards, and growth over security.

In sum, this literature posits entrepreneurs as economically motivated individuals who have a psychological predisposition to strike out on their own in the private economy, while managers are risk-averse individuals (Amihud and Lev 1981), conservative in their thinking and committed to maintaining power structures and the status quo. Managers are further seen as conformist (Pettigrew 1973) and predictable in their economic decision making (Barnard 1968; Hofer and Schendel 1978). If entrepreneurs are psychologically disposed to creative innovation and forging new paths, managers follow directives and maintain organizational order.

There are many obvious and fatal problems with the literature on psychological difference; a few are worth mentioning here. Buried at the foundation of the psychological difference literature is a set of atomistic economic assumptions about how individual economic actors behave. Psychologists and economists typically assume that individual action can be reduced to the internal workings of the human mind and the internal motivations that, on a fundamental level, define individuals in the economy. The literature on the psychological differences of entrepreneurs posits that individuals who choose this course are simply closer to the classical notion of what individual economic actors are. Structure, opportunity, and the sociopolitical world in which economic actors are embedded have fallen completely out of the equation. Yet many examples of research on economic action show clearly that social structure shapes economic action in fundamental ways. Whether these structures are the social networks in which economic actors are embedded (Granovetter 1985; Uzzi 1996) or the environments that are shaped by state institutions (Fligstein 1990; Dobbin et al. 1993; Guthrie and Roth 1999; Guthrie 1999), it is inconceivable that social structure does not play a role in the decisions and practices of would-be entrepreneurs. It is simplistic to say, for example, that risk taking (or risk aversion) is an individual trait, independent of the social obligations or opportunities that a given individual faces.

In addition, as much as entrepreneurs are reified in this literature, the reality is that the line between entrepreneurs and managers is significantly more fluid than advocates of the psychological view of entrepreneurs assume. Entrepreneurs themselves, if successful, often *become* managers. Further, and this is particularly true in cases of dramatic uncertainty, managers, for their part, are often forced to behave in an entrepreneurial fashion, seeking creative avenues for economic expansion and social, economic, and organizational reform.

A second category of research on who becomes an entrepreneur takes a more structural approach to the distinction between managers and entrepreneurs. Sexton and Bowman-Upton (1991), for example, have argued that, while entrepreneurship and management are fundamentally different, the distinctions derive from differences in the use and control of resources: entrepreneurs exploit resources, taking advantage of material opportunities as they become available, where managers oversee resources owned by the firms they run. Thus, this line of research acknowledges the extent to which organizational structure and an individual's relation to material resources have important implications for the notion of entrepreneurship.

Other studies similarly acknowledge the importance of firm structure in entrepreneurial behavior, but view managers and entrepreneurs as often having more in common than previous studies have assumed. Miner (1990) has argued that the extent to which managers are free to act like entrepreneurs depends upon the structure of the organization in which they are embedded. Recently, a number of scholars have developed the argument that, under certain circumstances, managers within organizations often act like entrepreneurs; accordingly, entrepreneurial managers have been labeled "intrapreneurs" (Pinochot 1985; Cornwall and Perlman 1990; Low and McMillan 1988; Wortman 1987). Covin and Slevin (1988) have argued that top management in corporations often shares the following traits with entrepreneurs: proactiveness, risk taking, and innovation. A number of other scholars working in this area have helped define the notion of entrepreneurship and its relation to management, emphasizing competitiveness and perception of opportunity (Cornwall and Perlman 1990; Sinetar 1985; Stevenson and Gumpert 1985). Geisler (1993) has extended the literature on "intrapreneurship" to the study of middle managers.

In sum, if we look beyond the jargon-laden terminology in this body of literature (*intrapreneurs?*), we find that scholars working in this area have contributed to the study of entrepreneurship in two important ways. First, research in this area has moved away from a psychological explanation of managers to one that places organizational structure and the structure of opportunity at the center of entrepreneurial action. At the same time, the identifiers of entrepreneurial action have shifted from personality traits (the "rugged" individual) to the practices of individuals, irrespective of whether these individuals are starting new enterprises or managing large firms. These practices include proactive, innovative, risk-taking behavior, and managers acting within this framework are viewed as entrepreneurs in their own right. Second, research in this area recognizes that the line between managers and entrepreneurs is blurry and that, under certain circumstances, managers can act like entrepreneurs and vice versa. This is an important step in the research on entrepreneurs, because it has broken down the hard boundary between managers and entrepreneurs, allowing us to think more generally about managerial and entrepreneurial action irrespective of occupational categories. Entrepreneurs may be employed in start-up ventures they began or they may be managers of large industrial firms; what is distinctive about them as a group of individuals is the practices and strategies they adopt.

Entrepreneurial Managers: The Structural View

While the move away from psychological views of entrepreneurial action among managers is a positive one, we are still left with the notion that entrepreneurial action is located at the individual level. If individual managers are innovative, proactive, or risk-taking in their business practices, they bear the stamp of the entrepreneur. Yet this view of the entrepreneur-manager is still incomplete—entrepreneurial action may, in part, be an individual phenomenon, but it is also structurally defined. Further, there is a tautological reasoning in this understanding of entrepreneurs: if we can define what the practices of entrepreneurial behavior are, then individuals who adopt these practices can be defined as entrepreneurs. A sociological view of this phenomenon leads us to inquire after the structural, social, and individual factors that might lead to entrepreneurial behavior among managers.

Several studies in economic sociology have posited that markets are social worlds, and that individual actors and organizations adopt practices in accordance with the social and structural nature of markets.[5] Harrison White's (1981) account of the fact that actors in markets set prices not according to a cost calculus but rather in accordance with their views of the practices of other actors in the market is an excellent analysis of the fundamental ways in which organizations and the managers that run them are shaped by the institutional and social environments in which they are embedded. This was a radical step forward in analyses of organizational behavior, as White's analysis showed empirically the importance of the social in economic decision making. DiMaggio and Powell (1983) further developed this idea in their theoretical treatise on institutional isomorphism in organizational fields. Arguing that organizations adopt practices that they see as successful models in the marketplace, DiMaggio and Powell expanded the notion of innovative action far beyond cost-benefit analyses of efficient action to the realm of the social.[6] Burt (1992) has argued that structure relates directly to the emergence of economic and entrepreneurial opportunities in the marketplace. And Fligstein (1990), Dobbin and Sutton (1998), and Guthrie and Roth (1999) have all argued that the structural constraints imposed by the state shape the extent to which managers can act in an entrepreneurial fashion in molding and reshaping the organizations they inhabit. All of these studies are relevant for the study of managers and entrepreneurs because they raise the notion that, while organizational structure—control of resources, decision-making power, and the like—is an important factor in understanding managers and entrepreneurs, other aspects of social structure are also critical.[7] The social world outside of the firm plays a critical role in the ways that managers and entrepreneurs lead their firms.

Entrepreneurial Managers in Shanghai

In this section, I will illuminate the discussion above through an analysis of the decisions and practices of managers in industrial Shanghai in the mid-1990s. My focus is the elaboration of a number of different ways that managers adopt new economic strategies in China and how these strategies relate to the behavior that we typically associate with entrepreneurial action. The focus of the research is organizational practices in the mid-1990s in China. While the data were gathered through in-depth interviews with general managers in Shanghai, the analysis begins with organization level data gathered in a random sample of eighty-one factories from four industrial sectors in Shanghai.[8]

Variables in the Analysis: Managerial Background and Social Structure in China

To begin this discussion, it is necessary to take a detour into a few empirical aspects of social structure in industrial Shanghai. For each of the aspects I will discuss below, a complex set of parameters shapes the constraints under which managers operate; however, in the analyses that follow, I focus on three critical variables: the background of the general manager, the social networks in which these managers are embedded, and a firm's position vis-à-vis the institutional structure of the state.

Personal Background

Personal background of the general manager is measured by looking at the effect of a general manager's education. There are many ways to think about a manager's background, but education plays a central role in the ways that managers think about the mandates and opportunities before them. Before the economic reforms began, it was very common for managers to come from a technical background, usually with a college education in engineering. In China today, after two decades of economic reform, many forward-thinking managers climbing China's new corporate ladders have backgrounds in business or economics. Thus, I examine the issue by looking at whether managers who have an education in business or economics (an option that was nonexistent in the prereform era) guide their firms differently than other managers in the reform era.

Social Networks

Like educational opportunities and the changing emphasis of educational programs, there are many ways that social networks are changing under China's economic reforms. One of the most important ways social networks are changing in China revolves around the foreign presence there. Foreign investment has many effects on the economic climate in China. In this study, I analyze the effects that formal relations with foreign investors have on the economic practices that are emerging in China. Relationships with foreign companies can be of many types, from formal joint venture relationships to cooperative licensing agreements to casual social networking. As a gauge of the organization's formal relations with foreign companies, I focus on whether an organization has a joint venture factory (*hezi qiye*) with a foreign investor. I use the joint venture investment because it is the most formal of the relations and the most complex in terms of cooperatively working out the details of the joint venture factory. Joint ventures involve the construction of a new organization (a separate legal entity) that is jointly owned by both the foreign and Chinese organizations.[9] As such, the process of constructing a joint venture requires the Chinese organization to work side by side with the foreign investor, hammering out the details of what is often a long-term relationship, in a way that is not necessary in most licensing agreements or other types of less formal agreements. If there are social network effects of relationships with foreign investment partners, it is most likely that we will see them here. Forty-eight of the firms in my study had at least one joint venture with a foreign partner.

The Institutional Structure of the State

Where a firm is situated in the administrative hierarchy of the former command economy not only had profound effects on how the organization experienced the command economy but also on how it is experiencing the economic transition (Walder 1992, 1995a; Guthrie 1997, 1999). Previously, I have argued that this institutional structure is *the* key structure shaping the decisions that managers make in reform-era China. Figure 7.1 represents this structure of the industrial hierarchy graphically. I operationalize the effect of this institutional structure on organizational practices (and therefore managerial decisions). Because firms under the jurisdiction of municipal bureaus are experiencing the transition much differently than firms under the jurisdiction of municipal and district companies, I look specifically at the effects that location under these different levels of state administration have on firm practices. The result is that I am able to analyze whether a firm's position vis-à-vis the central government has consequences for the strategies the firm adopts in the reform era.

The Entrepreneurial Decisions of Shanghai's Managers

Chinese industrial firms have been transformed in dramatic ways over the course of China's economic reforms. Perhaps the most important change

Figure 7.1   **The Institutional Structure of China's Command Economy**

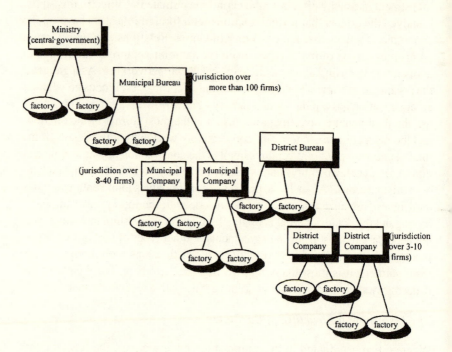

came when the state handed economic decision making over to industrial managers (Naughton 1995; Guthrie 1999). And, while some of the organizational changes in industrial firms are in direct response to the hundreds of new directives and economic laws being promulgated by the state, many of the changes in Chinese industrial firms come from decisions made by autonomous managers, who are transforming their firms by force of creativity, will, and, in some cases, pure desperation. In the uncertain environments of China's newly emerging markets, managers have been impelled to innovate, create, strategize, and improvise their way through the economic reforms. Many of these managers learned the ways of markets, competition, and economic survival through experimenting with and implementing the new organizational strategies and structures their firms were adopting in this period.

While I have analyzed many of the new strategies being adopted throughout Chinese firms in previous work (see esp. Guthrie 1999), in this chapter I consider how these strategies reflect entrepreneurial behavior in industrial managers in Shanghai. In previous work, I conceived of these firm-level changes as organizational strategies, yet that conception fails to account for the agency of managers in this process of change. The transformation of Chinese industrial firms is just as much a reflection of managerial decision making as it is of some abstract notion of organizational strategies, because it is largely the general managers (along with the local bureaucrats in some administrative jurisdictions) who are running the show in China today. These firm-level changes are very much about innovation, experimentation, and finding creative solutions to organizational problems; they are thus driven by the entrepreneurial decisions of the general managers who run these firms. In the sections that follow, I will examine the adoption of new organizational structures, the adoption of the Company Law, price-setting practices, and the reliance on connections in markets in this light. In addition to discussing how these organizational innovations reflect the entrepreneurial behavior of industrial managers in Shanghai, I will also push toward an analysis of the structural and social aspects of the environments in which managers are embedded to illuminate the circumstances under which entrepreneurial behavior is encouraged and common.

Intraorganizational Structure: Dismantling the Old and Creating the New

Organizational structure is an important site of innovation and change in China's transforming economy, and it reflects important strategic decisions made by industrial managers. The first dramatic change on the part of aggressive managers is a clearing of the decks. Wiping out the old system has been an important step in enterprise reform in China, but it has not been an easy one. As industrial enterprises under the command economy served as the nation's social security system, dismantling this system of extensive benefit packages amounted to a fundamental transformation of the labor relationship and the meaning of work in China. It is useful first to examine which managers and enterprises have been willing to implement these changes.

Table 7.1 shows two associations that are relevant for our discussion here. The first is that economic constraints appear to matter in significant ways if individual firms have moved aggressively against the systems of the past. The extent to which firms are burdened with retired workforces can determine whether managers are willing to take a scalpel to the expensive institutions that formerly defined employment relations.[10] Managers who feel greater economic pressure to implement reforms are more likely to begin dismantling the institutions of the former command economy, and this approach might constitute entrepreneurial behavior in its own right. These managers are creating new organizational forms through the destruction of old institutions. In this table, it is also clear that the variables that measure the social

Table 7.1

Ordinal Logit for the Determinants of the Total Number of Benefits Offered by Organizations in Four Industrial Sectors, Shanghai, 1995

Independent Variables	B	S.E.
Control variables[a]		
Chemicals	−2.41***	0.89
Electronics	−3.36	0.88
Garments	−0.49	0.60
Active employees (ln)	2.06***	0.40
Employee ratio	−3.92**	1.64
Organizational health	0.50	0.83
Profit margin (average 1990–1994)	−0.06*	0.02
Losses 1990	−1.07	0.67
Critical variables for the analysis		
General managers with business economic background	−1.18***	0.49
Joint venture	2.03***	0.63
Municipal bureau	0.76***	0.27
Municipal company	0.96***	0.33
Pseudo R^2	0.37	
Number of cases	79	

Notes:
*p <.01; ** p < .05; ***p < .01 (2-tailed tests).
See Appendix, Table 7.6, for discussion of variables. B is the coefficient effect, S.E. is the standard error. Benefits included in the dependent variable are housing, medical coverage for family members, medical clinic, child care, kindergarten, retail shop, commuter bus, and library.
[a]Reference category for sector is foods.

and institutional environments in which firms are embedded (joint ventures and bureau governance) are both statistically significant.

A second dramatic change in Chinese firms is the shift to newly emerging organizational structures and forms. Since the late 1980s, we have witnessed the emergence of bureaucratic structures that look strikingly like the organizational structures we find in Western economies. The construction of these new "intra-organizational" structures in Chinese firms over the last decade has required innovation, experimentation, and imagination by industrial managers. One industrial manager in Shanghai described these changes in the following way:

> The early 1990s were really the important years for the internal systems and rules of our organization. These were years of significant change in the organizational rules and the way we did things. Until 1990 everything

Table 7.2

Ordinal Logit for the Overall Institutional Structure of Organizations in Four Industrial Sectors, Shanghai, 1995

Independent Variables	B	S.E.
Control variables[a]		
Chemicals	−2.87**	1.16
Foods	−1.83***	0.60
Electronics	0.03	0.74
Active employees (ln)	0.36	0.33
Organizational health	0.21	0.22
Employee ratio	−0.17	0.15
Losses 1990	−1.24**	0.59
Losses 1990		
Critical variables for the analysis		
General managers with business		
economic background	−1.22***	0.50
Joint venture	1.18**	0.58
Municipal company	0.74***	0.28
Pseudo R^2	0.25	
Number of cases	81	

Notes:
** $p < .05$; *** $p < .01$ (2-tailed tests).
See Appendix, Table 7.6, for discussion of variables. B is the coefficient effect, S.E. is the standard error.
[a]Reference category for sector is garments.

was simply based on the state allocation system. But when the government stopped operating by this system, we had to come up with our own ways of organizing workers and making rules. Now we are very developed in this area. (Interview #53, 1995)

Today, evidence of these new institutions and structures abounds in the Chinese economy, yet industrial managers have embraced these changes at varying rates. Table 7.2 shows the types of firms that have aggressively adopted new organizational forms in China's transforming economy.[11] The analysis shows three associations that are relevant for our discussion. First, the background of general managers has a significant impact on the extent to which they actively reshape the organizations they run. Firms run by managers with a background in business and economics are more likely to adopt economic structures associated with the economic reforms. In other words, from the entrepreneurial framework, I contend that such general managers are more likely to act in an entrepreneurial fashion with respect to organizational restructuring than their counterparts with training in other areas or no formal training at all. Second, the social world—and the economic models in that social world—plays a significant role in the aggressive adoption of new organizational forms in China. Firms that have joint ventures with foreign companies are significantly more likely to adopt economic structures associated with the reforms. Third, the institutional structure in which a firm is embedded also plays a significant role in the adoption of new organizational structures and forms. Firms positioned under the jurisdiction of municipal companies tend to be aggressive adopters of the new organizational forms.[12]

The Company Law: Adopting New Corporate Forms

As general managers lead their firms to take advantage of the institutional opportunities created by the state, a second area of aggressive development and entrepreneurial reform can be seen. I have argued previously (Guthrie 1999) that, as the state inundates society and the market with a horde of new laws and institutional rules, the really interesting question becomes which of these institutional changes have meaning for society. Which of these institutional reforms do the economic actors in the marketplace adopt? Which are simply ignored? In the end, the institutional reforms that have meaning are those that are aggressively adopted by actors in the economy. And it is often entrepreneurial managers taking advantage of—or in some cases avoiding—the institutional changes who define and enliven these reforms.

A fascinating case in point is that of the Chinese Company Law. Adopted by the National People's Congress on December 29, 1993, the Company Law provides the first legal basis in the history of the PRC for private, collective, and state enterprises to exist as autonomous legal entities. It is an institutional change that continues the process of separating—both legally and operationally—enterprises from the state redistributive system of the former command economy. Yet, while the law now exists in China, there is still considerable variation in the extent to which organizations have chosen to incorporate this change into their daily operations. Managers must choose to transform their firms into companies if they want to take advantage of the Company Law—they must apply to the Economic Commission to take on company status; and aggressive managers have seen this as an opportunity to become part of the "modern enterprise system" [xiandai qiye zhidu]. They must act as entrepreneurs with respect to this new institution, apply for this change in status, figure out what it means for their organization, and adopt the changes that come with this economic transformation. One entrepreneurial general manager described this process:

In 1986, business in our factory really started picking up. Before, we were a planned economy. But after the economic opening, our factory was one of the earliest to integrate a market economic approach. That year was actually the year that our profits really started picking up. Then last year we applied to have our factory changed from an enterprise to a company. So now we are under the Company Law, and our scope of business is much wider. It's really a much better situation for us in terms of development now. (Interview #82, 1995)

What types of managers and firms are transforming their organizations in this way? Table 7.3 shows that two of the variables are significant for explaining the social context in which entrepreneurial managers operate. First, managers whose organizations are embedded in formal relationships with foreign companies are more likely to adopt the Company Law. Firms that are engaged in relationships with—and therefore under the influence of—foreign partners are more likely to pursue economic strategies that the state has defined as part of the "modern enterprise system." A general manager's decision to adopt the Company Law is not significantly related to the firm's profit margins or its overall organizational health, variables that would presumably be proxies for economic success; in other words, this change itself has little to do with past economic success. I think the stronger interpretation of the joint venture effect is that a foreign partner provides a Chinese firm with up-close examples of how foreign firms operate. The "modern enterprise system" is, in many ways, a rhetorical stand-in for Western-style management practices. Managers that are exposed to the concept of the "modern enterprise system" through contact with foreign companies and through setting up a joint venture company are more likely to see the institutional advantages (real or perceived) of broadening the organization's scope of operation and becoming an independent legal entity. Entrepreneurial managers pursue this change as a way of shepherding their firms into the modern economy.

The second finding that emerges from Table 7.3 is that firms at the highest level of the government administrative hierarchy are more likely than those under more local governmental offices to adopt the Company Law: position at the highest level of the government increases the likelihood by more than four times ($\exp[1.5] = 4.48$) that general managers in these positions will pursue this strategy. Bureau offices, with jurisdiction over many enterprises, do not have the administrative resources to monitor and offer administrative advice or help to the firms in the large organizational fields under their jurisdictions (Guthrie 1997, 1998a). As a result, firms under municipal bureaus experience a greater sense of being set adrift in the economic transition.

Table 7.3

Logistic Coefficients for the Adoption of the Company Law by Organizations in Four Industrial Sectors, Shanghai, 1995

Independent variables	B	S.E.
Control variables[a]		
Chemicals	−0.80	0.51
Electronics	−0.83	0.47
Garments	−0.48	0.45
Active employees (ln)	0.15	0.37
Organizational health	−0.02	0.08
Profit margin (average 1990–1994)	0.05	0.03
Percent products exported 1990	−0.01	0.01
Critical variables for the analysis		
General managers with background in		
business economics	−0.38	0.29
Joint venture	0.63*	0.36
Municipal bureau	1.50*	0.90
Municipal company	0.44	0.38
Jurisdiction size (ln)	—	—
Constant	−2.13	2.48
χ^2		20.37**
Number of cases		80

Notes:
* p < .1; ** p < .05.
See Appendix, Table 7.6, for discussion of variables. B is the coefficient effect, S.E. is the standard error.
[a] Reference category for sector is foods.

They are thus encouraged—or they feel the impetus—to pursue economic strategies on their own. Adopting the Company Law and thereby broadening the scope of action in China's growing markets is one such strategy that firms, especially those under bureaus, are taking. Firms under the jurisdiction of district companies, on the other hand, are much more closely monitored by their government organizations (relative to those under bureaus), and these firms are offered a significant amount of administrative help and attention in the economic reform. The result is that, when the opportunity to apply to become a company and adopt the Company Law arose, managers under high level governmental offices had the autonomy (and the impetus) to move their firms toward adopting this institutional change.

Price Setting: Flexibility and Competition in the Market

A crucial issue in the transition from a command to a market economy pertains to the setting of prices. Under the command economy, all price-setting in large industrial organizations was controlled by the state. Reforming price-setting practices would prove to be a central issue of the economic transition. Price reform has followed the course of gradualism that is indicative of China's economic transition, laden with politics, experimentation, and piecemeal implementation.[13] Managers, for their part, have responded to the price reforms in China in a variety of ways—some have simply remained passive, following the market, but pursuing few strategies in negotiating that can often allow prices to shift in a market, while others have viewed price reform as an opportunity to bargain aggressively with customers in the market. I view the latter as an example of entrepreneurial management in the economic reforms. One manager explained the practice of negotiations over price in the following way:

> We negotiate prices with customers—especially larger customers—when we need to. It's a complicated problem; we try to set a fair price from the beginning, one that takes into account the situations of our customers. But we also need the business, so we will negotiate prices if we have to in order to keep customers, especially larger customers. (Interview #103, 1995)

Another manager noted,

> We negotiate prices with customers if they want to. In the market economy now, we have this competition problem (*jingzheng wenti*). If we can't compete in terms of price, we won't be able to do the volume of business we need to. So sometimes we have to negotiate. (Interview #59, 1995)[14]

Table 7.4 shows how important position in the state hierarchy is in the ways that managers adopt pricing practices in the reform era. Managers of organizations that are at higher levels of the state industrial hierarchy are significantly more likely to negotiate prices with customer organizations. As I have noted above, organizations at this level of the industrial hierarchy are ultimately more free from state monitoring and control than their counterparts at lower levels of the industrial hierarchy, and managers of firms at this level of the industrial hierarchy encourage entrepreneurial behavior in the marketplace. This view turns on its head the perception that organizations at the highest level of China's industrial hierarchy (many of them the large SOEs that are still far from solvent) are still operating under the old system; on the contrary, I argue that these factories are among the most aggressive adopters of new economic strategies.[15] I would push this notion further in arguing that entrepreneurial managers play a central role in the extent to which their firms are aggressively embracing the reforms, but there is a structural aspect to this story. Managers of firms that have been set adrift by the

Table 7.4

Logistic Coefficients for the Practice of Negotiating Prices with Customers for Organizations in Four Industrial Sectors, Shanghai, 1995

Independent variables	B	S.E.
Control variables[a]		
Chemicals	−0.27	1.19
Foods	−0.48	1.07
Garments	1.19	1.23
Active employees (ln)	−0.01	0.48
Employee ratio	−1.27	2.01
Organizational health	0.27	0.22
Profit margin (average 1990–1994)	0.01	0.04
Losses 1990	0.64	0.91
Percent products exported 1990	−0.002	0.01
Government control of pricing	−1.84*	0.95
Input pricing system	−0.66	0.88
Critical variables for the analysis		
General managers with background in		
business economics	−0.02	0.68
Joint venture	−0.65	0.85
Municipal bureau	2.83**	1.34
Municipal company	1.70*	0.86
Constant	1.64	3.36
χ^2		27.47**
Number of cases		81

Notes:
* $p < .1$; ** $p < .05$ (2-tailed tests).
Note: See Appendix, Table 7.6, for discussion of variables. B is the coefficient effect, S.E. is the standard error.
[a] Reference category for sector is electronics.

state are guiding their organizations along a flexible and entrepreneurial path in terms of setting prices, among other economic practices.

Social Connections in Markets: Building Alliances

One of the issues that consistently emerges in the research on economic reform in China is the question of the role that social connections and networks play in China's transforming economy. In earlier work (Guthrie 1998b, 1999), I have argued that, while the use of connections to circumvent administrative barriers (i.e., the use of connections for corrupt practices) is declining in reform-era China, the use of connections to establish economic relations in markets is alive and well. Entrepreneurial managers take advantage of the social networks to which they have access in order to gain advantages in the market economy. They further work to cultivate these connections as a way of gaining advantages in China's rapidly changing economic system. One manager explained his reasons for cultivating relationships in the following way:

> In markets, relationships and connections are very important. Before, in the planned economy, business had nothing to do with connections or relations with customers. But now we are in a market economic system, and competition and relationships are very important. If you know me and trust me, I can communicate to you about our products and service more. You can tell me about any concerns or areas where you're unsatisfied. We still try to focus primarily on quality and price, but connections are also an important part of it. (Interview #93, 1995)

Another manager put it this way:

> I think that connections in markets are even more important than they are in procedures. If you have some customers whom you have been working with for a long time, this is the best situation for business. If you have a new product, they will trust you that it is a good product because they have worked with you for a long time. They might even do some advertising for you. It's as if you are old friends helping each other out. These types of relationships are really important in business. (Interview #68, 1995)

Table 7.5 shows that two relevant variables influence the extent to which entrepreneurial managers are actively adapting to a system of networks and connections in markets. First, general managers with backgrounds in business or economics are significantly more likely to view connections as important in the emerging market economic system. Individuals that are trained (educationally) in similar settings and under similar market principles are likely to view the world in similar ways and to guide their organizations to act in similar ways. The result is that general managers with similar types of educational backgrounds are significantly more likely to view networks and social relationships as an important part of doing business in the economic transition. Second, general managers of organizations that have joint ventures with foreign partner organizations are more likely than those without joint ventures to view social networks in markets as important for business in the reform era. Joint venture relationships are complicated relationships among foreign and Chinese organizations that are often forged over several months or even years. For many organizations, joint ventures are among the most important economic relationships in which the firm is engaged. Whether the venture means a new factory site (usually built by capital from the for-

Table 7.5

Logistic Coefficients for Determinants of the View that *Guanxi*—Social Relationships—Is Important in Markets Among Managers in Organizations in Four Industrial Sectors, Shanghai, 1995

Independent Variables	B		S.E.
Organizational variables[a]			
Chemicals	0.98*		0.58
Foods	0.88*		0.50
Electronics	0.71		0.49
Active employees (ln)	−0.40		0.35
Organizational health	0.09		0.08
Percent products exported	0.003		0.01
Overall institutionalization[b]	−28.00		0.18
Critical variables for the analysis			
General managers with business			
economics background	0.55*		0.30
Joint venture	0.71**		0.34
Municipal bureau	0.39		0.37
Constant	4.57*		2.34
χ^2		16.58*	
Number of cases		78	

Notes:
* p < .1; ** p < .05 (2-tailed tests).
See Appendix, Table 7.6, for discussion of variables. B is the coefficient effect on the dependent variable, S.E. is the standard error.
[a] Reference category for sector is garments.
[b] For discussion of the variable "overall institutionalization," see Guthrie (1999).

eign partner), the transfer of technology, or a relationship that will eventually lead to greater access to international markets, the joint venture is crucial for the future of the firm. General managers of organizations that have joint ventures have learned firsthand that good relations with prospective business partners are an important ingredient of successful business deals. It is likely that these types of business deals and the relationship work that went into forging them are foremost in the minds of these managers. Thus these managers are much more likely to view social connections as an important part of the economic transition than managers of organizations that do not have joint venture relationships.

Discussion and Implications

In this final section, I will relate the findings presented above to the notion of entrepreneurial management in China's economic reforms. Ultimately, the autonomy and innovation of managers in the transformation of the industrial workplace have played central roles in the extent to which new economic practices and new organizational forms are emerging in China. They are the individuals who are proactively transforming economic behavior in China.

In the discussion above, I argued that the concept of the entrepreneur is not very informative when it is attached to a clearly defined occupational category or to an individual's psychological constitution. In the first case, we miss a great number of the individuals who act like entrepreneurs—whether as innovators, risk takers, creators of new business models—despite the fact that they might work in large organizations in the industrial economy. In the second case, we are led down a path of psychological reductionism that ties entrepreneurialism to internal, individual traits rather than to the structural constraints and social pressures entrepreneurs face. In the findings presented here, I have attempted to show some of the ways that radical reform is occurring in large firms in China's transforming industrial economy and to make the case that these examples of radical reform at the organizational level are also examples of entrepreneurial management by the general managers implementing these changes. Whether we are talking about the institutionalization of new procedures and practices in firms or the adoption of the Company Law, entrepreneurial managers in China are leading the charge toward new economic practices. They are innovating, experimenting, and creating new organizational environments in their firms: the behavior of these managers is nothing if not entrepreneurial. For example, managers who are dismantling the costly institutions of the prereform era (extensive benefits packages, lifetime employment, etc.) and replacing these institutions with the rational bureaucratic structures that describe the "modern enterprise system" are taking an active role in leading their organizations into the modern era. Similarly, managers who are aggressively adopting the new institutional forms that define enterprise structure in China, such as the new Chinese Company Law, are proactively taking advantage of new possibilities for organizational structure and form. And managers who are actively leading their companies in examining and understanding the meaning of markets—and the practices that define them—are entrepreneurial in their adoption of new economic practices in the reform era.

I have also attempted to show how some of these behaviors might be viewed structurally rather than conceived of as individualistic tendencies. The structural aspects of the Chinese economy I have focused on are a firm's structural position vis-à-vis the state and its exposure to foreign investors. The first is important because firms at different levels of the administrative hierarchy of the command economy are experiencing the reforms in different ways. Those at the upper levels of this administrative hierarchy experience the greatest amount of

Table 7.6

Characteristics and Variables for Organizations from Four Industrial Sectors in Shanghai, 1995

	Mean	S.D.	Definition
Dependent variables			
Formal organizational rules	0.642	0.482	1 = organization has formal (written) organizational rules; 0 = no formal organizational rules.
Formal job descriptions	0.568	0.499	1 = organization has formal (written) job descriptions; 0 = no formal job descriptions.
Formal grievance filing procedures	0.642	0.482	1 = organization has formal grievance filing procedures; 0 = no formal grievance procedures.
Mediation institution in firm	0.556	0.500	1 = organization has an internal mediation institution; 0 = no mediation institution.
Institutionalized WRC mtgs.	0.852	0.358	1 = organization has institutionalized Workers' Representative Committee meetings in a formal way; 0 = meetings have not been institutionalized.
Promotion test	0.284	0.454	1 = organization uses promotion tests for worker advancement; 0 = no promotion tests.
Pay scale	0.642	0.482	1 = organization has a formal pay scale; 0 = no formal pay scale.
Formal hiring procedure	0.269	0.503	1 = organization has formal hiring procedures; 0 = no formal hiring procedures.
Overall institutionalization	3.630	1.907	Sum across all dummy variable categories for formal firm structure; the range of this variable is 0-7.

Housing	0.531	0.502	1 = organization currently offers housing as a benefit for workers; 0 = housing is not offered as a benefit.
Medical insurance	0.975	0.157	1 = organization offers medical insurance as a benefit for workers; 0 = medical insurance is not offered as a benefit.
Family coverage	1.148	0.050	Multinomial; 2 = organization offers full family coverage; 1 = partial coverage for family members; 0 = no coverage for family members.
Medical clinic	0.346	0.479	1 = organization has a medical clinic on site as a benefit for workers; 0 = no medical clinic.
Cafeteria	0.815	0.391	1 = organization has a cafeteria on site as a benefit for workers; 0 = no cafeteria.
Child care	0.173	0.380	1 = organization offers child care as a benefit for workers; 0 = no child care.
Kindergarten	0.136	0.345	1 = organization has a kindergarten as a benefit for workers; 0 = no kindergarten.
Retail shop	0.469	0.502	1 = organization has a retail shop as a benefit for workers; 0 = no retail shop.
Commuter bus	0.198	0.401	1 = organization offers commuter bus service as a benefit for workers; 0 = no commuter bus service.
Library	0.210	0.410	1 = organization has a library as a benefit for workers; 0 = no library.

(continued)

Table 7.6 (continued)

	Mean	S.D.	Definition
Total benefits	5.000	2.716	Sum across all of the benefit categories for the organization, where each category is assigned the value of the variable; the range of this variable is 0 to 11.
Guanxi in markets	487.000	0.503	1 = General manager affirms that connections are important in business relations; 0 = General manager views connections as unimportant
Organizational variables			
Chemicals	0.185	0.391	Proportion of firms in sample located in chemicals sector.
Electronics	0.284	0.454	Proportion of firms in sample located in electronics sector.
Foods	0.259	0.441	Proportion of firms in sample located in foods sector.
Garments	0.272	0.448	Proportion of firms in sample located in garments sector.
Organizational size	1,580.840	3,724.745	Number of active (not retired) employees, year end, 1994.
Organizational size (ln)	6.058	1.475	Natural log of active employees.
Employee ratio	0.754	0.176	(active employees)/(active + retired employees).
Organizational health (in millions)	120.000	443.000	Revenues less labor cost less money paid into national pension fund; variable is then standardized to average value for sector, to control for sectoral variation in input costs. See text for discussion of this variable.

Profits (in millions)	22.000	120.000	Profits for year end, 1990, renminbi.
Profits (in millions)	20.554	113.078	Profits for year end, 1994, renminbi.
Profit margin (1994)	0.070	0.085	Profits divided by revenues.
Profit margin (average 1990–1994)	0.073	0.097	Average profit margin for 1990 and 1994.
Losses 1994	0.259	0.441	1 = firm lost money in 1994; 0 = no losses.
Percent products exported 1994	25.815	35.845	Percentage of products exported in 1994.
Joint venture	0.593	0.494	1 = firm has a joint venture with a foreign firm; 0 = no joint venture.
Governance variables			
General manager with business economic background	1.198	0.813	1 = General manager has background in management or economics; 0 = no background in business or economics.
Municipal bureau	0.296	0.459	1 = firm under jurisdiction of municipal bureau; 0 = other.
Municipal company	0.296	0.459	1 = firm under jurisdiction of municipal company; 0 = other.
District company	0.321	0.470	1 = firm under jurisdiction of district company; 0 = other

autonomy from state governing offices, which creates a great deal of uncertainty for these firms (Guthrie 1997, 1998a, 1999). Thus, managers at this level of the administrative hierarchy have the greatest incentive to innovate and experiment with new economic strategies in the reforms.

The second issue—the significance of relationships with foreign investment firms—illuminates the importance of the social networks in which firms are embedded. Firms that have formal relations with foreign companies are shaped by these economic relationships in fundamental ways. Because many foreign investors in China are more interested in long-term investments (to capture market share) than they are in cheap labor, they generally seek Chinese partners that are predictable, stable, and knowledgeable about Western-style business practices and negotiations. Chinese factories, for their part, want desperately to land these partnerships, and they position themselves as suitable investment partners, fit to link up with the international community (a very popular concept among managers in China today) by adopting reforms that Western partners will recognize as stable, reform-minded business practices. Among these are the adoption of Western-style bureaucracies (which often include grievance filing procedures), Western organizational forms (i.e., the Chinese Company Law), and a recognition of the importance of relationships in markets.

Over the course of two decades of economic reform in China, while the reform of China's industrial economy has been gradual and incremental, managers have nevertheless increasingly been given the autonomy to act independently of state control. They have been given the space to make the decisions about how to guide their firms in the transition from a planned to a market economy. Yet not all managers have followed this course in the same way—some have been slow to transform their firms in the marketplace, while others have been aggressive and proactive in adopting new economic strategies and models of action. It is the latter group, I have argued, that reflect the behavior that we typically associate with entrepreneurs. Through the strategies they adopt and the approaches they take to transforming their firms in the era of economic reforms, they are, in many ways, every bit as entrepreneurial as the individuals striking out in the private economy. Understanding the strategies they adopt as well as the social and institutional factors that guide their decisions tells us a great deal about what it means to be entrepreneurial in China's transforming economy.

Appendix

This study is based upon a stratified random sample of eighty-one factories from four sectors in industrial Shanghai. Data were gathered through in-depth interviews with the general managers of these firms. Table 7.6 presents the means, standard deviations, and definitions of the variables that are relevant for the study conducted here. For more information on the data and research design, see Guthrie (1999).

Notes

Prepared for the conference "Entrepreneurs, Entrepreneurialism and Democracy in Communist and Post-Communist Societies," University of California, Berkeley, CA, May 19–20, 2000. Address correspondence to Doug Guthrie, Department of Sociology, New York University, 269 Mercer St., 4th Floor, New York, NY 10003; *doug.guthrie@nyu.edu.*

1. In general, defining gains and losses in terms of income seems extremely narrow, given that wages were typically *not* the way that individuals gained power and remuneration in the command economies. Many studies have drawn conclusions about cadre advantage based on income data (e.g., Nee 1989, 1991, 1996; Róna-Tas 1994; Bian and Logan 1996; Parish and Michelson 1996). Strangely, in this body of research, despite the fact that cadres most often enjoy advantages through nonwage benefits and other perquisites that are hidden from income data, few studies have diverged from the focus on income as the primary indicator of returns to political capital (for an exception, see Walder 1995b).

2. In his insightful article "Local Governments as Industrial Firms," Walder (1995a) brought to light many of the structural features of China's transforming industrial economy by acknowledging that local state-owned township and village enterprises and the officials who run them are very much like firms and managers, respectively, although a rigorous classification would not allow for such an analytical perspective. My purpose in thinking about managers and officials as entrepreneurs is analogous to Walder's view of local governments as industrial firms.

3. Indeed, there has been so much ink spilled pondering this question that Harwood (1982, p. 92), anticipating the position I will take below, was prompted to write: "After so much has been written on this subject, one might fairly conclude that it is not really so important to know what or who the entrepreneur is, rather, one ought to examine the habitat of this mysterious creature. Let the definition hunters abandon their futile pursuit after these elusive animals! Know them instead by the environmental variables that mold their behavior and determine their range!"

4. I should note here that this literature almost exclusively revolves around empirical studies and theoretical inquiries into the structure of the U.S. economy. It is thus not surprising that the "who gains, who loses" question or the "social implications" question, both of which are so common in research on transforming socialist economies, are not nearly as relevant here. It is more surprising, however, that scholars of entrepreneurship have not paid closer attention to and engaged this literature on the level of who becomes an entrepreneur or on the question of the relationship between entrepreneurs and managers, as transforming socialist economies have a good deal to say about both of these issues.

5. While economic sociology has made many important inroads into this literature, this is of course not to say that many scholars who preceded economic sociology were making arguments about the relationship between individuals and their institutional environments. For example, in several classic studies, Joseph Schumpeter (1934, 1949) argued for an analytical framework that linked individuals to the institutional environments in which they were embedded.

6. DiMaggio and Powell (1983) articulated three pressures that lead to institutional isomorphism in the marketplace—mimesis, coercion, and norms. It is the first of these three that I am referring to here.

7. While these studies and others have been useful for understanding the social nature of economic action among firms, a common—and legitimate—critique of these studies relates to the lack of agency depicted in these theories (see, e.g., DiMaggio 1988). Guthrie and Roth (1999, p. 43) have noted, "While [institutional] theory has convincingly shown the importance of institutional environments for organizational strategies and structures, research in this area sometimes fails to emphasize the agency of economic actors in responding to their institutional environments."

8. The data upon which this chapter draws come from 155 in-depth interviews with officials, managers, and experts in China's transforming economy. Eighty-one of these interviews were conducted with the general managers of a random sample of 81 industrial organizations in four industrial sectors in Shanghai. For a complete report of the data and data-gathering methodology, see Guthrie (1999).

9. In some cases the new organization is set up on the factory grounds of the Chinese partner. Even in these cases, however, the new organization is a separate legal entity.

10. This effect is captured in the "employee ratio" variable. The variable increases in proportion to the number of retired workers the firm must support. Thus, the positive association here indicates that the greater the economic burden for the firm, measured through the size of the retired workforce the firm supports, the more likely the firm is, ceteris paribus, to reduce the number of benefits offered to its employees.

11. The dependent variable for this analysis is based on an additive index of the presence or absence of the following organizational structures (all of which are new to firms in the reform era): organizational rules, grievance procedures, mediation committees, job descriptions, workers' representative committees, promotion tests, and formal hiring procedures.

12. In many ways, firms at this level of the industrial hierarchy are proving to be much more successful in reform than those at other levels of the urban industrial economy. For example, my study suggests that firms under municipal companies have not only adopted the most extensive changes in intraorganizational structure, but they have also been the most productive in Shanghai's urban industrial economy (Guthrie 1999).

13. Government control of pricing began to change officially with general reforms in 1979 and then more specifically with the October 1984 Reform Declaration. Implementing a market pricing system may not have been a central part of the financial rationalizing system that was being promoted by Zhao Ziyang, but it was an important issue on the table for many years of the reform and often advocated by Zhao himself. The "price reformers" certainly saw the issue as crucial to the success of the reforms, and even if the "enterprise reformers" were antagonistic to the idea, the liberalization of prices was an issue central to the debates that raged between these two reform-minded groups. But progress on the issue was slow. By the end of 1984, factor prices were still unreformed, and product prices had not yet been realigned. For discussion of the 1984 Reform Declaration, the "price reformers" and "enterprise reformers," and the lack of reform by the end of 1984, see Naughton (1995, pp. 136, 188–96, 248).

14. It is interesting to note here the conception of competition in markets as a "problem." As I have discussed in other work (Guthrie 1999), many managers in

China's economic reforms are actually quite ambivalent about the emergence of markets in China.

15. The confusion over this issue comes from the focus on productivity as the primary indicator of reform. Scholars have mistakenly assumed that a lack of gains in productivity implies a lack of reform. The reality, however, is that even though firms at the upper levels of China's planned economy are not showing gains in productivity, they are among the most aggressive adopters of reforms.

Bibliography

Amihud, Y., and B. Lev. 1981. "Risk Reduction as a Managerial Motive for Conglomerate Mergers." *Bell Journal of Economics* 12: 605–17.

Barnard, Chester. 1968. *The Functions of the Executive.* Boston: Harvard University Press.

Begley, T.N., and D.P. Boyd. 1987a. "Psychological Characteristics Associated with Performance in Entrepreneurial Firms and Small Businesses." *Journal of Business Venturing* 2 (1): 79–93.

———. 1987b. "A Comparison of Entrepreneurs and Managers of Small Business Firms." *Journal of Management* 13: 99–108.

Bian, Yanjie, and John R. Logan. 1996. "Market Transition and the Persistence of Power: The Changing Stratification System in Urban China." *American Sociological Review* 61: 739–58.

Brockhaus, R.H. 1982. "The Psychology of the Entrepreneur." Pp. 39–56 in *Encyclopedia of Entrepreneurship*, edited by C. Kent, D.L. Sexton, and K.H. Vesper. Englewood Cliffs, NJ: Prentice Hall.

Brockhaus, R.H., and P.S. Horowitz. 1986. "The Psychology of the Entrepreneur." Pp. 25–48 in *The Art and Science of Entrepreneurship*, edited by D. Sexton and R. Smilor. Cambridge, MA: Ballinger.

Brockhaus, R.H., and R. Pohlman. 1987. "Entrepreneurship Research Populations: Who Are They?" Pp. 22–24 in *Frontiers in Entrepreneurship Research*, edited by R. Ronstadt, J. Hornaday, R. Peterson, and K.H. Vesper. Wellesley, MA: Babson College.

Burt, Ronald. 1992. *Structural Holes: The Social Structure of Competition.* Cambridge, MA: Harvard University Press.

Busenitz, Lowell, and Jay B. Barney. 1997. "Differences Between Entrepreneurs and Managers in Large Organizations: Biases and Heuristics in Strategic Decision-Making." *Journal of Business Venturing* 12: 9–30.

Carland, J.W., F. Hoy, W.R. Boulton, and J.A.C. Carland. 1984. "Differentiating Entrepreneurs from Small Business Owners: A Conceptualization." *Academy of Management Review* 19 (2): 354–59.

Cornwall, Jeffrey A., and Baron Perlman. 1990. *Organizational Entrepreneurship.* Homewood, IL: Richard Irwin Publishers.

Covin, J., and D. Slevin. 1988. "The Influence of Organization Structure on the Utility of an Entrepreneurial Top Management Style." *Journal of Management Studies* 25 (3): 217–34.

DiMaggio, Paul. 1988. "Interest and Agency in Institutional Theory." Pp. 3–22 in *Institutional Patterns and Organizations: Culture and Environment*, edited by Lynne Zucker. Cambridge: Ballinger.

DiMaggio, Paul, and Walter Powell. 1983. "The Iron Cage Revisited: Institutional Isomorphism and Collective Rationality in Organizational Fields." *American Sociological Review* 48: 147–61.

Dobbin, Frank, and John Sutton. 1998. "The Strength of a Weak State: The Rights Revolution and the Rise of Human Resources." *American Journal of Sociology* 104 (2): 441–76.

Dobbin, Frank, John R. Sutton, John W. Meyer, and W. Richard Scott. 1993. "Equal Opportunity Law and the Construction of Internal Labor Markets." *American Journal of Sociology* 99: 396–427.

Fagenson, Ellen A. 1993. "Personal Value Systems of Men and Women Entrepreneurs versus Managers." *Journal of Business Venturing* 8: 409–30.

Fligstein, Neil. 1990. *The Transformation of Corporate Control.* Cambridge, MA: Harvard University Press.

Geisler, Eliezer. 1993. "Middle Managers as Internal Corporate Entrepreneurs: An Unfolding Agenda." *INTERFACES* 23 (6): 52–63.

Ginsberg, A., and A. Buchholtz. 1989. "Are Entrepreneurs a Breed Apart? A Look at the Evidence." *Journal of General Management* 15 (2): 32–40.

Gold, Thomas B. 1989a. "Guerilla Interviewing among the Getihu." Pp. 175–92 in *Unofficial China: Popular Culture and Thought in the People's Republic,* edited by Perry Link, Richard Madsen, and Paul Pickowicz. Boulder, CO: Westview.

———. 1989b. "Urban Private Business in China." *Studies in Comparative Communism* 22 (2–3): 187–201.

———. 1990. "Urban Private Business and Social Change." Pp. 157–78 in *Chinese Society on the Eve of Tiananmen: The Impact of Reform,* edited by Deborah Davis and Ezra Vogel. Cambridge, MA: Harvard University Press.

———. 1991. "Urban Private Business and China's Reforms." Pp. 84–103 in *Reform and Reaction in Post-Mao China: The Road to Tiananmen,* edited by Richard Baum. New York: Routledge.

Granovetter, Mark. 1985. "Economic Action and Social Structure: The Problem of Embeddedness." *American Journal of Sociology* 91: 481–510.

Guthrie, Doug. 2000. "The Emergence of Market Practices in China's Economic Transition: Price Setting in Shanghai's Industrial Firms." In *Managing Organizational Change in Transition Economies,* edited by Daniel Denison. Mahwah, NJ: Lawrence Erlbaum Associates.

———. 1999. *Dragon in a Three-Piece Suit: The Emergence of Capitalism in China.* Princeton, NJ: Princeton University Press.

———. 1998a. "Organizational Uncertainty and Labor Contracts in China's Economic Transition." *Sociological Forum* 13(3): 457–94.

———. 1998b. "The Declining Significance of *Guanxi* in China's Economic Transition." *China Quarterly* 154: 31–62.

———. 1997. "Between Markets and Politics: Organizational Responses to Reform in China." *American Journal of Sociology* 102: 1258–1303.

———. 1996. "Organizational Action and Institutional Reforms in China's Economic Transition: A Comparison of Two Industries." *Research in the Sociology of Organizations* 14: 181–222.

Guthrie, Doug, and Louise Marie Roth. 1999. "The State, Courts, and Maternity Leave Policies in U.S. Organizations: Specifying Institutional Mechanisms." *American Sociological Review* 64 (1): 41–63.

Harwood, Paul. 1982. "A Psychological Assessment of Managers and Entrepreneurs," *Journal of Business Management* 5: 85–103.

Hofer, C., and D. Schendel. 1978. *Strategy Formulation: Analytical Concepts.* St. Paul: West.

Hsing, You-tien. 1998. *Making Capitalism in China: The Taiwan Connection.* New York: Oxford University Press.

Kaish, S., and B. Gilad. 1991. "Characteristics of Opportunities Searches of Entrepreneurs vs. Executives: Sources, Interests, and General Alertness." *Journal of Business Venturing* 6: 45–61.

Low, M.B., and I.C. MacMillan. 1988. "Entrepreneurship: Past Research and Future Challenges." *Journal of Management* 14: 139–62.

McGarth, R., I. MacMillan, and S. Scheinberg. 1992. "Elitists, Risk-Takers, and Rugged Individualists? An Exploratory Analysis of Cultural Differences Between Entrepreneurs and Non-Entrepreneurs." *Journal of Business Venturing* 7: 115–35.

Miner, John. 1990. "Entrepreneurs, High Growth Entrepreneurs, and Managers: Contrasting and Overlapping Motivational Patterns." *Journal of Business Venturing* 5: 221–34.

Naughton, Barry. 1995. *Growing Out of the Plan: Chinese Economic Reform, 1978– 1993.* New York: Cambridge University Press.

Nee, Victor. 1996. "The Emergence of a Market Society: Changing Mechanisms of Stratification in China." *American Journal of Sociology* 101: 908–49.

———. 1991. "Social Inequalities in Reforming State Socialism: Between Redistribution and Markets in China." *American Sociological Review* 56: 267–82.

———. 1989. "Theory of Market Transition: From Redistribution to Market in State Socialism." *American Sociological Review* 54 (5): 663–81.

———. 1985. "Peasant Household Individualism." Pp. 164–90 in *Chinese Rural Development: The Great Transformation,* edited by William Parish. Armonk, NY: M.E. Sharpe.

Ohe, Takeru, Shuji Honjo, and Ian MacMillan. 1990. "Japanese Entrepreneurs and Corporate Managers: A Comparison." *Journal of Business Venturing* 5: 163–76.

Parish, William L., and Ethan Michelson. 1996. "Politics and Markets: Dual Transformations." *American Journal of Sociology* 4: 1042–59.

Pearson, Margaret M. 1997. *China's New Business Elite: The Political Consequences of Economic Reform.* Berkeley: University of California Press.

Pettigrew, Andrew. 1973. *The Politics of Organizational Decision-Making.* London: Tavistock.

Pinochot, Gifford. 1985. *Intrapreneuring.* New York: Harper and Row.

———. 2000. *Intrapreneuring: Why You Don't Have to Leave the Corporation to Become an Entrepreneur.* New York: Berrett-Koehler.

Róna-Tas, Akos. 1994. "The First Shall Be Last? Entrepreneurship and Communist Cadres in the Transition from Socialism." *American Journal of Socialism* 100 (1): 40–69.

Schumpeter, Joseph A. 1934. *The Theory of Economic Development.* Translated by Redvers Opie. Cambridge, MA: Harvard University Press.

———. 1949. "Economic Theory and Entrepreneurial History." In *Essays on Entrepreneurs, Innovation, Business Cycles, and the Evolution of Capitalism,* edited by Richard Clemence.

Sexton, D., and N. Bowman-Upton. 1991. *Entrepreneurship: Creativity and Growth.* New York: Macmillan.

————. 1990. "Female and Male Entrepreneurs: Psychological Characteristics and Their Role in Gender Discrimination." *Journal of Business Venturing* 5: 29–36.

————. 1985. "The Entrepreneur: A Capable Executive and More." *Journal of Business Venturing* 1 (3): 129–40.

Shapero, Albert. 1985. *Managing Professional People: Understanding Creative Performance.* New York: Free Press.

Shi, Xianmin. 1993. "Beijing's Privately Owned Small Businesses: A Decade's Development." *Social Sciences in China* 114 (Spring): 153–64.

Sinetar, M. 1985. "Entrepreneurs, Chaos and Creativity: Can Creative People Really Survive Large Company Structure?" *Sloan Management Review* 26 (1): 57–62.

Siu, Helen. 1989. "Socialist Peddlers and Princes in a Chinese Market Town." *American Ethnologist* 16 (2): 196–212.

Stevenson, H. and D. Gumpert. 1985. "The Heart of Entrepreneurship." *Harvard Business Review* 63 (2): 85–94.

Szelenyi, Ivan. 1988. *Socialist Entrepreneurs: Embourgeoisement in Rural Hungary.* Madison: University of Wisconsin Press.

Unger, Jonathan. 1996. "Bridges: Private Business, the Chinese Government, and the Rise of New Associations." *China Quarterly* 147 (September): 795–819.

Unger, Jonathan, and Anita Chan. 1995. "China, Corporatism, and the East Asian Model." *Australian Journal of Chinese Affairs* 33 (January): 29–53.

Uzzi, Brian. 1996. "The Sources and Consequences of Embeddedness for the Economic Performance of Organizations: The Network Effect." *American Sociological Review* 61: 674–98.

Walder, Andrew G. 1996. "Markets and Inequality in Transitional Economies: Toward Testable Theories." *American Journal of Sociology* 4: 1060–73.

————. 1995a. "Local Governments as Industrial Firms: An Organizational Analysis of China's Transitional Economy." *American Journal of Sociology* 101: 263–301.

————. 1995b. "Career Mobility and the Communist Political Order." *American Sociological Review* 60: 309–28.

————. 1992. "Property Rights and Stratification in Socialist Redistributive Economies." *American Sociological Review* 57: 524–39.

Wank, David. 1999. *Commodifying Communism: Business, Trust, and Politics in a Chinese City.* New York: Cambridge University Press.

————. 1996. "The Institutional Process of Market Clientelism: *Guanxi* and Private Business in a South China City." *China Quarterly* (September): 820–38.

————. 1995b. "Bureaucratic Patronage and Private Business: Changing Networks of Power in Urban China." Pp. 153–83 in *The Waning of the Communist State: Economic Origins of Political Decline in China and Hungary,* edited by Andrew Walder. Berkeley: University of California Press.

White, Harrison C. 1981. "Where Do Markets Come from?" *American Journal of Sociology* 87: 517–47.

Wortman, M. 1987. "Entrepreneurship: An Interpreting Typology and Evaluation of the Empirical Research." *Journal of Management* 13 (3): 259–79.

Yang, Mayfair Mei-hui. 1989. "Between State and Society: The Construction of Corporateness in a Chinese Socialist Factory." *Australian Journal of Chinese Affairs* 22 (July): 31–60.

8

Entrepreneurial Strategies and the Structure of Transaction Costs in Russian Business

Vadim Radaev

Introduction

In this chapter I examine newly emerging Russian entrepreneurship from the standpoint of new institutionalist theory, according to which enterprise behavior is constrained and enabled by formal and informal institutions (Williamson 1985; North 1992). The operations of enterprises inevitably lead to positive (nonzero) transaction costs, which are distinct from the costs of production. Transaction costs include costs associated with:

1. Acquisition of property rights and access to resources
2. Evaluation of resources and specification of property rights
3. Preparation of contracts and contract enforcement
4. Protection of property rights
5. Collection of data and advertising

Main Assumptions

There are several widely shared assumptions regarding the role of transaction costs in entrepreneurial behavior and their specific character in post-communist societies.

1. Transaction costs are very high in emerging markets in post-communist economies.
2. A large portion of transaction costs results from extortion by officials and racketeers.
3. Minimization of transaction costs is the main criterion for entrepreneurial decisions.

4. State policy should be aimed at removing barriers and helping entrepreneurs to decrease transaction costs.

All of these assumptions are highly doubtful or at least seriously controversial. First, the structure rather than the level of transaction costs is most important, given that transaction costs are very diverse. Second, the structure of transaction costs in Russian business is basically distorted. Some of these costs are overblown while others are lower than we would expect. A large proportion of transaction costs in the formal economy were replaced by alternative costs in the informal economy. Third, many transaction costs do not necessarily result from extortion. Entrepreneurs pursue active strategies aimed to increase certain of these costs. Fourth, entrepreneurs are often driven by a variety of motives other than minimization of transaction costs. These include finding a new market niche, saving on production costs, establishing networks, and increasing private gain by managers. Fifth, policy for supporting entrepreneurship should stimulate reduced transaction costs in some areas and increased spending in others. I develop this argument by focusing on microrelationships among Russian entrepreneurs.

Measurement Problems

Statements that transaction costs are high or low in the Russian economy cannot be verified in this general formulation. These costs are difficult to calculate due to the following factors:

1. Many transaction costs are closely connected with shadowy dealings. Entrepreneurs may be reluctant to disclose the details of their double bookkeeping.
2. Some of these costs cannot be measured monetarily. For example, it is not easy to measure the cost of time wasted queuing to see officials.
3. It is often difficult to distinguish transaction and production costs. For instance, an entrepreneur can do a favor for an official by giving a job to his or her relative. Formally these transaction costs are reported as salaries.
4. Transaction cost is a very general term inclusive of many different elements. It is not reasonable to aggregate all of these elements.

Thus, we must be very cautious with any generalizations regarding transaction costs. It would be more correct to assess different elements of transaction costs on the microlevel.

Data Sources

Our analysis is based on data from two surveys, conducted from 1997 to 1998, of nonstate enterprise managers and entrepreneurs (we do not differentiate between entrepreneurs and managers in this study). These surveys, which especially focused on transaction costs, are based on a standardized survey of 227 entrepreneurs from twenty-one regions of Russia and a set of ninety-six in-depth interviews with entrepreneurs. The standardized questionnaires provide quantitative and quasi-quantitative data revealing the distribution of various phenomena, while the semistandardized interviews focus on detailed mechanisms of transaction arrangements. The surveys were conducted by the author in conjunction with a research team from the Center for Political Technologies (headed by I. Bunin). The U.S. Center for International Private Enterprise (CIPE) funded the research.

The Shadow Economy and the Virtual Economy

The business environment largely determines the character of transaction costs. I argue that the level and structure of transaction costs in Russia are largely determined by the squeezing of the economy between its shadow and virtual sides.

The shadow economy is defined as the set of economic activities that are not displayed in official reporting and/or formal contracting due to deliberate concealment or noncoverage in official statistics. The shadow economy results from:

1. Nonregistration of enterprises
2. Exclusion of transactions from official accounting books
3. Employment without formal labor contracts
4. Concealment of profits and revenues

In total, the shadow economy is estimated to comprise 20 to 40 percent of the Russian economy at the present. We can estimate the elements of the shadow economy using data from a survey conducted by the Russian Independent Institute of Social and Ethnic Studies in summer 1999 covering 1,200 small enterprises in nine regions of Russia. According to these data, there remain in the shadow:

1. 10–20% of small firms
2. 20–30% of sales
3. 25% of workers and employees
4. 30–35% of wages (Ne preuspet'–khotya by vyzhit' 1999).

The shadow economy is one part of the more inclusive informal economy. The other part of the informal economy is not hidden in the shadow, although it is closely connected with shadow segments. Recently a new term was coined to distinguish this sort of activity, that is, the *virtual economy*. It is defined as the set of activities that is displayed in formal agreements and accounting books but in a basically distorted way. The virtual economy includes the fictitious economy and the overvalued economy. In the fictitious economy, transactions are reported that are actually absent (for example, a money transfer is made for goods that are not delivered). In the overvalued economy, the price of goods in exchange is inflated in relation to consumer demand.

In the Soviet time, the shadow economy did not play a significant role, while the virtual economy was flourishing. The command system was targeted to fulfill administrative plans. Strong pressures on enterprises stimulated intentional overvaluation of output (*pripiski*). *Pripiski* was a widely spread instrument helping to meet requirements of the plan and thus secure additional resources and wage funds for both managers and workers.

In the post-Soviet era, there is no need for *pripiski*. The virtual economy is based on quite different principles and is closely connected with barter exchange and payment arrears, which originate from the lack of "live" money. The Soviet barter economy comprised only 2 to 6% of industrial output. In the post-communist economy, barter has reached 50 to 70% (for different estimates, see Makarov and Kleiner 1999, p. 82).

Theoretically, barter supplies should be discounted in relation to cash payment. But post-Soviet reality is different. Bartered goods are normally overvalued because the price of delivered goods is not constrained by the purchasing power of clients (Gaddy and Ickes 1999).

The outcome of barter and payment offsets is controversial. On the one hand, offsets solve at least a part of the problem of payment arrears. On the other hand, they provide a biased picture of the economic situation. First, a distorted signaling system leads to disorientation of economic agents. Second, overvalued prices include inflated wages and tax payments. Accumulation of virtual wages and taxes pushes the economy into further circuits of payment arrears.

Barter exchanges and offsets also result in significant transaction costs for intermediaries that arrange mutual payments. According to data of the Russian Federation Ministry of the Economy, these firms charge 10 to 20% of the recovered sum (Gritsenko 1999).

The virtual and shadow economies are closely interrelated. Overvaluation of goods is an instrument for arranging shadow payments. Normally, these functions are fulfilled by intermediaries and one-night firms specially

Table 8.1

Problems with Market Entry by Type of Enterprise (in percent)

	Type of enterprise	
	Privatized	Nonstate
Serious problems with registration and licensing	11	27
Bribe-taking for permits for economic activity	56	64

created for these purposes. The latter raise prices and convert surplus value into cash, which creates a source of shadow revenue. A portion of these revenues goes to managers who sign contracts as their commission (*otkat*). The burden of additional transaction and production costs is left to the enterprise or accumulated in further wage and tax arrears.

The shuttling of value between the shadow and virtual sides is an essential characteristic of the Russian economy today. This phenomenon structures transaction costs.

Now we turn to the entrepreneurial strategies pursued in such a complex environment. We consider relationships with controlling authorities, tax inspectors, business partners, and protection and consulting agencies.

Fees and Bribes

Market Entry

Administrative barriers present challenging problems for market entry. To start up a firm the entrepreneur is supposed to visit 25 to 30 agencies and sign from 50 to 90 formal documents. In total, the process could take 3 to 6 months (*Biznes dlya Vsekh* 1997, p. 2).

Official fees for bureaucratic services normally are not high. But procedures are time-consuming and complicated, creating fertile ground for bribe taking. In our survey, almost two-thirds of respondents claim that they must make additional nonofficial payments to acquire permits for economic activity (Table 8.1). This is more characteristic of new nonstate enterprises, especially those most recently established. Demand for bribes was reported more frequently by firms in wholesale trade (70%) and less frequently by firms in industrial production (56.5%), science, health care, and culture (50%).

Complicated formal procedures for market entry lead to significant informal transaction costs. The total transaction costs of market entry for a small enterprise are estimated at the level of US $1,500 to $2,000 when no sophisticated licensing is required.

Entrepreneurs can save a great deal of time and probably some money if they use commercial services. A large number of firms specialize in resolving problems of registration and licensing. In Moscow they charge from $300 to $700 for registration. Licensing costs may be much higher. As a result, increasing numbers of entrepreneurs use commercial services, paying simultaneously for:

1. Fees for the state
2. Bribes for officials
3. Commissions for intermediaries

It is remarkable that exit from the market may be even more complicated than market entry. Official closure of the enterprise presents a greater problem than initial registration. The entrepreneur is supposed to pass numerous checkups. And transaction costs are relatively high, about $1,000 for firm closure. In the end, many enterprises are simply left open with a zero payment balance to avoid difficulties.

Access to Premises

Acquiring premises presents one more barrier for the start-up (34% of surveyed entrepreneurs pointed to this problem). Rents did decrease after the 1998 crisis.

When we asked whether entrepreneurs needed to bribe officials to access premises, 22.5% answered affirmatively. Managers of firms in retailing, catering, and consumer services acknowledged a necessity to "stimulate" officials more often (32%). Those in science, health care, and culture follow (27%). Firms in construction, transportation, and communications face this issue less frequently (6%).

Space rental relationships are also deeply connected to the shadow economy, especially in the case of subleasing. While minimal payment rates are declared in formal contracts, more than 50% of rent is delivered in brown envelopes.

Administrative Inspections

Relations with officials do not cease after firm start-up. Officials conduct numerous spontaneous inspections. To evaluate the scale of administrative control, we asked entrepreneurs how often state authorities inspect their firms. According to the data, firms average two checkups per month, although variance is high. At one-fourth of enterprises these controlling visits are virtually

Table 8.2

Expenditures on Informal Business Services and Personal Experience of Bureaucratic Extortion (in percent)

Expenditures on informal business services	Bureaucratic extortion		
	Frequent	From time to time	Absent
Significant	33	13	8
Insignificant	48	52	37
Absent	19	35	55
Total	100	100	100

Table 8.3

Types of Payments for Bureaucratic Services

	Compulsory fees	Voluntary fees
Legal requests	Official registration	Additional services
Illegal requests	Legal barriers evasion	Individual privileges

absent, while for another fourth they take place weekly or even more often. A comparative survey of small shops in Moscow and Warsaw demonstrated that the rate of inspections in Russia was double that in Poland, that is, 18.5 vs. 9 checkups per year respectively (Frye and Shleifer 1997, p. 357).

Inspections are a playground for bureaucratic extortion. Two-thirds of our survey respondents report subjection to extortion in their day-to-day activities: 20% report that extortion happens frequently, 45% report that it happens from time to time, and 35% report that extortion does not happen. In turn, subjection to bureaucratic extortion is correlated with expenditures on "informal business services," which no doubt include bribes. This linkage is quite explicit in Table 8.2.

Bribes may vary from "small presents" of several hundred U.S. dollars up to 20% of a subsidy or contract provided by the official. These practices are certainly not confined to civil service relations. Commission payments to bank managers providing loans to enterprises are also widespread. Informal rewards can easily be 10% of the loan, and 21% of survey respondents claim that it is necessary to give bribes to get credit.

Types of Payment

Payments for bureaucratic services may be categorized as in Table 8.3.

First, there are official payments for formal services. Remarkably, some of these services have been commercialized. Authorities have a right to use "contract prices" for some of their services. Besides, they are able to impose services of affiliated commercial firms. For example, to get a permit the entrepreneur might have to pay for training courses at a training agency appointed by the authorities. Thus, official fees include some compulsory payments for "market" services.

Second, the civil servant charges informal fees for speeding up bureaucratic procedures. This payment is voluntary and leaves room for entrepreneurial choice. These fees are informal but not illegal in that legal rules are not violated.

Third, fees are charged for evading legal barriers. Here the civil servant ignores the violation of the law, and the bribe is compulsory.

Fourth, the entrepreneur gives bribes for additional services, which bring individual privileges and competitive advantages. Often it is not possible to receive a contract or to win in a tender without bribing corrupt officials. However, the entrepreneur chooses between official fees and bribes here.

Let us add that fees normally increase moving from the first to the fourth type of payment.

Business Strategies

Dependence on authorities' decisions leads entrepreneurs to corruption-like activity. However, these additional fees and bribes do not necessarily result from extortion. Apart from paying off bureaucrats, the entrepreneurs proactively and intensively network with officials. The larger one's business, the more one needs to affiliate with civil servants and to pay for their services. Apart from protection, entrepreneurs seek individual privileges and state contractual orders. Bribe taking is flourishing in the latter arena.

> "The main bribes are given for guaranteed sales. Not bribes for tax evasion, but bribes for getting contracts, are most important. It is fantastic to receive contracts which provide a stable, secured profit" (head of holding).
> "It is one thing when a bribe is offered for services which should have been done for free. It is completely different when the bribe is given to receive a big contract. The mechanism of bribing is most powerful here" (head of production enterprise).

Despite the fact that authorities monopolize the "market" for bureaucratic services, it is possible politically to avoid both administrative pressures and transaction costs for bureaucratic services. Political solutions presume informal patronage of the firm by a state institution or an influential civil servant.

"If everyone knows that some firm belongs or indirectly is connected with the interests of a high-level official . . . naturally there will be no check-ups, no police, no sanitary control" (head of firm dealing with the supply of fuel).

Political capital, including partnerships and friendships with decision makers, saves on production costs, for instance, receiving privileged rates for electricity. Tax payments could be converted into virtual offsets. Many administrative barriers may be removed. However, the entrepreneur cannot entirely avoid transaction costs because some mutual services are normally expected for such patronage.

In conclusion, transaction costs for market entry and dealings with authorities are high indeed. Bribes and forced commercial fees here supplement official payments. At the same time, many entrepreneurs deliberately increase some of these costs to gain competitive advantages and save on production costs.

Contract Enforcement and Business Networks

Traditional utilitarian economic theory presumes "legal centralism," or the existence of efficient legislative rules and relatively costless state and arbitration control over their implementation (Williamson 1985). The state as powerful neutral party punishes for violation of rules. The weakness of such an assumption is evident, especially in the Russian case, in which legal constraints on opportunistic behavior are obviously not developed. Thus, the enforcement of business contracts by economic agents on the ground level is principal.

Contract Infringement

The high probability of contract infringement creates risk and uncertainty in Russian business. According to our survey data, 82% of entrepreneurs report that they have been victims of such infringement in their own economic activity, and 32% of them have had this bad experience frequently.

Apart from immediate economic losses, infringement of business contracts produces distrust in business relationships, which, in turn, leads to transaction costs of three sorts:

1. Costs of collection of data on the reliability of business partners
2. Costs of having sanctions against opportunists
3. Opportunity costs connected with lost potential profit and inefficient allocation of resources

Table 8.4

Personal Experience of the Infringement of Contracts and Informal Expenditures of the Firm (in percent)

| Informal expenditures | Infringement of business contracts | | |
	Frequently	From time to time	Absent
Significant	27	9	7
Insignificant	46	48	40
Absent	27	43	53
Total	100	100	100

A large part of actual costs are informal. The linkages of "informal expenditures" of the enterprise to market failure caused by malfunctioning business partnerships are demonstrated in Table 8.4.

No formal contract is a panacea for market failure. First, the culture of formal business contracting is not highly developed in Russia. Second, formal agreements cannot cover all necessary issues and anticipate all possible factors. Third, having signed a contract, the entrepreneur still is by no means secure against opportunism.

"No doubt it is necessary to sign contracts in any case. But anyway, implementation of this contract depends on the person" (head of real estate firm).

Business Networks

Insofar as formal means of contract enforcement are not very effective, entrepreneurs investigate their potential partners thoroughly. However, data collection costs both time and money. Besides, even very detailed investigations cannot guarantee desired outcomes. Hence, contracts are largely enforced via personal business networks.

A business network can be defined as a stable and relatively closed set of interpersonal links between regular business partners. Russian businessmen have become more selective in dealing with other agents in recent years. The intention to stay within "your own" business circles excludes most newcomers. We have grounds to assume that these networks are playing an increasing role in Russian business (Radaev 2000a).

"We give goods on credit only to permanent clients. We would never give it to any others. . . . If you are making purchases you should deal with your own acquaintances. Otherwise, you have no guarantees. They will sell distorted goods to you" (head of a wholesale firm).

"It is vitally important to have permanent partners now. They are valuable not because they make payments on time, but because they are paying back in principle" (head of a firm selling fuel).

Business networks fulfill several interconnected functions, namely:

1. Serving as channels of confidential information
2. Forming business reputations
3. Establishing trust and decreasing uncertainty
4. Providing systems of mutual assistance
5. Arranging barter exchanges and mutual offsets

Some network effects were revealed in our survey data. For example, those who started up in a new area of business suffered considerably from the unreliability of partners. Being outsiders, they often lack necessary connections; therefore, their risk of failure is high.

Business networks are often not institutionalized in any formal way. Numerous business associations and unions exist in all regions of Russia. But they are not very influential. No statistical correlation was revealed between membership in these associations and the market situation of the firms.

Business networks lower the risks of dealing with strangers and save transaction costs on information. However, maintenance of the business network is not costless itself. Apart from presentation expenses, the entrepreneur is expected to provide privileges to long-term business partners individually. A majority of entrepreneurs do offer such privileges when signing and/or enforcing business contracts: 25% do so on a permanent basis, 57% from time to time, and 15% never offer such privileges. What are these privileges? They include:

Offering discounts on prices—55%
Not requiring prepayments—44%
Tolerating delays with payments—39%
Providing additional free services—30%
Providing goods and services of better quality—14%
Others—3%

Entrepreneurs provided even more substantial support to other agents in their networks. We asked whether they would lend a considerable sum of money to the firm of a regular partner who is confronting financial difficulties. Only one out of five entrepreneurs responded negatively. A majority would give a loan, although the conditions differ:

No-interest loan—27%
Low-interest loan—25%
Market-interest loan—3%
No loan—20%
Hard to say—25%

Managers of new nonstate firms and those active in the informal economy (who have significant "informal expenditures") are more inclined to provide this sort of informal financial support to their permanent partners.

In general, we would conclude that transaction costs spent on enforcement of formal contracts are largely replaced by the cost of supporting informal networks. This argument is further developed in the next section of the chapter.

Rule of Law and Rule of Force

In spite of all efforts, entrepreneurs are not able to prevent opportunism by their business partners. What sort of sanctions do the entrepreneurs apply to unreliable partners?

Negotiate with and persuade partners—55%
Address the arbitration court—24%
Try to use force—11%
Try to win back later—3%
Do nothing—4%

Private and Legal Enforcement

We see that informal negotiation is the main instrument of dispute settlement. The choice of negotiation rather than litigation is not a unique preference of Russian businessmen. For example, studies of business relations in the United States show that entrepreneurs tend to settle disputes without appealing to court. Lawsuits for breach of contract are rare, for suing a partner is considered a poor strategy (Macaulay 1992, pp. 273–274, 279). Still, differences are substantial. In developed Western countries, negotiations are based on latent references to existing legal codes. Even if actual sanctions are not taken, these references are a good basis for effective informal agreements. In the case of Russian business, references to legal sanctions are not so effective. In this sense, the rule of law is not well established.

One-fourth of surveyed businessmen welcome the idea of going to the arbitration court. Managers of older age and heads of privatized establishments choose this route more frequently than younger managers and heads of newly established businesses. Firms in construction and transportation are most active here. Attitudes toward obeying the law positively correlate with the appeals to court (we asked several separate questions on obedience to the law).

The number of formal appeals to court has tended to increase recently in Russia. Still, many entrepreneurs are reluctant to use the court. Why? Arbitration procedures are lengthy and expensive, costing from 1.5 to 5% of the disputed sum. Besides, there is no guarantee that justice will be enacted. There are many gaps and controversies in existing legislation that prevent the resolution of many disputes. And even if entrepreneurs win in court, their losses will not necessarily be recovered. According to one respondent, "It is worthwhile to appeal to the Arbitration Court only if you are dealing with a reputable business organization" (head of trading firm).

Apart from inefficient arbitration procedures and high expenses (especially for small enterprises), there are informal boundaries of customary law, which persuade entrepreneurs to solve delicate issues among themselves. This logic of negative solidarity counterposing "us" (businessmen) and "them" (authorities) is still influential. And formal appeals to the state are judged frequently on moral grounds as attempting to break someone down.

Attitudes toward cheating depend on the character of business networks. The firms involved in mutual financial support through an informal credit market would be less likely to start a lawsuit against business partners. The norm of negative solidarity is stronger here.

Interestingly, our findings partially coincide with the outcomes of another 1997 study of 328 Russian enterprises (Hendley et al. 1999). According to this study, 56% of enterprise heads prefer to hold meetings with their partners to prevent or resolve problems, while 25% of them would appeal to the arbitration court. This almost exactly corresponds with our data. K. Hendley and coauthors also asked another set of questions regarding the effectiveness of legal procedures. They claim that legal methods of enforcement are preferred to private methods, contradicting our conclusion. This difference can be explained by the prevalence of privatized enterprises (77%) in their sample, which tend to deal with the court more often than new private businesses. As mentioned earlier, in our survey managers of privatized establishments do appeal to the arbitration courts more frequently than managers in the new businesses.

Sanctions against cheating are connected with transaction costs. Enterprise heads with insignificant expenditures for business protection negotiate with their partners to settle disputes (65%). If expenditures on protection services are virtually absent, managers tend to go to the arbitration court. In turn, those who have more informal expenditures do not often appeal to arbitration bodies (12.5%).

Use of Violence

Given the frequent infringement of business contracts, entrepreneurs have to look for alternative ways to protect their property. Violence is an additional instrument for settling disputes.

The lack of security in business relationships is evident in post-communist Russia. About 40% of entrepreneurs in our survey claim that they have been subject to threats and force in their own economic activity. Thus, the rule of law is often replaced by the rule of force.

Use of threats and force results in additional transaction costs for the parties involved in coercive actions. Many firms are forced to pay legal and/or criminal agencies for protection services. These expenditures may include:

1. Wages of the enterprise's own security department
2. Fees for contractual services of security agencies
3. Fees for additional services associated with use of violence

In the first case, which is more appropriate for bigger companies, transaction costs of protection are transformed into production costs.

We asked entrepreneurs to evaluate their expenditures on business protection. More than half (53%) of our respondents declare that they do have such expenditures. Two-thirds of them consider these costs to be insignificant for their enterprises; for one-third the cost is significant. The level of expenditures not surprisingly correlates with the frequency of violence in business relations.

Statistical analysis also reveals that expenditures on business protection are normally connected with transaction costs for advertising (Table 8.5), since advertised businesses more frequently receive protection "offers."

There is a relatively developed market for protection services in Russia. About 11,000 security agencies were registered in Russia by the beginning of 1999. They employ nearly 160,000 licensed personnel having 71,000 registered guns (Andreyev 1999). Services include:

1. Protection of business and businessmen
2. Establishing control over transactions
3. Collecting data on business partners
4. Using connections to resolve administrative and business issues

To get these services, one has to establish connections with protection agencies. This is certainly easier for state-run and large businesses. Maintenance of these links is an important business strategy overall. The time of rack-

Table 8.5

Enterprise Expenditures on Business Protection and Advertising
(in percent)

Expenditures on business protection	Expenditures on advertising		
	Significant	Insignificant	Absent
Significant	36	11	2
Insignificant	33	40	29
Absent	31	49	69
Total	100	100	100

eteers has gone, with mere extortion supplanted by strategic alliances between business partners.

Apart from protection of life and property, private and semiprivate protection agencies actively enforce contracts. Protection agencies play the role of influential third parties to whom entrepreneurs delegate control over big transactions (*soprovozhdeniye sdelok*). This sort of forced control has become a necessary element of business life (Volkov 1999).

Security groups (both legal and criminal) provide additional special services. They are widely hired to deal with unreliable and dishonest partners, especially for recovering debts. Prices for these "services" are high: criminal groups (*bratv*) may demand half of recovered debt. Legal security agencies charge from 15 to 40% of the sum in question (Polianski 1996, p. 20).

Security agencies may suggest a complex of services for regular "insurance fees." For legal agencies, these fees may vary from $100 to $600, depending on the size of the firm and the range of services (Andreyev 1999). If security agencies are more seriously involved in business affairs, the transaction costs of business protection can constitute 10 to 15% of revenues and can be even higher in cases where security agencies invest their own capital into a business apart from regular protection services.

When being cheated, only 11% of entrepreneurs tend to use force and probably deal with criminal and semicriminal groups. But implicit references to force are made by a much wider group of businessmen. By and large, use of force has been integrated as a "normal" element of economic relations.

In conclusion, I would underline that private methods of contract enforcement prevail over legal methods. Entrepreneurs prefer to negotiate informally rather than appeal in court. Use of violence is yet another important instrument of contract enforcement. Resources for protection are not so frequently extorted at present. Rather, businesses and protection agencies build strategic alliances. Bigger companies having their own security departments convert these transaction costs into production ones.

Professional Services and Double Bookkeeping

Here we consider transaction costs for professional services, including business information, counseling, financial auditing, and legal advice.

Business Information

Some types of transaction costs are not high in Russian business. Business information is an example. Theoretically, no one would deny the importance of information in today's world. However, the majority of surveyed Russian entrepreneurs do not consider business information a vital need. Only 14% of respondents pointed to the lack of information as one of the most serious problems while starting up. Financial issues are a much greater concern.

Data collection requires additional expenditures. Sixty percent of enterprises have insignificant expenditures for searching for and purchasing information. Only one-fifth (22%) of entrepreneurs declare significant information costs. And for 18% of firms, such expenditures are virtually absent. Remarkably, new nonstate enterprises spend relatively more on data collection than privatized enterprises (24% and 13%, respectively, have significant expenses). Firms in finance and market services are more likely to claim significant expenditures of this sort (40%). Insignificant expenditures are more frequently declared in wholesale trade and industrial production (70% and 67% respectively). The enterprises in retailing, catering, and consumer services avoid these expenses more often than others (27%).

Representatives of development agencies complain that Russian entrepreneurs tend to ignore opportunities for data collection. They are also reluctant to pay for it. They have learned from the Soviet experience that material resources have a certain pecuniary value while information does not. The latter is largely collected via personal networks and therefore has no explicit price.

Business partners are widely used as sources of information by 88% of entrepreneurs (used frequently by 49%), especially by small firms and nonstate businesses. Professional consulting and information agencies are used by only half of entrepreneurs, and only one out of eight respondents uses them frequently.

In sum, Russian entrepreneurs prefer professional over public sources of data. At the same time, relatively cheap and confidential informal dissemination channels are more important than formal ones.

Legal and Auditing Services

A special type of transaction cost is connected with legal and auditing services. These services are important because Russian legislation is incom-

Table 8.6

Use of Financial Auditing and Legal Advice by Size of the Firm (in percent)

	Size of enterprise	
	Large and medium	Small
Attracting auditors		
On permanent basis	30	5
From time to time	28	22
No contacts	42	73
Attracting lawyers		
Full-time employment	60	7
Long-term agreement	10	10
Specific consultations	23	53
No contacts	6	30

plete, the taxation system is highly unstable, and accounting is sophisticated. Thus, a high demand for professional services would be expected. And demand for full-time, skilled accounting officers is high indeed. On the contrary, market services of freelancers and counseling firms are used less frequently. Only 10% of enterprises have significant expenditures for consulting firms and specialists hired on a short-term contractual basis. These costs are insignificant for 45% of respondents and absent for the remaining 45%. This indicator is the lowest among all types of transaction costs.

Businesses in finance are no doubt spending more on these issues. Such expenses are insignificant for enterprises in industrial production and wholesale trade. Firms with retailing, catering, and consumer services are more represented among those with no such expenditures.

Now let us consider financial auditing more specifically. How many entrepreneurs use these services for evaluation of their resources? Ten percent reported using these services regularly, 23% from time to time, and 67% never. As far as sectoral divisions are concerned, industrial producers invite auditing firms most often, followed by firms in retailing; catering and consumer services are most reluctant. Larger enterprises employ such services more often than small ones do (Table 8.6).

What does financial auditing cost? In 1997 the average charge was $50 to $100 per hour, varying from $15 to $20 per hour for smaller companies to $250 to $500 for the top six companies. Auditing within one week cost $4,000 on average (*Biznes dlya Vsekh* 1997, p. 15). After the 1998 crisis, prices decreased, but still they are considered unaffordable by many firms.

A similar situation is observed in the case of legal advice. On the one hand, three-fourths of enterprises have some legal support. On the other hand, only 10% of them have long-term contracts with lawyers. Eighteen percent of enterprises have hired full-time lawyers. Regarding external market services, enterprises normally do not ask for more than a one-time consultation. Large and medium-sized companies prefer to employ lawyers full-time, while small firms can afford only consultations on specific issues or do not have legal support at all.

In general, contractual relations with auditors and lawyers are not widespread. Why do entrepreneurs avoid these professional market services? Nearly one-quarter claimed that high prices for the services of lawyers and auditors (22% and 27% respectively) prevent the enterprise from using them. About one-tenth pointed to low quality of services (7% and 10% respectively). The majority of entrepreneurs (71% to 73%) prefer to cope with financial and legal issues themselves.

This "self-reliance" is rather controversial. Our interviews demonstrate that entrepreneurs are not able to resolve many issues on their own, leading to numerous mistakes and financial losses. There must be some hidden reasons for avoiding market services. In our opinion, the most serious reason is that the entrepreneurs are reluctant to share secrets of their double accounting and shadow business deals with external experts. Since many practice at least some elements of double bookkeeping, they fear being reported to tax inspectors or criminal groups.

Thus, low trust limits such transaction costs, which are converted to production costs if the firm has enough funds for it. Being involved in the double bookkeeping inherent to the shadow economy, businessmen prefer to hire their own staff rather than invite professionals on a short-term contractual basis.

Tax Payments and Commissions

Taxation policy is one more important element of the entrepreneurial environment. In all surveys, entrepreneurs bemoan the high taxation level and frequent changes in taxation policy in Russia. They respond rationally, inventing dozens of legal and illegal ways to avoid tax payments. Smaller firms simply evade payments. Larger enterprises bargain with regional or federal authorities over tax exemptions. As a result, an increasing number of tax payments are paid as mutual offsets and barter deliveries. Taxes become a part of the virtual economy.

Tax evasion is undoubtedly the most widespread example of shadow economy dealings at present, mentioned by 84% of entrepreneurs when answering an open-ended question. Ten percent of respondents also mentioned "other financial violations," which may be closely connected with tax issues. As a result, 25 to 40% of state budgeted tax payments remain uncollected. Directly concealed revenues account for 20% (according to the Russian Ministry of Finance estimates). According to Government Working Center for Economic Reform estimates, only 1 to 2% of enterprises formally record all transactions and pay all taxes (Glinkina 1997, p. 50).

In sum, everyone seems to attempt to avoid at least some tax payments, which is viewed as a "legitimate" practice both by entrepreneurs and by public opinion. There is a well-established view that it is absolutely impossible to pay all taxes without ruining the enterprise. More importantly, the actors are in fact allowed not to pay. However, the argument of a "weak state" that is not able to collect taxes does not explain this phenomenon. Formal claims of state officials on cash flows are replaced by informal ones. Taxes are replaced by informal services and bribes (Shleifer and Vishny 1993, pp. 602, 611–612).

Some methods for tax avoidance are encouraged by state agencies. These are not confined to "primitive" bribing of tax inspectors, although that does take place. According to specific rules of the game introduced by controlling bodies, entrepreneurs should:

1. Follow formal requirements and fill out accounting forms properly regardless of whether they have something to hide.
2. Compromise with the tax authorities. For instance, it would be reasonable to let inspectors disclose some minor distortions in the entrepreneur's balances and to collect small fines. This may help conceal much more serious violations and avoid more significant losses.
3. Establish good personal relationships with the tax officials and, thus, make them "less attentive" and more tolerant of occasional failures, which are almost unavoidable.

Tax evasion may be connected to significant transaction costs. For instance, one is supposed to pay 2 to 5% for acquiring cash (*obnalichivaniye*). This charge is as high as 10% in some regions. Rates depend on the scale of the transaction and the quality of services, that is, the level of risk and the destination of money. In spite of these costs, acquiring cash is highly beneficial economically, for one can avoid payments of 40% of the wage fund to the state-regulated funds. Some firms specialize in *obnalichivaniye*. They operate for three months and then are abandoned.

> "They establish a new firm which is to disappear in three months without taxation reporting . . . Large legal firms, being aware of all the details of our inconsistent legislation, are working on this . . . The regular chain is as

follows: Russian firm–Western firm. Money is transferred to the West. And everything is absolutely in accordance to laws. They charge from 2 to 5% for their services" (head of multiprofile firm).

A similar story is observed with customs payments for imported goods. According to State Customs Committee data, smuggling constitutes up to 30% of all imports to Russia. The scale of shadow transactions increased dramatically after the 1998 crisis. There are special, high-priced firms registered as official customs brokers, who charge, for example, $3,000 to $5,000 for a truck with twelve tons of cargo (Pianykh 1999). But the benefits of these shadow custom dealings are evident. They decrease the price of importing goods by 20 to 30% compared to official customs procedures, and up to 100% for some items (Dobrov et al. 1999).

When most economic agents do not pay taxes, the entrepreneur rationally decides not to pay them either. This practice creates additional transaction costs for illegal and semilegal commissions and bribes. However, these transaction costs help to maintain the competitiveness of the firm and generate private gain.

Conclusions

1. We have to be cautious in generalizing about transaction costs and assessing their general level. Transaction costs are very diverse, and some are not easily calculated. Thus, the structure rather than the level of transaction costs is most important. This structure in Russian business is basically distorted. Some types of transaction costs are very high, while others are relatively low.

2. The structure of transaction costs is determined by the complex, extensive mixture of the shadow and virtual economies. The shadow economy is the set of economic activities that are deliberately concealed or not covered by official statistics. The virtual economy includes reported but nonexistent transactions and transactions that are overvalued in relation to consumer demand.

3. Many transaction costs do not result from extortion. Entrepreneurs pursue active strategies aimed to increase certain of these costs to increase their competitive advantage and private gain.

4. Transaction costs of surmounting administrative barriers and dealing with regulatory bodies are high in Russian business. Bribes and forced commercial fees supplement official payments and fines. At the same time, many entrepreneurs deliberately increase some of these costs to gain competitive advantages and save on production costs.

5. Contract infringement is widespread in the post-communist economy. Entrepreneurs try to protect themselves from opportunistic actions by building relatively closed business networks, stable and relatively closed sets of interpersonal links among regular business partners based on a combination of formal control and exchange of informal services. These networks are increasingly significant in Russian business. Transaction costs for enforcement of formal contracts are largely replaced by the cost of supporting informal networks.

6. Given the inefficiency of arbitration courts and many firms' reluctance to use third parties to settle disputes, Russian entrepreneurs must elaborate their own horizontal means of contract enforcement. Entrepreneurs prefer informal negotiations to court appeals. Use of violence is another important instrument for contract enforcement. Businesses and protection agencies build strategic alliances. In sum, private methods of contract enforcement prevail over legal methods.

7. The need for business information is not considered a vital demand by the majority of Russian entrepreneurs. And transaction costs for collection of business data as a rule are not significant. Russian entrepreneurs prefer professional rather than public sources of data. Informal network channels for cheap and confidential information are more important than official and commercial sources.

8. Auditors and lawyers are not usually hired on a contractual basis. Apart from complaints about high charges and low quality of these services, there is a more serious reason for rejecting professional services. Entrepreneurs are reluctant to disclose the secrets of their double accounting and shadow business dealings to external experts. They try to avoid the risk of being reported to tax inspectors or criminal groups.

9. Given that the majority of peers do not pay taxes, the entrepreneur cannot afford paying them and stay in business. In turn, this creates additional transaction costs for illegal and semilegal commissions and bribes. However, the total costs of legal business transactions are often much higher than those of semilegal business. It raises a general and important issue of how strong incentives for legalization could be created when legality of business does not fully pay.

Bibliography

Alimova, T., et al. (1997), Kak reguliruyetsya razvitiye predprinimatelstva v Moskve [How Is Enterprise Development Regulated in Moscow], *Biznes dlya Vsekh*, No. 16–17, July, p. 5.
Andreyev, N. (1999), Okhrana i "krysha": kto obespechit biznesu zhizn' bez strakha

[Security and "Krysha": Who Will Provide Life Without Fear for Business], *Izvestiya*, 5 February, p. 5.

Biznes dlya Vsekh (1997), No. 26, December, pp. 2, 15.

Chepurenko A., et al. (1998), Malyi Biznes Posle Avgusta 1998 g.: Problemy, Tendentsii, Adaptatsionnye Vozmozhnosti [Small Business after August 1998: Problems, Trends, Adaptive Capacities], in: M.K. Gorshkov, A.Yu. Chepurenko, F.E. Sheregi (eds.), *Osennyi Krizis 1998 goda: Rossiiskoye obschestvo do i posle* (Autumn Crisis of 1998: Russian Society Before and After). Moscow: ROSSPEN, pp. 101–183.

Dobrov, D., K. Gorsky, and G. Pianykh (1999), Pristupit' k tamozhennoi ochistke [Start Customs Operations], *Kommersant-Dengi*, No. 15.

Frye, T., and A. Shleifer (1997), The Invisible Hand and the Grabbing Hand, *American Economic Review, Papers and Proceedings*, Vol. 87, No. 2, pp. 354–358.

Gaddy, C., and B. Ickes (1999), A Simple Four-Sector Model of Russia's "Virtual" Economy. http://econ.la.psu.edu/bickes/ickres.htm.

Glinkina, S. (1997), K voprosu o kriminalizatsii rossiiskoi ekonomiki [The Issue of Criminalization of the Russian Economy], *Politekonom*, No. 1, pp. 56–63.

Gritsenko, G. (1999), Esche odin zachet, esche odna popytka [One More Set-Off, One More Attempt], *Delovoi express*, No. 12.

Hendley, K., P. Murrel, and R. Ryterman (1999), Law Works in Russia: The Role of Legal Institutions in the Transactions of Russian Enterprises (manuscript).

Macaulay, S. (1992), Non-Contractual Relations in Business: A Preliminary Study, in: M. Granovetter, R. Swedberg (eds.), *The Sociology of Economic Life*. Boulder, CO: Westview Press, pp. 265–283.

Makarov, V., and G. Kleiner (1999), Barter v Rossii: Institutsionalny etap [Barter in Russia: Institutional Stage], *Voprosy Ekonomiki*, No. 4, pp. 79–101.

Ne preuspet'–khotya by vyzhit': Malyi biznes Rossii posle avgustovskogo obvala [Not to Prosper–Just to Survive: Small Business in Russia after the August Collapse], (1999), *Biznes dlya Vsekh*, No. 22–23, September, p. 7.

North, D.C. (1992), *Institutions, Institutional Change and Economic Performance.* Cambridge: Cambridge University Press.

Pianykh, G. (1999), Neispravimaya i legendarnaya [Uncorrected and Legendary], *Kommersant-Dengi*, No. 15.

Polianski, A. (1996), Vyshe kryshi [Above the "Roof"], *Expert*, No. 2.

Radaev, V. (1993), Emerging Russian Entrepreneurship As Viewed By the Experts, *Economic and Industrial Democracy*. London: Sage. Suppl. to Vol. 14, No. 4, pp. 55–77.

——— (1997), Practicing and Potential Entrepreneurs in Russia, *International Journal of Sociology*, Vol. 27, No. 3, pp. 15–50.

——— (1998a), Regional Entrepreneurship: The State of Small Business, in: *A Regional Approach to Industrial Restructuring in the Tomsk Region, Russian Federation*. Paris: Organization of Economic Co-Operation and Development Proceedings, pp. 275–319.

——— (1998b), *Formirovaniye novykh rossiiskikh rynkov: transaktsionnye izderzhki, formy kontrolya i delovaya etika* [Formation of New Russian Markets: Transaction Costs, Forms of Control and Business Ethics]. Moscow: Center for Political Technologies.

——— (1999), Rossiiskii biznes: Struktura transaktsionnykh izderzhek [Russian

Business: The Structure of Transaction Costs], *Obschestvennye Nauki i Sovremennost,* ´No. 6, pp. 5–19.

—— (2000a), Setevoi mir [Network World], *Expert*, No. 12, 27, March, pp. 34–37.

—— (2000b), Corruption and Violence in Russian Business in the Late 90s, in: A. Ledeneva and M. Kurkchiyan (eds.), *Economic Crime in Russia.* London: Kluwer Law International, pp. 63–82.

Shleifer, A., and R.W. Vishny (1993), Corruption, *Quarterly Journal of Economics,* Vol. 108, No. 3, pp. 599–617.

Volkov, V. (1999), Violent Entrepreneurship in Post-Communist Russia, *Europe-Asia Studies,* No. 5.

Williamson, O.E. (1985), *The Economic Institutions of Capitalism: Firms, Markets, Relational Contracting.* New York: Free Press.

Williamson O.E., and S. Masten (eds.) (1999), *The Economics of Transaction Costs.* Cheltenham: Edward Elgar.

9

The Embedded Politics of Entrepreneurship and Network Restructuring in East-Central Europe

Gerald A. McDermott

Since the decline of mass production models in the 1970s, scholars and policy makers alike have debated over the forces that promote the creation of new firms (i.e., entrepreneurship) and the contribution of small- and medium-sized firms (SMEs) to growth and innovation.[1] Some analysts focused on the individual entrepreneur as arbitrageur and advocated the importance of policies that promoted the free movement of resources and market competition. Others focused mainly on the characteristics of interfirm networks that promoted resource sharing and cooperation.[2]

The events of the last decade in East-Central Europe offer scholars and policy makers a unique opportunity to evaluate these arguments in two important ways. First, because of communism's adherence to the economies of scale model, for both political and economic reasons, and the virtual absence of the private sector and SMEs, economic renovation in the region is closely linked not only to the restructuring of inherited state firms but also the creation of new SMEs.[3] Second, but in sharp contrast to the reorganization of industries in advanced countries, economic transformation in East-Central Europe is also wedded to the wholesale creation of market-based and democratic institutions. Thus, the changes in East-Central Europe deepen previous debates on SMEs by linking firm creation to institutional creation: how do approaches to institutional creation impact the creation of firms?

This chapter theoretically and empirically explores this question in light of two major analytical traditions on firm creation and SMEs while offering a third, alternative approach. On the one hand, Kirznerian views of entrepreneurship are reflected in reform approaches that understand transformation as discontinuous change from communism to capitalism and advocate the rapid privatization and liberalization of the economy.[4] In these approaches, economic renovation hinges on the ability of private individuals with secure ownership and creditor rights to "read" clear price signals and become arbitrageurs to fill both market and institutional gaps. On the other hand, economic sociology views of entrepreneurship and innovation are reflected in reform approaches that emphasize the continuity of past social structures determining strategy and policy choices.[5] Firms remain embedded in old socioeconomic networks, which are the sources of trust and reciprocity that facilitate the flow of resources and information needed for the firm restructuring and creation. In this view, policy should be directed at preserving the relationships of networks.

While building on the views of economic sociology, this chapter attempts to offer an alternative understanding of firm and institutional creation that accounts for both continuity and change. The conceptual point of departure from both approaches is that firms and entrepreneurial activity are embedded in both social and political ties that link the necessary *reorganization* of networks with institutional change. In this view, industrial networks were politically constructed by distinct groups of firm and public actors to obtain resources and develop informal regimes of authority for the coordination of improvised routines under the uncertainties of shortage. Similar to the literature in economic sociology, this view understands change as evolutionary, where new firms largely emerge not from a tabula rasa but as part of the reorganization of networked assets. While interlinked assets curb individual discretion, the experimental process of asset reorganization also impedes cooperation via contractual methods. Yet this view departs from much of the economic sociology literature in understanding that existing networks only function in a specific, in this case previous, political-institutional context. Historical social bonds can fail as well to mediate change and conflict over asset reorganization since they are derived from previous political relations with public institutions that provided key resources and bases of network authority structures. In turn, the experimental process of asset reorganization extends to the simultaneous experimental process of creating new roles for public institutions.

To clarify the deficiencies in the aforementioned dominant approaches and the advantages of my alternative, *embedded politics* approach to firm and institutional creation, this chapter seeks to explain the stark differences between the Czech Republic (CR), Poland, and Hungary in terms of entrepreneurial performance during the last decade. The first section offers summary data on the differences between these countries, a critique of the two dominant approaches, and a brief review of an embedded politics approach. Despite their gradual approach to privatization, Poland and Hungary clearly outperform the CR in terms of industrial output growth and the creation of manufacturing SMEs. The next two sections then explore these arguments empirically, using network and institutional data from the two extreme cases, the CR and Poland. The upshot, as discussed in the conclusion, is that institutional experiments based on public actors becoming financial partners and conflict mediators enhance the ability of network actors to learn and monitor one another and thus experiment with new forms of organization. Poland facilitated such institutional experiments not only in the ways it approached the creation of market institutions, but also in the ways it decentralized power and resources to local and regional political actors.

Explaining the Divergence in Growth and Firm Creation

By the mid-1990s, the Czech Republic was viewed as the crowning success of the depoliticization model advanced by those who viewed transformation as one of epochal change—a leap from one complete set of organizing principles to another.[6] In this view, communist countries were essentially composed of a unified party-state hierarchy commanding atomized firms or individuals. During transformation, an insulated state alone can and should define and impose a new institutional order upon a tabula rasa of atomized, self-interested actors. Depoliticization is the ability of the state to eschew negotiations with economic actors about the initial institutional designs and their subsequent revisions by cutting off a powerful "change team" from society to impose rapidly a new set of rules that directly guide actors toward efficient resolution of restructuring conflicts.[7]

Three key factors enabled the Czechs to achieve depoliticization: optimal starting conditions, an autonomous, powerful change team, and policies for rapid liberalization and privatization.[8] Because of their orthodox political and economic policies, the Communists left the Czech Republic with a stable macroeconomy, low foreign debt, weak social and political groups, and a central government with virtually complete legal control of assets. A coalition led by Vaclav Klaus used these conditions to virtually eliminate the powers of regional and local governments and construct a strong policy apparatus that cut itself off from potential "rent seekers," such as parliament and special interest groups. In turn, the Czech government rapidly liberalized trade and most prices, enacted conservative monetary and fiscal policies, created bankruptcy laws based on liquidation of defaulting debtors, instituted a limited, rule-based, recapitalization of banks, and, above all, privatized over 1,800 firms and four of the five main banks in less than four years through its now famous voucher method.[9]

In contrast, Hungary and Poland were deficient in all three areas.[10] Policies of partial economic and political liberalization, particularly in the 1980s, left both countries with relatively large fiscal deficits and foreign debt and relatively strong social groups and competing political parties. These economic factors created multiple goals for privatization, such as maximizing sales revenues and maintaining employment, rather than simply keeping privatization focused on the rapid delineation of private ownership rights. The political factors allowed organized groups and parties to contend for policy control and enabled stakeholders, such as workers' councils, managers, and local governments, to intervene in, if not exercise veto rights over, the privatization of assets. The governments were then forced to include several potentially conflicting aims into privatization and banking policies as well as engage in the arduous task of reclaiming full control over assets in order to privatize them. In turn, Hungary and Poland experienced stop-and-go policies in privatization and the reforms of banking and commercial laws. For instance, between 1990 and 1995, Hungary underwent three reorganizations of its privatization agency and policy, three revisions of bankruptcy law, and a series of problematic bank bailouts. During the same period, Poland was unable to initiate mass privatization and dealt with large industrial firms and banks mainly through a complex, state-backed plan for the restructuring of bank debt.

The depoliticization agenda rests on two key premises regarding firm creation.[11] First, in its emphasis on speed and discontinuous change, the depoliticization agenda views the main social and institutional ties under communism as promoting cancerous bargaining between firm managers and central state officials. Optimal asset reorganization and firm creation can come about only when these ties are destroyed and the state is no longer permitted to enter into economic activities; otherwise prices and incentive will remain distorted. Second, mass privatization allows various claimants to assets to strike "efficient bargains" so that resources can be quickly directed to the enterprising investors. These bargains are typically the consolidation of control rights over assets and cash flows, the liquidation of loss makers and delinquent debtors, the breakup of large firms, and the creation of enforceable contracts for outsourcing and alliances.

These two premises echo common market-based understandings of entrepreneurship. First, the emphasis on destruction of past forms of economic organization is a strong reminder of conventional interpretations of Schumpeter that creation of the new can come only by first destroying the old.[12] Second, the importance of clear price signals and property rights for individuals to be able to create "efficient bargains" through secondary market arbitrage is in direct line with Kirzner's argument that equates wealth and firm creation with "the daring, imaginative, speculative actions of entrepreneurs who see opportunities for pure profit in conditions of disequilib-

Table 9.1

Divergence in Privatization

	Czech Republic	Hungary	Poland
% of GDP in private hands (1995)	70	60	60
% of industrial output in private hands (1995)	93	65	60

Sources: EBRD (1996), Pohl et al. (1997).

rium."[13] Indeed, this convergence of ideas between the two literatures may come as no surprise, as Dusan Triska and Tomas Jezek, the architects of Czech privatization, based their understanding of economic activity, like Kirzner, heavily on the work of von Mises and Hayek.[14] Triska and Jezek's philosophy served the Czechs well in receiving praise from both independent scholars and such organizations as the International Monetary Fund (IMF), World Bank, and the European Bank for Reconstruction and Development (EBRD).[15] As can be seen in Table 9.1, by 1995 the Czech adherence to depoliticization had allowed the country to race ahead of Poland and Hungary in the transfer of property from state to private hands, especially in industry. The Czech gains in private sector creation indeed boosted confidence in using the depoliticization model elsewhere, including Russia.[16]

A Closer Look at the Data

The eventual outcomes of these contrasting approaches to transformation, however, conflicted significantly with the expectations of the depoliticization model. First, it has now been well documented by both independent scholars and even the World Bank that Czech mass privatization did not facilitate firm restructuring and new firm formation.[17] Rather, the evidence shows that the combination of rapid delineation of private ownership rights and weak capital market and banking regulation created incentives for short-term gains through equity arbitrage in the secondary market and not for investment into corporate governance and reorganization. At best, the subsequent creation of dominant investment funds with cross-holdings in the main Czech banks led to mismanagement of assets, with financiers concerned about blocking outside investors and unwilling to bear the risks of leading corporate reorganizations. At worst, new Czech entrepreneurs manipulated lax rules on shareholder protection and public oversight to reap profits through insider trading schemes and asset stripping. Such actions not only impeded potential new firms from making productive use of existing assets and from gaining contracts, but also

Figure 9.1 **Industrial Production in the Czech Republic, Hungary, and Poland**

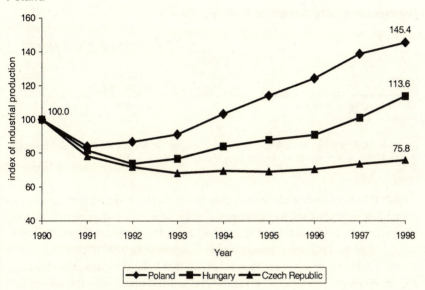

Source: OECD (1999) in Spicer et al. (2000).

thwarted the development of a capital market as a source of financing for both established and new firms. For instance, by 1998, no firm, old or new, used the Czech bourse to raise capital, while Poland saw a substantial rise in the liquidity and amount of capital raised in its bourse.[18]

Second, the divergence in the performance of financial entrepreneurs was matched by that of industrial entrepreneurs. Despite the rapid increase in private control over GDP and industry, the Czech Republic significantly lagged behind Hungary and Poland in the growth of both industrial output and manufacturing SMEs.[19] (See Figure 9.1 and Table 9.2.[20])

The two sets of evidence clearly present explanatory problems for the depoliticization approach to transformation and the Kiznerian view of entrepreneurship. The collapse of the Czech capital market, the strengthening of the Polish market, and the significant differences in industrial output and manufacturing SME growth undercut the argument that rapid state withdrawal from the economy and rapid delineation of property rights lead to growth and firm creation. One way to save the depoliticization approach is to argue that contrasting banking policies allowed Hungarian and Polish start-ups to have better access to bank credit than their Czech counterparts. Yet the existing evidence, particularly during the first half of the decade, shows that Czech SMEs and start-ups had relatively greater access to bank loans.[21]

Table 9.2

Divergence in SME Growth in Manufacturing

	Firms with Fewer than 250 Employees		
	Czech Republic (1995)	Hungary (1998, 1997)	Poland (1997)
Share of employment (%)	35	50.2	52.5
Share of sales (%)	29.5	37	37

Sources: Zemplinerova (1998), Polish Foundation for SME Promotion and Development (1999), and Institute for Small Business Development (1999).

Another way to save the tabula rasa understanding of transformation is to argue that firm creation has little to do with the existing state sector, as long as governments pursue strict fiscal and monetary policies, liberalize markets, and protect private property rights.[22] A good example of this view is the work of Johnson and Loveman, who argue that Poland's growth comes from the development of *de novo* private SMEs and not necessarily the reform and privatization of the existing state firms. *De novo* firms adapt relatively better and faster to the new conditions than existing state firms since they start from scratch and are smaller. That is, lacking the organizational baggage of existing firms and utilizing their relatively small size, *de novo* firms can quickly resolve the "complementarity" problem—the simultaneous reorganization of the strategy, structure, and compensation systems of a firm's operations.[23]

While it may be true that new, small firms have relative adaptability advantages over existing large firms, this argument becomes self-defeating. The basic problem is that in order to sustain the importance of clear property rights and mass privatization, Johnson and Loveman must argue that the development of new private firms has no connection to existing state firms, other than that the latter free up resources. First, this argument ultimately ignores the fact that Poland's government made significant interventions into the restructuring of the financial and industrial sectors and followed a gradualist path of transforming ownership, capital markets, and governance institutions. These actions not only violated rules of clear property rights and incentives but were also critical background conditions for the creation of new firms (see below). Second, Johnson and Loveman's own empirical evidence shows government assistance with debt reduction as key to the restructuring of transforming state firms and the importance of linkages between existing state firms and new private manufacturing firms as channels of sales, supplies, facilities, and personnel.[24]

The upshot is that one cannot explain dynamic new firm formation without understanding the linkages between the past and the present, the inherited state sector and the emerging private one, as sources of incubation and resources. Indeed, one of the few recent multicountry econometric analyses of *de novo* firms suggests this.[25] Moreover, even if one tries to base the relative performance differences on Poland and Hungary's former *second economies*, the research on this small private sector under communism clearly shows that it was intimately woven into the operations of state firms.[26]

Continuity and the Role of Socioeconomic Networks

Much of the work in economic sociology has focused on the importance of interfirm networks, as opposed to markets or hierarchies, in determining the ability of firms to adapt and innovate. In this view, the different structure, density, and strength of interfirm ties gauge the ability of firms to cooperate, access new information, maintain market positions, and innovate.[27]

The work of David Stark is the most prominent in extending the field into analysis of post-communist countries.[28] First, Stark was among the first scholars who showed that communist economies were less collections of atomized firms hierarchically commanded by the party state and more akin to constellations of firms embedded in a variety of horizontal and vertical social and economic ties that grew out of improvised responses to the uncertainties of the shortage environment. Second, he argues that after the collapse of communism, firms remained embedded in these ties, thus emphasizing the continuity of past socioeconomic structures. The reproduction of network ties not only promoted a diversity of experiments for firms to "recombine" assets but also provided them with norms of reciprocity and reliable channels of information and resources vital for generating and selecting restructuring strategies.

This approach is extremely useful in that it directs comparative analysis away from the use of idealized images of modern capitalism as benchmarks for reform to the use of midrange analytical categories that highlight the distinctive patterns of economic organization created within and across countries during transformation. Moreover, in demonstrating that the network, rather than the firm, was the unit of analysis, Stark reveals how old ties turn Johnson and Loveman's "complementarity" problem into an interfirm issue that links existing state firms to the creation of new firms. However, in his emphasis on the preservation of network relations and on the disconnection of the process of asset recombination from that of network reorganization, Stark reveals the limitations of economic sociology in explaining the divergence in growth and firm creation, and in general the relationship between firm creation and institutional transformation.

First, although Stark shows how networks can impact asset recombination, his emphasis on continuity overdetermines the ability of old ties to govern asset reorganization under new uncertainties in ways that lead to productive outcomes, rather than, say, to self-dealing or mismanagement. For instance, Stark argues that the Czech case is a prime example in which past informal network relationships were best preserved and formalized into sound governance institutions writ large by a responsive government. His evidence is the emergence of the complex interlocking ownership and financial links among the main Czech banks, their investment funds, and the overlapping portfolios of privatized state firms. In light of the evidence on Czech privatization discussed above—both the aggregate economic data as well as the virtual collapse of the Czech capital market—one must question whether the reproduction of old school ties is a sufficient mechanism for governing restructuring. Although the investment funds of the main Czech banks did not appear responsible for the most glaring cases of asset stripping, any vestiges of associationalism were apparently insufficient to help the banks and funds cooperate, select restructuring projects, and invest in the corporate governance of jointly controlled firms.[29]

Such empirical problems reveal a second, theoretical limitation to the work in economic sociology. In focusing on socioeconomic ties among firms, this approach is remarkably silent about how institutional change may interact directly with network reproduction, other than emphasizing institutional policies that preserve past network ties. For instance, Stark argues that reversals in Czech policies to partially suspend bankruptcy laws and to use public finances to net out chains of interfirm debt were positive recognitions of the importance of interfirm networks. Yet to what end? The evidence shows that the netting-out policy did little to lower debt and was canceled, since firms were unwilling to cooperate and fully reveal their liabilities.[30] Conversely, evidence that Polish SMEs use relatively high levels of interfirm credit and leasing arrangements, without creating unmanageable leverage, suggests that Polish policies have not only preserved but also reorganized intranetwork relations.[31] In turn, if past norms were insufficient to aid firms to cooperate over restructuring and debt reduction, then either the inherited network relationships had been altered in some significant way or they lacked qualities in and of themselves to help firms adjust to the new uncertainties. In either case, one would have to surmise that institutional factors can have a direct impact on the ability of networks to alter themselves and on the ways network actors select a set of restructuring strategies over another. But this would lead one to move beyond the purview of economic sociology, since conventional network analysis largely ignores changes in networks and does not integrate institutional-political factors into its understanding of the origins of interfirm networks.

An Embedded Politics Approach

The alternative, embedded politics approach advanced in this paper attempts to identify factors that continue to shape and constrain firm strategy, such as economic and social links that tie actors to common assets, as well as factors that can alter the structure and cohesion of inherited networks, such as specific institutional supports for networks. This approach departs, then, from conventional network analysis in understanding that firms are embedded in sociopolitical networks that are constructed and reconstructed by specific firms and public actors under different political-economic regimes. By clarifying the factors that shape the movement from one equilibrium to another, one can begin to specify the conditions that promote or impede firm formation in post-communist countries.

The basis for advancing an embedded politics approach to entrepreneurship in postcommunism is twofold. First, there is increasing evidence from a variety of East European countries that industrial networks include not just firms but also regional bank and party council officials.[32] For instance, my own research has shown that even in the relatively orthodox communist Czechoslovakia, planning experiments allowed midlevel institutions, such as industrial associations (VHJs) and regional councils, to take on greater decision-making rights over, respectively, production and the provision of social-welfare services.[33] Distinct patterns of industrial networks grew around different VHJs. Constituent suppliers, customers, managers, and work groups formed alliances with local state bank branches and party councils to gain privileges from the state center and create informal channels of coordination to adjust to the uncertainties of the shortage economy. These alliances solidified the network authority structure, since they were sources of political and financial risk sharing to limit central intervention and facilitate the autarky and improvisation needed to adapt to an ineffective institutional structure.

Second, much of the research on the importance of interfirm networks in advanced industrialized countries came out of the work on industrial districts.[34] This research emphasized not only the determining influence of different network characteristics on firm behavior but also the political-institutional architecture that was interwoven with interfirm relationships.

In the embedded politics approach, a key variable is power. The power a firm or plant may have over assets and the creation of formal and informal rules of interfirm relations is derived not only from one's position in the value-chain, such as a critical supplier or purchaser, but also from the strength of one's ties to local public actors, such as bank and party-council officials during communism. A network may be more hierarchical or more egalitarian, depending on the mix of these two factors. This understanding of the construction of the authority structures of economic networks becomes critical for post-communist restructuring in two ways.

First, alterations in the authority structure of a network emerge from both changes in the economic environment, like the relative importance of a particular product, and changes in the political-institutional environment, like privatization rules, financial regulations, and public sector reforms. Under new uncertainties, interdependent firms may be unable to cooperate over the reorganization of common assets, since the ability of one member to impose its will on or give reliable guarantees of compensation to another member depends not only on the risk associated with the investment and the historical bonds between them but also on the support of public actors who may be no longer available. For instance, in the Czech Republic, firms often lost their authority and access to resources when the centralization of policy-making power virtually eliminated regional and local councils and when the rapid privatization of banks and the new financial regulations gave the banks little incentive to finance restructuring.

Second, in linking institutional and asset-reorganization experiments, the approach can clarify the conditions that promote cooperation and lead to dynamic firm creation. As suggested already by my discourse, the recombination of network assets is an iterative negotiating process at two levels: the selection of restructuring projects and the creation of rules (formal or informal) about monitoring one another. Akin to workouts, this process is fraught with questions of how risk is shared and how the process is governed. The history of Western capitalism has shown that workouts for both financial institutions and firms demand that public actors share some of this risk and adjudicate conflicts over the control of assets and liabilities.[35] This history has also shown that the creation of institutions to facilitate workouts, be they directed by a central bank, a ministry, or the courts, has been an experimental one, in which public and private actors enact one set of rules, analyze the results, and reform the existing rules. In turn, the restructuring of existing networks that lead to growth and firm formation in East-Central Europe will depend largely on both the ability of public actors to become risk sharers and conflict mediators and the ability of the political system to allow public actors to experiment and learn to take on these new roles.

The rest of this chapter will empirically illustrate this argument, by applying this approach first to analyze the fragmentation and demise of a potentially prosperous Czech machine-tool network and then to analyze the respective political-institutional conditions that facilitated network restructuring and firm creation in Poland. Although the data presented here, particularly with respect to the latter cases, is somewhat incomplete, the evidence suggests that Polish growth was due to two key factors: the initiation of policies that allowed public and private actors to engage jointly in the gradual reorganization of assets and policies that fostered the participation of local public actors in restructuring. Rather than drawing bright lines between the public and the private, between the center and the periphery, such policies understood restructuring as a negotiated process, in which rules of participation helped public and private actors share information and learn how to monitor each other's use of common assets.

The Fragmentation of Old Ties

Czech machine tool firms form a vital part of the country's machinery and equipment sector, which was the engine of industry for Czechoslovakia and the Austro-Hungarian Empire and which continued even during the decline of the 1990s to account for the largest share of manufacturing employment and the second largest share of manufacturing value added in the CR.[36] The Czech firms were also the premier machine tool suppliers within the Communist bloc trade regime (CMEA) and among the top eight nations in machine tool production in the world for much of the post-World War II period.[37] Since the mid-1970s, scholars have viewed the machine tool industry worldwide as a paradigmatic example of SME creation and flexible specialization.[38] With their decades of experience and skill, Czech machine tool firms were poised to join this trend in 1990. Moreover, the traits of the network of these firms and their embrace of rapid privatization pointed in their favor.

First, by 1990 the machine tool industry was already organized into many legally independent firms, as opposed to a few large, vertically integrated firms as were common in other branches.[39] During communism, the VHJ known as TST managed the large majority of firms and plants that produced machine tools and many of their key components. By the late 1980s, TST had over twenty firms, comprising about 30,000 employees and a rather broad production profile of machines and components. When Czechoslovakia dissolved the VHJ system in 1987–88, TST members (including many plants) chose to become legally independent state firms. This movement toward deconcentration grew out of TST's polycentric network, which possessed many qualities associated with networks that facilitate the transfer of tacit knowledge, flexibility, and access to new information and resources.[40] (See Figure 9.2.) Structurally, there were several central firms that worked with the directorate on a consensual basis, and members had retained considerable decision-making powers and independent financial accounts. Relationally, although members had a deep history of overlapping, direct social and professional ties, they were usually horizontally associated with limited direct operational links and had often generated their own links out-

Figure 9.2 **Polycentric Network (e.g., TST VHJ)**

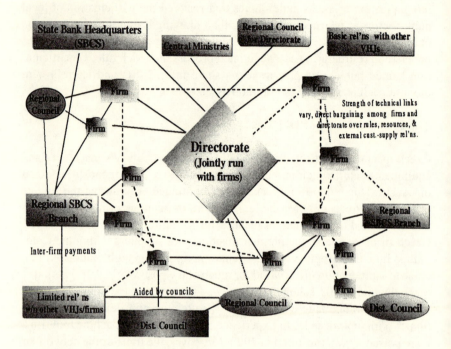

Source: McDermott (2002)
Note: Solid, bold lines denote relatively stronger channels of communication and coordination; broken and light lines denote relatively weaker channels.

side of TST. For instance, a TST firm typically focused on a certain class of machines, had several plants, and produced over 80 percent of its inputs in-house. While parts like hydraulics, pneumatics, and ball bearings, as well as specific metal castings, came from other members, the firms acquired certain electronic components from other VHJs jointly via the TST directorate or directly, depending on the quality of their local professional linkages. A key reason for the development of this polycentric network with its combination of rich social ties and potential "brokerage" opportunities for members[41] was that most member firms developed direct links to regional bank branches and regional/district administrative–Communist Party councils. These linkages aided firms in managing interfirm debts, mediated delivery disputes with non-TST firms in the region, and were sources of countervailing bargaining power vis-à-vis one another, the TST directorate, and the central state ministries.

Second, in 1990 and 1991 and in the face of the dissolution of regional councils, the weakening of local councils, strict banking laws, and rapid privatization, the ex-TST firms took advantage of their network structure by embracing privatization, spinning off new firms, and grafting indirect equity alliances onto their inherited social ties. The firms and plants entered privatization individually (mostly via vouchers). In 1991, ex-TST firms had already broken themselves up into forty firms, with the six largest allowing their plants to operate as semiautonomous profit centers and prepare themselves for eventual spin-offs. At the same time, ex-TST firms sought to balance individual autonomy with group cohesion by bolstering past professional ties with new equity and financial ones. In particular, members sought to combine social and equity links help manage areas in which they lacked individual resources and know-how, such as in foreign trade, common trademarks, critical supplies, vocational training, and development loans. They converted the former TST directorate into the support headquarters of a new machine tool association, SST, in which each firm was an owner. SST, in turn, used its historical ties to actors in the trade and financial sectors to take a 30 to 40 percent equity stake in one of the major trade houses, Strojimport, and build an alliance with members of the foreign trade financial group, FINOP, and the Czech Republic's main trade bank, CSOB. With FINOP, and CSOB, SST created a new private bank, Banka Bohemia, and an equity investment company, ISB, whose engineering fund bought strategic stakes in SST member firms and important suppliers/customers.[42] The result of this elaborate equity and financial alliance can be seen in Figure 9.3. Member firms would renew past direct ties with one another and have a collective brokerage link outside the group via SST. While member firms owned SST, SST ran the boards of Strojimport and the engineering fund, provided strategic information to its members, and aided members in negotiations with banks, notably via Banka Bohemia.

By mid-1996, however, the industry had fragmented into insolvency. The attempt by SST members to preserve their past social relationships, reinforce them with new governance mechanisms of equity and contracts, and also replace past public external partners with new private financial ones did little to promote cooperation and restructuring.

First, the uncertainties of new production experiments demanded a reorganization of existing network ties and undermined the cooperation between member firms. As each firm began to experiment with new products or alterations of existing ones, they turned to one another for the development or subcontracting of certain components and the cost sharing of exporting and importing (especially for computer numerically controlled [CNC] electronics). Since these

Figure 9.3 Network Ties in the Czech Machine Tool Industry

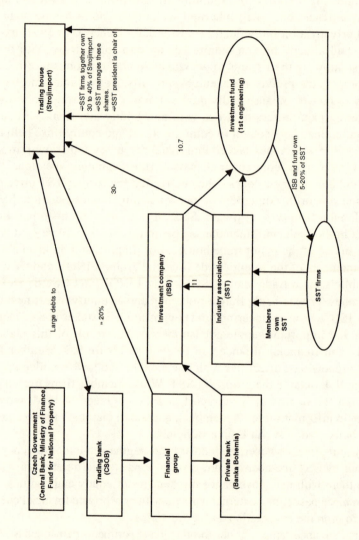

Note: Direction of arrow denotes direction of ownership. Percentages denote ownership share.

experiments were highly uncertain and often conflicted with one another, no firm could give the guarantees to the others to forgo their own plans and invest in those of the solicitor. For instance, with the collapse of trade in the CMEA and the domestic recession, SST firms sought new market niches based on short pilot production runs. Even when the solicitor demonstrated that the trial runs were for a credible international client, these runs were often too short and had too poorly defined future revenue streams to instill confidence in other members to prioritize their own component production for the given project. Experimentation had also led member firms often to encroach on one another's product lines in such a way that firms feared that collaboration would undermine individual export revenues.[43]

Secondly, the supporting equity alliances failed to provide needed financing to overcome the hold-up problems among members. As one of the five main Czech banks, CSOB was the critical financial link in the alliance. Yet the collapse of CMEA trade left CSOB and Strojimport with a large stock of nonperforming credits and weak capital bases. CSOB, in turn, refused to initiate the restructuring of Strojimport and provide credit lines to Banka Bohemia and SST firms. A typical option would be the use of institutional workout mechanisms, in which public actors share some of the risks and create rules for the multiple parties to assets to negotiate iteratively over the restructuring of both operations and financing. Czech transformation policy eliminated any role for extended participation by public actors and any mechanism for joint management of assets, other than voluntary contracts. For instance, bank restructuring was reduced to a one-time, partial recapitalization and debt removal, leaving banks on their own to deal with troubled firms. Bankruptcy was reduced to a fast track to liquidation, which has now been well documented to be ineffective.[44] Given the tight interdependencies between the banks and industrial firms, the big Czech banks found it too risky to lead bankruptcies or restructuring, and SST firms languished. Indeed, in 1994, four of the five largest *de novo* banks, including Banka Bohemia, were seized by regulators and closed.

Neither the old social relationships among firms nor the new equity alliances with financial and trade organizations were sufficient to provide credible structures for negotiated management of claims to common assets, be they production plants or import-export ventures. The next best option for a firm is to forgo collaboration, vertically integrate needed assets, and, ultimately, resort to financial manipulation. This scenario reached even the most successful SST firm, ZPS.

Between 1992 and 1995, ZPS more than doubled its total sales and exports. The firm penetrated new export markets for final products, such as redesigned horizontal machining centers and multispindle lathes, as well as for semifinished goods, such as steel castings and pallet exchangers.[45] A key factor in ZPS's success was its ability to renew its own local sociopolitical network and use it to build new channels of financing and export contacts. In contrast to other SST firms, ZPS did not discard civic-social assets (health clinic, power station, apartments, community center) that the Communists had typically put on the books and sites of firms. Rather, ZPS comanaged and cofinanced them with the local government and entrepreneurs. Coupled with the management's active participation in the country's "velvet revolution," these actions afforded ZPS significant social and political capital in the Zlin district, which it converted to socioeconomic capital. For instance, ZPS gained financing from employees and local citizens in 1991–92 when other firms had little via a company-based credit union and a locally placed bond issue. Also, employee shares and a community voucher fund together held about 20 percent of equity in ZPS, over which management had de facto control. From this base, ZPS management cultivated a network of local and foreign entrepreneurs who were former ZPS or big bank employees. This network opened up new export markets to ZPS and helped create a set of allied, medium-sized investment funds and banks that channeled strategic information and financing to ZPS. To sustain the growth and increase the revenue streams from its component plants, the heavily leveraged ZPS had originally planned to gradually spin off upstream operations and utilize other SST firms for more areas of subcontracting. Yet, as SST relationships fragmented and firms bordered on default, ZPS found it too risky to engage in such a strategy.[46] Instead, ZPS sought to acquire other SST firms by mid-1995. The question, of course, was how it would obtain control of the other firms, given that the big five Czech banks and the dominant investment funds had proven useless as sources of direct financing.

The answer is that a well-placed network can be used for self-dealing and domination as easily as it can be used for collaborative production. And when there are no institutions to help actors extend the time horizons and reformulate their methods of mutual monitoring and project selection through joint deliberation, the former strategy is optimal. ZPS and its local allies, in turn, used their elaborate network of new small banks and investment funds to channel financing from the banks' depositors and a poorly monitored state insurance company to ZPS, to gain strategic control of ZPS shares, and to manipulate share prices of ZPS and other companies. At the same time, ZPS sought to control the SST board and the engineering investment fund mentioned above. With its new finances, manipulation of share prices, and influence over SST's fund, ZPS management orchestrated a series of takeovers of several of the fledgling SST member firms. The idea was that continued refinancing of existing debt and potential income streams as an oligopolist would reduce its leverage over time. This scheme came crashing down in late 1996 when two of ZPS's allied banks went insolvent and regulators seized the insurance company because its weakness threatened the stability of the financial system.

In many respects, the inability of private contractual and ownership methods to resolve the holdup and collective action problems is well known already in the work on uncertainty, incomplete markets, and common asset management.[47] But much of this literature also argues that the first steps toward collaboration would often depend on preexisting social structures and a patterned history of mutual exchange.[48] Clearly, this shift in the literature opens the door for the continuity approaches to transformation that stress the importance of the reproduction of past social capital and certain interfirm network structures as determinants of collaboration and performance. Yet despite the structural and relational qualities of the SST network and the conscious efforts by members to fortify them, SST firms came to view one another as competitors. Neither the old school ties nor positions on the various boards were sufficient to convince assumed financial and trade allies to divert dwindling resources to the SST firms.

One can begin to make sense of the failure of past social relations and equity ties to mediate the disputes among SST firms if one integrates political and institutional constructs into the definition of social capital and networks. As depicted in Figure 9.2, the alliances that TST firms had with regional and district administrative councils and bank branches were key sources of mediation and authority that supported the polycentric network. While the council and branches collaborated with relevant firms to provide resources and coordinate economic activity, they also provided countervailing power vis-à-vis other strong member firms and the directorate of TST. In this view, the political and financial capital of councils, for instance, helped allied firms not only to engage in strategies of forced substitution and autarky but also to maintain the firms' level of autonomy and influence in bargaining within TST. The Czech agenda of depoliticization altered this equilibrium in three fundamental ways.

First, bent on centralizing power, the central government not only cut off regular communication with firms but also literally and figuratively eliminated traditional external partners of the firms—the local governments. Second, the agenda offered firms only a few private actors with existing resources as new external allies. Third, the agenda offered no framework for public support of extended multiparty negotiations for asset recombination, be it through a workout mechanism or through regional development initiatives.

On the one hand, the limited number of potential allies shifted the authority structure of SST's network. Whereas previously the polycentric structure and quasi-brokerage positions of various members emanated from ties to district and regional bank branches and councils, after 1990, as shown in Figure 9.2, the new alliances with banks and trade companies were concentrated via the SST directorate. The effectiveness of these new alliances depended in part on a level of cooperation and confluence of interests among SST firms that had existed only when firms had their own bases of resources and political leverage via, notably, the councils. On the other hand, the new external allies alone lacked the political and financial capital to credibly mediate intra-SST disputes and share risk with these firms—and thus reconstruct the social ties and authority structure of the network. The only institutional means available were voluntary contracts, liquidation, and poorly regulated investment funds. As already mentioned, the combination of uncertainty and interdependencies between banks and industrial firms made bank-led restructuring too risky. Rather, banks and their funds minimized investment in corporate governance and focused on arbitrage activities in the secondary equity markets. In turn, SST relations fragmented and new resources were unavailable for spin-offs or start-ups in the industry.[49]

To a certain degree, one can interpret ZPS actions as generated from its advantageous "brokerage" position and capital, which emerged via ZPS's conscious efforts to rebuild and convert its own local sociopolitical network into a source of sales and financing. These actions were sufficient for ZPS to restructure itself and begin new lines of potentially lucrative products. Brokerage, however, is a two-way profession and depends still on the integration of supporting public institutions. On the one hand, the broker needs a reasonably stable core network (SST) to put existing assets and information to new uses without taking full responsibility for them. On the other hand, as the core network collapses and total control becomes paramount to the broker's entrepreneurial aspirations, the broker (ZPS) demands ever more resources to consolidate its position (and avoid default). Local public actors could no longer participate, as they lacked resources and a political framework to coordinate actions with other SST localities or the central ministries. Moreover, without institutionalized mechanisms to encourage existing financiers to share the risk in the broker's consolidation, the broker's private allies must mirror the broker's domination strategy to capture any available financial resources. For ZPS's allies, this meant a short-term strategy of manipulating the values of their own investment portfolios and for ZPS to gain debt-finance via their own banks and the Czech insurance company. Notice that the brokerage strategy ends in a domination strategy—of both the broker's former core network and its financial channels—when there are no adequate institutions to facilitate extended negotiation and multiparty risk sharing. Ultimately, the incentives lead to systemic failure, when the state can no longer ignore the damage. Creditors seized the banks of the allies and the Czech insurance company, and ZPS was forced to enter a new state-administered restructuring agency in 1999.

Enabling Restructuring and Institutional Experiments in Poland

The Czech failures suggest that asset recombination between interlinked parties forces two levels of experimentation—with the reorganization of the network and with new roles for public actors, particularly at the regional levels. First, the reorganization of the network challenges the existing authority structure and its existing terms of cooperation. Restructuring can advance then with institutional mechanisms that facilitate extended multiparty deliberations—deliberations that may at first explore and select new projects but, in turn, generate new modes of mutual monitoring and asset control. Second, because public actors are integral to existing networks and tend to be vital players in such deliberations elsewhere in the world, network reorganization is intimately linked to the exploration of new roles for public actors. As with differences between "law on the books" and "law in practice," the definition and enforcement of institutional mechanisms is as much about power and resources as it is about the trial-and-error process.[50] In turn, the development of any institutional mechanisms promoting multiparty deliberations will demand not only government initiative but also the delegation of, at least, powers for different public actors to experiment with new roles and define what a new policy, law, or whole institutional framework may become.

The Polish approach to transformation has contrasted sharply with the Czech approach on both of these levels of experimentation. The Poles created mechanisms that enabled stakeholders and outsiders as well as public and private actors to negotiate over time the reorganization of assets and the redefinition of property rights. First, rather than focus on rapid mass privatization, the Poles created legal vehicles that tied ownership transformation to the restructuring of assets. Second, central, regional, and local governments played significant roles in initiating, financially supporting, and monitoring the negotiated transformation of property rights and the restructuring of assets—for both large and small firms.

In short, one can explain relative strength in Polish industrial growth and manufacturing SMEs by a set of policies that helped network actors to reorganize their overlapping claims to assets over time. These policies had two key traits. First, while private property rights remained blurred, the government, at all three levels, delegated public authority for asset restructuring to private actors. This authority was linked to a set of rules and incentives to induce monitoring via continuous, multiparty deliberations over experiments with reassignments of asset control and use. Second, the use of government political and financial capital helped not only to initiate the reorganizational process but also to maintain it, since the capital enabled resources to continue flowing from large, state firms to smaller spin-offs and *de novo* ones. Together the two traits resemble the main properties of workout vehicles found in advanced industrialized countries: breathing space for the parties to assets to experiment with reorganization projects and rules that promoted mutual monitoring through iterative, disciplined negotiations. The rest of this chapter examines these different policies in Poland and their impact on the recombination of network assets.

Polish Privatization and SMEs

The very political forces and the 1990 law on privatization of state enterprises that legalized the veto powers of employee councils and effectively blocked rapid, mass privatization led to an approach that focused less on defining clear private ownership rights and more on delegating use rights and getting assets reorganized. The first part of the approach opened two routes that focused mostly on medium-sized firms, empowered stakeholders, and facilitated the transfer of assets to existing network actors. One route, "liquidation," sent firms through a bankruptcy procedure.[51] For instance, the most prominent liquidation route (Article 19) included 1,464 firms, or over 26 percent of all and 37 percent of nonagricultural firms subject to ownership transformations by the end of 1996.[52] Although the details of the data lack clarity, previous research shows that as much as half of these assets of completed projects were partially restructured, kept as going concerns, and sold or leased to stakeholders and outsiders.[53] The downside of these court-based proceedings has been their slowness. For instance, as of December 1996 about only 34 percent of Article 19 projects were completed.

The other route, probably the most efficient and dynamic, came through Article 37 of the 1990 law and is commonly known as "direct privatization."[54] This law allowed employee councils to legally dissolve the state firm and then have the assets sold or leased to a new company, often comprised of insiders.[55] By December 1996, 1,247 firms, or over 22 percent of all and 31 percent of nonagricultural firms subject to ownership transformation, entered direct privatization. Direct privatization accounted for almost 30 percent of all nonbank privatization revenues.[56] Almost 40 percent of firms were in manufacturing. By the end of 1996, 97.9 percent projects in direct privatization were completed, far surpassing the completion rates for "liquidation" and especially the "indirect privatization" paths of commercializing firms and then selling them case by case or via the voucher investment funds (14.9 percent). The lease option has accounted for over two-thirds of direct privatization projects and by the end of 1995 accounted for more employees than those in the "indirect" path.[57] This option was effectively a way for stakeholders to create a management-employee buyout (MEBO) through state-subsidized financing. The new company had to have at least 50 percent of the employees of the original firm and make an initial down payment of 20 percent of book value. In return, it received a below-market interest rate and could defer payments for one to two years. Research has shown that MEBOs and firms in direct privatization in general have performed well: the financial, productivity, and output indicators of the firms surveyed tend to be better than national and sectoral averages, and by 1998 only twenty-three MEBO firms had defaulted on their lease payments.[58] The studies also show that the majority of firms were undertaking organizational, process, and product innovations.

The use of Articles 19 and 37 for ownership transformation, particularly MEBOs, made three critical contributions toward network reorganization. First, as opposed to focusing on delineation of ownership rights, these routes made asset restructuring and the reordering of property simultaneous and gradual. Not only were assets often partially cleaned up and made available for stakeholders of the old or related firms, but also the leasing arrangements effectively were incentive contracts that tied the option for full ownership to the reorganization and the efficient use of assets.

Second, these routes set a general tone that multiparty negotiations and consultations were necessary for linking restructuring and ownership change. For instance, Article 37 required that a majority of employees approve the process and, for MEBOs, form the new company. Article 19, though apparently less efficient, effectively avoided zero-sum outcomes by forcing creditors (banks and suppliers) and managers to generate a basic restructuring plan and find a new owner that was willing to also accept the existing workforce. Given often the legacy of tight linkages between firms and plants and the use of social relationships among them to coordinate decisions, this implicitly meant a degree of interfirm negotiation about such actions.[59] Moreover, public actors, notably the forty-nine *voivodships* (regional administrations) that received responsibility over most firms as their "founders," became central in facilitating dispute resolutions and consultations among firms. As the founder of an enterprise, the voivodship could initiate or block a liquidation petition, was charged with screening and vetting direct privatization projects before they were passed to the central Ministry of Ownership Transformation for final approval, and negotiated with MEBO candidates about certain terms of repayment. As such, the voivodship was negotiating with and mediating between the various stakeholders and competing claimants to assets. Moreover, as an agent of the central government charged with monitoring compliance with the various agreements, it collaborated with other public agencies, firms, and banks to pool information and learn more about the activities and problems of firms in the region.[60]

Third, the central and regional governments shared the risk of restructuring and so provided breathing space for firms to experiment with restructuring strategies and a way to learn how to effectively monitor the users of subsidies. For instance, Article 19 provided an initial experiment for firms to receive debt relief and for banks and voivodships to follow the results. The leasing option was an innovation on SME subsidies, not only due to the use of an incentive contract but also due to the delegation of powers to the voivodships, which were better positioned than central authorities to pool local information and develop *ex ante* and *ex post* monitoring capabilities.

Polish Privatization and Workouts of Large Firms

Another consequence of the blocking of a Polish form of voucher privatization was a shift in policy toward the largest firms and banks. With case-by-case privatizations and existing bankruptcy procedures taking much time, the government had to become more proactive and address large firm restructuring as a key part of more gradual ownership change. In turn, the government initiated two simultaneous policies: a state-backed workout regime and a strong regulatory framework for both capital markets and a limited use of vouchers. Together, these two sets of policies were based on the three principles just discussed: tying restructuring to ownership transformation, creating government-monitored mechanisms to promote extended deliberations on restructuring among parties to assets, and using public actors to share some of the risk of restructuring. These policies had arguably an important, though often indirect, impact on SME creation and network restructuring: they kept a flow of resources moving via large firms to SMEs, they bolstered the use of the capital market for IPOs (initial public offerings), and they helped interlinked banks, large firms, and SMEs address restructuring collectively.

Facilitating Workouts

Recall that Czech rejection of extended government participation in transformation impelled the Czech government to delink ownership change from restructuring: firm restructuring would emerge once private ownership and the new bankruptcy law were established, and bank restructuring was based on rapid privatization and a one-time, partial recapitalization and debt relief with no involvement of the concerned firms. In contrast, the Poles sought to tie both ownership change and restructuring as well as bank and firm restructuring. Some of these objectives were met in using from the outset bankruptcy mechanisms as a course of privatization. But these mechanisms were still slow, due to common problems of court-based workouts in East-Central Europe. In turn, the Polish government took the innovative step of creating the Enterprise and Bank Restructuring Program (EBRP) in 1993—originally thought of as a way to address the growth of bad debts while prepping banks and firms for privatization and initiating debt-equity swaps. The program was innovative for three reasons. First, while EBRP aimed to address the growing bad debt crisis and prepping seven of the nine main commercial banks for privatization, it purposefully linked bank and large firm restructuring. Second, in becoming the initiator of this process, the government recognized not only that market incentives were insufficient but also that the government itself was a key stakeholder in both firms and banks, not least of all due to its responsibilities as lender of last resort and as a creditor to both (via taxes). Third, in linking the restructuring of the two and thus taking charge of establishing and monitoring the criteria thereof, the government was to become an extended participant as a financial partner and conflict mediator to the parties involved.

The design of EBRP was rather simple. The government offered the seven banks (which held about 60 percent of outstanding enterprise debt) a one-time recapitalization sufficient to deal with classified debts that originated prior to 1992. In return, the banks had to establish workout departments and had to reach a debt resolution agreement with their debtors by March 1994, to be fully implemented by March 1996. Such an agreement allowed for five paths, including demonstration of full debt servicing (about 40 percent of the 787 total firms), bankruptcy, liquidation, debt sale, and a new regime called "bank conciliation." This last route became the most popular method of dealing with problem firms (23 percent of firms and 50 percent of debt) and has been widely judged as a successful, innovative policy that not only improved the financial and operational performance of banks and firms but also provided a strong foundation for rejuvenating the governance of relations between financial institutions and firms.[61]

Bank conciliation was a state-backed vehicle, in which the government, banks, and firms exchanged financial assistance for property rights and reorganizational actions. The policy and the process itself had two critical impacts on network reorganization. First, in linking restructuring of firms to debt relief, bank conciliation enhanced the ability of network actors to recombine mutual claims and of SMEs to grow. On the one hand, the restructuring of large firms' finances and operations provided a flow of resources and thus breathing space for larger firms and their interconnected smaller firms to experiment with new uses of facilities and assets and new methods of contracting. Moreover, since bank conciliation forced operational restructuring, it provided a framework in which large firms could begin negotiations with suppliers and customers about initiatives in spin-offs, leasing, subcontracting, and production changes. On the other hand, government intervention not only broke an existing stalemate between banks and firms, similar to that in the Czech Republic, but also provided a vehicle in which banks could learn more about serving clients and the problems manufacturing firms faced. For instance, in his detailed analysis of the heavily industrialized Lodz region, Dornisch notes that perhaps the most important outcome of EBRP in general, and bank conciliation in particular, was that the regional bank learned how to tap back into interfirm networks and use them to create what he calls "project networks" for more efficient *ex ante* and *ex post* monitoring of the financing of new and existing firms. The project networks were vital to the regional bank's successful development of regional equity and venture capital funds.[62]

Second, in using the principles of delegation and deliberation, bank conciliation helped both public and private actors learn how to use negotiated solutions of common asset problems and learn how to develop their new roles in network restructuring. For instance, bank conciliation was a conscious effort by the government to overcome market inefficiencies and centralized administration. The government first provided financial support to the banks (and to the firms under a separate agreement on unpaid taxes and wages) while delegating restructuring authority to them, mainly to a lead bank. At the same time, it set clear rules of restructuring criteria, termination dates, and negotiating principles that it used to monitor bank and firm compliance. Within this framework of rules, the banks and firms negotiated the terms of restructuring and in some cases (about 10 percent) debt-equity swaps. During implementation, all three actors had to reveal to one another regularly information on the progress of their actions and thus begin to learn how to monitor one another and devise new roles for themselves.

Regulating Mass Privatization and the Capital Markets

In late 1995, the government initiated the privatization of 512 medium- to large-sized firms by placing them within fifteen government-created National Investment Funds (NIFs), which would be owned by citizens and managed by top investment banks. Besides the limited scope of the program, three key differences with the Czech program have been attributed to the strengthening of incentives by funds to restructure assets (and not simply trade them) and the creation of a vibrant capital market for financing existing and new firms.[63] First, while citizens via vouchers were majority owners of funds, the government created incentive contracts for fund managers that tied their revenues to firm performance and value creation. Second, the Poles took their time in developing a rigorous regulatory regime for securities markets that focused on public disclosure and protection of minority rights. Third, the government temporarily held 25 percent of equity in each firm.

The combination of controlling stakes by the NIFs and the state and the strong regulatory laws not only blocked the path of Czech-type arbitrageurs but also helped build the credibility of a new method of finance during the fragile, nascent period of the implementation of a new institutional regime. In turn, the credibility of both restructuring incentives and the capital market in general helped network restructuring and SMEs in two ways: restructuring provided a continued flow of resources via large firms (i.e., purchases, supplies, subcontracting, etc.) to SME development and new firm formation, while capital market credibility facilitated the creation of perhaps the best IPO market in the region and thus a vital source of SME financing.

When one combines EBRP with the privatization policies, one can see that at both the macro and micro levels, the Polish government was facilitating negotiated solutions to network reorganization and project selection by becoming an interim financial partner to restructuring and utilizing the principles of delegation and deliberation. At the macro level, in both EBRP and mass privatization, the government was delegating restructuring responsibilities to private actors. Delegation overcame first mover problems by forcing firms and banks to take action and providing a public financial commitment (i.e., recapitalization and NIF contracts) that enhanced the credibility of the action. Notice that delegation is distinct from the private property rights approaches since ownership and creditor rights are conditional; and it is distinct from traditional economic-sociological approaches since it overtly attempts to break the existing pattern of relations. Deliberation occurred directly and indirectly. It was direct in EBRP through the simultaneous creation of performance criteria and rules for iterative, collective review by the parties of each other's actions. It was indirect in the NIF program and the new regulatory regime through the restructuring incentives and through the government monitors regularly reviewing with the firm and NIF managers their performance and compliance. Notice again that deliberation attempts to order common asset governance, and not deny it, as the property rights approaches would like; and it facilitates a process of multiparty negotiation over authority and the reorganization of interactor ties, which the traditional network approaches would not view as necessary.

At the micro level, this process was also present via direct privatization. MEBOs were given limited financial support and delegated the authority over certain assets. At the same time, the lease agreements demanded that ownership transfer would be possible only if asset restructuring was sufficient in paying out the lease. One could argue that the government indirectly instilled a similar process of gradual adjustment of interfirm ties by inducing the gradual change of asset control. In sum, the Polish approaches to privatization and debt restructuring did not simply have the government preserve existing networks, as Stark and Bruszt would argue, but also provided incentives and rules that guided network actors to reorganize the authority structure and operational relations among themselves.

Local Government

The importance of the interactive relationship between public actors and network restructuring can be brought into sharper focus when one considers a third fundamental difference between the Czech and Polish approaches to transformation: the role of regional and local governments. Both Polish and Czech reformers were highly concerned about continued control by communist apparatchiks of regional and local councils and maintaining a unitary state. But their methods of dealing with them contrasted sharply. As mentioned earlier, the Czech approach centered on concentrating power into an elite change team within the central government and debilitating local power. Consequently, regional governments were dissolved and reinstated only in 1998, while district-level powers diminished and municipalities fragmented. In Poland, the labor union Solidarity had developed a strong grassroots organizational network and believed that strengthening local democracy was vital to negating the legacy of communist centralism. In turn, the Poles not only maintained the forty-nine regional governments (voivodships) but also strengthened the role and accountability of local governments (*gminas*).

Consequently, significantly different institutional settings emerged. The CR has fragmented into numerous small, largely uncoordinated municipalities and weak districts. Poland's municipalities, the *gminas*, are considerably fewer and larger, and are coordinated by both the sociopolitical ties of Solidarity and entrepreneurial voivodships.[64] Although Czech and Polish municipalities have roughly similar aggregate revenue and expenditure structures, the Polish *gminas* and voivodships have significantly more autonomy on the setting of tax rates and on the use of funds and organizational resources that allowed them to be relatively proactive. For instance, whereas the Czech central government established only two regional development agencies (RDAs) in the regions with the highest unemployment, the Polish voivodships and *gminas* had created sixty-six RDAs by 1996 throughout the country. While privatization and economic restructuring rested solely in the hands of the central government in the CR, voivodships and to some degree *gminas* were from the beginning given significant responsibilities, particularly in becoming the legal "founders" of many manufacturing firms. Indeed, the Polish *gminas* have been consistently cited for their improvement in services and their unique ability to create a vibrant municipal bond market. Moreover, recent research in Poland reveals high and strong correlations between the implementation of development policies and the density and diversity of public-private institutions in voivodships, on the one hand, and relatively high rates of industrial restructuring, participation in direct privatization (especially via MEBOs), SME creation, and the reception of foreign direct investment (FDI) on the other.[65]

One clearly cannot overstate the impact on restructuring of a particular administrative law or budgetary indicator. Indeed, voivodships have also been criticized for lacking local accountability via direct elections and sufficient financial resources and autonomy to aid economic restructuring.[66] Nonetheless, despite their limitations, voivodships and *gminas* have played important roles, less as profound managers of the economy, than as agents of institutional experimentation to become active participants and forums for strengthening and reshaping the network ties among firms, banks, and one another. This insight is critical when one considers that the Czech counterparts were literally or figuratively eliminated from playing any role in privatization and restructuring. In separate but equally detailed and extensive research on the role of voivodships in industrial restructuring, Hausner and Dornisch show how voivodships were able to harness their limited, but nonetheless existing, political and organizational capital to revitalize informational, social, and economic links among private and public actors.[67]

First, in exploring their legal roles as founders of many state firms and as overseers of regional development, voivodships were most effective when they focused first on becoming an effective monitor of firms in their jurisdictions. To do so, they combined their relative authority and organizational resources with the social, informational, and human resources of regional banks, firms, consultants, *gminas*, and the local offices of the central tax agency. These initial steps toward pooling diverse sources of knowledge and information became first and foremost a resource for economic actors to expand their portfolios of strategies, collaborators, and project screening capabilities. For instance, when EBRP was launched, the regional banks lacked effective monitoring capabilities. They began to make up for their deficiencies by participating in regular regional council meetings and accessing the voivodship database, particularly on the firms that were in EBRP and had the voivodship as their founder. The regional banks, in turn, began to consider the strategic goals of the voivodship, the regional labor bureau, and the tax authority regarding the firms directly and indirectly under their control.

Second, this interaction via information sharing allowed participants to begin to learn about each other's capabilities and interests and define some basic areas of joint action and risk and resource pooling. For instance, the pilot experience in restructuring firms in EBRP, and in some case becoming co-owners of them, led the Lodz Bank and Lodz voivodship to comanage a closed World Bank investment fund for initially twenty firms. A tie such as this fortified horizontal links among related public and private actors.[68]

Third, it is vital to note that these developments were gradual and that initiatives often failed. But it was the continued presence and efforts of the voivodships and *gminas* as well as the impulse coming from programs like EBRP and direct privatization that allowed the actors to learn from the failure and recombine pieces of the potential interorganizational networks. The actors learned not simply how to evaluate a particular project but also how to define a reasonable set of common projects and how to assess each other's actions and contributions. As Dornisch emphasizes in his analysis of the revitalization of Lodz, a voivod that was transformed from a rust belt into one of the most vibrant regions of SME development and restructuring, learning about project selection was intimately connected to learning how to monitor each other and share authority over common assets. Just as private and public actors were assessing the prospects of new projects, they were also gaining experience about what were the most effective roles they could play.

Concluding Remarks

This chapter has had two related arguments. First, it appears that new firms arise via a reorganization of existing interfirm networks. The existing approaches to transformation and firm creation have difficulties capturing this process. On the one hand, the depoliticization approaches, based on property rights and Kirznerian views of entrepreneurship, collapse in the face of the failures of the Czech policies and the relative success of Polish policies that limited mass privatization and enhanced the roles of central and regional governments. On the other hand, the fragmentation of a potentially dynamic Czech machine tool network and the collapse of Czech investment funds points to weakness in standard economic-sociology approaches that ignore network change.

Second, an *embedded politics* approach may prove more useful in analyzing restructuring and firm creation, at least in East-Central Europe. Its core argument is that networks are sociopolitical entities, whose authority structure is constructed by economic and public actors under specific political-institutional regimes. Reforms in public institutions can destabilize industrial networks and inhibit cooperation between firms and banks (and limit new firm creation). But the interlinked experimental processes of asset restructuring and network reorganization depend largely on the formation of new institutional workout mechanisms that facilitate risk sharing and continuous, disciplined deliberations among the parties to assets. Since public actors are both constituents to networks and often key players in such institutions, identification of workout institutions comes not simply from reference to laws. Rather, my approach focuses on the ways that public actors, particularly at the regional and local levels, are given the legitimacy and resources to engage firms and explore their roles as risk sharers, initiators, and monitors of firm and bank negotiations over restructuring strategies and asset control.

Implicit in this argument is that, via network reorganization, firm creation depends on linking monitoring and learning. At one level, interlinked firms and banks are attempting to learn how to construct new formal and informal methods of mutual monitoring and project selection. This is where asset restructuring is tied to network reorganization. At another level, public actors, be they central agencies or regional governments, are learning how to provide financial and organizational support to firms and banks while experimenting with different ways to monitor the latter. In turn, the embedded politics approach argues that public actors are most effective in combining learning and monitoring, for themselves and for economic actors, when transformation policies are based on the principles of delegation and deliberation, rather than simply providing subsidies or drawing a bright line between the public and the private.

Notes

An initial version of this chapter was presented at the conference "Entrepreneurs, Entrepreneurialism, and Democracy in Communist and Post-Communist Societies" at the University of California–Berkeley, May 19–20, 2000. The author is grateful for the comments from conference participants, David Dornisch, Grzegorz Ekiert, Anna Grzymala-Busse, Mauro Guillen, Vit Henisz, Yoshiko Herrera, Chip Hunter, Bruce Kogut, Katharina Pistor, Andrew Spicer, David Woodruff, and Rick Woodward.

1. For reviews of the debate, see Piore and Sabel (1984), Acs and Audretsch (1990), Sengenberger, Loveman, and Piore (1990), and Pyke and Sengenberger (1992). In general, the debate dates back to the works of Schumpeter (1934) and Marshall (1923).

2. For the former, see Kirzner (1973, 1997) and Gilder (1984). For the latter, see especially, Piore and Sabel (1984), Powell (1990), Burt (1992), Sengenberger, Loveman, and Piore (1990), Locke (1995), Herrigel (1996), and Saxenian (1994). For

an insightful analysis and overview of the network-entrepreneurship link in the organizational theory literature, see Larson (1992).

3. For an East-West comparison of industrial structures, the role of scientific management, and the potential for SMEs in industrial restructuring, see Acs and Audretsch (1993) and McDermott and Mejstrik (1992). Whereas SMEs accounted for about 1 percent of industrial employment in communist Czechoslovakia, SMEs comprised about 10 percent of industrial employment in Hungary and Poland.

4. See, in particular, Kirzner (1973, 1997), Johnson and Loveman (1995), Boycko, et al. (1995), Sachs (1990, 1993), and North (1990) for these views on firm and institutional creation. For a review of these and other similar works on this issue, see Spicer, McDermott, and Kogut (2000).

5. For general discussions of the relationship between firm creation, innovation, and networks, see the debates between Burt (1992) and Coleman (1990) as well as Granovetter (1985), Larson (1992), Powell (1990), and the special issue of *Strategic Management Journal* (January 2000). The work of David Stark (see below) is one of the few conscious efforts to incorporate this literature into the East Europe debate.

6. See Olson (1992), Murrell and Olson (1991), Boycko et al. (1995), Shleifer and Vishny (1994), Frydman and Rapaczynski (1994), Sachs (1990), Camdessus (1995), and World Bank (1996). Depoliticization is also evident in the works associated with developmental statists. See Amsden (1992), Amsden et al. (1994), Haggard and Kaufman (1992, 1995), and Moon and Prasad (1994).

7. See McDermott (1998, 2002) for a discussion of the depoliticization approach as it appears in various schools of thought, including economics, rational choice, and developmental statism.

8. Discussions on the formation of policy and the conditions in the Czechoslovak Federated Republic and the Czech Republic and on the optimal conditions for reforms in general can be found in McDermott (2002, Chapter 3), Hayri and McDermott (1998), OECD (1996), World Bank (1996), Moon and Prasad (1994), Haggard and Kaufman (1992, 1995) and Amsden et al. (1994).

9. Note that regarding policies of privatization in the region, I am concerned only with the so-called large privatization programs and not those focused on shops and restaurants.

10. For discussions of the different social, political, and economic conditions and policies in Poland and Hungary, see World Bank (1996), Frydman and Rapaczynski (1994), Dabrowski et al. (1991), Levitas (1994), Stark and Bruszt (1991, 1998), Ekiert and Kubik (1999), Wittenberg (1997, 1999a, and 1999b), and Antal-Mokos (1998).

11. Again, see McDermott (1998, 2002) for an extensive discussion of this view. See also Boycko et al. (1995), Schleifer and Vishny (1994), Sachs (1991), Camdessus (1995), and Frydman and Rapaczynski (1994).

12. The clearest connections are made in Boyco et. al. (1995), Sachs (1990, 1993), and Johnson and Loveman (1995).

13. Kirzner (1997, 68).

14. Jezek (1989), Klaus and Jezek (1991), and Klaus and Triska (1989).

15. See, for instance, Frydman and Rapaczynski (1994), Boycko et al. (1995), World Bank (1996), Nellis (1999), Camdessus (1995), EBRD (1995).

16. See, for instance, Boycko et al. (1995), Frydman and Rapaczynski (1994), Nellis (1999), and World Bank (1996).

17. For U-turns by its advocates, see World Bank (1999), Johnson and Shleifer

(1999), and Nellis (1999). For other critiques, see Coffee (1995, 1996, and 1998), Spicer et al. (2000), and McDermott (1997, 2002).

18. See Johnson and Shleifer (1999) and Coffee (1999).

19. Although surveys by the EBRD (1995) and OECD (1996) show Czech SMEs having a greater share of employment and GDP, most of the growth in Czech SMEs was in trade, tourism, and some services (Zemplinerova (1995, 1998). These are hardly sources of long-term growth and stability. Moreover, mainstream studies of SMEs focus on the manufacturing sectors (Acs and Audretsch (1990, 1993).

20. While some may argue that it is problematic to compare the Czech 1995 SME data with the Polish and Hungarian 1997–98 SME data, I would argue that such a comparison should give a comparative advantage to the Czechs, especially for advocates of the depoliticization model. First, 1995 marks the greatest divergence between the CR and the other two countries in terms of private sector shares of GDP and industrial output. Second, 1994–95 was the period of strongest GDP growth for the CR, with the later years, especially 1997–99, seeing negative growth. In turn, both factors would in many ways tend to overstate the growth of SME share relative to other years.

21. The idea here is that the ability of the Hungarians and Poles to sell off many of their banks in the mid-1990s made them more efficient. There are two problems here. First, not only were these sell-offs relatively late in the 1990s, but also the Czech state had minority positions in the main banks by 1994. Second, analyses, though limited in their sample sizes, show that Czech SMEs and start-ups had greater access to credit than their Polish and Hungarian counterparts. See Bratkowski et. al. (1999) and EBRD (1995).

22. This argument originates from the work of Janos Kornai (1990).

23. Johnson and Loveman (1995, pp. 104–105).

24. See in particular Chapters 3–6.

25. Bilsen (1998) shows that de novo firms in Romania and Bulgaria outperform those in Hungary. A key reason for this result is not in spite of but rather because of Hungary's SME sector and market liberalization being at later stages of development. That is, whereas Romanian and Bulgarian firms can reap quick growth benefits by simply entering sectors where there are few firms, Hungary's initial rapid growth in SMEs filling the void in markets has already passed, causing the performance of Hungarian new firms to depend in many ways on the restructuring of existing state firms and institutional development.

26. The notable works on this are Gabor (1990), Szelenyi (1988), Seleny (1993) and Stark (1986, 1989).

27. See, for instance, Granovetter (1985), Nohria and Eccles (1992), Powell (1990), Uzzi (1996, 1997), Rowley et al. (2000), Kogut (2000), and Kale et al. (2000). For analysis on the relationship between different types of networks and entrepreneurship, see Larson (1992) and Burt (1992).

28. Stark (1986, 1996, 1999), Stark and Bruszt (1998), and Grabher and Stark (1997).

29. See World Bank (1999), Coffee (1996), and McDermott (2002, Chapters 3 and 4) for analyses of the collective action problem that the dominant funds and banks face in investing into firms.

30. See McDermott (2002, Chapter 3).

31. Bratkowski et al. (1999), Johnson et al. (2000), and Jarosz (1999).

32. For work on the former USSR, Poland, German Democratic Republic, and Hungary, see, for instance, Prokop (1996), Woodruff (1999), Dornisch (1999), Jacoby (2000), Seleny (1993), Szelenyi (1988), and Levitas (1994, 1999). Even within the work of Stark and Bruszt (1998), there are strong suggestions of the interconnection between local political actors and managers (see, for instance, pp. 112–115).

33. Hayri and McDermott (1998), and McDermott (1997, 2002).

34. See for instance, Saxenian (1994), Locke (1995), Piore and Sabel (1984), Sabel and Zeitlin (1997), Herrigel (1996), and Grabher (1993).

35. For insightful analyses on the development of U.S. institutions for bankruptcy, limited liability, insurance, and lender of last resort, see Cui (1995) and Moss (1996a, 1996b, 1998).

36. The Czech machinery and equipment sector is classified as NACE 29. OKEC-NACE is the Czech classification system that roughly corresponds to the International System of Industry Classification (ISIC). Division 29 includes: (291) manufacture of machinery for the production and use of mechanical power, (292) manufacture of other general-purpose machinery, (293) manufacture of agricultural and forestry machinery, (294) manufacture of machine tools, (295) manufacture of other special-purpose machinery, (296) manufacture of weapons and ammunition, (297) manufacture of domestic appliances n.e.c. While most firms discussed below are in NACE 294, some are in 295. As late as 1997, even with the decline of industrial employment and output, these industries and the sector as a whole remained at the heart of Czech manufacturing. For instance, NACE 294 and 295, respectively, accounted for 11 percent and 29 percent of sales within NACE 29. NACE 29 as a whole accounted for almost 15 percent of total manufacturing employment (the largest of the eleven sectors in manufacturing) and about 12 percent of total manufacturing value added (second only to food processing). See publications and data by Ministry of Industry and Trade of the Czech Republic, 1998, at http://www.mpo.cz.

37. For a brief history of the Czech machine tool industry, see McDermott (2002, Chapter 2).

38. See, for instance, Piore and Sabel (1984), Herrigel (1996), Friedman (1988), Carlsson (1989), Carlsson and Taymaz (1994), Acs et al. (1991), and Acs and Audretsch (1990).

39. The following analysis of the machine tool network is based on McDermott (2002, Chapters 2 and 5). An analysis of other branches that possess tightly integrated, hierarchical networks can be found in Hayri and McDermott (1998) and McDermott (2002, Chapter 4).

40. See, in particular, Rowley et al. (2000), Kogut (2000), Larson (1992), Uzzi (1996), Locke (1995), Burt (1992, 2000), Kale et al. (2000).

41. See Larson (1992), Rowley et al. (2000), and Burt (2000) for the ways these apparently opposing traits can be optimal for firms in turbulent conditions and entrepreneurial settings.

42. The variation in the stake held by SST in Strojimport is due to changes in the structure of the firm and to ongoing negotiations about share price. As the network fragmented (see below), SST firms ultimately returned the shares to the state. Also, given the shareholding regulations and dispersion of ownership in the Czech Republic, the 3 to 20 percent equity stakes acquired by ISB enabled SST, on behalf of ISB, to gain a seat on the management or supervisory board of the respective firms.

43. A similar fate met the vocational training system, which severely hurt the ability of member firms to retain existing craftsmen and train new ones. Vlacil et al.

(1996) show that the combination of the government policy to make training centers self-financing and the liquidity constraints of machine tool firms led to the virtual collapse of vocational training in the industry.

44. See Hoshi et al. (1998) and McDermott (1997, 2002).

45. For a detailed discussion of ZPS and its strategies with various banks, funds, and the insurance company, see McDermott (2002, Chapter 5).

46. The problems of spin-offs were common to other industries as well (Hayri and McDermott, 1998). Indeed, econometric analysis shows that there were relatively few cases of Czech industrial spin-offs, and they performed substantially worse than their former parent firms. See Kotrba (1994) and Lizal et al. (1995).

47. See, for instance, Stiglitz and Weiss (1981), Cui (1995), Ostrom (1990), and Bates (1988).

48. See especially Bates (1988), Ostrom (1995), Putnam et al. (1993). Indeed much of the management literature on networks came from those working on strategic alliances. See Larson (1992), Uzzi (1996), Kale et al. (2000), and Kogut and Zander (1992).

49. Note that even though there was considerable downsizing in the industry, new start-ups would still be hindered by the depression of the industry. Start-ups would have, for instance, few chances to buy or lease equipment and obtain sales.

50. See Coffee (1999) for an insightful argument about why the issue of law in practice and regulatory regimes may be the crucial issue for capital market development in East-Central Europe.

51. I am speaking here mainly of Article 19 of the 1981 law on state enterprises and to a lesser degree the amended 1934 bankruptcy act.

52. See Blaszczyk and Woodward (1999) and Nuti (1999) for data on privatization. As of December 1990, there were 8,441 state enterprises. By December 1996, 5,592 enterprises had entered a track of ownership transformation. By this date, 662 of these firms had entered the process of the bankruptcy act.

53. See Gray and Holle (1998a) and Blaszczyk (2000). I also confirmed this estimate with the research team at CASE Foundation, Warsaw.

54. See Jarosz (1999), Nuti (1999), and Blaszczyk and Woodward (1999) for details.

55. Sales could be sold for cash or as an in-kind contribution to an existing company. Alternatively, the assets could be leased with an option to buy to a company established by at least 50 percent of the employees of the original firm.

56. This figure is generated from total nonbank privatization revenues through the direct and indirect paths of privatization. See Jarosz (1999, p. 35, Table 4).

57. By the end of 1995, leased firms accounted for over 170,000 employees, whereas firms in indirect privatization accounted for about 158,000 employees.

58. There were two major systematic studies of 200 of these firms (across industries and regions) in 1995 and 1998 (Jarosz, 1996, 1999). One drawback has been the slow rate of investment, largely due to the lack of immediate ownership of the assets.

59. See Dornisch (1997).

60. See Jarosz (1999, Chapters 2, 4, 10), Dornisch (1997, 1999) and Hausner et al. (1995, 1997, 1998).

61. See Van Wijnbergen (1997), Gray and Holle (1998b), Dornisch (1997, 2000), and Montes-Negret and Papi (1996). I draw on these works for the following paragraphs as well.

62. See Dornisch (1997, 2000).

63. See Coffee (1999), Pistor (1999), and Johnson and Schleifer (1999).

64. See OECD (1996b), Hausner et al. (1995, 1998), Baldersheim et al. (1996), Blazek (1993), Levitas (1999). The basic structural differences are stark. For instance, the number of Czech municipalities grew by 50 percent by 1991 to 6,237, with an average size of 1,700 inhabitants, while Polish *gminas* maintained most of their integrity (2,466 *gminas* with average size of 15,000 inhabitants). While Czech and Polish municipalities have similar, proportional financial data, the Polish *gminas* were given significantly more autonomy on the use of funds and organizational resources to pursue (i.e., investment, infrastructure, regional development, etc.). For analyses of regional development agencies in the region, see Halkier et al. (1998).

65. On these issues, see OECD (1996b), Hausner et al. (1995, 1997, 1998), Dornisch (1997, 1999, 2000), and Jarosz (1999).

66. For instance, the central government has several areas of control over voivodships, including appointing the governor, controlling the budgets, and restricting autonomy in the use of funds. See Hausner et al. (1995, 1997), Levitas (1999), OECD (1996b), and Dornisch (1999, 2000).

67. For the following discussion, see Hausner et al. (1995, 1997) and Dornisch (1997, 1999).

Bibliography

Acs, Z., and Audretsch, D. 1990. *Innovation and Small Firms.* Cambridge: MIT Press.
———. eds. 1993. *Small Firms and Entrepreneurship: An East-West Comparison.* Cambridge: Cambridge University Press.
Acs, Z., D. Audretsch, and B. Carlsson. 1991. "Flexible Technology and Firm Size," *Small Business Economics,* 3(4): 307–321.
Amsden, A. 1992. "A Theory of Government Intervention in Late Industrialization." In Dietrich Rueschemeyer and Louis Putterman, eds., *State and Market in Development: Synergy or Rivalry?* Boulder: Lynne Reiner.
Amsden, A., J. Kochanowicz, and L. Taylor. 1994. *The Market Meets Its Match: Restructuring the Economies of Eastern Europe.* Cambridge: Harvard University Press.
Antal-Mokos, Z. 1998. *Privatisation, Politics and Economic Performance in Hungary.* Cambridge: Cambridge University Press.
Baldersheim, H., M. Illner, A. Offerdal, L. Rose, and P. Swianiewicz. eds. 1996. *Local Democracy and the Processes of Transformation in East-Central Europe.* Boulder, CO: Westview Press.
Bates, Robert. 1988. "Contra Contractarianism: Some Reflections on the New Institutionalism," *Politics and Society,* 16: 387–401.
Bilsen, V. 1998. "Job Creation, Job Destruction, and Growth of Newly Established, Privatized, and State-Owned Enterprises in Transition Economies: Survey Evidence from Bulgaria, Hungary, and Romania," *Journal of Comparative Economics,* 26: 429–445.
Blaszczyk, B. 2000. "The Privatization Program and Post-Privatization Ownership Evolution in Poland," unpublished manuscript from the CASE Foundation Project, "Secondary Privatization: The Evolution of Ownership Structure of Privatized Companies," Warsaw.
Blaszczyk, B., and R. Woodward, eds. 1999. "Privatization and Company Restructuring in Poland," CASE Reports No. 18, Center for Social and Economic Research, Poland.

Blazek, J. 1993. "Changing Local Budgets in the Czech Republic—Half Way Over?" Paper presented for the conference "Regional Organization and Administrative Performance in Central Europe," Prague, September 27–30.

Boycko, M., A. Shleifer, and R. Vishny. 1995. *Privatizing Russia.* Cambridge: MIT Press.

Bratkowski, A., I. Grosfeld, and J. Rostowski. 1999. "Investment and Finance in De Novo Private Firms: Empirical Results from the Czech Republic, Hungary, and Poland," Working Paper No. 236, William Davidson Institute, University of Michigan Business School.

Burt, R. 1992. *Structural Holes: The Social Structure of Competition.* Cambridge: Harvard University Press.

———. 2000. "The Network Structure of Social Capital." *Research in Organizational Behavior,* Vol. 22.

Camdessus, M. 1995. *Russia's Transformation at a Turning Point.* Address presented at the Conference of the U.S.-Russia Business Council, Washington, DC., March 29.

Carlsson, B. 1989. "Small-Scale Industry at a Crossroads: U.S. Machine Tools in a Global Perspective," *Small Business Economics,* 1(4): 245–261.

Carlsson, B., and E. Taymaz. 1994. "Flexible Technology and Industrial Structure in the U.S.," *Small Business Economics,* 6(3): 193–210.

Coffee, J. 1996. "Institutional Investors in Transitional Economies: Lessons from the Czech Experience." In R. Frydman, C.W. Gray, and A. Rapaczynski, eds., *Corporate Governance in Central Europe and Russia,* I: 111–186. Budapest: Central European University Press.

———. 1999. "Privatization and Corporate Governance: The Lessons from Securities Market Failure," Working Paper No. 158, Center for Law and Economic Studies, Columbia Law School.

Coleman, J. 1990. *Foundations of Social Theory.* Cambridge: Harvard University Press.

Csaki, G., and A. Macher. 1997. *Ten Years of Privatization in Hungary.* English-language manuscript.

Cui, Z. 1995. "The Dilemmas of the Soft Budget Constraint: Three Institutions that Challenge the 'Invisible Hand' Paradigm," Ph.D. Dissertation, Department of Political Science, University of Chicago.

Dabrowski, J.M., M. Federowicz, and A. Levitas. 1991. "Polish State Enterprises and the Properties of Performance: Stabilization, Marketization, Privatization," *Politics and Society,* 19(4): 430–437.

Dornisch, D. 1997. "An Ecology of Projects: Economics Restructuring and Network Recombination in Post-Socialist Poland," Ph.D. Dissertation, Department of Sociology, Cornell University.

———. 1999. "Project Networks vs. Networks of Cooperation: Regional Restructuring and Governance in Post-Socialist Poland," *BISS Public,* 27: 73–103.

———. 2000. "The Social Embeddedness of Polish Regional Development: Representative Institutions, Path Dependencies, and Network Formation." Unpublished manuscript.

EBRD. 1995, 1996, 1997, 1998. *Transition Report.* London: European Bank for Reconstruction and Development.

Ekiert, G., and J. Kubik. 1999. *Rebellious Civil Society: Popular Protest and Democratic Consolidation in Poland, 1989–1993.* Ann Arbor: University of Michigan Press.

Ellerman, D. 1998. *Voucher Privatization with Investment Funds: An Institutional Analysis.* Working Paper No. 1924, Development Economics Unit, World Bank.

Friedman, D.H. 1988. *The Misunderstood Miracle: Industrial Development and Political Change in Japan.* Ithaca: Cornell University Press.

Frydman, R., and A. Rapaczynski. 1994. *Privatization in Eastern Europe: Is the State Withering Away?* London: Central Europe University Press.

Gabor, I.R. 1990. "On the Immediate Prospects for Private Entrepreneurship and Reembourgeoisement in Hungary," Working Paper No. 90.3, Cornell University, Ithaca, NY.

Gilder, G. 1984. *The Spirit of Enterprise.* New York: Simon and Schuster.

Grabher, G., ed. 1993. *The Embedded Firm: On the Socioeconomics of Industrial Networks.* London: Routledge.

Grabher, G., and D. Stark, eds. 1997. *Restructuring Networks in Postsocialism: Legacies, Linkages, and Localities.* Oxford: Oxford University Press.

Granovetter, M. 1985. "Economic Action and Social Structure: The Problem of Embeddedness," *American Journal of Sociology,* 91: 481–510.

Gray, C., and A. Holle. 1998a. "Classical Exit Processes in Poland: Court Conciliation, Bankruptcy, and State Enterprise Liquidation." In L. Balcerowicz, C. Gray, and I. Hoshi, eds., *Enterprise Exit Processes in Transition Economies.* Budapest: CEU Press.

———. 1998b. "Poland's Bank-Led Conciliation Process." In L. Balcerowicz, C. Gray and I. Hoshi, eds., *Enterprise Exit Processes in Transition Economies.* Budapest: CEU Press.

Haggard, S., and R. Kaufman. 1992. "The State in the Initiation and Consolidation of Market-Oriented Reforms." In D. Rueschemeyer and L. Putterman, eds., *State and Market in Development: Synergy or Rivalry?* Boulder, CO: Lynne Reiner.

———. 1995. *The Political Economy of Democratic Transitions.* Princeton: Princeton University Press.

Halkier, H., M. Danson, and C. Damborg. 1998. *Regional Development Agencies in Europe.* Philadelphia: Jessica Kingsley.

Hausner, J., T. Kudlacz, and J. Szlachta. 1995. *Regional and Local Factors in the Restructuring of Poland's Economy.* Krakow: Krakow Academy of Economics.

———. 1997. "Restructuring in South-Eastern Poland." In G. Grabher and D. Stark, eds., *Restructuring Networks in Postsocialism: Legacies, Linkages, and Localities.* Oxford: Oxford University Press.

———. 1998. "Regional Differentiation of Factors Conditioning the Growth of Innovativeness in Poland's Economy." In R. Domanski, ed., *Emerging Spatial and Regional Structures of an Economy in Transition.* Warszawa: Wydawnictwo Naukowe PWN.

Hayri, A., and G. McDermott. 1998. "The Network Properties of Corporate Governance and Industrial Restructuring: A Post-socialist Lesson," *Industrial and Corporate Change,* 1: 153–193.

Herrigel, G. 1996. *Reconceptualizing the Sources of German Industrial Power.* New York: Cambridge University Press.

Hoshi, I, J. Mladek, and A. Sinclair. 1998. "Bankruptcy and Owner-Led Liquidation in the Czech Republic." In L. Balcerowicz, C. Gray, and I. Hoshi, eds., *Enterprise Exit Processes in Transition Economies.* Budapest: CEU Press.

Institute for Small Business Development. 1999. *State of Small and Medium Sized Business in Hungary.* Budapest: Institute for Small Business Development.

Jacoby, W. 2000. *Imitation and Politics: Redesigning Germany.* Ithaca: Cornell University Press.

Jarosz, M., ed. 1996. *Polish Employee-Owned Companies in 1995*. Warsaw: Institute of Political Studies, Polish Academy of Sciences.

———. 1999. *Direct Privatization: Investors, Managers, and Employees*. Warsaw: Institute of Political Studies, Polish Academy of Sciences.

Jezek, T. 1989. "The Assumptions of Symmetry as a Methodological Problem of Comparative Organizational and Society Analysis," Internal Working Papers, Prognosticky ustav, CSAV, Prague.

Johnson, S., and G. Loveman. 1995. *Starting Over in Eastern Europe: Entrepreneurship and Economic Renewal*. Boston: Harvard Business School Press.

Johnson, S., J. McMillan, and C. Woodruff. 2000. "Entrepreneurs and the Ordering of Institutional Reform," *Economics of Transition*, 8(1): 1–36.

Johnson, S., and A. Shleifer. 1999. "Coase vs. the Coasians: The Regulation and Development of Securities Markets in Poland and the Czech Republic," Working Paper, Social Science Research Network.

Kale, P., H. Singh, and H. Perlmutter. 2000. "Learning and Protection of Proprietary Assets in Strategic Alliances: Building Relational Capital," *Strategic Management Journal*, 21: 217–237.

Kirzner, I. 1973. *Competition and Entrepreneurship*. Chicago: University of Chicago Press.

———. 1997. "Entrepreneurial Discovery and the Competitive Market Process: An Austrian Approach," *Journal of Economic Literature*, 35 (March): 60–85.

Klaus, V., and T. Jezek. 1991. "Social Criticism, False Liberalism, and Recent Changes of Czechoslovakia," *East European Politics and Society*, 5(1): 26–40.

Klaus, V., and D. Triska. 1989. "The Economic Center, Reform and Equilibrium," *Czechoslovak Economic Digest*, 2: 34–56.

———. 1994. "Review Article of Janos Kornai's *The Socialist System: The Political Economy of Communism*," Buchs, October.

Kogut, B. 2000. "The Network as Knowledge: Generative Rules and the Emergence of Structure," *Strategic Management Journal*, 21: 405–425.

Kogut, B., and A. Spicer. 1998. "Chains of Embedded Trust: Institutions and Capital Market Formation in Russia and the Czech Republic," unpublished manuscript.

Kogut, B., and U. Zander. 1992. "Knowledge of the Firm, Combinative Capabilities, and the Replication of Technology," *Organization Science*, 3: 383–397.

Kornai, J. 1980. *Economies of Shortage*. Amsterdam: North Holland.

———. 1990. *The Road to Economic Freedom*. New York: Norton.

Kotrba, J. 1994. "Czech Privatization: Players and Winners," CERGE-EI Working Paper No. 58.

Larson, A. 1992. "Network Dyads in Entrepreneurial Settings: A Study of the Governance of Exchange Relationships," *Administrative Science Quarterly*, 37: 76–104.

A. Levitas. 1994. "Rethinking Reform: Lessons from Polish Privatization." In V. Milor, ed., *Changing Political Economies: Privatization in Post-Communist and Reforming Communist States*, 99–114. London: Lynne Riener.

———. 1999. "The Political Economy of Fiscal Decentralization and Local Government Finance Reform in Poland 1989–99," Research Triangle Institute, unpublished manuscript, Warsaw.

Lieberman, I. 1997. "Mass Privatization in Comparative Perspective." In I. Lieberman, S. Nestor, and R. Desai, eds., *Between State and Market: Mass Privatization in Transition Economies*, 1–18. Washington, DC: World Bank.

Lizal, L., M. Singer, and J. Svejnar. 1995. "Manager Interests, Breakups, and Performance of State Enterprises in Transition." In J. Svejnar, ed., *The Czech Republic and Economic Transition in Eastern Europe*. San Diego: Academic Press.

Locke, R. 1995. *Remaking the Italian Economy: Local Politics and Industrial Change in Contemporary Italy*. Ithaca: Cornell University Press.

Marshall, A. 1923. *Industry and Trade: A Study of Industrial Technique and Business Organization, and of Their Influences on the Conditions of Various Classes and Nations*. London: Macmillan.

McDermott, G. 1997. "Renegotiating the Ties That Bind: The Limits of Privatization in the Czech Republic." In G. Grabher and D. Stark, eds., *Restructuring Networks in Postsocialism: Legacies, Linkages, and Localities*. Oxford: Oxford University Press.

———. 1998. *The Communist Aftermath: Industrial Networks and the Politics of Institution-Building in the Czech Republic*. Ph.D. Dissertation, Department of Political Science, MIT, Cambridge, MA.

———. 2002. *Embedded Politics: Industrial Networks and the Institutional Change in Post Communism*. Ann Arbor: University of Michigan Press. Forthcoming.

McDermott, G., and M. Mejstrik. 1992. "The Role of Small Firms in the Industrial Development and Transformation of Czechoslovakia," *Small Business Economics*, 4 (3): 179–200.

Montes-Negret, F., and L. Papi. 1996. "The Polish Experience in Bank and Enterprise Restructuring," Financial Sector Development Department, World Bank, unpublished manuscript.

Moon, C., and R. Prasad. 1994. "Beyond the Development State: Networks, Politics, and Institutions," *Governance: An International Journal of Policy and Administration*, 7(4): 360–386.

Moss, D.A. 1996a. *Socializing Security: Progressive-Era Economists and the Origins of American Social Policy*. Cambridge: Harvard University Press.

———. 1996b. "Government, Markets, and Uncertainty: An Historical Approach to Public Risk Management in the United States," Harvard Business School Working Paper No. 97–025, October.

———. 1998. "Limited Liability and the Birth of American Industry: Theory Meets History," Harvard Business School Working Paper No. 98–079, March.

Murrell, P. 1992. "Conservative Political Philosophy and the Strategy of Economic Development," *East European Politics and Society*, 6: 3–16.

Murrell, P., and M. Olson. 1991. "The Devolution of Centrally Planned Economies," *Journal of Comparative Economics*, 15: 239–265.

Nellis, J. 1998. "Time to Rethink Privatization in Transition Economies?" Discussion Paper No. 38, International Finance Corporation.

Nelson, R., ed. 1993. *National Innovation Systems: A Comparative Analysis*. New York: Oxford University Press.

Nelson, R., and S. Winter. 1982. *An Evolutionary Theory of the Firm*. Cambridge: Belknap Press of Harvard University.

Nohria, N., and R. G. Eccles, eds. 1992. *Networks and Organizations: Structure, Form, and Action*. Boston: Harvard University Press.

North, D. 1990. *Institutions, Institutional Change and Economic Performance*. Cambridge: Cambridge University Press.

Nuti, D.M. 1999. "Employee Ownership in Polish Privatizations." In P. Hare, J. Batt, and S. Estrin, eds., *Reconstituting the Market: The Political Economy of Microeconomic Transformation*. Amsterdam: Harwood Academic.

OECD. 1996a. *The Czech Republic*. Paris: Organization for Economic Cooperation and Development.

OECD, 1996b. *Transition at the Local Level: The Czech Republic, Hungary, Poland, and the Slovak Republic*. Paris: Organization for Economic Cooperation and Development.

OECD. 1998a. *Czech Republic*. Paris: Organization for Economic Cooperation and Development.

OECD. 1998b. *Economic Surveys: Poland 1997–1998*. Paris: Organization for Economic Cooperation and Development.

OECD. 1999. *Main Economic Indicators*. Paris: Organization for Economic Cooperation and Development. CD-ROM.

Olson, M. 1992. "The Hidden Path to a Successful Economy." In C. Clague and G. Rausser, eds., *The Emergence of Market Economies in Eastern Europe*. Cambridge: Blackwell.

Ostrom, E. 1990. *Governing the Commons: The Evolution of Institutions for Collective Action*. New York: Cambridge University Press.

———. 1995. "Self-Organization and Social Capital," *Industrial and Corporate Change*, 4 (1): 131–159.

Peng, M., and P.S. Heath. 1996. "The Growth of the Firm in Planned Economies in Transition: Institutions, Organizations and Strategic Choice," *Academy of Management Review*, 21: 492–528.

Piore, M., and C. Sabel. 1984. *The Second Industrial Divide*. New York: Basic Books.

Pistor, K. 1999. "The Regulatory Framework for Equity Markets in Transition Economies," Working Paper, Social Science Research Network.

Pistor, K., and A. Spicer. 1997. "Investment Funds in Mass Privatization and Beyond." In I. Lieberman, S. Nelson, and R. Desai, eds., *Between State and Market: Mass Privatization in Transition Economies*. Washington, DC: World Bank.

Pohl, G., R. Anderson, S. Claessens, and S. Djankov. 1997. "Privatization and Restructuring in Central and Eastern Europe: Evidence and Policy Options," World Bank Technical Paper No. 368, World Bank, Washington, DC.

Polish Foundation for Small and Medium Enterprise Promotion and Development. 1999. *Report on the Condition of the Small and Medium-Size Enterprise Sector in Poland for the Years 1997–1998*. Warsaw: PAB-Font.

Powell, W. 1990. "Neither Market nor Hierarchy: Network Forms of Organization." In L.L. Cummings and B.M. Staw, eds., *Research in Organizational Behavior*, CD-ROM, Vol. 12, 295–336. Greenwich, CT: JAT Press.

Powell, W., and P. DiMaggio. 1991. Introduction in W. Powell and P. DiMaggio, eds., *The New Institutionalism in Organizational Analysis*. Chicago: University of Chicago Press.

Prokop, J. 1995. "Industrial Conglomerates, Risk Spreading, and the Transition in Russia," *Communist Economies & Economic Transformation*, 7 (1): 35–50.

———. 1996. Marketization in Russia's Regions, 1990–1994. Ph.D. Dissertation, Department of Government, Harvard University.

Putnam, R., R. Leonardi, and R. Nanetti. 1993. *Making Democracy Work: Civic Traditions in Modern Italy*. Princeton: Princeton University Press.

Pyke, F., and W. Sengenberger, eds. 1992. *Industrial Districts and Local Economic Regeneration*. Geneva: Institute for Labour Studies.

Ragin, C. 1987. *The Comparative Method: Moving Beyond Qualitative and Quantitative Strategies*. Berkeley: University of California Press.

Rowley, T., D. Behrens, and D. Krackhardt. 2000. "Redundant Governance Structures: An Analysis of Structural and Relational Embeddedness in the Steel and Semiconductor Industries," *Strategic Management Journal*, 21: 369–386.

Sabel, C. 1992. "Studied Trust: Building New Forms of Co-operation in a Volatile Economy." In F. Pyke and W. Sengenberger, eds., *Industrial Districts and Local Economic Regeneration*. Geneva: Institute for Labour Studies.

———. 1993. "Constitutional Ordering in Historical Perspective." In F. Scharpf, ed., Games in Hierarchies and Markets. Boulder, CO: Westview Press.

———. 1994. "Learning by Monitoring: The Institutions of Economic Development." In N. Smesler and R. Swedberg, eds., *The Handbook of Economic Sociology*. Princeton: Princeton University Press.

Sabel, C., and J. Zeitlin. 1997. "Stories, Strategies, Structures: Rethinking Historical Alternatives to Mass Production." In C. Sabel and J. Zeitlin, eds., *Worlds of Possibility: Flexibility and Mass Production in Western Industrialization*. Cambridge: Cambridge University Press.

Sachs, J. 1990. "Eastern Europe's Economies," *The Economist*, January 13.

———. 1993. *Poland's Jump to the Market Economy*. Cambridge: MIT Press.

Saxenian, A. 1994. *Regional Networks: Industrial Adaptation in Silicon Valley and Route 128*. Cambridge: Harvard University Press.

Schumpeter, J. 1934. *The Theory of Economic Development: An Inquiry into Profits, Capital, Credit, Interest, and the Business Cycle*. Cambridge: Harvard University Press.

Seleny, A. 1993. *The Long Transformation: Hungarian Socialism, 1949–1989*. Ph.D. Dissertation, Department of Political Science, MIT.

Sengenberger, W., G. Loveman, and M. Piore, eds. 1990. *The Re-Emergence of Small Enterprises: Industrial Restructuring in Industrialised Countries*. Geneva: Institute for Labour Studies.

Shleifer, A., and R. Vishny. 1994. "Privatization in Russia: First Steps." In O. Blanchard, K. Froot, and J. Sachs, eds., *The Transition in Eastern Europe: Restructuring*, 2: 137–164. Chicago: University of Chicago Press.

Spicer, A., G. McDermott, and B. Kogut. 2000. "Entrepreneurship and Privatization in Central Europe: The Tenuous Balance Between Destruction and Creation," *Academy of Management Review*, 25 (3): 630–649.

Stark, D. 1986. "Rethinking Internal Labor Markets: New Insights from a Comparative Perspective," *American Sociological Review*, 51: 492–504.

———. 1989. "Coexisting Organizational Forms in Hungary's Emerging Mixed Economy." In V. Nee and D. Stark, eds., *Remaking the Economic Institutions of Socialism*. Stanford: Stanford University Press.

———. 1996. "Recombinant Property in East European Capitalism," *American Journal of Sociology*, 101: 993–1027.

———. 2001. "Ambiguous Assets for Uncertain Environments: Heterarchy in Postsocialist Firms." In P. Di Maggio, D. Stark, and E. Westney, eds., *The Future of the Firm: The Social Organization of Business*. Princeton: Princeton University Press.

Stark, D., and L. Bruszt. 1991. "Remaking the Political Field in Hungary," *Journal of International Affairs*, 45(1): 201–246.

———. 1998. *Post-Socialist Pathways: Transforming Politics and Property in Eastern Europe*. New York: Cambridge University Press.

Stiglitz, J. 1994. *Whither Socialism?* Cambridge: MIT Press.

————. 1999. *Whither Reform? Ten Years of the Transition.* Keynote address, World Bank Annual Conference on Development Economics, Washington, DC., April 28–30, 1999.

Stiglitz, J., and A. Weiss. 1981. "Credit Rationing in Markets with Incomplete Information," *American Economic Review*, 71: 393–410.

Szelenyi, I. 1988. *Socialist Entrepreneurs.* Madison: University of Wisconsin Press.

————. 1989. "Eastern Europe in an Epoch of Transition: Toward a Socialist Mixed Economy." In D. Stark and V. Nee, eds., *Remaking the Economics Institutions of Socialism.* Stanford: Stanford University Press.

Uzzi, B. 1996. "The Sources and Consequences of Embeddedness for the Economic Performance of Organizations: The Network Effect," *American Sociological Review*, 61: 674–698.

————. 1997. "Social Structure and Competition in Interfirm Networks: The Paradox of Embeddedness," *Administrative Science Quarterly*, 42: 35–67.

Van Wijnbergen, S. 1997. "On the Role of Banks in Enterprise Restructuring: The Polish Example," *Journal of Comparative Economics*, 24: 44–64.

Vlacil, J., I. Hradecka, I. Mazelkova, and G. McDermott. 1996. "Politics, Skills, and Industrial Restructuring." Working Paper No. 96:8, Sociologicky ustav, AVCR, Prague.

Walder, A. 1994. "Corporate Organization and Local Government Property Rights in China." In V. Milor, ed., *Changing Political Economies: Privatization in Post-Communist and Reforming Communist States.* London: Lynne Riener.

Wittenberg, J. 1999a. "The 1994 Hungarian Election in Historical Perspective." In G. Toka and Z. Enyedi, eds., *The 1994 Election to the Hungarian National Assembly.* Berlin: Sigma.

————. 1999b. *Did Communism Matter? Explaining Political Continuity and Discontinuity.* Ph.D. Dissertation, Department of Political Science, MIT.

Woodruff, D. 1999. *Money Unmade: Barter and the Fate of Russian Capitalism.* Ithaca: Cornell University Press.

World Bank Development Report. 1996. *From Plan to Market.* New York: Oxford University Press.

World Bank. 1999. *Czech Republic: Capital Market Review.* Washington, DC: World Bank.

Zemplinerova, A. 1998. "Malé podniky v ekonomice a jejich financování" (Small firms in the economy and its financing), CERGE-EI, Prague, unpublished manuscript.

10

Social Capital and Entrepreneurial Success

Hungarian Small Enterprises Between 1993 and 1996

György Lengyel

Introduction

The aim of this paper is to examine, with sociological tools, the social conditions facilitating the failure and success of small enterprises. I intend to use the term "small enterprise" in a broad sense to include micro- and small enterprises as well as the self-employed. This work draws on survey research, launched in 1993 (Czakó et al. 1994) and repeated in 1996, that targeted the economic and social characteristics of Hungarian nonagricultural enterprises employing fewer than fifty people. The panel survey contains personal and business figures for the self-employed (with or without employees) and the leaders of small incorporated firms, weighted by settlement type and legal form. These data reveal that one-third of the 1,407 small enterprises closed down between 1993 and 1996. At the same time, some one-sixth of the operating small ventures expanded their profile, about one-eighth enlarged their markets, and more than one-tenth increased their staff.

In this chapter, liquidation and expansion are the primary indicators of the failure and success of an enterprise. Although liquidation and expansion provide, at best, tentative measures of failure and success, they are nevertheless visible and relatively reliable. By comparison, data about the profits of small enterprises are often unreliable and unavailable, because entrepreneurs want to hide or minimize profits in their reports to ensure tax avoidance and for other reasons. Data on entrepreneurial income are also unreliable. The very fact of survival may be a sign of serious achievement for many of the start-ups, even when profitability cannot be ascertained. Similarly, among firms that have survived, expansion can generally be interpreted as a measure of success.

Two types of analysis can be discerned in studies that focus on the causes underlying the liquidation or expansion of firms: first, the direct experiences of entrepreneurs, and second, the cultural, demographic, or socioeconomic phenomena that may act as probable, though not necessarily causative, factors in the survival chances of an enterprise. Both types of analysis rely on the subjective interpretation of facts, and the two supplement rather than invalidate each other. Due to the nature of the survey data used in this study, however, I focus mostly on the second type.

Anthropological research reveals that interpretations of entrepreneurial failure and success in social terms are often a local matter. For example, when village dwellers in the Hungarian Great Plain were interviewed about unsuccessful entrepreneurs, their answers were formed in social terms. The respondents identified very few cases of failure, and neighbors typically named those entrepreneurs whose social and economic status collapsed for noneconomic reasons: alcoholism, divorce, or chronic illness (Tóth 1997). In a West Hungarian industrial city, local politicians recommended a small entrepreneur to interviewers as an example of a success story. He nearly went bankrupt because a foreign chain bought out the shops in his region that used to sell his product. Nevertheless, he was still active in the local chamber of commerce and on different committees, partly because such participation was always his habit and partly because it helped him to keep his social status and to reorganize his business (Kelemen and Lengyel 1998). In political terms, he remained successful, despite his beleaguered entrepreneurial efforts. All in all, we have to keep in mind that failure and success are interpretive categories.

Conceptual Frames: Types of Capital

The theory of types of capital is important for empirical research. First, it offers a paradigm for the interpretation of social reality. Second, and perhaps more important, it helps us to understand that certain resources may be important in explaining the action potential and life chances of entrepreneurs, apart from the possession of material goods.

Social capital is used here in the sense applied by James Coleman in his study entitled "Social Capital in the Creation of Human Capital" and in his later work, which is fundamental reading in social theory (Coleman 1988, 1990). According to this theory, the social capital types are resources of rational social action that exploit certain elements of the social structure. Social capital is productive when it facilitates the attainment of certain goals. It is only partly fungible, as special social capital types correspond to specific goals.

Social capital is the least tangible of all capital types. It is a characteristic of networks of interpersonal relations rather than persons, unlike the incorporated variant of cultural capital. It differs from physical capital types, since it is embodied in relations, or in personal and official connections. Coleman emphasizes three forms of social capital: obligations, information, and norms.

In the dimension of obligations, expectations and trustworthiness can be taken for a sort of "credit slip" in Coleman's interpretation. Their operativity depends on the truthfulness of the environment and the spread of obligations. As for information capital, it is valuable not because it may be cashed in like credit, but because it provides access to otherwise costly information that may be an effective tool of the workings of networks of social relations. Paradoxically, norms and effective sanctions may be both very powerful and very fragile.

Alternative interpretations of the concept of social capital (Bourdieu 1997; Anheier et al. 1995; Nan Lin 1988; Burt 1988; Portes and Sensenbrenner 1993) go beyond the scope of this paper. Nor can we touch upon its elaboration in Francis Fukuyama's work about trust, whose relevant argumentation is also partly based on Coleman (Fukuyama 1997). The common element in all of these approaches is the proposition that there is an unevenly distributed kind of resource in the society that is embedded in informal and formal social relations and norms.

It should be noted, however, that although social capital is a major source of security, at certain points solidarity-based social ties might be disadvantageous for entrepreneurs. Summarizing their findings of a survey of Zambian entrepreneurs, Andrew A. Beveridge and Anthony R. Oberschall state that most entrepreneurs tried to separate business and kinship. Though at times they availed themselves of the services of relatives in seeking out market possibilities or rendering technical assistance, they usually avoided the employment of relatives for reasons of work discipline (Beveridge and Oberschall 1979). The theoretical implications of empirical research concerning social capital and social structure are intensively discussed in the debate about socialist and postsocialist economies (Walder 1995; Szelényi and Kostello 1996; Oberschall 1996; Róna-Tas 1997; Zhou 2000a, 2000b; Cao and Nee 2000; Walder et al. 2000). Victor Nee took a sample of Chinese peasant households to study how market reforms influenced the income of households and what factors influenced their market orientation. One of his hypotheses is that with the shift of the resources of power from redistribution to the market, cadres have slight, if any, advantage when launching a private enterprise. This hypothesis was, however, disproved by Nee's findings. Although the great majority of households with market income were noncadre households, cadres (in this case, typically brigade leaders) had more advantageous opportunities to set up in their own businesses than did other groups (Nee 1989).

In my analysis of social conditions, I attribute special significance to the networks of entrepreneurs and, more broadly speaking, to various types of social capital, since the entrepreneurs themselves called our attention to the importance of these factors and since several research findings also point in this direction (Granovetter 1994; Whitley 1992). But there is no realistic assessment of the effects of social capital, including networks and norms, unless they are compared to the effects of other groups of factors. Such groups include cultural and economic capital (Bourdieu 1997; DiMaggio and Mohr 1985).

As far as cultural capital is concerned, different conceptualizations might be equally useful for empirical analysis, as demonstrated by studies in the new economic sociology (Fernandez Kelly 1995; DiMaggio and Mohr 1985; Anheier et al. 1995). Below I interpret the term "cultural capital" after Pierre Bourdieu (Bourdieu 1978, 1997; Bourdieu and Wacquant 1992), although I do not focus on conversion and symbolic forms.

Bourdieu's main argument for extending the notion of capital in this direction claims that anything capable of producing profit and reproducing itself is capital. He differentiates three kinds of cultural capital: incorporated, objectified, and institutionalized. The incorporated form of cultural capital is the disposition of mind and body, which requires personal time input and cannot be transferred like money. The connection between incorporated capital and economic capital derives from the time spent on acquiring the former. The objectified form of cultural capital refers to material objects and the media that are closely connected to the incorporated form and may have had a formative effect in a childhood environment. The institutionalized form of cultural capital is embodied in qualifications such as academic titles, enabling the conversion of cultural capital into economic capital.

Although such interpretations of social and cultural capital may serve as inspiring starting points, they do not encompass all the factors to be taken into account when an enterprise contracts or expands. At least one obvious further group of factors must also be considered: economic capital, or, more generally, the economic conditions of an enterprise.

Operationalization of Types of Capital

Social Capital

Following Coleman's reasoning, I measure obligations by the extent of formal and informal relations. (The description of variables and models can be found in the Appendix.) Although Coleman interprets the types of social capital as interpersonal relations and hence as public goods, one may, when the unit of analysis is the individual, operationalize social capital by measuring individual rates of participation in various types of social capital. Membership in interest-protecting and professional organizations and political parties and connections with local and central authorities, banks, and agencies are all types of participation considered as *official connections*. Contacts with business partners—meeting with them at family or social events, borrowing or lending equipment, asking or providing loans or favorable conditions of payment—these are all treated as *interest-based personal connections* here. Finally, according to Coleman (1988), family background may include elements of social as well as cultural capital, but I intend to focus on the social aspects. Therefore, survey variables on the involvement of family members, relatives, and friends in solving business problems are treated as evidence of *solidarity-based personal relations*.

The measurement of norms presents the greatest problem. Our survey provides some information about the adherence to norms in the form of hard work, measured by whether or not the respondent works early in the morning and late at night, as well as on weekends. A question on whether "you must breach some rules if you want to get on" also sheds light on norm-violating behavior. These opinions about norms were measured in 1993, which precludes circular reasoning and may illumine causal connections. However, opinions based on closed questions obviously record less thoroughly deliberated or lasting judgments (Schuman and Presser 1996). All this needs to be considered when effect mechanisms and their strength, duration, or direction are studied.

Cultural Capital

The incorporated form of cultural capital is measured by education, by experiences in managerial jobs or the second economy, and by unemployment. The objectified form is operationalized as the possession of cultural goods (CD player, video recorder, computer, paintings) and the education of children as well as the way of life (foreign study trips, music, ballet, elite sports). The institutionalized form of cultural capital can be operationalized by taking into account academic qualifications and the number of professional qualifications and skills.

Economic Capital

The following indicators of economic capital are included: which branch does the respondent work in (trade or other fields), how large a market does the enterprise supply, to what extent is the capacity of the enterprise utilized, how big is it, when was it founded, is it a one-person firm or an associated company? Material capital is measured by the value of buildings, machines, equipment, and stocks as of 1995 or at the moment of liquidation.

Results

Factors Rendering the Liquidation of a Firm Probable

Social Capital

Our research suggests that social capital greatly affects whether an enterprise is liquidated or survives (Table 10.1a)*. Just as might be expected, hard work as a norm had a positive effect and the approval of rule-violation had a negative effect upon survival chances. As for obligations and expectations, personal contacts with business partners had a positive effect, while dependence on strong ties had a negative influence. Not that friends are worse advisers than business partners, but those entrepreneurs who fail to go beyond the narrow circles of trust based on solidarity will be at a disadvantage in regard to both available capital proper and attainable information. Consistent with the above-mentioned arguments of Beveridge and Oberschall, reliance on solidarity-based personal relations (with relatives, etc.) diminished survival chances, whereas interest-based personal relations (with business partners) enhanced them. Official connections, on the other hand, proved to be insignificant in this respect. Our statistics also show that former Socialist Party membership did not significantly influence the liquidation of firms (Table 10.3).

At this juncture, one may mention the findings of a case study of entrepreneurs in a West Hungarian village (Kovács 1997). The analysis of the extent of entrepreneurial networks has shown that local origin does not play an important role. The extent of interest-based networks of leaders of associated companies was more than double those of their self-employed colleagues. A considerable number of entrepreneurs heading incorporated companies were newcomers, the majority of their relations reaching beyond the settlement.

Cultural Capital

Cultural capital provides a comparatively weak explanation for the survival chances of enterprises. This is also reflected in the fluctuation in the general mood of the intellectuals. In the late 1990s, intellectuals testified to well-

---

*Tables appear in an appendix at the end of the chapter.

above-average inclinations toward entrepreneurship, but by the mid-1990s there had been a decline and the picture grew more unclear. Today, university graduates are far less willing to go into business than college graduates.

On the whole, entrepreneurs who set up on their own because of real or threatening unemployment have above-average chances of preserving their businesses, as our earlier research findings have proved. Among these entrepreneurs, there is a huge difference between those who drifted into unemployment and entrepreneurship on the one hand, and, on the other, those who, sensing the threat of joblessness, responded to the challenge by taking a decisive step in time. What we have here—even if the challenging market opportunity is a negative one—does remind one of the phenomenon that Israel Kirzner called alertness in his theory of entrepreneurship (Kirzner 1973).

Entrepreneurs often believe that a stroke of luck is necessary for success in the founding of an enterprise. As the interviews conducted by Erzsébet Őrszigethy (1999) reveal, the large role of chance in business requires of the entrepreneur an adaptable character, good communicative skills, and an ability to take advantage of circumstances. Small entrepreneurs also benefit from alacrity, flexibility, reliability, an autonomous business mentality, and a respect for independent work.

Beyond personality traits, elements of one's professional career history such as comparative autonomy, former experience in auxiliary production or the second economy, and former managerial experience play a role. As expected, earlier involvement in the second economy has a strong positive influence on the survival of an enterprise. Former managerial experience also has a positive effect upon survival chances (Table 10.1b). Comparative research on Eastern Europe has revealed that former managerial experience has relevance for entrepreneurial inclination (Róna-Tas and Lengyel 1997–98). Managers display an above-average tendency to set up their own enterprises, regardless of whether they come from the state or the cooperative sector. Our earlier investigations of entrepreneurial inclination suggested that in the late 1980s and early 1990s, past experience as a cadre in the planned economy had no significant influence upon the recruitment basis of entrepreneurs (Kuczi and Lengyel 1996). Our more recent research findings, however, indicate that various personality traits required by cadre existence have been utilized in different ways. One component of the cadre past—loyalty ensured by party membership—did not substantially influence the survival of small firms. By contrast, the other component of the cadre past—managerial experience— does affect the survival chances of an enterprise. These findings are consistent with arguments for the institutional heritage bequeathed by the planned economy, which tend to suggest that one's past as a cadre is not a neutral but a substantial component of business chance during the market transition.

Economic Capital

The economic capital proper was weakly positively correlated with survival chances according to bivariate statistics (Table 10.3), but proved insignificant in the logistic regression model (Table 10.1c). As far as economic conditions are concerned, the date of foundation as well as the number of employees and employers proved insignificant in relation to survival. A market radius stretching beyond one's settlement or immediate surroundings more than doubled the survival chances, while being self-employed or a retailer halved them. Although not included in the models, entrepreneurs' own explanations for the liquidation of their businesses are highly instructive. In response to open-ended questions, there were substantial differences between the opinions of those whose companies closed down and those who continued to run their firms but pronounced upon the fate of their less successful fellow- entrepreneurs. The majority of those who closed their firms blamed defects of the market; those whose firms remained open accused deficiencies in economic policy for the liquidation. Also, owners of failed firms mentioned subjective factors such as their age, state of health, and family background as causes, while the active businessmen attributed the failure of their colleagues to lack of expertise or competence. The latter group also noted that the firms that were liquidated probably lacked the required capital.

It pays to compare these findings with surveys of public opinion on entrepreneurial tendencies in the late 1980s and early 1990s. In the late 1980s, among those who rejected the personal possibility of setting up a business of their own, the great majority named subjective reasons—mainly lack of ability, avoidance of risk, and, to a lesser extent, age. But by the mid-1990s, the first experiences of widespread entrepreneurship modified the arguments against it. There was a massive reduction in answers referring to risk avoidance and lack of talent, while those who blamed shortage of capital and age increased heavily. Interestingly, less than 10 percent blamed flawed economic policy (high tax rates, social policy contributions, incalculable economic regulations) and even fewer cited defects of the market (shrinking markets, lost deals, growing expenses) as reasons for rejecting an entrepreneurial career at both points of time. In other words, while there was a shift from subjective to objective reasons for refusing entrepreneurial paths, people did not blame policy and market institutions directly. Nevertheless, it might be expected that the importance of lack of capital as an obstacle to entrepreneurial careers and success will grow, highlighting the role and responsibility of policy and market institutions in raising capital.

Factors Influencing the Expansion of Enterprises

The general characteristics of expanding firms in the study are as follows. Sixteen percent of active enterprises reported an expansion of activity, 13%

the widening of their market, and 11% a staff increase. Inclusive of overlapping cases, that amounts to somewhat over one-quarter, or 27%, of firms that survived in the period between 1993 and 1996. For one thing, growing firms had an above-average number of staff (related to the fact that they were incorporated companies), and they employed specialists, especially bookkeepers and solicitors. Two-thirds of growing firms employed a bookkeeper and about a quarter employed a lawyer. Among firms not undergoing any expansion, bookkeepers were employed by two-fifths and solicitors by one-tenth. Well overrepresented among growers were those with a built-up infrastructure (office, workshop, transport vehicles), those who took up bank loans, and those who invested most of their reserves into the venture. Leaders of growing firms were younger than the average entrepreneur.

The trust-based relations and competitive drive of small enterprises substantially differ from those of large firms, especially if the former are not subcontractors in production or services. A survey of large Hungarian enterprises in the first half of the 1990s revealed that the contractual contacts of these firms with the users were closer to the model based on duties and interest-based trust than to one relying on short-term deadlines and formal, arm's-length relations (Whitley et al. 1996). Large firms that dominate an entire economic branch can more easily cooperate with users and subcontractors owing to this asymmetry than can enterprises subject to greater competition.

In analyzing the cases of market expansion and growth, Ágnes Vajda has shown that firms set up as incorporated companies are more likely to grow: more than two-fifths of incorporated companies have grown, against one-fifth of self-employed enterprises (Vajda 1997). This growth was particularly typical of wholesale trading and consulting firms. By contrast, expansion was way below average for enterprises dealing in retail trade, catering, transportation, education and health services, and real estate trade. As for these branches, the nature of activity already delimits demand for growth, and signs of the saturation of the market can also be spotted.

As regards industrial and construction firms, the tendency of growth was at the average level. Investigations highlighting market relations also confirm this. The small firms that displayed a well-above-average tendency for expansion were the ones in contact with other firms (particularly Western firms or state enterprises) instead of the consumer. This repeatedly warns that interenterprise trust requires specific attention in view of growth.

Social Capital

Various forms of social capital have considerable influence upon the growth of a firm, which is measured here through the extent of business activities, the size of markets, and the number of employees (Table 10.2a) Friendly relations with business partners, celebrating family holidays or social events together, asking them for favors, or providing favorable conditions for them pays in terms of expanding the scope of business activities. Official connections to authorities, political parties, and nonbusiness partners were insignificant in terms of the scope of activities and market radius and actually had a negative effect on the growth of the staff. This, however, may have to do with the fact that this variable is correlated with the variable measuring work ethic. Acceptance of norm-breaching behavior is more typical of stagnating than of growing enterprises.

The only form of social capital that seems to encourage market expansion is the involvement of family members, relatives, and friends in the solution of business problems. The growth of the staff is also positively influenced by solidarity-based strong ties. This result is, at first glance, surprising when we recall that dependence on solidarity-based ties was more likely among liquidated ventures. Among surviving ventures, however, involvement of friends, relatives, and old colleagues proved especially characteristic of growing firms. The explanation might be that in the first case entrepreneurs are locked into primordial relations, while in the second they can exploit the strong ties, most likely benefiting from personal connections. The role of personal ties in entrepreneurial success might therefore be best understood in these models as a factor that may reinforce the effect of economic/physical and norm-based habitual endowments. The entrepreneurial attitude internalizes external possibilities; underlying the entrepreneurial inclination, one finds intuition, presentiments, habits, and judgments based on abilities, experiences, and external endowments.

Networks of small firms based on norms and attitudes are important for the inspiration of confidence. These networks connect firms with similar endowments, which constrains any behavior aimed at deceiving the partner and leads to sharing information and lending help. Instead of the statement "I don't know how to do it so I have to trust you," Perrow says, small firm networks, linking up enterprises based on similar techniques and procedures, depend on the statement "I know how to do it so I trust you" (Perrow 1993). The value of hard work and norm-abiding behavior positively influences the expansion of enterprises, although their impact is greater upon liquidation and survival. These habitual elements are better suited to separating entrepreneurial and nonentrepreneurial makeups, being overgeneralized for the inner differentiation of each entrepreneurial type.

Cultural Capital

The components of cultural capital only weakly explain the variants of expansion. Possessing cultural goods (CD player, video recorder, etc.) is related to all three forms of growth, which derives from the fact that incorporated companies and entrepreneurs of professional background are overrepresented among growing ventures. The second economy has no effect on any forms of expansion of firms. Previous experience of unemployment, however, positively influences the expansion of markets and the number of activities. Here again, just as in the case of the strong ties, unemployment correlates both with liquidation and growth. In this case, the likely explanation is that the former unemployed need an intensive period of adjustment and learning to find the proper form of activity and market. Unemployment has no connection, however, with the growth of the staff. Interestingly, those entrepreneurs who escaped forward into entrepreneurship before becoming unemployed—and who survived in great proportion—usually don't expand their businesses. Accumulated experience and skills have a positive effect in the explanation of survival chances but fail to significantly explain expansion chances. The incorporated cultural capital measured by education correlates with growth and has a positive but weak connection with expansion of activities and markets in the logistic regression models (Table 10.2b).

Economic Capital

The model of economic circumstances highlights two factors that have a particularly powerful influence upon a firm's growth: market share and the legal form of the enterprise (Table 10.2c). Incorporated firms with economic activity in several settlements and a large market share typically display signs of expansion. The utilization of capacities, total capital, and the youth of the company all have a positive but less important impact on the forms of expansion.

As we saw earlier, trading companies were overrepresented among closed-down firms. It can, however, also be demonstrated that merchants are more inclined to expand their businesses than firms on the average. At first glance, the two criteria of success—survival chances and expansion chances—contradict each other in the case of this particular group of enterprises. However, an above-average rate of fluctuation of retail dealers may fit into the picture of above-average expansion potential of wholesale trading companies among survivors.

Summary

One third of enterprises with a staff below fifty in our survey were liquidated between 1993 and 1996. Liquidation was primarily typical of commercial ventures, the self-employed, and those who heavily relied on friends and relatives, as well as those who were unemployed at some time (Table 10.3). Based on research results, social capital constitutes one of the most powerful groups of factors explaining liquidation, but economic capital also proved important. Norm-keeping behavior and adoption of the value of extensive (late night and early morning) work increased the survival chances of a firm. Social capital was particularly important for incorporated firms: as case studies of entrepreneurs reveal, the size of the network of incorporated entrepreneurs was far larger than that of the self-employed.

Small entrepreneurs who relied on primordial personal bonds in solving problems were vastly overrepresented in the liquidated category. Interest-based personal relations had a positive effect, while solidarity-based personal connections had a very strong negative effect on survival chances of small enterprises.

Former second-economy and managerial experience had a positive influence on survival. Yet the models of cultural capital had a weak explanatory force, which may derive from the fact that these elements promote formalized knowledge and the related patterns of survival or liquidation. Research findings suggest that we have to separate the impacts of the cadre past: while loyalty proved by party membership had no impact on the social processes of entrepreneurial selection, managerial experiences were connected with the chances of survival. Forced entrepreneurship had two components as well. Those who were unemployed before becoming independent generally were unsuccessful as entrepreneurs, but among those who did succeed, growth potential was above average. Those who sensed the threat of unemployment and escaped forward into the enterprise survived in a great proportion.

Next we considered expansion of surviving enterprises. About a quarter of the enterprises active between 1993 and 1996 displayed some growth. Among these, about a sixth of small firms expanded their activity, a fourth enlarged their markets, and slightly more than a tenth increased the staff. One-fifth of the self-employed and more than two-fifths of the incorporated companies expanded. Highly above-average growth was only typical of small ventures that produced for other firms and not for the ultimate consumer. Overrepresented in this regard were wholesale traders and special consultants. The expanding small ventures had an above-average employment and capacity-exploiting policy, were incorporated, and to a large extent invested most of their surplus in the enterprise (Table 10.4.). Highly overrepresented among the growing small ventures were those who employed specialists, had elaborate infrastructures, and acquired credit.

Among the groups of factors considered, the model of social capital had the greatest significance in the extension of staff. Both solidarity-based connections and indicators of norm-keeping behavior were important in explaining the growth of the number of employees. Extension of market radius and the number of activities are also most influenced by solidarity-based strong ties.

Dependence on solidarity-based strong ties was found among expanding and closed-down firms alike. The explanation of this might be that in the latter case, solidarity means a kind of network reduced to friends and relatives, while in the former it is firm support of wider trust-based market operations. The drive for independence is shared by both groups, the former being also connected to a profit-oriented attitude and the ability to establish mutually advantageous contacts. The value of hard work had no impact on the extension of market radius or the scope of activities. One may venture to say that the habitual elements are better suited to marking entrepreneurial and nonentrepreneurial dispositions off from each other: norms have a far smaller influence on the growth of an enterprise than on its survival or liquidation.

Appendix

Table 10.1a

Logistic Regression Models of Survival of Enterprises
Social Capital (Dependent variable = SURVIVAL)

Independent Variables	B	Exp (B)
HARDWORK	0.96	2.60
RULEVIOL	−0.40*[1]	0.67
BUSITIES	0.94	2.57
PERSTIES	−1.95	0.14
OFFTIES	n.s.	
Constant	0.60	
N	732	
−2LL	764.70	
Model Chi sq.	167.67	

Notes:
SURVIVAL: fate of the enterprise in 1996 (0 = liquidated, 1 = working)
HARDWORK: works early morning and late night, 1993 (0 = no, 1 = yes)
RULEVIOL: to get ahead must breach certain rules, 1993 (0 = disagree, 1 = agree)
BUSITIES: any of the following: meeting with business partners for birthday parties, family, or social events; borrowing equipment or asking for a loan or favorable conditions of payment or modification of deadlines from business partners; lending equipment, allowing modification of a deadline, providing a loan or favorable conditions of payment for business partners on a friendly basis, 1993 (0 = no, 1 = yes)
PERSTIES: whom can entrepreneur rely on in solving problems, 1993 (0 = works alone or other; 1 = family, relatives, friends, old colleagues)
OFFTIES: any of the following: official connections with local authorities, ministries, banks, political parties, privatization agencies, labor offices, foundations, entrepreneurial centers, safeguarding bodies, educational institutions, foreign enterprises, state enterprises, cooperatives, 1993 (0 = no, 1 = yes)
[1] Hereinafter significance levels differing from 0.0001 are signed separately (0.05 = *, 0.01 = **, 0.001 = ***)

Table 10.1b

Cultural Capital (Dependent Variable = SURVIVAL)

Independent Variables	B	Exp (B)
NUMQUAL	0.11*	1.11
MGREVER	0.23*	1.26
UNEMPL	−0.87	0.42
SECECON	0.40***	1.48
CULTGOOD	0.60	1.83
Constant	−0.39	
N	1,364	
−2 LL	1,638.71	
Model Chi sq.	88.17	

Notes:
SURVIVAL: fate of the enterprise in 1996 (0 = liquidated, 1 = working)
NUMQUAL: number of qualifications
MGREVER: ever held a managerial position (0 = no, 1 = yes)
UNEMPL: ever unemployed (0 = no, 1 = yes)
SECECON: had experiences in the second economy (0 = no, 1 = yes)
CULTGOOD: owns CD player, video recorder (0 = no, 1 = yes)

Table 10.1c

Economic Capital (Dependent Variable: SURVIVAL)

Independent Variables	B	Exp (B)
NUMEMPL	n.s.	
ENTVALUE	n.s.	
SELFEMPL	−0.77**	0.46
SIZEMARK	0.74***	2.09
TRADE	−0.59**	0.55
USECAPAC	0.02	1.02
BEGYEAR	n.s.	
Constant	0.98	
N	737.00	
−2 LL	722.93	
Model Chi sq.	91.11	

Notes:
SURVIVAL: fate of the enterprise in 1996 (0 = liquidated, 1 = working)
NUMEMPL: number of employers and employees in the last year
ENTVALUE: value of buildings, machines, equipment, and stocks owned by the enterprise in 1995 or in the year of liquidation (Ft)
SELFEMPL: self-employed (0 = company, 1 = self-employed)
SIZEMARK: size of the market in the last year (0 = one settlement, 1 = more than one settlement area)
TRADE: involved in trade (0 = no, 1 = yes)
USECAPAC: use of capacity in 1993 (%)
BEGYEAR: year enterprise was founded

Table 10.2a

Logistic Regression Models of Expansion of Enterprises
Social Capital (dependent variables: ACT, MARKET, STAFF)

Independent variables	Extension of activities		Markets		Number of employees	
	B	EXP(B)	B	EXP(B)	B	EXP(B)
HARDWORK	n.s.		n.s.		1.70**	5.46
RULEVIOL	–0.71*	0.49	n.s.		–0.55*	0.58
BUSITIES	0.81	2.25	n.s.		n.s.	
PERSTIES	0.94**	2.55	0.97	2.6282	2.24	9.37
OFFTIES	n.s.		n.s.		–1.36**	0.26
Constant	–2.59		–2.45		–3.62	
N	487		487		487	
–2 LL	356.42		349.46		273.30	
Model chi sq.	21.15		14.46		59.01	

Notes:
ACT: extended the activities between 1993 and 1996 (0 = no, 1 = yes)
MARKET: enlarged the market between 1993 and 1996 (0 = no, 1 = yes)
STAFF: increased the number of employees between 1993 and 1996 (0 = no, 1 = yes)
HARDWORK: works early morning and late night, 1993 (0 = no, 1 = yes)
RULEVIOL: to get ahead must breach certain rules, 1993 (0=disagree, 1=agree)
BUSITIES: any of the following: meeting with business partners for birthday parties, family, or social events; borrowing equipment or asking for a loan or favorable conditions of payment or modification of deadlines from business partners; lending equipment, allowing modification of a deadline, providing a loan or favorable conditions of payment for business partners on a friendly basis, 1993 (0 = no, 1 = yes)
PERSTIES: whom can entrepreneur rely on in solving problems, 1993 (0 = works alone or other; 1 = family, relatives, friends, old colleagues)
OFFTIES: any of the following: official connections with local authorities, ministries, banks, political parties, privatization agencies, labor offices, foundations, entrepreneurial centers, safeguarding bodies, educational institutions, foreign enterprises, state enterprises, cooperatives, 1993 (0 = no, 1 = yes)

Table 10.2b

Cultural Capital (Dependent Variables: ACT, MARKET, STAFF)

Independent variables	Extension of activities		Markets		Number of employees	
	B	EXP(B)	B	EXP(B)	B	EXP(B)
NUMQUAL	n.s.		n.s.		n.s.	
YEAREDUC	0.06*	1.06	0.10**	1.10	n.s.	
MGREVER	n.s.		n.s.		n.s.	
UNEMPL	1.33	3.80	1.08	2.96	n.s.	
SECECON	n.s.		n.s.		n.s.	
CULTGOOD	0.69**	1.99	.52*	1.69	0.69***	1.98
CULTKIDS	0.57**	1.76	n.s.		n.s.	
Constant	−3.05		−3.85		−2.64	
N	886		886		886	
−2 LL	722.92		649.31		623.70	
Model chi sq.	56.73		35.46		15.29	

Notes:
ACT: extended the activities between 1993 and 1996 (0 = no, 1 = yes)
MARKET: enlarged the market between 1993 and 1996 (0 = no, 1 = yes)
STAFF: increased the number of employees between 1993 and 1996 (0 = no, 1 = yes)
NUMQUAL: number of qualifications
YEAREDUC: years in school
MGREVER: ever held a managerial position (0 = no, 1 = yes)
UNEMPL: ever unemployed (0 = no, 1 = yes)
SECECON: had experiences in the second economy (0 = no, 1 = yes)
CULTGOOD: has CD player, video recorder (0 = no, 1 = yes)
CULTKIDS: children attended foreign schools or took paid courses in music, ballet, riding, or sailing (0 = no, 1 = yes)

Table 10.2c

Economic Capital (Dependent Variables: ACT, MARKET, STAFF)

Independent variables	Extension of activities		Markets		Number of employees	
	B	EXP(B)	B	EXP(B)	B	EXP(B)
SELFEMPL	−0.62*	0.54	−0.82**	0.44	−0.59	0.56
TRADE	1.32	3.75	0.91**	2.48	n.s.	
SIZEMARK	1.02***	2.76	1.27	3.57	1.39***	2.83
USECAPAC	0.01*	1.01	n.s.		n.s.	
ENTVALUE	n.s.		n.s.		5.7E-05**	1.00
BEGYEAR	0.07*	1.08	0.08*	1.08	0.14**	1.15
Constant	−9.10		−9.01		−15.30	
N	575		572		572	
−2 LL	470.99		437.87		379.47	
Model Chi sq.	44.41		42.22		59.59	

Notes:
ACT: extended the activities between 1993 and 1996 (0 = no, 1 = yes)
MARKET: enlarged the market between 1993 and 1996 (0 = no, 1 = yes)
STAFF: increased the number of employees between 1993 and 1996 (0 = no, 1 = yes)
SELFEMPL: self-employed (0 = company, 1 = self-employed)
TRADE: involved in trade (0 = no, 1 = yes)
SIZEMARK: size of the market in the last year (0 = one settlement, 1 = more than one settlement area)
USECAPAC: use of capacity in 1993 (%)
ENTVALUE: value of buildings, machines, equipment, and stocks owned by the enterprise in 1995 or in the year of liquidation (Ft)
BEGYEAR: year enterprise was founded

Table 10.3

Proportion of Liquidated Enterprises in Different Categories

Category	%	Cramer's V (Phi)	N
Average	33.1	–	1,407
RULEVIOL (agrees that whoever wants to get ahead must violate certain rules)	37.7	0.11**	761
HARDWORK (works early morning and late night)	30.1	0.14	761
BUSITIES (hasn't obligatory relations with business partners on friendly basis)	46.6	0.18	745
OFFTIES (hasn't official connections with authorities, parties, banks, etc.)	37.9	n.s.	743
PERSTIES (relies on family, relatives, friends, old colleagues in solving problems)	47.3	0.29	1,407
PARTY (ever was a Hungarian Socialist Workers Party member)	26.6	n.s.	1,407
EDUCATION:			
Elementary	52.8	0.21	111
Vocational	30.6		304
Secondary	34.1		543
College	30.6		254
University	22.7		188
MGREVER (ever fulfilled managerial position)	28.0	0.10	1,398
UNEMPL (ever was unemployed)	47.9	0.14	1,402
ENTFORCE (forced entrepreneur—was unemployed or was afraid of being unemployed)	21.7	0.17	1,391
SECECON (had experiences in the second economy)	26.2	0.13	1,397
CULTGOOD (has CD player, video recorder, computer, or paintings)	22.1	0.18	1,407
CULTKIDS (children attended foreign schools or took paid courses in music, ballet, riding, or sailing)	24.7	0.07	1,407
REGION:			
Countryside	33.2	n.s.	992
Budapest	32.9		415
SELFEMP (self-employed)	37.4	0.19	1,407
TRADE (engaged in trade)	50.1	0.23	1,407
BEGYEAR (year of starting: 1991–)	42.9	0.10**	1,202
LOWCAP (economic capital, below average)	30.7	0.35	983
AVGCAPAC (use of capacity, 50%–)	12.6	0.29	1,092
LOWHOURS (working hours below average)	41.7	0.14	746
BIGMARK (size of the market: more settlement, greater area)	21.7	0.22	1,325

Table 10.4

Proportion of Growing Enterprises in Different Categories

Category	Expansion of activities		Expansion of the market		Expansion of the staff		
	%	Cr's V (Phi)	%	Cr's V (Phi)	%	Cr's V (Phi)	N
Average	15.8	—	12.7	—	11.3	—	942
RULEVIOL (agrees that whoever wants to get ahead must breach certain rules)	10.1	0.10*	13.3	n.s.	9.2	n.s.	508
BUSITIES (hasn't obligatory relations with business partners on friendly basis)	8.1	0.08*	11.8	n.s.	6.8*	0.08	497
OFFTIES (hasn't official connections to authorities, parties, banks, etc.)	9.3	n.s.	13.3	n.s.	9.6	n.s.	493
HARDWORK (works early morning and late night)	12.6	n.s.	12.1	n.s.	12.0	0.07*	508
PERSTIES (relies on family, relatives, friends, old colleagues in solving problems)	23.2	0.16	19.2	0.15	22.6	0.28	942
PARTY (ever was a Hungarian Socialist Workers Party member)	16.4	n.s.	12.6	n.s.	12.0	n.s.	942
EDUCATION							
Elementary	3.2	0.16***	6.3	0.13*	3.1	0.16	52
Vocational	9.1		8.4		4.7		211
Secondary	16.5		11.5		12.6		357
College	18.8		16.7		13.5		176
University	24.5		19.5		18.0		145
MGREVER (ever fulfilled managerial position)	16.2	n.s.	15.5	0.07*	14.3	0.08	942
UNEMPL (ever was unemployed)	31.7	0.15	24.4	0.12***	11.0	n.s.	942
ENTFORCE (forced entrepreneur—was unemployed or was afraid of being unemployed)	14.2	0.09	12.7	n.s.	9.2	0.12***	926

Variable							N
SECECON (had experiences in the second economy)	18.4	n.s.	15.8	0.07	13.4	n.s.	942
CULTGOOD (has CD player, video recorder, computer, or paintings)	20.5	0.14	15.8	0.10**	14.3	0.10**	942
CULTKIDS (children attended foreign schools or took paid courses in music, ballet, riding, sailing)	25.3	0.12	12.7	n.s.	13.8	n.s.	942
REGION							
Countryside	15.2	n.s.	13.7	n.s.	11.6	n.s.	663
Budapest	17.3	0.10**	10.2	0.17	10.5	0.21	279
SELFEMP (self-employed)	13.9	n.s.	9.6	n.s.	7.6	0.09	942
TRADE (engaged in trade)	18.2	0.13***	11.1	0.08	5.5	n.s.	942
BEGYEAR (year of starting: 1991–)	19.7	n.s.	15.3	n.s.	13.4	0.13	737
LOWCAP (economic capital, below average)	15.8	0.12	12.7	0.11**	8.1	0.16	778
AVGCAPAC (use of capacity, 50%–)	20.0	0.08*	14.7	n.s.	15.0	0.07	785
LOWHOURS (working hours below average)	13.3		11.3		9.8		942
BIGMARK (size of the market: more settlement, greater area)	21.2	0.16	19.1	0.19	16.6	0.18	897
SUB (subcontracting firm)	17.7	n.s.	17.0	0.06	16.6	0.08*	933
INVEST (invested the reserve into the venture)	19.4	0.12	17.6	0.18	15.8	0.17	935

Bibliography

Angelusz, Robert (ed.). 1997. *A társadalmi rétegződés komponensei* [Components of social stratification]. Budapest: Új Mandátum K.

Anheier, Helmut K., Jürgen Gerhards, and Frank P. Romo. 1995. Forms of Capital and Social Structure in Cultural Fields: Examining Bourdieu's Social Topography. *American Journal of Sociology* 100 (4): 859–903.

Beveridge, Andrew A., and Anthony R. Oberschall. 1979. *African Businessmen and Development in Zambia*. Princeton: Princeton University Press.

Bourdieu, Pierre. 1978. Az osztályok pályája és a valószinûségi okság [The orbit of classes and probability causality]. In *A társadalmi egyenlőtlenségek újratermelődése* [Reproduction of social inequalities]. Budapest: Gondolat, pp. 237–310.

———. 1997. Gazdasági tőke, kulturális tőke, társadalmi tőke [Economic capital, cultural capital, social capital]. In R. Angelusz (ed.), *A társadalmi rétegződés komponensei* [Components of social stratification]. Budapest: Új Mandátum K., pp. 156–177.

Bourdieu, Pierre, and Loic J.D. Wacquant. 1992. *An Invitation to Reflexive Sociology*. Cambridge, UK: Polity Press.

Burt, Ronald S. 1988. A státusz/szerepegyüttesek mint kvázi-hálózati poziciók vizsgálata nagy népességek felvételeiben [Examining status/groups of roles as quasi-network positions in surveys of large samples]. *Szociológiai Figyelő* 3, 61–78.

Cao Yang and Victor G. Nee. 2000. Comment: Controversies and Evidence in the Market Transition Debate. *American Journal of Sociology* 105: 1175–1189.

Coleman, James. 1988. Social Capital in the Creation of Human Capital. *American Journal of Sociology* 94, Supplement: 95–120.

———. 1990. *Foundations of Social Theory*. Cambridge, MA: Belknap Press.

Czakó, Ágnes, Tibor Kuczi, György Lengyel, and Ágnes Vajda. 1994. *Vállalkozások és vállalkozók, 1993* [Enterprises and entrepreneurs, 1993]. Budapest: KSH-BKE.

DiMaggio, Paul, and John Mohr. 1985. Cultural Capital, Educational Attainment and Marital Selection. *American Journal of Sociology* 90: 1231–1261.

Fernandez Kelly, M. Patricia. 1995. Social and Cultural Capital in the Urban Ghetto: Implications for the Economic Sociology of Immigration. In Portes Alejandro (ed.), *The Economic Sociology of Immigration: Essays on Networks, Ethnicity and Entrepreneurship*. New York: Sage, pp. 213–247.

Fukuyama, Francis. 1997. *Bizalom* [Trust]. Budapest: Európa K.

Granovetter, Mark. 1994. Business Groups. In Richard Swedberg and Neil Smelser (eds.), *The Handbook of Economic Sociology*. Princeton: Princeton University Press, Russell Sage Foundation, New York.

Kelemen, Katalin, and György Lengyel. 1998. Interview with R.S., entrepreneur (manuscript).

Kirzner, Israel M. 1973. *Competition and Entrepreneurship*. Chicago: University of Chicago Press.

Kovács, Róbert. 1997. A gencsapáti vállalkozások kapcsolatrendszere [The network system of enterprises in Gencsapati] (manuscript).

Kuczi, Tibor, and György Lengyel. 1996. Vállalkozók és vállalkozói hajlandóság Kelet-Európában [Entrepreneurs and entrepreneurial inclination in Eastern Europe]. In György Lengyel (ed.), *Vállalkozók és vállalkozói hajlandóság* [Entrepreneurs and entrepreneurial inclination]. Budapest: BKE, pp. 259–280.

Nan Lin. 1988. Társadalmi erőforrások és instrumentális cselekvés [Social resources and instrumental action]. *Szociológiai Figyelő* 3: 79–92.

Nee, Victor. 1989. A Theory of Market Transition: From Redistribution to Market. *American Sociological Review* 54: 663–681.

———. 1996. The Emergence of Market Society: Changing Mechanism of Stratification in China. *American Journal of Sociology* 101: 908–949.

Oberschall, Anthony. 1996. The Great Transition: China, Hungary and Sociology Exit Socialism into the Market. *American Journal of Sociology* 101: 1028–1041.

Őrszigethy, Erzsébet. 1999. Egy kisváros vidéki pillérei [Provincial pillars of a town]. In György Lengyel (ed.), *Kisvállalkozások megszűnése, bővülése és kapcsolatrendszere* [Liquidation, expansion and networks of small enterprises]. Budapest: BKE Műhelytanulányok.

Perrow, Charles. 1993. Small Firm Networks. In Richard Swedberg (ed.), *Explorations in Economic Sociology*. New York: Russell Sage Foundation, pp. 377–402.

Portes, Alejandro, and Julia Sensenbrenner. 1993. Embeddedness and Immigration: Notes on the Social Determinants of Economic Action. *American Journal of Sociology* 99: 1320–1350.

Róna-Tas, Ákos, and György Lengyel (eds.). 1997–1998. Entrepreneurship in Eastern Europe I-II. *International Journal of Sociology* 27: 3–4.

Schuman, Howard, and Stanley Presser. 1996. *Questions and Answers in Attitude Surveys*. London: Sage Publications.

Szelényi, Iván, and Eric Kostello. 1996. The Market Transition Debate: Toward a Synthesis? *American Journal of Sociology* 101: 1082–1096.

Tóth, Lilla. 1997. Entrepreneurial Careers and Networks in a Large Village. In György Lengyel (ed.), *Megszűnt és működő vállalkozások, 1993–1996* [Wound-up and working enterprises]. Budapest: MVA, pp. 103–122.

Vajda, Ágnes. 1997. A kisvállalkozások növekedéséről [On the growth of small enterprises] (manuscript).

Walder, Andrew G. 1995. Career Mobility and the Communist Political Order. *American Sociological Review* 60: 309–328.

Walder, Andrew G., Bobai Li, and Donald J. Treiman. 2000. Politics and Life Chances in a State Socialist Regime: Dual Career Path into the Urban Chinese Elite, 1949 to 1996. *American Sociological Review* 65: 191–209.

Whitley, Richard. 1992. Societies, Firms and Markets: The Social Structuring of Business Systems. In R. Whitley (ed.), *European Business Systems*. London: Sage.

Whitley, Richard, Jeffrey Henderson, Laszlo Czaban, and György Lengyel. 1996. Trust and Contractual Relations in an Emerging Capitalist Economy: The Changing Trading Relationships of Ten Large Hungarian Enterprises. *Organization Studies* 3: 397–420.

Zhou Xueguang. 2000a. Economic Transformation and Income Inequality in Urban China: Evidence from Panel Data. *American Journal of Sociology* 105: 1135–1174.

———. 2000b. Reply: Beyond the Debate and Toward Substantive Institutional Analysis. *American Journal of Sociology* 105: 1190–1195.

11

Entrepreneurial Governmentality in Postsocialist Russia

A Cultural Investigation of Business Practices

Alexei Yurchak

Entrepreneurial Governmentality

According to a classical understanding of entrepreneurship, young Soviets in the late 1980s were not supposed to be good at inventing and running private businesses because their generation was raised in a society in which private business was practically nonexistent. And yet, in the late 1980s, great numbers of young people quickly started creating new private businesses and turned out to be exceptionally good at it. Clearly, the mere adoption in the Soviet Union of the laws on individual private activity (1986) and on cooperatives (1988) could not teach anyone overnight how to be a businessman. These people acquired particular entrepreneurial knowledge and skills long before the collapse of the Soviet state, not necessarily by acting as managers in Soviet industry or dealers on the black market, but by having to operate within the Soviet system itself. How did this happen? To answer this question, I will use an analytical tool that is broad enough to encompass under one rubric of "entrepreneurship" diverse and seemingly disconnected phenomena from both the Soviet and post-Soviet contexts. To create this analytical tool, I will consider the concept of entrepreneurship through the angle of Foucault's concept of governmentality (1991), emphasizing the aspects of entrepreneurship that involve organizing and governing people, institutions, relations, objects, and ideas.

In the classic sense, the term "entrepreneurship" refers to the industrious, systematic activity of organizing and operating a profit-making business venture and assuming the risks of possible failure.[1] In a narrow reading, this definition speaks about business activity, markets, and economic profit. We may also read it in a wider sense as referring to an activity that belongs to the family of governing processes. To think of entrepreneurship in this way, I will turn to Foucault's concept of "governmentality."

This term was coined by Foucault as a synonym for what he called the "art of government" or "rationality of government" (Foucault 1991). "Government," according to Foucault, is "a form of activity aiming to shape, guide or affect the conduct of some person or persons." This activity can involve different types of relations: "the relation between self and self, private interpersonal relations involving some form of control or guidance, relations within social institutions and communities and, finally, relations concerned with the exercise of political sovereignty." Governmentality, then, is "a way or system of thinking about the nature of the practice of government (who can govern; what governing is; what or who is governed), capable of making some form of that activity thinkable and practicable both to its practitioners and to those upon whom it was practiced" (Gordon 1991: 2–3).

Considering the activity of entrepreneurship as a form of governmentality, I will use the category of entrepreneurial governmentality to organize my analysis. In Foucauldian terms, then, to be an entrepreneur is to have entrepreneurial governmentality that makes it "thinkable and practicable" to relate to different aspects of the world—people, relations, institutions, the state, laws—in terms of symbolic commodities, risks, capital, profits, costs, needs, demands, and so on. It is a way of knowing what an entrepreneurial act is, who can act entrepreneurially, and what or whom can be acted upon in an entrepreneurial way. The category of entrepreneurial governmentality will allow me to speak about entrepreneurship in a context in which there was no private market or business. For example, Komsomol secretaries in the Soviet period acted as entrepreneurs in the field of ideological production in which ideological texts, speeches, rituals, social programs, educational sessions, and professional contests were produced.[2] To be a Komsomol secretary, especially during the late Soviet period, was to apply very particular "technologies" of entrepreneurial governmentality that allowed one to fulfill projects and achieve goals by conducting procedures, organizing people, relating to institutions, and so on.

What made these entrepreneurial technologies unique had to do with their particular setting vis-à-vis the state in a socialist context. No relationship between the individual and the state is marked only by official codes. The state's institutions, laws, and ideologies everywhere are related to in a mixture of terms that allows individuals to "officialize" or "personalize" them depending on the context. However, the Soviet state, especially during late socialism, was an exceptional case of this mixture of terms. Drawing from Bakhtin's notion of "hybridity,"[3] I posit that in the Soviet context the officialized and personalized relations between the individual and the state were marked by an extreme form of hybridity. This translated, in everyday practice, into the necessity to constantly switch back and forth between the officialized and personalized terms in one's relations with the state.

The socialist entrepreneurial technologies were organized precisely around an ability to switch between these distinct forms and meanings in different public contexts. These technologies proved crucial, I argue, for the development of private business in the first post-Soviet years. Understanding this hybrid cultural model is important for understanding how business practices have evolved since the fall of socialism. For example, this perspective will show that the concept of "corruption," which is used to describe much of business practice in Russia today,[4] often is a misnomer. This concept hinges on a flattened view of human action in terms of rational-choice behavior.[5] We cannot brand practice as immoral or irrational without first studying it ethnographically and historically.

The hybrid social system has a rhyme and reason of its own. Like many other systems, it has provided its actors with various choices of ethical and unethical behavior. Indeed, the view of the Russian state in accordance with this hybrid model allows small business owners to circumvent some state laws that they understand as antidemocratic, while still genuinely aspiring to a society that is based on the democratic "rule of law." In fact, I will argue, it is precisely the entrepreneurs of small business who are particularly willing and prepared to serve as a foundation for the development of civil society in Russia.[6] Conducting an ethnographic analysis of the practices, expectations, and desires of these people is crucial for the understanding of what the rule of law and civil society will mean in the Russian context and how they may develop.[7]

Methods and Informants

The research for this chapter was part of a larger anthropological study of the culture of the "last Soviet generation." To find informants for that larger project, I placed a number of ads in St. Petersburg newspapers *Chas Pik* and *Nevskoe Vremia* in 1994. The ads explained that I was interested in investigating how my generation of Russians—people who grew up and came of age just before the changes of perestroika—adapted to the dramatic social changes of the last ten years. These ads yielded a wide response, and I was able to collect several extensive diaries and correspondences dating from the 1980s and to conduct many interviews, in which their authors described how they experienced the period of change. Originally, I did not intend to study post-Soviet entrepreneurs. However, it soon became apparent that an increasing number of the people in their thirties whom I interviewed for my research had changed their previous occupations and turned to private business activities in the 1990s. The topic for this chapter emerged out of that realization.

To embark on a more extensive study of private business in St. Petersburg, I joined the private advertising agency Market Point where, for a year, in 1994 and 1995, I worked as a copywriter. This work put me in contact with a large number of businesses and entrepreneurs in the city. I conducted long, semistructured interviews with twenty-six entrepreneurs (see the full list of the informants in the Appendix). Five of these people (the first five names on the list) I interviewed repeatedly over the course of six years, from 1994 to 1999. I also conducted participant-observation research in four businesses: most extensively in a computer sales and maintenance firm (Yurii), and on a more limited scale in an advertising firm (Lena), a public relations firm (Leonid), and a car importing business (Mikhail). In this chapter I explicitly quote several interviews and use many more interviews, as well as my field notes, as background for the discussion.

Anthropological ethnographic methods, especially participant observation, can offer unique insights into the analysis of entrepreneurs' understandings and practices in the post-Soviet context. These methods have the ability to highlight contradictions and inconsistencies between what people say that they do and what they in fact do, providing a perspective on subtle and crucial shades of meaning that may remain invisible to methods based on structured interviews and questionnaires.

The Last Soviet Generation

The largest group of successful entrepreneurs that emerged in the first post-Soviet decade belongs to one generation. Today they are in their thirties to early forties,[8] and most of them own small and medium-sized businesses, that is, firms with fewer than 100 workers.[9] These people were born between the mid-1950s and late 1960s and came of age, became educated, and started their adult lives during the Brezhnev period, before the changes of perestroika began in 1986. We may call this cohort the last Soviet generation. The following discussion concerns mostly the cultural understandings and practices of that generation.

The analysis of changing cultural dynamics among generations, "cohort analysis," has occupied a prominent position in anthropology, especially during the past two decades. By focusing on the temporal dimension, this approach fits well with current anthropological views of culture as dynamic, contested, and nonhomogeneous. As many recent anthropological studies have argued, "coming of age at particular moments creates telling fault lines through which meaning is transformed" (Rofel 1999: 22). As we will see, the early experiences of the members of the last Soviet generation significantly affected how they understood, practiced, and shaped the activity of private business in the late Soviet and early post-Soviet years. This analysis starts in the 1970s and 1980s, before private business was officially born but when diverse conditions for its future development were shaped. I will then trace the evolution of some forms of entrepreneurial governmentality into the present.[10]

Most of the first private entrepreneurs of the last Soviet generation followed three trajectories from socialism to post-Soviet business: from Komsomol activism to business, from industry and science to business, and from the black market to business. I will concentrate on the first two trajectories since they are particularly widespread: in 1996 almost 40% of all entrepreneurs came from leading positions in the Komsomol and another 40% came from the Soviet industry (Kryshtanovskaia 1996; Medvedev 1998).

The period of late socialism, from the mid-1960s to mid-1980s, witnessed a shift toward a particular cultural logic of the individual's relationship with the state. This was a shift from the idealism of the Khrushchev period toward more pragmatic cultural values and an ambivalent or "hybrid" view of the official ideology (Yurchak 1997, 2000b). The Komsomol, the ideological institution of the younger generation, during late socialism proved particularly instrumental in shaping new forms of entrepreneurial governmentality. The spheres of activity where economic, cultural, and ideological production intersected—for example, the spheres managed by the Komsomol committees—proved to be the most fertile ground for the future growth of private firms. These activities taught Komsomol members a new pragmatic understanding of work, time, money, skills, and professional relations and particular hybrid understandings of the official plans, rules, laws, and institutions of the party-state. I will discuss these understandings below.

Here I will describe just a few of these spheres of activity. One of these was the youth construction brigades, which built houses or cowsheds in the collective farms outside of cities in which college students and young industrial employees participated throughout the late socialist period. These brigades were organized under the auspices of the Komsomol and took different forms, from official student companies (*stroiotriad*) to quasi-private *shabashkas*.[11] The latter conducted work based on private arrangements with employers and were considerably more efficient and better compensated than was usual in the socialist economy.

The cultural dynamic within these construction brigades can serve as a lens through which we can observe shifting personal relations with the party-state in the late socialist period. To provide an outline of that cultural shift, I will quote from a diary that was written in Moscow in the late 1970s.[12] The diary's author, Vladimir, compares his experiences of the summer construction brigades in two periods, the late 1950s and the 1970s. Vladimir was born in 1939 and belongs to the technical intelligentsia and to the generation of the "sixtiers" (*shestidesiatniki*), whose identities were defined during the decade of the 1960s. These people started as young supporters of the Communist Party's democratizing reforms under Khrushchev but later became increasingly disillusioned by the retreat from reform under Brezhnev. As a result, many of them combined an affinity to communist ideals with a criticism of the shortcomings of the Soviet system.

At the height of Khrushchev's reforms, in 1957, Vladimir, an eighteen-year-old student in a Moscow technical college, joined a student construction brigade. He romanticized this form of work and chose to participate in it not for profit but for the Komsomol enthusiasm, communal spirit, and heroic labor. At the end of that summer, the participants in the brigade returned to Moscow to be greeted at the train station as heroes by a crowd of fellow students. Vladimir compared his experience in the 1957 brigade with a "labor commune" (*trudovaia komunna*):

> We worked in a Kustanai Soviet farm as a brigade at the central manor, doing various types of work, especially construction. Our conditions were somewhat similar to the contemporary shabashka brigades and student construction brigades: we lived as a commune, shared food and housing, worked on assignments, and at the end of the season equally divided among all participants the money that the brigade earned as a whole. . . . We hardly made enough to cover the cost of our food, but this did not sadden us—we were prepared to work even for free.

Vladimir took part in several more brigades in the late 1950s while at college. In the 1970s, summer construction brigades, in which students and young employees of state enterprises participated, became a much wider phenomenon. At the same time, a more pragmatic model of such brigades became common—*shabashka* brigades that operated as temporary quasi-private enterprises. Such brigades worked all over the Soviet Union, often traveling across the whole country to the sites of their short-term employment. Due to a shortage of labor in some regions of the country, a particular organization of the work process, and special relations with the employers, these brigades often managed to earn unusually high wages by completing their jobs in a much shorter time and with fewer people than was provided for by the official plan.

In 1974, after a fifteen-year break, Vladimir, now a thirty-five-year-old college instructor, applied to participate in a summer *shabashka* brigade organized at his college. Vladimir writes that although he and his wife were in dire straits (they had just had their second child), he was embarrassed to admit that he applied to the brigade for the money. In fact, he was keen to recreate the spirit of the labor commune that he came to know in the late 1950s.

The brigade traveled from Moscow to the region of Khabarovsk, close to the Pacific coast, to construct buildings for a local collective farm. Vladimir described the brigade as consisting of two distinct generations: college students between ages nineteen and twenty-one (members of the last Soviet generation), one of whom, Seryozha, was the brigade's organizer and leader, and college instructors and researchers in their mid-thirties (the generation of the sixties). Vladimir described what he perceived as a symptomatic cultural shift between the two generations in their understanding of collective and individual interests, personal worth, the value of labor, money, and time.

At the end of the summer, when the members of the *shabashka* brigade returned to Moscow, it was time to pay individual salaries by dividing the sum received by the brigade. Vladimir and other older members expected the division according to the "collective principle" with which they were familiar: everyone is paid equally. Seryozha and his peers disagreed: they wanted to assign salaries according to the "individual principle" by calculating the "personal worth" of everyone's work to the brigade. Seryozha decided to subjectively assign everyone a "quotient" reflecting the kinds of labor performed, the person's skills, speed, attitude to work, and so on. Moreover, to avoid any disagreements, Seryozha, as the brigadier, decided on everyone's quotients himself. This decision at first led to a silent conflict between "the young" and "the old." However, the older generation was extremely embarrassed to initiate a public confrontation over the issue of money—a reluctance of which, according to Vladimir, Seryozha was well aware and which he used. As a result, Vladimir and his peers complied. Vladimir offers a telling analysis of the cultural dynamic manifested in this event, as he and his older peers perceived it:

> It seems to me that the conflict between Seryozha and his friends, on the one hand, and the "teachers," on the other, is a conflict of generations. The collective and hopeless idealism of the people who were educated in the old Komsomol traditions is being replaced by the generation of Seryozha and his friends—calculating [*raschiotlivye*), tough, brazen, individualist, and exploiting, within allowed limits, not only of themselves but also of any "fool" around. For the "older generation" [*dlia starshikh*) money is a "tainted prose of life" [*'prezrennaia proza zhizni'*) and is acceptable only as an additional recognition of the importance of their labor. For the "younger generation" [*dlia 'molodykh'*) money is the main measure of value [*glavnyi meritel' tsennostei*). For them money does not "smell" [*den'gi ne pakhnut*), and any means for making it is acceptable. . . . Until recently,

I myself, with all my guts, belonged to the older generation educated in the old Komsomol ways.

The importance of the collective socialist values to the older generation, however, did not imply a blind belief in all ideological dogmas. On the contrary, their idealism involved an engaged interest in the workings of the Soviet system and was often accompanied by an outspoken criticism of its shortcomings. The young, on the other hand, were less critical of the system because they no longer experienced its ideological claims as ideas to be taken at face value. Ideology for them had become an unavoidable context within which to pursue other, not strictly ideological, goals and interests and to create their own alternate universe of meaning. From the perspective of the younger generation, one could be both a conscientious person who cares about the common good and a pragmatic person who cares about one's own interests, and most of them wanted to be neither an ardent supporter of nor a dissenter against the system. Vladimir writes:

> Incidentally, a critical attitude [to the Soviet system] cannot serve as a criterion for distinguishing between these two generations. In fact, the "teachers" generally criticize the authorities (*vlasti*) much more fiercely and profoundly than do the "young," who are indifferent (*bezraslichny*) to common problems and to the fate of their country, and who would consider [how to correct] mistakes in the conduct of the socialist economy (*oshibki v khoziaistvovanii*) only if that served their practical purposes and personal goals. The former [older generation] are great idealists, the latter [younger generation] are mostly realists.

In the late 1970s and early 1980s, the *shabashka* brigades increasingly resembled quasi-private firms which their organizers, like Seryozha, managed in an increasingly entrepreneurial manner. For an illustration, consider the work of a *shabashka* brigade in the early 1980s. At that time, Yurii (born in 1960), a student in a Leningrad engineering college, became a frequent *shabashka* organizer and participant. Because of his personal talents, he performed a peculiar entrepreneurial task, increasing the brigade's efficiency by circumventing the typical problems and obstacles associated with the Soviet economy of shortage and the state's forms of political control. Yurii explains:

> How was the official system of production organized? You could almost never receive any supplies in time. In construction there were constant delays with the shipments of cement, and builders were often idle for long

periods of time. How did we avoid this? We sent a person from our brigade to the cement plant and he paid everyone in cash—the foreman, the person who loaded the cement, the truck driver, and so on. Their official salaries were maybe 150 rubles a month, and we paid them that whole amount right away. Of course, they worked like crazy bringing us anything we needed.

When the brigade was building a wooden house, it urgently needed a supply of logs:

> According to the official method we needed to place an order for logs at the sawmill, they would enter us into their plan, then we would wait for ages for our turn, and eventually they would saw the logs for us. Instead, our whole brigade would go to the logging area of the forest, pay the loggers in cash, ourselves load the logs on the truck, hire the truck to bring them to the sawing shop, pay the sawing shop in cash to let us saw the logs ourselves, and then hire another truck to bring them to the construction site.

Yurii's brigade fulfilled the official norms several times over. The practices of such *shabashka* brigades were organized by applying particular "hybrid" technologies of entrepreneurial governmentality, which included formal and informal ways of managing time, resources, methods of work, relations, and so on. I provide the discussion of the *shabashka* brigades as just one example of a much wider phenomenon of organizing quasi-private work based on an application of these technologies of entrepreneurial governmentality. I will discuss such technologies in more detail in the next sections.

Many members of the last Soviet generation, especially men, experienced these forms of work in the 1970s and 1980s. They learned that by applying these governmental technologies, they could organize and manage an efficient work process and achieve required goals despite the obstacles associated with the economy of shortage and its political regulations. They also learned that such work could be not only socially meaningful but also personally profitable even in the context of state socialism. In the late 1980s, many of these people became involved in the process of inventing the newly legalized private business. Yurii and four of his colleagues registered a construction cooperative in 1988 and later transformed it into a successful computer business (see below).

Officialized-Public Sphere and Personalized-Public Sphere

Different states are not similar institutions that happen to function in different cultural and historic contexts, but rather institutions that are themselves always historically and culturally constructed and imagined by their subjects. Directly borrowing conceptual tools developed for the analysis of modern Western states, which can provide analytical rigor to the analysis of some aspects of non-Western states, nevertheless runs the risk of glossing over other crucial culturally specific aspects of these non-Western states. As theorists of the postcolonial states have argued, "the legacy of Western scholarship on the state has been to universalize a particular cultural construction of 'state-society relations' in which specific notions of 'statehood' and 'civil society' are conjoined."[13] This cultural construction involves, for example, such dichotomies as public vs. private, legal vs. illegal, and state vs. civil society.

The nature of the Soviet state and its relationships with Soviet society and Soviet subjects cannot be grasped by such dichotomies.[14] As Oleg Vite has argued, during the late Soviet period the public sphere of everyday Soviet life became increasingly reorganized into two public spheres that Vite calls *publichanaia* (public sphere proper) and *privatno-publichnaia* (private-public) (Vite 1996; Voronkov and Chikadze 1997: 74–75). These two public spheres corresponded to two distinct ways of understanding and shaping public practices and relations in everyday life. The practices in the former were regulated by the written laws and rules of the state that were represented in the official Party and state texts and documents, and could be compared to "statute law." Unwritten cultural understandings and nonofficial agreements that could be compared to "customary law" regulated the practices in the latter sphere.

Vite's insight about the distinct nature of the two public spheres in the late Soviet period is helpful for our analysis. His discussion has one problem, however: by emphasizing the rules and understandings as a way of distinguishing between the two public spheres, Vite reproduces, albeit in a new form, the familiar private-public dichotomy. His two public spheres are fixed and strictly separate from each other. Unlike Vite, I prefer to distinguish between the two public spheres in the late Soviet period by the types of *action* in which people were involved and that resulted in routine "personalization" or "officialization" of the individual's relations with the state. To emphasize action, I define the two public spheres as *officialized-public sphere* and *personalized-public sphere*.[15] This emphasis allows me to speak of them not in terms of fixed and divided topographical spaces, but rather in terms of two types of practices that could coexist and overlap in the same space and context. In other words, the officialized and personalized public spheres should be seen not in terms of dichotomy and divide but, as mentioned above, in terms of dialogic coexistence or hybridity.[16]

The relationship of the Soviet person to the party-state also became based on this dialogical or hybrid cultural dynamic. People often participated in the Soviet system quite conscientiously by representing their practice within the officialized-public sphere in the official terms that were required by the party-state. At the same time, people routinely adjusted their practice in accordance with the conditions and understandings of the personalized-public sphere. Examples of this relation between the person and the state are well known from discussions of the socialist "economy of shortage." Managers in Soviet industry could officially report successful fulfillment of the plan. At the same time, most managers could not avoid being involved in diverse personalized arrangements with workers, suppliers, auditing committees, and others. These practices of the managers have been described as procuring, resource bargaining (Kornai 1980; Verdery 1996), *pripiski* (account padding*), and so forth. From the perspective of the officialized-public sphere, the plans were indeed fulfilled, and the official reports stated this fact. However, in the personalized-public sphere the nature of labor, the time, resources, relations, and ultimate results often were reinterpreted so dramatically that it would be impossible to understand the plans' "fulfillment" purely in terms of what the plans were officially designed to achieve.

This does not mean that the managers were not interested in doing good work and satisfying social needs. They simply learned how to do their official work by employing hybrid entrepreneurial technologies that took advantage of the distinctions between officialized-public and personalized-public spheres. In the post-Soviet period, it was these hybrid entrepreneurial technologies that informed the development of private business. Most of these hybrid technologies were organized around a particular semiotic procedure that I theorized elsewhere as *heteronymous shift* (Yurchak 2000b).** In the heteronymous shift of an official written report, political slogan, speech, plan, the form of the symbol (signifier) is meticulously reproduced but the meaning to which it refers in a concrete context (signified) is shifted. Heteronymous shift became a central mechanism of the subject's relation with the system during late socialism and first post-socialist years.

---

*On the practices of *pripiski*, see Radaev.

**The Greek term "heteronym"—a word of the same spelling (written representation) but different and unrelated meaning than another word—is used to emphasize that the meaning, for which the replicated forms of ideological signs stood in different contexts, always involved on element of *unpredictability*. Typical heteronyms in English include for example, *bass* (string instrument) and *bass* (fish), *lead* (metal) and *lead* (to guide), *minute* (60 seconds) and *minute* (tiny), *tear* (to rip) and *tear* (teardrop), and so forth.

The Work of Komsomol Secretaries

A similar reinterpretation of the official practice happened in the field of ideological production. Steven Solnick recently compared the Komsomol of the late Soviet period with a "primitive business school" (Solnick 1998: 118), because it taught organizational skills, provided access to official resources, and eventually allowed its members to make money by using them. However, we may add to this observation one crucial point: the Komsomol also helped to shape the particular late-socialist form of entrepreneurial governmentality. It did so by teaching the Komsomol administrators that to achieve official goals, in the context of the state-imposed obstacles and forms of control, they needed to organize and manage public practice according to the hybrid logic of the two overlapping public spheres.

In the 1980s, Andrei worked as an engineer in a Leningrad research institute and was active in its Komsomol organization. Born in 1955, Andrei, like Seryozha whom we encountered in the example above, was a member of the last Soviet generation. In 1982, Andrei was elected to the post of secretary of the institute's Komsomol committee and was required to conduct different forms of ideological work. In this work Andrei also learned a model of entrepreneurial governmentality. For example, one of the routine assignments that Andrei received from the Komsomol *raikom* (district committee) was to organize a system of *politinformatsii* (political-ideological lectures) at his institute. He had to choose ten rank-and-file Komsomol members, organize them as a *lektorskaia gruppa* (lecturers' group), and have them present about fifteen lectures over the course of the year in front of their colleagues.[17]

As Andrei expected, the prospect of making public political lectures proved vastly unpopular among young Komsomol members; most people had an inexhaustible supply of excuses for not participating. Andrei was well aware that he could not avoid organizing the lecture group altogether. In fact, as a conscientious secretary, he thought that having some lectures was important. However, he also knew that in the real context of his institute the number of lectures required by the official plan was completely unreasonable. Andrei, as an entrepreneur in the field of ideological production, worked under the conditions of the "ideological economy of shortage," which were parallel to those in the field of industrial production.[18] As such, Andrei faced the basic problem of a manager in that symbolic economy: he could neither avoid the official task nor achieve it in the officially prescribed way. Like industrial managers, he practiced diverse technologies of entrepreneurial governmentality for organizing production and fulfilling goals regardless of the "ideological shortages" and unrealistic plans.

In the case of the political lecture, Andrei's committee decided that in terms of the official reports the lecturing group would deliver all the required lectures, but in practice the number and seriousness of the lectures would be diminished to fit the real conditions. Andrei chose the leader of the lecturer's group, whose task was to keep the "system of reports" (*otchetnost'*) about both real and fictitious lectures. If the reports were reviewed by the Raikom, the leader was supposed to discuss them "with a competent look" (*s gramotnym vidom*). In practice only three political lectures, instead of fifteen, took place during the year. Such arrangements were so commonplace that they did not appear unusual either to the members of Andrei's Komsomol committee or to the rank-and-file Komsomol members with whom Andrei had to arrange various aspects of this work. Andrei's contacts in the *raikom* were also aware that the official task was hardly realistic and that some arrangement must have taken place, but did not ask for the details. The *raikom*, explains Andrei, "looked more at our paperwork, at how we kept the reports, and at who said what according to the reports."

As in the case of industrial managers, however, it would be a mistake to interpret this technique of ideological production as cynicism, opportunism, or complete lack of belief in socialist values among Komsomol secretaries. In fact, Andrei believed in some communist values and in the importance of the Komsomol in teaching these values to the young. However, as a pragmatic practitioner of ideological work, he also knew that to organize people and orchestrate events was not the same thing as to devise and require them on paper. He came to believe, like many other members of his generation, that some ideological tasks were more important than others and that some official requirements could be ignored without too much harm, while others had to be performed with all earnestness. Andrei distinguished between two types of Komsomol work. The first he called *proforma* (formality) and *ideologicheskaia shelukha* (empty ideological shell) and performed mostly at the level of the official reports. The second type he called *rabota so smyslom* (work with meaning) and found important and enjoyable; he often organized it on his own initiative. Examples of the second type of work were frequent professional initiatives organized by Andrei and the committee: contests among young employees of the institute for the best professional skills (*konkurs profmasterstva*), the system of apprenticeship (*nastavnichestvo*), work in agricultural farms and construction brigades, assistance to young families with housing or kindergarten for children, sports competitions, the museum devoted to the institute's role during the war, celebrations, hikes in the country, and other activities.

These initiatives won Andrei several honorary diplomas (*gramota*) "For Kosmomol Work," awards of which he was proud and which he kept on the wall in his office and later at home. For him these were not meaningless documents received in exchange for meaningless activities, but signs of public recognition for his organizing talents, creativity, and genuine concern for the social good. In his work, Andrei and other "entrepreneurs" in the field of ideological production learned that official obstacles and unreasonable requirements, imposed by the party-state could be reinterpreted and rendered meaningful or simply avoided. These complex hybrid practices—distinguishing between meaningful and meaningless types of work, organizing people to perform these types of work, juggling different meanings, producing different reports, and ultimately relating to the state's laws, institutions, and ideologies in these different ways—became "thinkable and practicable" precisely because of the particular form of late-socialist entrepreneurial governmentality.

The Invention of Komsomol Firms

At the end of perestroika, in the late 1980s, most active Komsomol secretaries, including Andrei, reinvented themselves as private businessmen, turning their committees into private banks and firms.[19] They managed to perform this transformation not only because of their privileged position, organizing skills, and access to resources, but also because they had learned a particular form of entrepreneurial governmentality. Unlike many other social groups, they were ready to relate to the changing world as entrepreneurial agents, continuing to shape that world, in new contexts, in terms that they found socially and personally meaningful. Since the late 1980s, Andrei has been instrumental in creating a number of successful private firms, at first in the entertainment and travel business and in the past several years in designing equipment for the metallurgical industry.

When the twentieth Congress of Komsomol, in 1987, introduced its long-ranging reform permitting district and later primary Komsomol committees to open and control their own financial accounts, many Komsomol secretaries did not just passively accept this innovation but started actively experimenting with it. As was typical of the regulations imposed by the party-state, these reforms were ambiguous and contradictory (Solnick 1998: 110–111). The secretaries implemented these reforms in practice by applying the hybrid entrepreneurial technologies that they had perfected in other spheres of Komsomol practice. In this process, many local secretaries managed to transfer the financial resources of the Komsomol into the starting capital for their future businesses, making these operations invisible to the higher Komsomol bodies and to the rank-and-file Komsomol members, depriving them of an opportunity to lay claim to these resources. It would be too simplistic, however, to interpret that process as opportunism or corruption on the part of the

Komsomol leaders. For many of them, the reforms provided new avenues for conducting what Andrei called "work with meaning," and they wanted to explore these new avenues entrepreneurially, without letting diverse actors and interests create obstacles in this process.

Marina (born in 1968), an instructor of a *raikom* in 1988–1989 and a co-organizer of a youth center, explains how some local secretaries of primary Komsomol organizations, supervised by her *raikom*, were kept uninformed about these transformations. Many of these primary secretaries (like Andrei in the examples above) traditionally did not display much initiative in their interactions with the *raikoms* and, as a result, were likely to remain badly informed of the new opportunities that the financial reform offered. For example, they were often unaware that the reform allowed them to gain complete control over the accounts of their primary organizations and of the large sums of membership dues that accumulated in these accounts. It was this information that the *raikoms* did not automatically offer to local secretaries, keeping local funds under the *raikoms'* control.

Eventually, members of the *raikoms*, and of the more informed local committees, officially secured the unclaimed Komsomol funds as starting capital for their first business projects—travel bureaus, entertainment agencies, and later private firms.[20] The entrepreneurial governmentality practiced by these ideological producers played a crucial role in the way the new financial resources were managed and the emerging institutions and structures of private business were shaped. As a result, in just a couple of years, a whole network of private businesses and an army of private entrepreneurs emerged all over the country. To illustrate this process, I will analyze the transformation of the Komsomol committee of the university in a middle-sized Siberian city. The committee's secretary, Sasha (born in 1966), explains:

> After the 20th Congress of Komsomol . . . I went to the local branch of the state bank, having absolutely no information, and said that I wanted to register our account there. The accountant asked me how I wanted to register it. I asked what were the options, and she explained that we could open an account from which we could make only noncash payments (*beznalichnaia oplata*) or an account from which we could withdraw cash. I said that I wanted the second type. We opened that account and started depositing into it the membership dues of the university Komsomol organization.

Sasha and members of his committee registered themselves in the city council as a *molodiozhnyi tsentr* (youth center), a new type of institution that the Komsomol reforms allowed to participate in rudimentary business. They also invented a hybrid name for their center, "Youth Center Komsomol

Committee," and ordered a stamp and a letterhead with this name.[21]

The two halves of that name, "Youth Center" and "Komsomol Committee," provided the new organization with a hybrid identity: in different contexts, different aspects of this identity were emphasized.[22] The phrase "Komsomol Committee" officialized the organization's identity, presenting it as an ideological state organization that functioned in the officialized-public sphere and therefore had legal access to state power—in Sasha's words, "it was easier to operate when you had the Komsomol behind you." The phrase "Youth Center" personalized the organization's identity, presenting it as a private firm that could officially take advantage of the resources of the personalized-public sphere and could provide services and make decisions according to its personal business rationale. This ability was inaccessible to other state institutions. The use of this creatively constructed identity in conducting business was a hybrid technology of entrepreneurial governmentality practiced by the Komsomol secretaries. This technology was also widely used by other newly formed institutions at the time, including the very top of the administrative apparatus—for example, the "Russian Privatization Center" that steered privatization in the early 1990s.[23]

In 1989, the department of foreign languages at Sasha's university needed to purchase several VCRs for its language lab. Officially the department could purchase products only from a state store by making a transfer from the university noncash (*beznalichnyi*) account. However, at the time it was not possible to buy this equipment in the state stores. VCRs were available from private persons who traveled to the West, but one had to pay cash, to which the department, as a state institution, had no access. Sasha's "Youth Center," on the contrary, could withdraw cash from its new account. Using this difference in the nature of the accounts, Sasha, like many other organizers of youth centers, devised the following business plan.

When, in 1989, students of Budapest University were planning to attend his university as part of the Komsomol student exchange, Sasha suggested that his center would pay for their airplane tickets to Russia if the Hungarians brought three VCRs from Budapest. For the center, this arrangement was profitable because at that time three VCRs in Russia cost twice the price of the airplane tickets. For the Hungarians, the relative prices were reversed. The department of foreign languages received its VCRs and made a noncash transfer to the youth center's account, most of which the center withdrew to cover the price of the Hungarian tickets, keeping the rest as a "service charge." This charge was the youth center's first financial profit from a business action. And, Sasha explains, "everything was completely legal. We simply bought airplane tickets as part of the Komsomol student exchange. The business side was not visible to anyone."

This model of entrepreneurial action was based not only on the new ability of youth centers to have independent accounts, but also on the secretaries' ability to create elaborately hybrid practices that acquired different forms and meanings in two different public spheres. By providing a way of cashing noncash transfers, the new bank account served as a "valve" connecting the two public spheres. The youth center's business was based on pumping money, products, identities, and meanings between the spheres through this valve. Importantly, from the perspective of the officialized-public sphere, everything was completely legal. In this example, the "law" itself is understood in hybrid terms: for Sasha, as for most entrepreneurs in the years to follow, it was important that in the officialized-public sphere the letter of the law was observed, even if in the personalized-public sphere the spirit of the law was violated. The operation of the financial account as a valve, the use of a hybrid name, and the treatment of the law as a hybrid—all these were particular late-socialist technologies of entrepreneurial governmentality.

The use of such technologies also allowed youth centers to develop one of the first business services in the late 1980s, which became known as "cashing" (*obnalichivanie*), the transformation of noncash funds into cash. Hastily founded youth centers around the country began offering this service to state enterprises (today a similar service of "cashing" is offered by banks—see below). Thanks to this service, state organizations (research institutes, factories, universities) were able to buy previously unobtainable foreign equipment, such as photocopying machines and personal computers, which a growing number of private Soviet travelers brought into the country from the West.[24] According to the official documents, within the officialized-public sphere, research institutes bought this equipment from youth centers, paying them in noncash transfers. The youth centers cashed these transfers through their accounts, paying part of the sum to the vendor and keeping part as a service charge. This element of the business action was performed in the personalized-public sphere and arranged through oral communication. Ultimately, all actors benefited, and they did so legally in terms of the interpretation of the law in the officialized public sphere.

These and other entrepreneurial activities of the youth centers created the conditions for the emergence of a whole class of new private entrepreneurs. To this new class, the youth centers provided a legal umbrella for private entrepreneurial action. Before the registration of private firms was officially allowed, many independent promoters, using the youth centers as their facades in the officialized-public sphere, organized their own business projects, such as tours for foreign visitors, concerts of independent music bands, video salons, and later imports of clothing, foodstuffs, and equipment. By providing unregistered entrepreneurs with the youth centers' name, letterhead, and stamp, the centers effectively sold the entrepreneurs access to the official state's resources. In the slang of the period, the centers acted as the entrepreneurs' *krysha* (roof or aegis). This *krysha* service was the first hybrid "protection technology" used in entrepreneurial activities: it protected independent entrepreneurs who acted in the personalized-public sphere from the official gaze of the state, allowing them to achieve results by providing their actions within the privatized-public sphere with a "legal" framework of the officialized-public sphere.

In the next several years, the range of protection technologies, such as *krysha*, and their spheres of application grew substantially. The term *"krysha"* also began to be used to refer to the "protection" provided to businesses, at first by criminal groups and later by private, state, and hybrid security organs (see below).

The Invention of Cooperatives

In 1989, following the adoption of the law on cooperatives, Yurii, who organized *shabashka* brigades in the early 1980s (see above), and four of his friends (two from Yurii's industrial enterprise and two from a Komsomol youth center) registered a "cooperative."[25] The Komsomol participants contributed most of the starting capital. At first, they officially registered themselves as a "construction cooperative," whose occupation was to build houses for state clients. After years of *shabashka* experience, most of them could imagine how to run such an operation. However, under the umbrella of the construction cooperative, they wanted to experiment with importing computers from the West. The computer business was an unknown territory and required a lot of preparation—learning about computers, studying demand, establishing contacts abroad, and so on.

According to Yurii, to make the business possible, at least in the beginning, they had to avoid paying unreasonably high taxes, the kind of taxes that entrepreneurs call "state-sponsored extortion" (*gosudarstvennoe vymogatel'stvo*). Whether this tax really would have made the business unfeasible is less important for this analysis than the fact that the entrepreneurs perceived that it would, thereby justifying their actions. That perception was based in part on their past experience of the meaning and function of the state's rules and regulations. The profit from selling computers in Russia at that time was extremely high, up to 200%. Yurii's main job, as the co-op's chairman, was to organize the whole operation so that this profit would not be visible and the high taxes would not destroy it. Yurii explains:

> The official invoice said that we bought the PC from a private person, usually an old lady pensioner, for 30,000 rubles. We paid her 50 rubles in

cash for putting her name and signature on the invoice. This allowed us to withdraw 30,000 rubles from our bank account. . . . In fact we bought the computer from someone else for 10,000 rubles. So now we had 20,000 in cash that was not taxed. We used that money for business development and for high salaries for ourselves—at that time all of us bought cars and apartments.

In 1989, the computer part of the business grew rapidly and the cooperative dropped "construction" as its main occupation and began developing a regular supply of computers. The work was designed to avoid the customs tax on equipment imported for business, a tax that was also seen as unrealistically high. At first the goal was achieved as follows:

We had friends in a Petersburg firm that was an authorized dealer of a U.S. computer manufacturer. Three or four times a month they drove to the manufacturer's Helsinki branch to receive a large shipment of laser printers and bring them to Russia. Because of the constant crossing of the Russian-Finnish border, they had established good personal relations with the Russian customs officials. Often they brought more printers than they declared, but the customs officer never searched their truck, checking only their customs declarations. . . . We made an arrangement with our friends in that firm: they put several boxes with our computers among their boxes on that truck, and we paid them in cash for the transportation. We simply jumped on their wagon. And everyone around us did something similar. This was why local computer vendors at the time could offer low prices.

Another method for reducing high customs taxes is *peresortitsa* (sort reshuffle)—products are represented on the official invoice as cheaper, less sophisticated, or in smaller quantities than they actually are. This is another technology of entrepreneurial governmentality, whereby the product acquires a hybrid identity, meaning different things in different spheres.

In 1992, Yurii's company received a shipment of new notebook computers from the United States. The official invoice represented the units as "electronic typewriters," which at the time looked sufficiently similar to notebook computers. As a result, the cost of each unit was stated as $200, one seventh of its actual price. In 1994–1995, another computer firm imported CD-ROM drives, representing them on the invoices as flexible diskette drives, a cheaper but similar-looking product.

Today, to give products these hybrid identities, the firms find middlemen (*posredniki*) abroad. The middleman buys the product from the original foreign seller, then, while the product is still abroad, changes its identity—its price or type—and then resells it to the Russian firm. The middlemen are usually ex-Soviets of the same generation who are based abroad and are friends or relatives of the entrepreneurs. The relations with the middlemen are constructed within the personalized-public sphere, are based on mutual trust,[26] and are usually unwritten and made over the phone. The middlemen's companies are registered abroad and are compensated for their business services unofficially. For example, throughout the 1990s, Yurii's company imported some of its computer products through a middleman in the United States, Yurii's school friend.

Yurii and other entrepreneurs claim that they became involved in creating new identities for the imported products not only because of high taxes but also because of the ambiguous and contradictory formulations of the law:

> The laws are written in such a way that the customs official may decide to take a customs tax of 5% or 45%. . . . It depends on what you name the product. If you register the computer as simply parts (*komplektuiuschee*) for a larger product, then you pay 5%. If you mention the computer as it is, a complete product, you pay 25%. If you bring it as a monitor, the tax is 40%. All this is decided completely by the customs official. This is why they work only with a certain familiar group of people and get rather large sums in bribes.

Dmitrii (born in 1957), the co-owner of a firm that imports Scandinavian foodstuffs, at some point used a Russian middleman based in Germany, whom Dmitrii had known from the time they both served in the army. That person bought ice cream from a Scandinavian company and resold it to the Russian company at half the original price. These operations were performed while the ice cream was still in its country of origin. Dmitrii explains: "In fact, our middleman never even traveled to Scandinavia from Germany or saw the ice cream." When the ice cream crossed the Russian border, the customs tax was therefore lower than it would have been otherwise. Dmitrii explained how that worked (in the mid-1990s):

> We paid [the Scandinavian company) $600,000 for four large refrigerator trucks of ice cream every week through our German middleman. Then he sold these four trucks of ice cream to us at half their price, for $300,000. . . . The customs tax was 20% of the price, plus the state tax was 34% of the price. Our profit was approximately 10%. . . . On each refrigerator truck of ice cream we saved 40 million rubles [$1,000] in customs taxes. And we drove four trucks of ice cream per week, saving $4,000. If the middleman operation did not work, our profit would be minimal, plus the price of the ice cream in the shops would have to go up. But with the middleman we managed to make our profits feasible and to decrease the price in the shops from $2 to $1.65 per ice cream.

According to Arkadii (born 1942, interviewed in 1998), who imports home appliances and sells them in several stores he owns, with time more "sort-reshuffling" began to occur, not abroad, where the middlemen conducted it, but right at the customs checkpoints as the product was crossing the border:

> There exists a system of customs clearance that is called *levaia rastamozhka* ["left" or informal customs clearance). We agree with the customs officers that one truckload of refrigerators will be registered on paper as costing $500 instead of $2,000 each. We prepare two invoices, one for the customs and another for our store. . . . One can arrange *levaia rastamozhka* if one has the right contacts at the customs. For this service one usually pays $500 to the customs officer.

In these examples, the companies' relations with the state (official reports, payment of taxes, customs declarations) are conducted in the officialized-public sphere. Here the product acquires an officialized identity stated in documents. The interactions between companies and their middlemen, as well as oral agreements with customs officers, are conducted in the personalized-public sphere, where the product acquires a personalized identity, which is unwritten and agreed upon in oral interactions.

To be able to continuously perform this shift between the two public spheres and the two sides of the products' hybrid identities, most firms have to keep hybrid accounting systems, consisting of a combination of "white accounting" (*belaia bukhgalteriia*) and "black accounting" (*chernaia bukhgalteriia*). White accounting corresponds to the identity of the business and the product in the officialized-public sphere; black accounting corresponds to these in the personalized-public sphere. White accounting is used in one's interaction with the state, black accounting is used in the interaction with other businesses. Neither the white nor the black side of these hybrid business operations is "fake." They are both real in their respective spheres and are mutually complementary. Without both, a "legal" and viable business would not be possible, at least in most cases. In one firm, I observed how a newly hired accountant was trained to keep both accounting systems simultaneously. There are also white and black cash, white and black computers, and even white and black ice cream.

Relations between businesses and banks also have developed around the need to shift identities, funds, and products between the two public spheres. For example, to keep the black and white accounting systems, private firms continuously need cash that is not officially registered. This means that banks, whose business depends on private firms, need to provide legal (in the officialized sense of the word) ways of pumping funds back and forth between the two spheres. This service of turning noncash accounts into cash (*obnalichivanie*) is performed by the banks' departments known in slang as "cashing firms" (*obnalichivaiushchaia kontora*). These services are similar to the first cashing operations invented by the Komsomol youth centers, the banks' predecessors, in the late 1980s (see above).

Business consultant Nikolai (born 1964) and bank manager Piotr (born 1962) independently described how the cashing firms work. A business signs an officially registered contract with a department of the bank (which is in fact a cashing firm) according to which that department provides the business with some service that is difficult to account for, the most common being "consulting services" (*konsul'tatsionnye uslugi*). Businesses pay cashing firms for this service by making an official noncash transfer to the bank's account. After that, the business receives its money back, now in cash, minus the cashing firm's service charge of 4–7 percent. The money switches from its officialized-public identity (officially registered noncash form) to its personalized-public identity (unregistered cash form). The bank, which serves as a valve connecting the two spheres, charges a fee for this service (as the youth centers did in the past).

Konstantin (born 1964), the owner of a courier business, explains (in summer 1998):

> The cashing firms do two things for companies. They help us to turn our black expenses into white. And they help us to get cash that we need for business development. So, ultimately, this is a good service that needs to be done. . . . Without it many businesses would not be able to operate.

The cashing firms are an example of middleman companies that exist for a short period of time—many of them declare bankruptcy at the end of each fiscal quarter.[27]

The Hybrid Identity of State Officials, the Hybrid Model of the State

In the late 1990s, local state officials' involvement in the business practices of entrepreneurs grew. This involvement followed the same hybrid logic, which can be illustrated by the development of the so-called car scheme. According to a recent law, Russian citizens who spent over six months abroad (and who are known in slang as *shestimesiachniki*, "six-monthers") could bring a foreign car into Russia by paying a very low customs tax,[28] while the regular tax on such cars was very high. The adoption of this law several years ago launched a vibrant business whose entrepreneurial technology was based on creating hybrid identities for the cars and switching these identities back and forth between the two public spheres. This procedure would be impossible unless the identities of the state officials, the relations with them, and the meanings of the law and money were understood in hybrid terms.

Car-importing businesses bought foreign cars in Western Europe, registered them in the names of Russians returning from abroad, brought the cars to Russia, and then resold them to the actual customers who awaited them. Thousands of cars were brought into the country every year through this arrangement. In this procedure, the car received a new identity in the officialized-public sphere, according to which it was not subject to a high tax. This arrangement saved several thousand dollars on each car, even though the Russian travelers, as well as the state officials involved in the procedure, were compensated for their services.

Mikhail (born 1964), a co-owner of a car importing business, officially imported cars (in 1997–1998) from Finland. During that period, Mikhail's company also constantly searched for Russian six-monthers returning from abroad. Originally Mikhail looked for them through friends and acquaintances, but he gradually established special relations with customs officers who put him in touch with returning travelers on a regular basis. The customs officers, explains Mikhail, were the first to see the passports of returning travelers and could easily identify who spent more than six months abroad by looking at the border-crossing stamps. They approached the appropriate travelers with the offer to register a car in their name and pay them between $500 and $1,500 for the procedure. Those who agreed were put in touch with the representatives of Mikhail's or similar car importers. One such Russian traveler explained how the official performed the actual switch between the two public spheres in the course of the interaction:

> In May 1998, I returned to Russia after a year spent abroad. The customs officer at the airport with professional and strict mannerisms carefully studied my passport and my declaration and searched one of my bags. He asked me questions in a very professional and strict tone. Then he studied my passport for the second time and suddenly changed his professional strict tone to a more quiet and "normal" one and asked me whether I was interested in bringing a car into the country and earning $500 for this. He pointed to a guy in plain clothes who was standing among the crowd on the Russian side of the customs. That guy had dollars in cash and would be ready to pay me right away. The customs officer also added that everything was perfectly legal because the law allowed me to bring a car for myself and then to sell it to someone else once it is in the country. Apparently they had cars in the warehouse at the airport waiting for such guys as myself to bring them through the customs.

That customs officer presented a perfect example of the hybrid identity of some state officials. In the officialized-public sphere, such officials conscientiously act as guardians of the state's law, making sure that no contraband is brought into or taken out of the country. At the same time, the same officials may act in ways that contradict the state's interests by transferring the official state's resources, to which they have unique access (state power, information, and protection provided to customs employees), into the personalized-public sphere. These officials use their position as a valve for connecting the two public spheres.

This example, like the previous ones, again illustrates the process of the personalization of the state. None of these business arrangements would work without the participation of many people of different occupations, both state officials and private actors. For example, the car importing business would not work without the participation of private citizens, customs officers, public notary officers, car registration officers, car inspectors, traffic police inspectors, and others. All of these actors perceive the state as a hybrid whose laws, documents, and representatives have hybrid identities. In this model of the state, its law has to be observed in the officialized-public sphere only. This is why such schemes as the car importing business are not perceived by many of these actors as necessarily "illegal." The officialized-public side of the law is not violated—from that perspective the cars are brought into the country by people who are *legally* tax-exempt and then are *legally* sold to others.

All these actors distinguish between those state laws that they perceive as meaningless and counterproductive and those that they perceive as meaningful and important. The former type of laws (e.g., unreasonably high taxes, constraints on the withdrawal of cash from accounts, privileges given to random groups of citizens) they treat as a formality that has to be followed in officialized-public terms only and that, in fact, can be subjected to hybrid entrepreneurial technologies. The latter type of laws they follow in earnest. Perceiving the state and its laws in accordance with this hybrid model means always expecting that some steps and regulations of the state will be positive and meaningful and some will be negative and unreasonable. The entrepreneurs have to relate to the state in this discriminating manner all the time, as did Andrei and other Komsomol secretaries of the recent past, who also distinguished in their Komsomol responsibilities between work with meaning and pure meaningless formality and also invented hybrid entrepreneurial technology when dealing with these distinct aspects of reality (see above).

The hybrid model of the state, and the ability to distinguish between its different sides, allows customs representatives to act and to see themselves as conscientious officials, who protect the meaningful interests of the state in earnest. Similarly, this model allows entrepreneurs to be involved in informal activities and at the same time have a genuine desire for the democratic rule of law in the country. It is clear then that the logic of such hybrid technologies differs from the logic of corruption. It should also be clear that for such a distinction to become evident, business practice must be analyzed in historically and culturally specific contexts.

Technologies of Protection and Insurance

From the perspective of Foucault's governmentality, insurance can be considered as a "technology of risk." Francois Ewald explains this technology as "an art of combining various elements of economic and social reality according to a set of specific rules. From these different combinations, there derive the different sorts of insurance institution" (Ewald 1991: 197). The technologies of entrepreneurial governmentality discussed in this chapter are not universal forms but are products of a concrete historical, economic, moral, and political environment. Similarly, concrete forms of the insurance and protection of business practice, as technologies of risk, are also historical constructs in every given environment. If the meaning of the state, its law, and its officials, as we have seen, is understood in hybrid terms, then the state's law alone cannot function as an adequate form of insuring and protecting business practice, especially those aspects of this practice that are organized in the personalized-public sphere. There must be other entrepreneurial technologies of managing the risks associated with this sphere. What are these technologies of risk in Russian business and how have they developed since the late 1980s?

During the early period of inventing and constructing business, many official rules and laws had not yet been adopted, were not known by everyone equally, or were simply contradictory. At the same time, the forms and regulations of business practice within the personalized-public sphere had not yet been normalized and shared among various actors either. In that context, a form of criminal protection of business practice emerged. That "criminal" technology of risk started as a chaotic and disorganized racket. Various criminal groups frequently approached small businesses, demanding protection fees and threatening businessmen with physical violence if they did not comply. At first businesses often had to pay protection fees to different groups and in unpredictable amounts. The criminal groups that claimed to be a business's protection were known in slang as its *krysha*, or roof (see the origin of this term above). These criminal groups created the risk of violence and offered a technology of *krysha*-protection to manage that risk. Basically, they offered businesses protection from themselves.

After a couple of years, in around 1993–1994 this situation transformed into a more or less normalized system of risk management that entrepreneurs started calling "the civilized *kryshas*" (*tsivilizovannye kryshi*)—still unavoidable but more predictable and less violent. Following the model of the early noncriminal *kryshas* (such as the youth centers), the criminal *kryshas* began to play a more involved role in business. They turned into a kind of guarantor of shared understandings and agreements between entrepreneurs in the personalized-public sphere and offered ways of "solving problems" in case of conflict (Shelly 1996, Volkov 1999, Humphrey 1999a). As a technology of risk, the *krysha* was transforming from pure protection to protection with insurance.

Katherine Verdery has suggested that the popular construction of the "Mafia" in the mid-1990s as a "civilized" and comforting presence (in Romania and in some countries of the former Soviet Union) gave "voice to an anxiety about statelessness, alongside other forms of insecurity" (Verdery 1996: 219). We may add that this anxiety and insecurity were experienced, first and foremost, as a lack of the familiar, shared, predictable understandings in the officialized-public sphere of the state, understandings to which different actors could refer in their business practice. It was due to that lack that the role of the personalized-public sphere in structuring practice became much more important for a time. Here the lack was filled by the "civilized *kryshas*," which provided not only protection and insurance but also mutually shared understandings of interactions, agreements, and contracts.[29] The words of the owner of an entertainment and music promotions agency, Igor (born in 1964), illustrate how entrepreneurs perceived this role of the *kryshas* at that time (summer 1996): "for *kryshas* everything is based on your word. . . . If you said something, you said it. Tricking someone is not even in the cards."

That did not, however, mean that the state was simply absent from the picture. As we have seen, the post-Soviet state has inherited a hybrid structure from the late Soviet period. This hybridity of the state quite soon, by the mid-1990s, caused the criminal *kryshas* to lose their original functions. Official state organs started providing private businesses with a combination of services within both the officialized-public and personalized-public spheres, effectively squeezing the *kryshas* out of the latter. In the past several years, entrepreneurs have increasingly claimed that criminal *kryshas* are a thing of the past.

Today most entrepreneurs themselves avoid contacting *kryshas* for solving problems because official state organs can now provide hybrid technologies of risk—that protect and insure entrepreneurs simultaneously in both the officialized-public and the personalized-public spheres. In this context, criminal *kryshas* cannot easily operate since state organs challenge them in both spheres simultaneously: the state fights *kryshas* as "organized crime" in the officialized-public sphere and confronts *kryshas* as business competitors in the personalized-public sphere. The owner of an entertainment agency, Igor, whom we encountered above, described how this hybrid technology of risk works in practice (in summer 1996):

> I have a very serious *krysha*—the anticrime unit of the MVD (police). . . . As a state anticrime organization, they provide official security to people and businesses. But they can also be your *krysha*, and like all other Mafia groups, they can intimidate people, recover your money, the whole thing. . . . So I have an official contract with them . . . I pay them 50,000 rubles a month ($10 at the time) as a state security organization. But of course you understand that this is a ridiculously low sum. So I also have an agreement with them, like I would with any *krysha*, and when I organize a concert I pay them $500 in cash to provide me with protection. This is called a gentlemen's agreement (*dzhentel'menskii dogovor*). . . . I am lucky to have this arrangement, because the same guys will protect me from the state and from bandits.

Leonid (born 1965), the owner of an advertising and public relations firm, explains other aspects of this hybrid technology of risk (in summer 1998):

> In the past couple of years Mafia *kryshas* have become less visible. Of course, they did not all disappear completely and will not disappear for a while. There are still niches. But now you have a choice of how to do things. Either you do them through legal state structures (*legal'nye gosudarstvennye struktury*), such as FSB (Federal Security Service), MVD, etc. Or you do them through the bandits. These two options provide identical functions. If you choose the legal option (*legal'nyi put'*), bandits will not harm you. They will be informed that you are protected by legal means (*legal'nym sposobom*). There are special phone numbers for solving such problems. Bandits will not shy away from calling the Department for Fighting Organized Crime (OBOP) to find out whether it really represents the interests of such and such firm.

Here the state organs are described as having hybrid identities. By calling state agencies "legal state structures" and by referring to their services as "legal option" and "legal means," Leonid refers only to the officialized-public side of these agencies' identity. At the same time, by describing special phone lines that such state agencies use to communicate with criminal groups, he refers to the personalized-public side of their identity, their *krysha* identity. In short, these state organs are able to manage risks and problems associated with a hybrid variety of actors—other state agencies, criminal groups, and business competitors. They provide protection and insurance by implementing hybrid technologies of risk that involve channeling official state power and information, to which these organs have unique official access, into the personalized-public sphere. They can also do the opposite channeling of power and resources.

Effectively, these hybrid technologies again perform a partial privatization of the state. For example, many entrepreneurs today enter the following relationship with local state agencies. Anton (born 1960), the general manager of a food and wine importer, explains (in summer 1998):

> The FSB and MVD provide formal and informal protection. You can hire an official contact in these structures called a security consultant (*konsul'tant po bezopasnosti*). Large companies also have their own employee called the chief of security service (*nachal'nik sluzhby bezopasnosti*). These two people are in contact with each other and this is how your company is warned about planned checkups. This contact also gives you access to computer databases. For example, you may look up who is on the founding board of some firm, check the account of the banking operations of your potential client, and so on.

Nadezhda, a businesswoman (born 1963) who owns a small company selling measuring equipment for the chemical industry, explains (in summer 1998):

> A new trend is simply to buy a cellular phone for your contact in the police and pay for the phone charges. Then you have regular access to any information about other businesses. Besides, if you had problems with criminals, you could call your direct line for a police unit.

Pavel (born 1959), manager of a telecommunications and Internet provider firm, explains (in May 1999):

> If a client company refuses to pay our bills month after month, claiming that they are having financial problems, we often turn to our security department to sort things out. The chief of the security department has contacts in the FSB, who are his personal friends from his previous career in the KGB. Through these channels he finds out what informal kinds of business our client may be involved in—every company here is involved in such things by definition—and then he uses this knowledge as a point of pressure on that company when negotiating the return of their debt.

The last quote illustrates that the knowledge about the inevitability of nonofficial business practices (as we have seen, most entrepreneurs claim they have to perform nonofficial practice if they want to conduct a viable business) can be used as a point of pressure against firms within both the officialized-public and personalized-public spheres.

Technologies of Enforced Protection and Insurance

In fact, state agencies may use this knowledge to blackmail entrepreneurs into "subscribing" to personalized-public relations with them.[30] In Yurii's words, "the *krysha* used to cover you from the problems associated with criminal structures. But today the main problem is to defend yourself from the state." If a firm refuses to comply with the demands imposed by a state organ, it can be punished through official methods. Basically, if a firm refuses to circumvent the official state law and transfer its relations with the state organ from the officialized-public to the personalized-public sphere, the firm may be punished *officially* by means of this very law.

Here is how the system works. In the summer of 1996, the following event took place in Yurii's firm. Representatives of an official law-enforcement organ, the district bureau of the OBEP (*Otdel Bor'by s Ekonomicheskoi Prestupnost'iu*, Department for Fighting Economic Crime) unexpectedly came to the firm's office and ordered it to close for an official checkup of its operations. Yurii explained:

> There were three of them, all in plain clothes. They stormed into our main office and shouted: "All hands on the tables, do not touch anything, do not push any buttons, and do not grab any phone receivers!" The main guy shows us his papers: captain of militsia [police], so-and-so. We are in shock, of course.

The OBEP officers started checking official invoices, accounts, and products. In such circumstances, state officials often do not even look for any serious mistake, but instead try to find examples of nonofficial procedures, which they know inevitably are practiced by most firms. In Yurii's firm, the officers claimed that although several American computers had certificates guaranteeing their safety to the U.S. consumers, they did not have safety certificates complying with the law of the Russian Federation. Although this was a conspicuously unreasonable charge, which the officers admitted themselves, it could be easily pressed if needed. The officers declared that the computers with no certificates had to be confiscated by the state. Yurii explains:

> They told us that if we supplied correct certificates to them in four days, the equipment would be returned. But we'd still have to prove that we had

not broken the law by bringing the equipment without Russian certificates into the country in the first place.

The total cost of the confiscated computers was $8,000, but the OBEP officers quietly explained that the computers could be returned if the firm paid half of this sum in cash to them. Entrepreneurs know from experience that confrontation with the OBEP in such situations can cause graver problems.[31] Yuri commented that "at that time we received most of our equipment through our middleman in the United States, which made some of our certificates semilegal anyway." This is why "we discussed the situation in our firm and decided to choose the nonconfrontational tactics":

> The next morning I went to see the OBEP officers in their district office. The main officer and I went outside and sat in his car. He asked me: "So, what have you decided?" I simply passed him the envelope. He put it in his pocket without looking inside, gave me the invoice of their checkup, and added: "Tear it up in front of me." I tore it up, returned him the torn pieces of paper, and we shook hands.

However, this was not the end but the beginning of a new relationship: "After we paid them, the chief of the OBEP office declared, 'Now we are *svoi*' (belong to the same circle). If you have any problems with the tax police, tax inspection, etc., call us and we will help to sort things out.'" In exchange, the firm was told to provide the OBEP office with a form of "sponsorship assistance" (*sponsorskaia pomoshch'*). First the firm received an official letter from the director of the district office of the UVD [Department of Interior Affairs), to which the district OBEP belongs, requesting that it purchase a refrigerator for the UVD office as a form of sponsorship. Now the firm regularly fixes the equipment and upgrades computers in the UVD offices at its own expense. Yurii explained: "All this is done for free and is registered in our accounting reports as sponsorship assistance. We even got a thank-you letter from the district bureau of the UVD for our voluntary help."

It is obvious in this example that the relations between the firm and the state organ are based neither simply on bribery and corruption nor on voluntary help,[32] although the initially extorted payment, which signaled the establishment of the special relations of *svoi*, clearly did take place. The term *svoi* here indicates a shift of the relations from the officialized-public to the personalized-public sphere.[33] The term "sponsorship assistance" represents the firm's coerced assistance in terms of the officialized-public sphere. Such relations between the firm and the state institution are an element of a much wider system of hybrid relations, which are based, as we have seen, on the practice of linking the officialized-public and personalized-public spheres. In fact the whole district bureau of the UVD, with its different bosses and officers, seems to be involved in this hybrid relationship. The OBEP office does not have sufficient access to equipment and money, since the resources of the state are limited. However, it has access to the power and knowledge of the officialized-public sphere, including insider information about reviews by other agencies, interpretation of laws, and tax procedures. The private firm, on the other hand, has access to equipment and money. The OBEP literally forces the firm to engage in a barter of these resources, pumping them back and forth between the two public spheres.

In that context, firms such as Yurii's often look for additional protection and insurance from unexpected raids by other state agencies. On advice from several small firms, Yurii and his colleagues looked for a contact in the higher leadership of the city's law-enforcement organs. With the disintegration of the KGB, many of its officers were hired by the state into new law-enforcement organs, including the FSB (Handelman 1995, Shelly 1996, Volkov 1999, Humphrey 1999a). As a result, many personal networks in these agencies have been reproduced from the Soviet period. Entrepreneurs know this fact well. Through a contact in the city law-enforcement organ, Yurii's firm found a group of former KGB officers, now working in the FSB, who "knew the chief of the city tax police personally." They agreed to use this connection to provide the firm with insurance and protection for a monthly fee of $1,000. Such fees are known in slang as "subscription charge" (*abonentskaia plata*). This name suggests that the payment is voluntary and distinguishes it from the extorted fees. It also suggests that the payment is regular, fixed, and functions as an insurance fee. This form of insurance is organized around the hybrid nature of the state's law enforcement organs. As a technology of risk, this insurance is based on pumping such resources as official state power and information and private money between the officialized-public and personalized-public spheres. Even before the managers in Yurii's firm ever encountered the workings of this insurance technology in action, they imagined it to be based on the familiar hybrid model, which one of them described like this:

> The state law-enforcement structures (*silovye struktury*) in the city have their own spider web with a spider sitting at the top. He has all the operative information about the city. Neither the tax police nor the anticrime agencies will ever visit your firm simply out of the blue. They have to be given an instruction from the top as to which firm has to be checked. It is that boss who gives the order to check firm X. . . . But simultaneously he may call someone down the web and say: "tomorrow such and such busi-

ness friends of yours will be visited by the organs for a checkup. Tell them to put their things in order, or everything may get confiscated." And then through the same chain some money goes up the web and ends up in his pocket.

In the months following the August 1998 crisis, the frequency of unexpected raids on small businesses by state agencies increased. At the end of 1998, Yurii's firm finally had a chance to see their "insurance service" in action—the firm was unexpectedly raided by fifteen members of the district bureau of the tax police. Yurii explains:

> It was clear that at first they were looking for unaccounted sums in cash. They were opening all the drawers, and demanding to see our safes. . . . But since they did not find anything . . . they confiscated our server [the main computer with the firm's business information) in order to analyze the information on its hard drive.

Without the server, the firm could not continue to do most of its business. However, the main problem was that the drive contained information of both white and black accounting (see above), which could easily be used to press charges against the firm. To decipher the information on the hard drive, the tax police needed a computer expert and it took several days to get one. During that time, the firm's "insurance" service solved the problem. Yurii explains:

> The former KGB men put us in touch with an officer from our district bureau of the tax police, where our server was, who told us what to do. The tax police started work at nine in morning. He brought our computer engineer to the building past the guard at the door at seven a.m. The engineer replaced the hard drive on our computer with an identical "empty" [containing no "black" files) hard drive. I was waiting outside in a car; in case someone unexpectedly entered the building I had to call our engineer inside on his cellular phone.

The operation was successful. However, for this additional insurance the firm started paying a "subscription fee" to the boss of the district bureau of the tax police:

> We hope to avoid further complications with them by paying $500 monthly directly to their chief. This would guarantee that from this side we won't be hit by anyone. But he made it clear that he can't guarantee we won't be hit from a higher level, say, from the city bureau of the tax police.

As we have seen, relations between private businesses and state agencies have gradually developed on different levels. At first, state agencies simply failed to recognize business practice performed in the personalized–public sphere and were sometimes paid to do it. Later they became engaged in that practice themselves. Soon state organs started selling access to official state power and resources. Then they started providing firms with various forms of official and nonofficial information about and protection/insurance from criminal *kryshas*, other state agencies, and business competitors. And finally some state agencies started literally forcing businesses to "subscribe" to their personalized services of risk management by creating situations in which firms have no choice but to seek out such subscriptions.

Conclusion

In light of this discussion, we may now reconsider the concept of the entrepreneurial governmentality that developed in late socialism and that shaped the practices and relations of various actors in the field of private business during the first post-Soviet decade. As I suggested in the beginning, to possess entrepreneurial governmentality is to know what an entrepreneurial act is, who can act entrepreneurially, and what or who can be acted upon in an entrepreneurial way. I have argued that at the core of important technologies of entrepreneurial governmentality in Russia has been a hybrid model of the state. This model provided conditions for the development of a particular agentive relation vis-à-vis the state among members of the last Soviet generation that involved reinterpretation and personalization of some of the state's official institutions, laws, and ideological meanings.

The paradox of late socialism was that this form of individual agency, which was required to achieve official goals of the party-state, increasingly escaped the control of that state and ultimately contributed to its demise.[34] This was a late Soviet illustration of Judith Butler's argument that the subject's agency exceeds the power, which, through external subjection, enables this agency in the first place: "[o]ne might say that the purposes of power are not always the purposes of agency" (Butler 1997: 15). This form of agency was based on various hybrid technologies in the individual's dealings with the state. That agency also allowed the new entrepreneurs of the 1990s to continue inventing and reinventing their personal projects and businesses in the post-Soviet context in spite of multiple obstacles and forms of control imposed by various powers, formal and informal. For that reason, to gloss over all of the various hybrid entrepreneurial practices that I discussed by one term—be it "corruption" (Kleiberg 1995) or "virtual economy" (Gaddy and Ickes 1998)—is to miss a crucial point. The most striking aspect of this form of entrepreneurial agency is that it is directed not so much at personal enrichment at any cost as at building a meaningful personal reality in different spheres of everyday activity and within different and quickly changing regimes of power.

When the Soviet Union collapsed at the end of perestroika, it was primarily the officialized-public sphere of the state—with its institutions, laws, and ideologies—that experienced the main crisis. In that context, the personalized-public sphere expanded into new areas of everyday life, and many of its relations and understandings became even more important. For example, the early models of post-Soviet business were based on the relations and understandings of that sphere. In this respect, speaking about the collapse of the party-state may be misleading because the state's personalized-public sphere did not collapse but rather re-adapted to the new situation much better than was obvious at the time.[35]

As we have seen in the examples above, the first entrepreneurial experiments conducted by youth centers and cooperatives implemented and further developed various hybrid technologies, which had already existed in late socialism. During the early period of experimentation with private business, this form of entrepreneurial governmentality was reproduced on all levels of business practice. Because of the crisis of the officialized-public sphere, the process of constructing new institutions, laws, relations, and ideologies of the state became informed with personalized relations and understandings on all levels. The hybridity of the relations between the individual and the state became perhaps even more omnipresent than was ever the case during socialism.

Obviously, in order to replace this hybridity with a distinction between the state and civil society, it is not sufficient simply to introduce market principles and economic incentives. Such an innovation, as we have seen, simply leads to the development of hybrid entrepreneurial technologies, thus reproducing the hybridity. Instead, one would need to change the ways in which people experience the state with its institutions, officials, laws, and ideologies. As Chris Hann and Elizabeth Dunn recently argued, it is only by shifting our "debates about civil society away from formal structures and organizations and towards an investigation of beliefs, values and everyday practices" that we can start to understand how state-society distinctions may be operationalized in concrete social contexts (Hann and Dunn 1996: 14).

How do entrepreneurs themselves today understand the "state" and its motifs and relations? Most of them turn to the hybrid model when they interpret the rationales behind the rules, laws, and actions of the state and its representatives.[36] Similarly, most state representatives also expect their relations with businessmen to be based on the hybrid model. A sociological study showed that one of the most striking recent changes in the interaction between businessmen and state bureaucrats is the incredible openness and matter-of-factness with which the latter have started offering to the former their "special" services (Radaev 1998: 46), which are based on the technologies of switching between officialized and personalized spheres that I have described.

The entrepreneurs continue seeing the state as being partly privatized by state officials. Even though I never specifically asked entrepreneurs what they thought about the state, they invariably offered comments like the following. Yurii, manager of the computer business (in winter 1999):

> Here the whole structure of the relations with the state is very similar to how it worked in Soviet times. They only refer to it differently today. Just look who is in power today, who leads this structure—they are all, from top to bottom, the same people, former Party and KGB functionaries. Of course, none of them are in today's Communist Party.

Nikolai, business consultant (in summer 1998):

> In this country the rules of the game (*pravila igry*) change once a day and even once a minute, in the whole country, and with different speeds. . . . This is why the government has no power. It has created a pyramid that everywhere consists of personal interests that come into conflict with state interests. The state cannot overcome this problem. This manifests itself anywhere you look.

Pavel, manager of the telecommunications and Internet firm (winter 1998):

> Now they [the state) have announced a new campaign for the honest payment of taxes. . . . But this is simply another political action designed to make it seem as though some kind of activity goes on. And in the end the attitude of those on the top is clear. They simply consider taxes their own property—the more they manage to collect, the more they put in their pockets. This is how most entrepreneurs, and also many state bureaucrats who work with finances, think.

Nadezhda, president of the firm selling equipment for the chemical industry:

> In my eyes the state and the bandits are the same thing. It is the state that reproduces these conditions and lives off them.

What is the main condition for the persistence of this understanding of the state and its motifs? Clearly, it is linked to the expectation of most Russian people, learned from years of experience, that for state laws and regulations to be applicable to everyday life they have to be reinterpreted in personalized terms. In the past years, this experience has been reinforced by endless, unpredictable shifts in the political and economic arenas. Many Russian people today are again confident, as in the years preceding perestroika, that all forms and levels of power in the country have already been redistributed and that now nothing in the society can be changed[37] As a result, most people believe, as they did in the past, that they can rely only on their own ingenuity for the success or even survival of their family or business. Everyday life in Russia currently is organized more and more around the relations, practices, and meanings of personalized-public spheres. Such widespread phenomena as barter, elements of "virtual economy," the growing political apathy, and the fact that common Russian people collectively keep billions of dollars in cash at home, unwilling to lend them to the state (Castells and Kiselyova 1998) are all manifestations of this shift.

On the one hand, it would seem that what gets increasingly lost in this process is the basis for "civil society," which cannot exist without at least some hope that popular discourse and action can instigate changes in the rules, institutions, and ideologies of the state. If the Russian people do not regain this hope, strictly economic or political reforms will not work. On the other hand, however, this shift itself may create potential for the development of civil society. As we have seen, today many Russian entrepreneurs are used to working in creative ways, inventing new techniques and networks of personalized-public relations that are literally withdrawn from the officialized spheres of the state.

Perhaps the most striking feature of the post-Soviet entrepreneurs and employees of private businesses is their perception of themselves as agents who depend on the state only in part. They inherited this self-perception from the late Soviet years. Most firms are involved in inventing entrepreneurial technologies in order to conduct a relatively efficient business in the ever changing environment, where the behavior of state representatives, the interpretation of laws, and the level of taxes are highly unpredictable. In other words, these people represent a group of active and creative agents who consciously try to stay relatively independent from the state and to insure themselves against its unpredictability. They engage in this entrepreneurial practice not simply to enrich themselves at any cost but to build a meaningful, independent, and "civilized" reality for themselves, at least partly *in spite* of the state.[38] It is among this group of people that a version of civil society may develop.[39]

In fact, these people imagine and regularly mention another model of the state, which they call the "civilized state" (*tsivilizovannoe gosudarstvo*) and in which, they claim, they would prefer to live. That state would be based on the predictable and impersonal rule of law. That kind of state is familiar to most Russians from the public discussions during perestroika and especially in the wake of the failed coup of August 1991. The entrepreneurs also often point out that they see the ultimate meaning of their work precisely in the creation of such a civilized state. Irina Hakamada, the head of the State Committee for the Support and Development of Small Business and herself a member of the last Soviet generation, summarized this view:

> My generation, however sad that may be, came to life only to build a road to the desirable world where the individual, the law, and the common sense would reign supreme. . . . Perhaps I jumped into entrepreneurship because of a feeling of hopelessness. I could no longer attend the Party meetings, where nothing was decided, the sessions of the university department, where nothing was taught, the discussions of the trade union, from which a common person could expect no benefits. . . . Money was of no particular interest for me. I chose independence. . . . Many people don't understand us, suspect us of being insatiably thirsty for money. But those who make money do it differently. Our life is a thirst for self-affirmation. It is a passionate desire to construct a new image of the society in which you act as an organic element in one big family. These are not the ambitions of one individual but of a whole social layer.[40]

It is striking how similar the values of some members of the last Soviet generation, according to Hakamada's text, are to the values of the previous generation, as described in Vladimir's diary in the beginning of this chapter. However, there is one fundamental difference between these descriptions—the relations between the state and the individual. The generation of the sixties—Vladimir and his peers—wanted to build "normal life" in the society working together with the state. Today many of the small business owners, representatives of the last Soviet generation, want to build "normal life" independently, in spite of the state.

However, for these people to become a social space in which civil society develops, they would need to imagine themselves as members of a unified social group, who share aspirations about a civilized state. Such an "imagined community" (Anderson 1983) could develop by means of a shared public discourse that is independent of the communicative tools of the state.[41] The most recent attempts of the Russian state to constrain independent media[42] can be seen as attempts to prevent such an imagined community from developing.

I hope that Castells and Kiselyova are right in arguing that today's fast-forwarded development of the "tools of information and communication" is likely to provide "new avenues of social transformation" by fostering a "decentered, networked, grass-rooted process of social change" (Castells and Kiselyova 1998). In that case, the three conditions in today's Russia—the growing importance in everyday life of the personalized-public sphere, the development of "network society," and the existence of the entrepreneurial governmentality that allows for inventing of practices that transcend officialized-public regimes of power—may be the necessary components of civil society. The question is whether and which "tools of information and communication" will emerge for this process.

Appendix: List of interviewed informants with birth date and occupation

(Last names are not mentioned and some first names are changed to protect the informants' identity.)

1. Andrei (born 1955)—former leader of Komsomol youth center, manager of music promotions agency, manager of firm designing equipment for the metallurgical industry (quoted)

2. Yurii (1960) manager of computer sales and maintenance business— (quoted)

3. Nadezhda (1963)—president of firm selling measuring equipment for the chemical industry (quoted)

4. Leonid (1965)—owner and director of advertising and public relations firm (quoted)

5. Nikolai (1964)—business consultant (quoted)

6. Marina (1968)—former employee of Komsomol youth center, co-owner of food importing business (quoted)

7. Sasha (1966)—former employee of Komsomol youth center, organizer of cashing firm (quoted)

8. Igor (1964)—entertainment and music promotions agency (quoted)

9. Dmitrii (1957)—manager of foodstuffs import business (quoted)

10. Konstantin (1964)—owner of courier service (quoted)

11. Anton (1960)—former Komsomol youth center, general manager of a food and wine importer (quoted)

12. Pavel (1959)—general manager of telecommunications and Internet provider (quoted)

13. Arkadii (1942)—director and co-owner of firm importing and selling home appliances (quoted)

14. Irina (1960)—owner of costume tailoring service for theaters

15. Lena (1965)—art director and co-owner of advertising firm

16. Rashid (1961)—director and co-owner of firm importing of telecommunications equipment from Europe

17. Mikhail (1964)—employee of car-importing business

18. Oleg (1961)—employee of hi-fi equipment chain of stores

19. Natalia (1965)—owner of beauty salon

20. Grigorii (1965)—former employee of Komsomol youth center, co-owner and director of public relations and translation services

21. Irina (1956)—owner of accounting consultations firm

22. Rem (1960)—food shop owner

23. Piotr (1962)—bank manager

24. Natasha (1958)—food shop owner

25. Vladimir (1939)—author of diary about 1957 and 1974 student construction brigades

26. Olga (1963)—owner of real estate dealership

Notes

An early version of this chapter was presented in a panel on organized crime in Russia (panel organizer Nancy Ries) at the Annual Meeting of the American Anthropological Association, Philadelphia, November 1998.

1. *The American Heritage Dictionary of the English Language*, 3d edition, New York, Houghton Mifflin, 1996.

2. See Faraday (2000) on cultural production and Yurchak (2000b) on ideological production in the late Soviet period.

3. Bakhtin uses the concept of hybridity in relation to his other term, "dialogism," which he introduces in the study of discourse (Bakhtin 1994: 304–305). Bakhtin's most general claim is that dialogism is "constitutive of human subjectivity as such" and "represents an inescapable component of any possible creative thought or deed" (Gardiner 1992: 73). For Bakhtin, modern subjectivity is not divided or fragmented but rather dialogic or hybrid—its multiple voices are never "self-enclosed or deaf to one another. They hear each other constantly, call back and forth to each other, and are reflected in one another" (Bakhtin 1984: 75; on hybridity, see also Bhabha 1994). The late Soviet and post-Soviet contexts provide fascinating examples of such dialogism.

4. In much of the Western discourse about Russia today, the term "corruption" seems to play the role once reserved for the term "communism." A recent op-ed piece in the *New York Times*, tellingly entitled "The New Russian Menace," remarked: "The struggle of the last half century was to defeat Communism; the challenge in the years ahead will be to constrain corruption. The second struggle may well prove more difficult, because avarice is a more fundamental aspect of human nature than the Communist precept that people are subject to historical determinist forces beyond the individual's control. . . . [W)e have an obligation to insure that the corrosive impact of foreign corruption is blocked from our shores. America may be as challenged today by the threat of a deterioration of values—galloping corruption—as it was yesterday by Marxist ideology" (James Leach, *New York Times*, September 10, 1999, p. A27).

5. See Eyal, Szelenyi, and Townsley for a critique (1998: 40).

6. Caroline Humphrey has also observed recently that "although the need for law is invoked by almost everyone, it is the small business people who really mean it" (Humphrey 2000: 181).

7. As Foucault argued, the distinction between the state and civil society is not a historical inevitability and should be seen, instead, "as a form of schematization" that distinguishes "a particular technology of government" (Foucault 1997: 75).

8. A study conducted by the Sector of Elites at Moscow Institute of Sociology revealed that in 1996 the average age of a Russian businessman was 36 (*Argumenty i fakty*, 1996, No. 44, p. 6). A recent rating of forty top managers of Russia includes thirty-six men and four women, most of them in their thirties, with the average age of 35.5 ("TOPografiia," in *Kar'era*, 1999, No. 12, December).

9. According to the Duma State Committee for the Support of Small Businesses, "in 1991 there were 268,000 small businesses [in Russia), in 1996 their number exceeded a million, but shrank down to 840,000 in 1997" (Dmitry Dokuchaev, "Small Businesses Are Ready to Fight for Their Rights" [Malyi biznes gotov srazhat'sia za svoye), *Izvestia*, October 1, 1998, p. 2). In Moscow alone, before the crisis of August 1998, there were 240,000 small businesses employing about 3 million people. After

the crisis, up to 50% of these businesses temporarily or permanently stopped their operations (Koriukhin and Gordeyev 1998). Recently the number of small firms has been growing substantially. For some sectors of small business the crisis turned out to be a blessing in the long run; for example, it led to a substantial growth in local production of foodstuffs and pharmaceutical and chemical products (see Natalia Kulakova and Vitalii Buza, "Banki vybrali dolzhnikov" [Banks have chosen debtors], *Kommersant Daily,* February 17, 2000, p. 8).

10. This study is limited mostly to St. Petersburg and Moscow.

11. From the slang verb *shabashnichat'* or *shabashit'*—to moonlight.

12. I discovered this diary in the *Narodnyi arkhiv* (People's archive) in Moscow in 1995 and wish to express gratitude to the archive for letting me use it.

13. Gupta (1995: 376). Also see Coronil (1997), Taussig (1994, 1997), Borneman (1997).

14. For a growing literature that critiques an uncritical treatment of modern dichotomies of private vs. public and formal vs. informal, see Humphrey (1999b: 28), Lampland (1995: 273, n. 1), Stark (1996: 1016), Vite (1996), Wedel (1998a: 7–8, 10), Levada (1993: 66), Voronkov and Chikadze (1997: 74).

15. The personalized-public sphere can be compared to David Stark's "recombinant zone," a hybrid sphere in postsocialist Hungary in which property bears aspects of both public and private property. Stark calls this type of property "recombinant property" (Stark 1996: 1016).

16. See note 3. For a more detailed discussion of this dialogic or hybrid relationship, see Yurchak (2000b).

17. The topics of such lectures had to fit the "ideological education" (*ideino— vospitatel'naia rabota*)—for example, explains Andrei, one could discuss the Komsomol movements in Hungary or the decisions of the recent Party Plenum.

18. For a similar parallel between industrial and cultural economy of shortage in state socialism, see Faraday (2000).

19. Many of the richest businessmen and political figures in Russia today also trace their financial empires directly to their high-ranking Komsomol positions. See "Chisto konkretnyi chelovek: Sergei Lisovskii vsegda stremitsya poluchit' maksimum udovol'stviia ot zhizni," *Nezavisimaia gazeta,* September 26, 1998; "Vysokii bankir v chernykh botinkakh" (Mikhail Prokhorov), in *Profil'* No. 25, July 6, 1998; "Vladimir Potanin ukhodit iz ONEKSIMa," *Profil'* No. 16, April 27, 1998; "Sergei Kirienko mechtal stat' pervym sekretarem TsK VLKSM," *Profil,'* No. 13, April 6, 1998; "Media Watch: Komsomol Media Network," *Moscow Times,* March 6, 1998; "The Business of Politics," *Monitor Times,* May 24, 1997; David Hoffman, "Kirienko: the Inside Story," *Washington Post Foreign Service,* Tuesday, March 31, 1998; Medvedev (1998). This fact is well known in Russia today and often leads to sarcastic remarks in the media and in everyday speech—see "Komsa bessmertna," *Nezavisimaia gazeta,* September 29, 1998.

20. For example, Marina and her husband, also a former secretary of a *raikom,* turned their Youth Center into their family business in the early 1990s.

21. The Komsomol Secretary Andrei, whom we met before, created a similar Youth Center in his research institute. His Center experimented with promotion business, organizing tours of St. Petersburg rock groups, film festivals, and exhibitions of local artists. Eventually the Center divided into several businesses that are still active in St. Petersburg today, varying their activity from publishing, to hotel business, to import of nonferrous metals.

22. For a discussion of similar hybrid techniques used in the invention of post-Soviet business names see Yurchak (2000a).

23. As a "flex organization," The Russian Privatization Center presented itself as both a "private" and a "state" organization. As the former, it gained privileged access to Western (especially American) aid funds and resources. As the latter, it gained access to insider government information through personal ties and networks widespread within the state apparatus. This "flex" identity put the center in a more advantageous position than any purely "private" or purely "state" organizations, allowing it "to influence and execute policies" on privatization of state property in Russia (Creed and Wedel 1997: 2001). Also see Wedel (1998a: 9–10, 1998b). Compare this hybrid identity with the dual meaning of what David Stark calls "recombinant property" in postsocialist Hungary (Stark 1996).

24. Private citizens were able to start traveling abroad relatively easily around 1988–1989, after the reforms of perestroika made the Soviet borders porous.

25. For a discussion of the invention of cooperatives, see Jones and Moskoff (1991).

26. On the role of trust based on friendship and kin in Russian business culture, see Nancy Ries (2002).

27. See Celestine Bohlen and Michael R. Gordon, "Russians Say Bank Scheme May Not Be What It Seems," *New York Times*, September 12, 1999.

28. That law was changed several times but was not abolished until recently.

29. Volkov (1999), analyzing the functional conditions for the emergence of the criminal control of business in the early 1990s, argues that the loss of the "monopoly of legitimate violence" by the collapsed Soviet state led to the appropriation of violence by organized crime. In this analysis, it is not clear what to make of the historical and cultural specificity of the modern state of the late-Soviet type. For example, what does the "monopoly of legitimate violence" mean in the state that functions, and is experienced by its subjects and representatives, as a hybrid model of officialized-public and personalized-public laws, networks, identities, forms of control, and forms of information? What happens if the officialized-public elements of that state collapse while the personalized-public elements experience a much weaker crisis, as happened in Russia? Janine Wedel, for example, argues that as a result of that collapse some elements of the Soviet state, which she calls "informal groups and networks" and which I call the personalized-public sphere of the state, accumulated even more power than in the socialist period (Wedel 1998a, 1998b). Michel Foucault's critique of the model of the modern state is illuminating for these postsocialist transformations of power: "to pose the problem in terms of the State means to continue posing it in terms of sovereign and sovereignty, that is to say in terms of law. If one describes all these phenomena of power as dependent on the State apparatus, this means grouping them as essentially repressive . . . relations of power, and hence the analysis that must be made of them, necessarily extend beyond the limits of the State . . . because the State, for all the omnipotence of its apparatuses, is far from being able to occupy the whole field of actual power relations, and further because the State can only operate on the basis of other, already existing power relations" (Foucault 1980: 122).

30. This is reminiscent of the tactics used in the recent past by criminal groups. Not surprisingly, many entrepreneurs today speak about the raids (*naezdy*) of the state organs using the language they once used to describe criminal *kryshas*. According to a recent sociological study, in the last two years 28% of private entrepreneurs have encountered more attempts by state organs to extort money from them, the majority

claimed that the sums of extortion have also increased, and 60% reported at least no decrease in extortions (Radaev 1998: 36, 44–45).

31. Yurii explains: "If we responded that we did not want any deals with them and wanted everything to be legal, they would simply reply: 'Fine, if you want everything to be legal, it will be legal. We are going to seal your office, take all your documents, and tomorrow you will come to our bureau for the investigation. This procedure is going to take up to a month, and your company will be closed during that time.'"

32. For an example of the argument that interprets entrepreneurs' activities as "corruption" and "lack of experience," see Kleiberg (1995).

33. For a discussion of the concept of *svoi*, see Wanner (1998) and Ledeneva (1998).

34. For a discussion of the role that individual agency played in this process, see also Yurchak (1997, 2000b).

35. Stark and Bruszt's recent observation—that the collapse of the party-state in Eastern Europe left behind not an "institutional void" but rather "partial ruins" that today continue providing "institutional building blocks" in the process of political, economic, and social transformation (1998: 6)—is also relevant for the Russian situation.

36. State Duma Deputy Ivan Grachev, a supporter of small businesses, thus described the situation after the 1998 crisis: "Unless a small company has a super-profitable project, the only way for it to survive is by moving 90 percent of their business into the shadow, as opposed to about 50 percent before the crisis" (Koriukhin and Gordeyev, 1998).

37. According to a survey conducted by Macro International in Russia within weeks of the crisis, most Russian people named "the loss of their dreams and the loss of confidence in Russia as the two things that were affected worst by the crisis" (Koriukhin and Gordeyev).

38. Caroline Humphrey calls it a desire to build "normal life" (Humphrey 2000: 181).

39. Mayfair Yang argues that in China of the early 1990s a type of civil society developed within the *guanxixue* networks, "'poaching' on the public domains monopolized by the state" and thus neutralizing "the power of official channels, state rules, and state regulators . . ." (Yang 1994: 308).

40. From Hakamada's homepage on the Internet: www.hakamada.ru/pozic.htm.

41. Steps in this direction have been made. Since the August 1998 crisis, a small business movement with sixty regional branches in the country has formed. Duma Deputy Ivan Grachev, who is leading the movement, remarked: "If the middle class indeed becomes a political force, it will be a useful fruit of the crisis" (Dmitry Dokuchaev, "Small Businesses Are Ready to Fight for Their Rights," *Izvestia*, October 1, 1998, p. 2).

42. For example, the arrest in Chechnya of Andrei Babitskii (*Radio Liberty*) and the continuous government attacks on Media Most corporation.

Bibliography

Anderson, Benedict. 1983. *Imagined Communities: Reflections on the Origin and Spread of Nationalism.* London: Verso.

Bakhtin, Mikhail. 1994. "Discourse in the Novel." In Michael Holquist (ed.), *The Dialogical Imagination: Four Essays by M.M. Bakhtin*, pp. 259–422. Austin: University of Texas Press.

————. 1984. *Problems of Dostoevsky's Poetics*. Edited and translated by Wayne C. Booth. Minneapolis: University of Minnesota Press.

Bhabha, Homi. 1994. *The Location of Culture*. London: Routledge.

Borneman, John. 1997. "State, Territory and National Identity Formation in the Two Berlins, 1945–1995." In Akhil Gupta and James Ferguson (eds.), *Culture, Power, Place: Explorations in Critical Anthropology*, pp. 93–117. Durham, NC: Duke University Press.

Bourdieu, Pierre. 1991. *Language and Symbolic Power*. Cambridge: Harvard University Press.

————. 1977. *Outline of a Theory of Practice*. Cambridge: Cambridge University Press.

Butler, Judith. 1997. *The Psychic Life of Power: Theories in Subjection*. Stanford: Stanford University Press.

Castel, Robert. 1991. "From Dangerousness to Risk." In Graham Burchell, Colin Gordon, and Peter Miller (eds.), *The Foucault Effect: Studies in Governmentality with Two Lectures by and an Interview with Michel Foucault*, pp. 281–298. Chicago: University of Chicago Press.

Castells, Manuel, and Elena Kiselyova. 1998. "Russia and the Network Society: An Analytical Exploration." Paper presented at conference, *Russia at the End of the 20th Century*, Stanford University, November 5–7, 1998.

Coronil, Fernando. 1997. *The Magical State: Nature, Money, and Modernity in Venezuela*. University of Chicago Press.

Creed, Gerald, and Janine Wedel. 1997. "Second Thoughts from the Second World: Interpreting Aid in Post-Communist Eastern Europe," *Human Organization* 56(3): 253–264.

Dokuchaev, Dmitry. "Malyi bienes gotov srazhat´sia za svoye [Small businesses are ready to fight for their rights). *Izvestia*, October 1, 1998, p. 2.

Ewald, Francois. 1991. "Insurance and Risk." In Graham Burchell, Colin Gordon, and Peter Miller (eds.), *The Foucault Effect: Studies in Governmentality with Two Lectures by and an Interview with Michel Foucault*, pp. 197–210. Chicago: University of Chicago Press.

Eyal, Gil, Ivan Szelenyi, and Eleanor Townsley. 1998. *Making Capitalism Without Capitalists: The New Ruling Elites in Eastern Europe*. London: Verso.

Faraday, George. 2000. *Revolt of the Filmmakers: The Struggle for Artistic Autonomy and the Fall of the Soviet Film Industry*. University Park: Pennsylvania State University Press.

Foucault, Michel. 1997. "The Birth of Biopolitics." In Paul Rabinow (ed.), *Ethics: Subjectivity and Truth. The Essential Works of Michel Foucault, 1954–1984*, vol. 1, pp. 73–79. New York: New Press.

————. 1997. "The Ethics of the Concern of Self as a Practice of Freedom." In Paul Rabinow (ed.), *Ethics: Subjectivity and Truth. The Essential Works of Michel Foucault 1954–1984*, vol. 1, pp. 281–301. New York: New Press.

————. 1991. "Governmentality." In Graham Burchell, Colin Gordon, and Peter Miller (eds.), *The Foucault Effect: Studies in Governmentality with Two Lectures by and an Interview with Michel Foucault*, pp. 87–104. Chicago: University of Chicago Press.

————. 1980. "Truth and Power." In Colin Gordon (ed.), *Michel Foucault: Power/ Knowledge: Selected Interviews and Other Writings, 1972–1977*, pp. 109–133. Brighton, UK: Harvester Press.

Gardiner, Michael. 1992. *The Dialogics of Critique: M.M. Bakhtin and the Theory of Ideology*. London: Routledge.

Gordon, Colin. 1991. "Governmental Rationality: An Introduction." In Graham Burchell, Colin Gordon, and Peter Miller (eds.), *The Foucault Effect: Studies in Governmentality with Two Lectures by and an Interview with Michel Foucault*, pp. 1–52. Chicago: University of Chicago Press.

Gupta, Akhil. 2000. "Spatializing States: The Integrated Child Development Services Program in India." Lecture delivered at University of California, Berkeley, February 16.

———. 1995. "Blurred Boundaries: The Discourse of Corruption, the Culture of Politics, and the Imagined State." *American Ethnologist* 22(2): 375–402.

Hakamada, Irina. 1999. Personal homepage: <www.hakamada.ru/pozic.htm>.

Handelman, Stephen. 1995. *Comrade Criminal: Russia's New Mafiya*. New Haven: Yale University Press.

Hann, Christopher, and Elizabeth Dunn (eds.). 1996. *Civil Society: Challenging Western Models*. London: Routledge.

Hoffman, David. 1998. "Kiriyenko: A New Breed of Russian." *Washington Post Foreign Service*, Tuesday, March 31.

Humphrey, Caroline. 2000. "Dirty Business, 'Normal Life,' and the Dream of Law." In A.V. Ledeneva and M. Kurkchiyan (eds.), *Economic Crime in Russia*, pp. 177–190. Boston: Kluwer Law International.

———. 1999a. "Russian Protection Rackets and the Appropriation of Law and Order." In Josiah McC. Heyman (ed.), *States and Illegal Practices*, pp. 199–232. Oxford: Berg.

———. 1999b. "Traders, 'Disorder,' and Citizenship Regimes in Provincial Russia." In Michael Burawoy and Katherine Verdery (eds.), *Uncertain Transitions: Ethnographies of Change in the Postsocialist World*. Lanham: Rowman and Littlefield.

Jones, Anthony, and William Moskoff. 1991. *Ko-ops: The Rebirth of Entrepreneurship in the Soviet Union*. Bloomington: Indiana University Press.

Kharkhordin, Oleg. 1999. *The Collective and the Individual in Russia: A Study of Practices*. Berkeley: University of California Press.

Kleiberg, Iulia. 1995. "Sotsial'nye otkloneniia molodezhi v usloviiakh rynka" [Social deviations of youth in the conditions of the market). In *Materialy mezhdunarodnoi nauchno-prakticheskoi konferentsii: molodezh' v usloviiakh sotsial'no-ekonomicheskikh reform*. [Materials of the International Scientific-Practical Conference: Youth in the Conditions of Socio-Economic Reforms]. Vypusk 2. St. Petersburg: St. Petersburg University, September 26–28, pp. 53–54.

Koriukhin, Kirill, and Alexander Gordeyev. 1998. "Small Firms Retreat into Shadow," *Moscow Times*, October 8.

Kornai, Janos. 1980. *Economics of Shortage*. Amsterdam: North-Holland.

Kryshtanovskaia, Olga. 1996. "Finansovaia oligarkhiia v Rossii." *Izvestiia*, No. 4, January 10.

Kulakova, Natalia, and Vitalii Buza. 2000. "Banki vybrali dolzhnikov," *Kommersant Daily*, February 17, p. 8.

Lampland, Martha. 1995. *The Object of Labor: Commodification in Socialist Hungary*. Chicago: Chicago University Press.

Ledeneva, Alena. 1998. *Russia's Economy of Favours: Blat, Networking and Informal Exchange*. Cambridge: Cambridge University Press.

Levada, Yurii. 1993. *Sovetskii prostoi chelovek: opyt sotsial'nogo portreta na rubezhe 90–kh*. [Soviet simple man: attempt of a social portrait at the turn of the 1990s). Moscow: Izdatel'stvo "Mirovoi Okean.

Medvedev, Roy. 1998. *Kapitalizm v Rossii?* Moscow: Prava cheloveka.

Radaev, Vadim. 2000. "Entrepreneurial Strategies and the Structure of Transaction Costs in Russian Business." Paper presented at conference, *Entrepreneurs, Entrepreneurialism and Democracy in Communist and Post-Communist Societies*, University of California, Berkeley, May 19–20.

———. 1998. *Formirovanie novykh rossiiskikh rynkov: transaktsionnye izderzhki, formy kontrolia i delovaia etika* [Formation of new Russian markets: transactional costs, forms of control, and business ethics). Moskva: Tsentr politicheskikh tekhnologii.

Ries, Nancy. 2002. "'Honest' Bandits and 'Warped People': Russian Narratives about Money, Corruption, and Moral Decay." In Carol Greenhouse, Elizabeth Mertz, and Kay Warren (eds.), *Ethnography in Unstable Places*. Durham, NC: Cornell University Press.

Rofel, Lisa. 1999. *Other Modernities: Gendered Yearnings in China After Socialism.* Berkeley: University of California Press.

Shelly, Louise. 1996. *Policing Soviet Society: The Evolution of State Control.* London: Routledge.

Solnick, Steven. 1998. *Stealing the State: Control and Collapse in Soviet Institutions.* Cambridge: Harvard University Press.

Stark, David. 1996. "Recombinant Property in East European Capitalism." *American Journal of Sociology* 101: 993–1027.

Stark, David, and Laszlo Bruszt. 1998. *Postsocialist Pathways: Transforming Politics and Property in East Central Europe.* Cambridge: Cambridge University Press.

Taussig, Michael. 1997. *Magic of the State.* New York: Routledge.

———. 1994. "Maleficium: State Fetishism." In Emily Apter and William Pietz (eds.), *Fetishism as Cultural Discourse*, pp. 217–247. Ithaca, NY: Cornell University Press.

Verdery, Katherine. 1996. *What Was Socialism, and What Comes Next?* Princeton: Princeton University Press.

Vite, Oleg. 1996. "Izbirateli—vragi naroda? (Razmyshleniia ob adekvatnosti elektoral'nogo povedeniia i faktorakh, xa ee uroven' vliiaiushchikh)" [Are voters enemies of the people? (Some thoughts: about the adequacy of electoral behavior and the factors that affect it). In *Etika uspekha* 9, 58–71.

Volkov, Vadim. 1999. "Violent Entrepreneurship in Post-Communist Russia." *Europe-Asia Studies*, July.

Voronkov, Viktor, and Elena Chikadze. 1997. "Leningradskie evrie: etnichost' i kontekst" [Leningrad Jews: Ethnicity and context). In *Biograficheskii metod v izuchenii postsotsialisticheskikh obshchestv. Materialy mezhdunarodnogo seminara* [Biografic method in the studies of postsocialist societies materials of the international seminar). St. Petersburg: Center for Independent Social Research, pp. 74–78.

Wanner, Catherine. 1998. *Burden of Dreams: History and Identity in Post-Soviet Ukraine.* University Park: Pennsylvania State University Press.

Wedel, Janine, 2001. "Transactions in the U.S.–Russia Relationship: Representational Fraud, Shifting Agency, and Russia's Decline." Paper presented at the conference "Ten Years Since the Soviet Union," School of Slavonic and East European Studies, University College London, November 10, 2001.

————. 1998a. "Informal Relations and Institutional Change: How Eastern European Cliques and States Mutually Respond." *Anthropology of East Europe Review* 16(1): 4–13.

————. 1998b. *Collision and Collusion: The Strange Case of Western Aid to Eastern Europe, 1989–1998*. New York: St. Martin's Press.

Woodruff, David. 1999. "Barter of the Bankrupt: The Politics of Demonetization in Russia's Federal State." In Michael Burawoy and Katherine Verdery (eds.), *Uncertain transitions: Ethnographies of Change in the Postsocialist World*, pp. 83–124. Lanham: Rowman and Littlefield.

Yurchak, Alexei. 2000a. "Privatize Your Name: Symbolic Work in a Post-Soviet Linguistic Market." *Sociolinguistics* 4(3): 406–434.

————. 2000b. "Hegemony of Form: The Unexpected Outcome of the Soviet Linguistic Project." Paper presented at Post-Soviet Center Carnegie Seminar, University of California, Berkeley, Fall.

————. 1997. "The Cynical Reason of Late Socialism: Power, Pretense, and the *Anekdot*." *Public Culture* 9(2): 161–188.

Yang, Mayfair Mei-hui. 1994. *Gifts, Favors and Bouquets: The Art of Social Relationship in China*. Ithaca, NY: Cornell University Press.

12

Marketing Civility, Civilizing the Market

Chinese Multilevel Marketing's Challenge to the State

Lyn Jeffery

In January 1998, Xingsha, a small town 10 km outside Changsha, Hunan (itself well known in China as Mao Zedong's hometown), was dubbed by a hostile media as China's first "multilevel marketing city." Multilevel marketing, otherwise known as direct sales or network marketing, is a system whereby vertically integrated networks of so-called distributors both consume and sell products.[1] Two years before, Xingsha had a population of 10,000, but when the Hunan Kangfubao Exercise Equipment Company started developing marketing networks in the area, everything began to change. Kangfubao was selling one of the Chinese multilevel marketing industry's most popular products, colloquially known as the "swaying machine" (*yaobai ji*). It was a plastic box the size of a smallish typewriter, with a pair of hollows where one's heels rested while lying supine on the floor. When turned on, the hollows shifted from side to side, gently wiggling the entire body in what was described as a goldfish-like movement. This type of "anaerobic" movement was said to increase the amount of oxygen in the blood, thereby curing any number of conditions, including among others heart disease, diabetes, cancer, stomach upset, skin disease, paralysis, and indigestion. As with most multilevel marketing (MLM) products, the Kangfubao machine cost more than double what it would in a state-owned store.

In late 1997 Kangfubao built large new headquarters in Xingsha. Within a few months an estimated 100,000 people had flocked to the town and its neighboring communities, packing local apartments and making landlords, merchants, and authorities rich. The *Nanfang zhoumo* (Southern Weekend) newspaper reported that an additional thousand arrived each day (Sun and Guo 1998). Corporate headquarters received ten thousand visitors a day, selling them hundreds if not thousands of machines. Kangfubao had its own security forces, in effect creating a small fiefdom outside local law.[2] The streets were lined with bookstalls selling the kind of motivational and get-rich-quick manuals that are attached to multilevel marketing around the world.[3] And as with MLM organizations around the world, the product attracting these crowds was not the swaying machine; rather it was the way the machines were being sold—in a pyramid-shaped network in which participants' profits came from recruiting product-purchasing members into networks "below" them.

In China, MLM, or *chuanxiao*, swept the country during the 1990s with a powerful entrepreneurial message of just-around-the-corner wealth and health. Old and young, male and female, urbanites and farmers alike were recruited into marketing networks where they purchased expensive health products that promised miracle cures, attended training sessions where they learned to talk, think, and move like salespeople, and then conducted their own recruitment activities. *Chuanxiao* mobilized and capitalized upon the well-known Chinese social networks (*guanxi*). The industry, introduced to China by American, Taiwanese, Hong Kong, and Japanese companies in 1990, had by 1997 sold an estimated US$7 billion of products (mainly health foods, supplements, cosmetics, and the like) through networks with some 10 million participants.[4] Since the vast majority of distributors had little or no background in sales and marketing, *chuanxiao* training focused on the transformation of the individual into a multilevel marketeer. As with MLM around the world, the consumption of products, and sales and recruitment from within personal relationships, were presented as opportunities for life-enhancement rather than as a commodification of social relations. Nevertheless, the industry and its practitioners were from the beginning viewed with suspicion by the majority of the population. For instance, I regularly heard derogatory comments from people outside the *chuanxiao* community. These comments, often based on direct experience with *chuanxiao* practitioners, focused on the way marketeers capitalized upon their personal relationships, "cheating family, cheating friends."[5]

Ideas about entrepreneurialism are fundamental to the global network marketing industry. Once having paid the fee to join, distributors are doubly positioned at a node in their "upline's" network and at the "top" of their own networks. The meaning of entrepreneurship and entrepreneurial identity, however, is always locally specific, rooted in particular cultural and historical contexts. In China the imperative to develop one's own network gave rise to a potent set of narratives that celebrated the free individual—no longer dependent upon the state for his or her livelihood—such as "being your own boss" (*zuo ziji de zhuren*) and "relying on oneself to support oneself" (*kao ziji yang ziji*). This emphasis on individual ambition stood in direct contrast to decades of anti-individualist, anticapitalist education received by many participants in the Maoist era (1949–1976).

If the Chinese state and marketers are crafting their own notion of entrepreneurship, the term remains highly contested within the global MLM industry itself. Some critics argue that network marketing is not entrepreneurial in the truest sense. As Stephen Butterfield writes in his scathing *Amway: The Cult of Free Enterprise*, "The 'entrepreneurs' who market the products are . . . totally dependent on the Corporation for supply, research, development, commissions, policies, rules and regulations, whole-sale price" (1985: 152). He goes on to describe MLM as an illusion of entrepreneurship and self-help: rather than managing, organizing, and assuming profit from their own businesses, distributors are actually working for a multinational corporation within a rigid, hierarchical system. Butterfield is attempting to distinguish between true and false, between entrepreneurial ideology and action, where the former is understood as that which obscures a nonentrepreneurial reality.

What I found in China, however, was a complicated picture in which different groups of marketers were able to generate a range of incomes for themselves based on their investments, their relationships with others, and their own labor. True, marketers were dependent on companies for product supply and the distribution of profits, but in the highly competitive Chinese direct selling industry, they also had many ways of circumventing corporate systems for their own benefit. For instance, distributors would join several companies at the same time, taking advantage of changing profit-taking policies; they would leverage their networks in one corporation against another, in effect treating them like personal assets; they would create their own promotional materials and sell them; they would lead their own for-profit training seminars; and in some cases they would produce the goods themselves rather than getting them from the company factory.[6] The majority of distributors were far from the eyes of corporate headquarters and proved nearly impossible to control.

Multilevel Marketing City

Kangfubao followed the example of other *chuanxiao* corporations: its main recruitment tools were marketing or "potential training" seminars (*qianneng xunlian*), which taught participants how to be both moral and competent entrepreneurs. In Xingsha, upwards of 6,000 people attended beginning, intermediate, and advanced training classes, held thrice daily for a nominal fee. There they squeezed into huge rooms where they were treated to a typical *chuanxiao* menu of loud disco music, dancing, group call-and-response ("How are the people from Shandong province doing?" "Great!" "How about the people from Henan province?"), and public self-introductions from excited new marketers. One bespectacled man in a suit stepped up and nearly dropped the mike in his nervousness. The crowd laughed. "I'm from the old revolutionary district of Jiangxi, my name is Zhang Bing [lit., soldier]," he said. "After coming to Xingsha my brain has finally burst into revolution. I now understand what real life is!" (Sun and Guo 1998).

In addition to attending seminars, people's daily work consisted of calling friends and family around the country and using any and all methods to convince them to come to Xingsha to become "downlines"—*xiaxian*, members from whose sales those above them would receive commissions. This is a highly unusual strategy in the MLM industry, where networks generally spread so quickly precisely because they are less tied to fixed locations than other industries. In most Chinese cases, local distributors would attend trainings with their upline sponsors (*shangxian*) until they were ready to conduct their own basic seminars in their villages or neighborhoods. True, other urban *chuanxiao* corporate headquarters were pilgrimage sites for highly mobile marketers, but Kangfubao was the only one to generate this kind of concentrated, located, central recruitment model.

The majority of would-be Xingsha distributors were nonelites from medium and small cities in relatively less developed provinces: middle-aged workers, peasants, and migrant workers without urban residence permits ("floaters"). A fairly typical group was six people from the same family in Hebei province, north of Hunan. The first of their family to come to Xingsha was a twenty-five-year-old man, originally a factory worker, who had lost his job and taken up repair work. Two months earlier, someone from his village had invited him to Xingsha to attend what he had thought would be a technical workshop. It was not until he arrived that he found out about MLM. He remained in Xingsha, succeeding in getting an uncle and four cousins to join him. "Facts prove that it was the right decision for me to stay here," he told a Chinese newspaper reporter. "Now my monthly salary is up to 3,000 yuan [$365]. And according to the regulations of the company I'll be a chief executive in six months, with a salary of 120,000 a month [$14,600]—more than the president of the United States!" Of course, "company regulations" contained no guarantee that this would happen. The fact that his "salary" was coming from the commissions he made from recruiting his relatives to join the network was not a problem. As he put it, "first of all we are professional colleagues and then we are relatives. I made money off of them but I have led them to the top of humanity's most glorious peak, [and] they will be grateful to me" (Sun and Guo 1998).

Unfortunately for him (although perhaps fortunately for the rest of his relatives), this was not to be. On April 21, 1998, the official Chinese news agency announced what many in the industry had been dreading and what the state had been threatening for years: from that day on, all direct sales activities including multilevel marketing were banned, with a final date of October 31 for corporations to wind up operations completely.[7] Thus began the kind of race to recoup losses that strikes fear into any investment organization, be it a bank or a pyramid scheme. Across China, angry, disappointed *chuanxiao* marketers saw their hopes for wealth disappear, and they wanted someone to take responsibility. As with any marketing network, those who had joined most recently, who were positioned at the bottom of the network, lost the most. No longer able to recruit others and make commissions, they were left only with their overpriced products, rage, and blame. Complicating the picture was the fact that they had entered the company through someone they knew, often a relative. This put millions of people in very, very awkward positions.

Some companies were able to placate their members, even to continue operating in a going-down-with-the-ship kind of way; many more were inundated with requests for refunds. However, since people were often trying to return merchandise that exceeded the one- to two-month money-back guarantee period, companies were unwilling and often unable to fulfill their requests. Other companies shut their doors and fled with what were rumored to be large amounts of cash. A year before, pro-MLM marketers and economists had contrasted *chuanxiao* to the kind of pyramid investment schemes in Albania whose disintegration led to civil war in that country. Now, similar feelings of rage and injustice were to engender violence in China.

While we will never know what happened to the small family group mentioned in the article above, perhaps they were left in the same predicament as many others in Kangfubao's "multilevel marketing city" and its environs. Thousands had borrowed money or sold possessions to raise the 5,000 yuan needed for travel expenses and purchase of the overpriced swaying machine— a sum equivalent to a year's salary for the average urban resident, much more than that for rural residents. With no hope of earning back any of their investment, they found themselves penniless, often without even the means to return home. According to newspaper reports, Kangfubao refused distributors' demands for refunds and reimbursement of expenses (Zhao 1998).

In the town of Pingtang, 3,000 Kangfubao distributors slept on the streets or crowded into unfurnished rented rooms, pooling their dwindling funds for a meager diet of rice porridge. In a small nearby building, five high-level Kangfubao distributors and an assistant general manager of the company's Changsha office were held hostage for four days immediately following the ban's announcement. The crowd—armed with clubs and iron bars—was unified in its demand that unless members were fully reimbursed there would be bloodshed. Pressed by authorities facing an increasingly unstable situation, Kangfubao finally announced that it would release 1 million yuan and that each distributor would be given 600 yuan for travel expenses—a far cry from the 5,000 that most had already spent. That afternoon, 300 police took the building and began to send protestors home (Zhao 1998).

The next day four people died and hundreds were injured in the nearby city of Zhangjiajie, when several thousand enraged Kangfubao distributors demonstrated in the main street, marching, singing, and breaking windows in the central department store. Pausing at the post office, some attempted to place free telephone calls and, when they were unable to do so, destroyed the equipment. Several hundred of them peacefully occupied a major intersection, but others beat a traffic policeman, overturned cars, and wielded sticks and knives in combat with what were described in a newspaper report as "a small number of local hoodlums" (*Zhongguo huagongbao zhoukan* [China Chemical Industry Weekly] 1998).

Why did the Chinese government move to shut down the multilevel marketing industry after eight years? From 1990 to 1998, MLM had exploded across the country, addressing the needs of the state in several important ways: it brought millions of dollars to local state commerce, tax, and public security bureaus; it provided some measure of employment for millions of laid-off workers and underemployed peasants; and it modeled Westernization, capitalism, and new entrepreneurial practices while paralleling the state's civilizing rhetoric on the importance of cultivating market competence in Chinese workers. Indeed, despite widespread popular condemnation, this is why MLM made sense to so many people: it fit perfectly within the state framework. The story of the state's response to *chuanxiao* has much to tell us about the changing meanings of socially productive work, proper social identity, and political participation in contemporary China. For while the party-state retains the authority to define the moral parameters of economic behaviors, a study of the multilevel marketing industry confirms the widespread emergence of institutions with the capacity to engender alternative political, social, economic, and moral allegiances—allegiances that might challenge the Chinese Communist Party (CCP). In the multilevel marketing instance, this challenge was met with a state crackdown.[8]

An understanding of these emerging institutions or movements must take into account how historically embedded cultural categories continue to shape the narratives and practices of both state officials and ordinary people. For instance, as David Kelly reminds us, "Orthodox Maoism continues to provide and propagate a discursive field, setting up the ways in which social and political reality is categorized, and thus the ways in which political problems are resolved" (1991: 21). In order to examine some of the central political and social themes played out in *chuanxiao*, we might first briefly review certain aspects of the Maoist-era state position on labor, proletarian consciousness, and political participation. Specifically, I will argue that labor was seen at least partly as a pedagogical tool for the production and distinction of virtuous political identities (the proletariat) with an exclusive right to political participation. Understanding this legacy allows us to make sense of the current party-state rhetoric on civilization (*wenming*) and quality (*suzhi*), which makes state-defined self-cultivation central to the national marketization project. The older meanings remain highly significant in shaping both state and popular actions and assumptions today—but only to a point. The critical link between the state-sanctioned category of socially productive labor and political agency—the promise and context in which labor was made meaningful for several decades and the foundation upon which the Chinese Communist Party established its moral authority—has yet to be elaborated by the party-state and is therefore unclear to everyday Chinese citizens. More than any other contemporary institution, MLM corporations attempted to fill this moral vacuum with a politics of self-cultivation and entrepreneurship—what I will argue is an inherently political move.

Labor, Proletarian Consciousness, and Political Identity in the Maoist Era

Maoist Chinese socialism was at least partly about inspiring people to conceive of and participate in labor in an unprecedented way. The goal was participation of 100 percent of the population in certain types of state-validated work and the eradication of invalidated types of work that fell within the category of exploitative capitalism. To succeed, the state needed to transform people's thinking, hence the focus on thought reform as outlined in Mao Zedong's two philosophical treatises, "On Contradictions" and "On Practice" (Rickett 1957: 199). As Maurice Meisner writes, "In place of the Marxian-defined economic and social prerequisites for socialism and communism, the Maoist faith in the future relied on the spiritual and moral transformation of people. 'If you are not completely reborn,' as Mao proclaimed, 'you cannot enter the door of communism.' . . . it was the 'transformation of the subjective world' that was regarded as the decisive factor in 'transforming the objective world'" (1982: 198). Maoist theory broke with conventional Marxist beliefs in the objective laws of history in this respect, advocating instead a voluntaristic faith in the power of human consciousness, action, and morality to produce and maintain revolutionary social change (Meisner 1982: 60).

It is therefore no surprise that the CCP dedicated vast efforts to the culti-

vation of the new socialist individual. In the periods both immediately before and after the 1949 revolution, people had to learn what "class" was and
where they stood within it, and who counted as a "worker" and what kinds
of political consciousness went along with that status. William Hinton details the land reform movement in the mid- and late 1940s, for instance,
when we see peasants being given new vocabularies with which to express
new political relationships (1966). And Gail Hershatter describes how much
"thought work" had to be done with urban prostitutes immediately after the
revolution, in order to get them to understand and identify themselves as
oppressed subalterns in the new terms of socialism (1993). But perhaps the
most important new cultural category was that of "labor." For as Lisa Rofel
writes, "in China, 'labor' . . . under socialism served as the principal cultural
site for the production of identities. . . . That is, the state made labor the
cultural arena in which women and men crafted the meaning of 'liberation,'
proved their socialist moral worth, expressed their nationalist sentiments,
and received their rewards—or punishments—from the state" (1998: 122).
For at least three decades, Maoist politics blurred the economic domain with
the politics of identity, making economic behavior—capitalist or socialist—
the primary measure of political virtue and immorality.

Prior to the economic reforms begun in 1978, the state embraced the Marxist notion that the portion of human activity classified as "productive work"
had certain profound effects on the individual: it functioned didactically to
produce correct revolutionary consciousness. The crucial classificatory notion of class (*jieji*) was based upon one's position in regard to labor and the
means of production. Those who participated in the right kinds of labor
(*laodong*) were said to have at the very least the potential for proletarian
consciousness. Conversely, it was thought that participation in the exploita-
tion of labor both produced and was produced by counterrevolutionary political commitments. In this understanding, modern, revolutionary consciousness
and politically authoritative proletarian standing were to be obtained by breaking through "feudal" consciousness (Perry 1997: 43). Participation in state-
sanctioned forms of labor was a crucial state instrument of political
mobilization (Yeh 1997: 71). This ability to define the moral discourse on
labor and political participation was a central aspect of state power.

We can see the operation of this vision of the didactic power of labor in
the use of prescriptive labor policies, ranging from the labor reform (*laodong
gaizao*) and reeducation through labor (*laodong jiaoyang*) systems that have
awaited Chinese criminals since the 1950s to the mass migration of urban
intellectuals to rural areas during the Cultural Revolution in the late 1960s.
These programs reflected the beliefs that labor was an important tool in the
project of thought reform, an education in a more righteous proletarian con-

sciousness, a cure for politically or socially undesirable habits and crimes, and, in the case of bourgeois prisoners, a right to be earned.

Published accounts such as the Ricketts' *Prisoners of Liberation* provide insight into the powerful effects of the Maoist-era model of labor, consciousness, and political identity, especially on those to whom virtuous political identity was denied. The document, published in 1957 by an American couple who spent four years in Chinese prisons in the 1950s on charges of espionage, has to be read as a complicated political statement to a hostile American public. The Ricketts were released from Chinese prison into a Cold War political environment in which their espousal of communist ideals could only be interpreted as brainwashing. In the following passage, Allyn Rickett describes how he and his cellmates began to gain a new perspective on the meaning of productive labor, in the midst of their "thought reform" process:

> The continuous progress of the revolution had a positive effect on the prisoners. Especially after 1953 the building of the new China absorbed the attention of almost all of them. Few could help but be infected with the spirit of challenge. While in the United States people grab their newspaper to find out the standing of their favorite ball team, in China interest was centered on the fulfillment of production goals. It was the same in our cell.
>
> The announcement of a new invention, the building of a new factory, or the surpassing of a production target would bring forth excited exclamations, and the news of a drought or flood would throw the cell into deep gloom. The activities and accomplishments of model workers, such as the railroad engineer Yo Sheng-wu and the girl textile worker Ho Jien-hsiu, were followed with the same interest as those of a Mickey Mantle or Grace Kelly here at home.
>
> . . . My cellmates were fired with the desire to be a part of the new China, and the feeling that they were criminals outside of it all weighed heavily on them. Thus there began to grow a new incentive to reform. No longer was it just a question of reforming simply to avoid punishment. Now there was the positive hope for a vital and fruitful future in helping to build their country.

Without suspending critical judgment, we can get from this passage a glimpse of labor as an act of political significance. For prisoners at least, participation in labor was desirable because through it the state conferred a virtuous, meaningful social and political identity:[9] through labor it was possible to remake oneself as a positive agent in the national modernization project. To be denied access to socially meaningful work was to be deprived of the tools for establishing one's political and moral authority.

Through the examples above, I have outlined the Maoist-era notion of the didactic power of proletarian labor, as well as the link between labor participation and political identity. How does this conceptual template continue to shape contemporary understandings of these categories? In China today, official discourse on productive work no longer directly privileges the agricultural and factory-based labor undertaken by the peasant and urban working class, and popular opinion now devalues the social identities of people who participate in them as "low quality" (*suzhi cha*) and uncivilized (*bu wenming*). Now enterprises are encouraged to focus on profit rather than social welfare, labor and property are being commodified, and individuals are allowed or forced to educate themselves with new, marketable skills. But this neoconservative state project is not yet a coherent socioeconomic political program (Fewsmith 1995). In redefining the category of labor thus, the state has been unable to maintain what has historically been one of its most important sources of authority: authorship of the conceptual link between political virtue and the performance of correct labor. Given the historical relationship between labor and political consciousness, what kind of virtuous political identity, conferring the right to what kind of political agency, is crafted through an individual's participation in entrepreneurial activities? It is in the state's response to movements like Chinese MLM that we see most clearly the tensions generated by this as-yet-unanswered question.

Work, Civility, and Political Identity in China Today

For the average citizen in contemporary China, the transition to capitalism is happening in a way similar to the earlier transition to socialism: through the acquisition and mastery of emerging rhetorics, the practice of new activities, and the experience of new social identities that come with them (Jeffrey 2001a). Unlike in the earlier period, however, the power of the CCP to define the parameters and significance of each of these realms is increasingly fragmented. The explosive growth of multilevel marketing is but one example of this. Yet as with any market institution in China today, *chuanxiao* owed its existence to the larger framework of economic reforms established by the state. Moreover, *chuanxiao* operated by mobilizing many of the same moral narratives about the market that we find in official discourse.

In *National Past-times*, Ann Anagnost (1997) presents a compelling vision of the kinds of political and cultural work undertaken by the CCP in its attempt to legitimize itself as the sole moral and political leader of the Chinese nation. "Civilization work" (*wenming gongzuo*) is central as a practice that produces a vision of both state and subjects: the Chinese people as an uncivilized, low-quality populace in constant need of moral and social guidance and a national pedagogy. In the 1990s, this official rhetoric was highly visible: massive billboards detailing the attributes of a civilized person (don't spit, don't swear, be polite to strangers, don't push in line, etc.), "Civilized Household" plaques dotting front doors, numerous newspaper articles about civilized enterprises and civilized workers, and the like.

Civility is imagined here "as an absence, as something lacking among the Chinese people that needs to be induced into being" (Anagnost 1997: 77). Just as the CCP needed to teach citizens what it meant to become part of the state socialist project in the Maoist era, now it needs to teach citizens how to be civilized in a state socialist market economy. "In this concern over the people's productivity," writes Anagnost, "we see the [Chinese Communist] party constituting itself as the historically necessary agent to lift the nation from a state of dependency and backwardness to autonomy and even world domination" (1997: 95). In other words, the kind of social actors necessary for Chinese economic global dominance do not yet exist, or, at best, they exist only in small numbers. According to state rhetoric, their creation remains, as in the previous era, a state project. The difference lies in the vision of how the Chinese people must be changed. Proletarian labor and revolutionary consciousness are no longer the state's goals; rather the goals now are wage labor, entrepreneurship, and "high-quality" citizens.

While civilization status is bestowed upon individuals, households, and enterprises by government agencies, the notion of an individual's "quality" (*suzhi*) places the civility problem squarely on the shoulders of everyday citizens.[10] Rather than questions of privilege, education, class, gender, ethnicity, regional identity, or social connections, low quality is often invoked in everyday conversation to explain why certain groups or individuals have not succeeded in participating effectively in the market economy. For instance, rural migrant workers are almost uniformly described as of low quality by urban residents, and drivers deplore the low quality of poorly behaved pedestrians and bicyclists. In multilevel marketing, downlines complained that they were inadequately trained by low-quality sponsors or, conversely, advertised their networks as full of high-quality people.

Like the category of revolutionary consciousness in the Maoist era, quality and civility are personal attributes linked to individuals' effective, productive employment in national modernization; as such, they are constructed by the state as virtues. However, neither quality and civility nor the wage labor they engender are state-sanctioned *political* identities. They cannot be used as effectively as state instruments of political mobilization because they do not confer rights to political participation in the ways that proletarian labor and consciousness did years ago. To cultivate one's quality, thus theoretically increasing one's chance of success in the market, does not lead to any clear-cut political enfranchisement.

By depoliticizing the links between moral virtue, state-sanctioned labor, and political agency, the state has severely weakened the historical basis of its own authority. The result is a wide variety of contestants for the moral and political loyalties of the Chinese people. Multilevel marketing was one such contestant. It was a particularly challenging contestant because it spoke in the language of the state, using a familiar grammar in which categories of economic, political, and moral action were made meaningful through one another, and thus highlighted the state's failure to make entrepreneurial activity significant in the political way that proletarian labor once did. While public opinion and the media saw *chuanxiao* as the worst sort of commodification of personal relationships, what it sold was no less than an education in how to raise one's own moral quality through self-cultivation, in order to become a successful marketeer. *Chuanxiao* did the work of making explicit the links between moral and entrepreneurial success, amidst a barrage of rather vague state proclamations on civility. Let us now examine some of the ways in which this was done.

Becoming a Civilized Marketer

"You've come here to learn how to be a proper person (*xuehui zuoren*). We are selling characters, not products!"[11] Ms. Zhao, a forty-something schoolteacher from Datong in central China, was full of pride and enthusiasm as she shouted this comment to the audience below her. She was acting as a teacher-trainer in a potential training, one of the seminars offered by *chuanxiao* corporations around the country. Throughout the 1990s, hundreds of thousands of people taught and participated in similar trainings, where they learned to conceive of and develop their potential via explicit methods for cultivating new psychological, physical, and emotional senses of self. [12] Trainings taught participants how to buy and sell effectively but also, more importantly, as Zhao's statement suggests, how to negotiate the moral aspects of entrepreneurship. For according to *chuanxiao* rhetoric, it was impossible to succeed without being morally upright.

In cities and larger towns there were many opportunities for seeing direct sales and marketing done in person, at different companies, and by dozens of different networkers, but in smaller towns and villages where one or two people brought in the entire concept, product, and company, marketeers had to learn from each other. In the absence of fully staffed, fully legal representative offices, there was a variable mixture of "product distribution centers" (*fahuo dian*), "classrooms" (*ketang*), and individual homes. To a large extent, *chuanxiao* education in these kinds of places was arranged and even led by powerful local distributors. Not surprisingly, many people found it easier to imagine a stranger as an instrument for change than their cousin whom they'd known all their lives. Therefore, print, audio and video materials were especially important sources of information.

In addition to trainings and lectures such as those that occurred daily in "MLM city," there was a plethora of print, audio, and visual information on selling, distributed free or at low cost through companies, then reprinted and redistributed by individual networkers. These educational instruments supplemented face-to-face learning for would-be distributors and were most useful for people at two different stages of their *chuanxiao* experience: first, those who had successfully accumulated a growing network that they needed to manage and educate, and second, those just starting out in cities, towns, and villages where there were no official corporate offices and who therefore had few local opportunities for education. Mr. Gao, a former factory worker from a large town near Shenyang in the northeast, was a good example of the former. When I met him at a training in Tianjin, a city not far from Beijing, he was proudly heading up an active network of almost a thousand people. He took the responsibilities and privileges of seniority very seriously, constantly trying to increase his knowledge in order to better teach his downlines. He took advantage of trainings near and far, but also found printed materials important in his work. As his network increased in size, he told me, so did his recognition of his own deficiencies in the areas of management and human relations. He was, in effect, running his own thousand-person company, with no formal training in business, economics, or marketing. Distributors like Mr. Gao, with plenty of disposable income, consumed large quantities of the books and monthly journals that targeted the *chuanxiao* audience.

Didactic multilevel marketing texts can be read in multiple ways: as ideal visions of what *chuanxiao* could do, as a series of answers to unspoken questions, as indicators of what networkers needed most to sell the practice, and perhaps most interestingly as road maps to the concept of improving one's quality for success in the market. There is much rich material in such texts; here I use them as a source of data on the centrality of self-cultivation in *chuanxiao*. An examination of the parameters of *chuanxiao*'s promised moral education has much to tell us about how state-constructed notions of quality and civility are subject to alternative interpretations. As we see in *chuanxiao*, these interpretations borrow from the authority of state discourse in order to establish themselves as authoritative institutions capable of generating moral, financial, and maybe, eventually, even political fealty.

Cultivating a Correct Mindset

In texts as in oral narratives, the notion of self-cultivation in *chuanxiao* is best apprehended through two terms: *xintai* (mindset) and *zuoren* (upright conduct). The first, *xintai*, means literally the "attitude" (*tai*) of the heart, mind, feeling, or intention (*xin*). In a decade in China, I had never noticed this word until I began my research on *chuanxiao*, where it was ubiquitous. *Xintai* is not listed in the standard mainland Chinese-English dictionary published in 1987 (indicating perhaps that it was not in common usage prior to the 1990s), but a 1993 mainland dictionary translates it as "psychology." As used in *chuanxiao*, a more accurate translation would be "mindset." *Xintai* constituted the part of individual consciousness that must be brought under control, regulated, and adjusted in order to succeed in the practice of *chuanxiao*. In fact, one of the industry's central, oft-repeated claims was that all you had to do was have the correct *xintai* and your success would be guaranteed. The difficulty of managing one's *xintai* is explicitly defined as *the* central problem of becoming a marketer.

The second important term is *zuoren*: literally, *zuo* (to make, produce, manufacture; to do, engage in; to be, to become) and *ren*, or person/human. The 1993 Shanghai Jiaotong University dictionary translates *zuoren* as "conduct oneself; behave; be an upright person." This Confucian phrase clearly emphasizes the fashioning or making of the decent self and is commonly heard in everyday usage outside of *chuanxiao* in the context of ethical and moral behavior. Network marketers were taught what correct *xintai* looked like and from this were supposed to gain a knowledge of how to *zuoren*— how to be and act like a decent human being. In the world of *zuoren*, humanity is not a universal attribute but rather something that can and should be learned, maintained, and evaluated by others.

I will first explore *xintai* through excerpts from a *chuanxiao* company manual that provided instructions on how to run an NDO meeting. NDO stood for "New Distributor Opportunity" sales sessions, which were always referred to by the English acronym. These corporate materials were prepared specifically for uplines who needed to educate their newly recruited distributors. In theory, NDOs were separate from the OPP, or "Opportunity" classes that were geared specifically for recruitment. In function, NDOs often merged with OPPs, as did potential trainings and product information sessions. Every *chuanxiao* experience was also a lesson in recruitment—but NDOs were especially set apart for new distributors to learn the basics of sales and marketing.

The following excerpt is part of an NDO outline offered to session leaders: in effect, a guide for the guides, or instructions on how to instruct others who had recently joined the company. On the first page, under the title "Sharing—Mindset and Concepts" and the subtitle "How to Take Your First Steps in MLM," the manual sets out the two goals for an NDO:

It is extremely important to establish a good mindset. This is the most difficult thing to resolve in *chuanxiao*.
The second key issue is to guide downlines in changing their perspectives.

New members did not need to be convinced of the importance of a correct mindset for success; this paradigm made sense within an older framework of labor and consciousness, even for younger participants. The difficulty was in establishing this correct mindset. Instructors were reminded here of the importance of their own mindset in instructing others. They were to act as a moral example, much in the manner of model workers in earlier political campaigns or social superiors in the Confucian mandate to act as models of morality for their inferiors.[13]

Just as in public discussions of quality and civility, an individual's "mindset" was posited as the central obstacle to market success, rather than class, gender, ethnicity, education, social connections, finances, or a host of other factors. In light of this, the new recruits' job was to master their own mind by first preparing it for study. "Returning the mind to zero," adopting the mindset of a five-year-old child, and making the mind an "empty glass" were some of the most commonly suggested techniques for self-preparation. As in earlier Maoist theories of the subject, subject-making began with the enlistment of individuals in the project of their own transformation.

The text goes on to explain what to teach new members about how mindset adjustment can be achieved:

> How to adjust the attitude: Eliminate the interference and worries of traditional consciousness; make yourself think of nothing at all, just emptiness; calm down completely; accept new concepts, new marketing ideas, new forms of marketing; reconsider, re-arrange your life, your study and your work; accept new information; don't accept any interference. The mental state at this moment is . . . like that of a Buddhist.[14] It is extremely difficult to reach. Through study, feeling, and practice, one can gradually adjust the mindset to the optimum condition. (Wuhan Xintian Baojianpin n.d.)

Maoist-era subjects had to break through "feudal consciousness" to experience themselves as socialist citizens. Today "traditional consciousness"—referring, ironically, to the consciousness and attitudes toward work inculcated by what was implicitly interpreted in *chuanxiao* discourse as a failed socialism—appears as psychological "interference" in successful self-cultivation.

"Once you have this mindset," the text told the NDO leader, "you'll never refuse new things again, or make snap judgments against things." Not refusing "new things," accepting new marketing techniques, and suspending judgment meant, of course, joining the network and buying the company's various products. It is not surprising that *chuanxiao* corporations would idealize this "mindset." This kind of teaching could work well in the production of compliant, even gullible network members, but it also worked well for the individuals who were willing to change themselves as effectively and quickly as possible. Indeed, the successful reproduction of this paradigm *could* lead to at least a modicum of success within the network, since one is never so persuasive as when one truly believes.

Print and oral narratives established the relationship between market success and a virtuous mindset characterized by the willingness to uncritically accept new practices and products, an interest in learning, the desire to help others achieve success, and the tenacity to stand up to the failure and condemnation one would certainly meet with along the way. The category of the bad mindset contained all the evils of market competition: stealing others' recruits, stealing people's bonuses, using downlines solely for recruitment fees and then never helping them achieve their goals, cheating, lying, fraud, misrepresentation of products or company backgrounds or bonus systems, gossip, slander—in short, the things that the most successful people had done to make it to the top of giant networks, the things that many of the companies did to make a profit. *Xintai* was used to evaluate someone's business practices as fair or unfair. One top distributor I knew constantly invoked the good mindset of the company's CEO as the reason that she chose to keep her large network with that company, rather than move it to another. When she eventually did leave for another more profitable firm, she explained that she had discovered that the CEO had been hiding an incorrect mindset all along.

Becoming Moral Through Marketing

Manuals also addressed the issue of correct moral conduct, or *zuoren*. As one excerpt stated, "*Chuanxiao* is the work of correct conduct [*zuoren de gongzuo*], and yet it is extremely difficult to change people's attitudes and perspectives" (Wuhan Xintian Baojianpin n.d.). In general, however, *zuoren* was articulated most clearly in trainings and lectures rather than in print. Stories of the moral transformations brought on by MLM trainings were legion. "You should have been at the last training in Datong," a teacher-trainer once told me:

> It was amazing. A young man who had just gotten out of prison really got into it. He told us a story about how his mother used to bring him food and

clothing in prison, and then stand outside the windows in the cold and rain so he could see her there, waiting for him. For the first time in his life, he understood the meaning of filial piety, and he promised he was going to go home, fall on his knees in front of his mother, and beg her forgiveness. He gave [the head trainer] so many kowtows that his forehead was bleeding. It was great!

At a Beijing-based company whose head lecturer was an experienced multilevel marketer from Taiwan, the rehabilitation of a wayward son was documented in photographs on the walls of the meeting room, while all the distributors used the story in their sales pitches. The man's mother was in her fifties, a heavyset woman with dark red hair who showed little interest in talking to a foreign anthropologist about her experiences. Her son was downright suspicious of me. But others were happy to tell me their tale. Her husband had left them when the boy was small, and as a result the child grew up wild and violent. He used to beat his mother, steal her money, and refuse to do honest work. One day she attended one of Mr. Wang's *chuanxiao* potential trainings and immediately saw that if she could convince her son to come in, she might have a chance of changing him. And in fact that is exactly what happened. Working as a team, with a network of several hundred people below them, they were held up as living proof of the power of *chuanxiao*'s moral message to transform recalcitrant social agents.

The process of transforming attitudes and perspectives, and the transmission of this process, was indeed a most desirable commodity—a product that promised that no matter who you were, all you had to do was try to think the right thoughts and success would be yours. It echoed a neoliberal rhetoric that placed the locus of success or failure squarely on the individual's capacity for moral change, thereby naturalizing the growing social inequalities. What I am most concerned with in this chapter, however, is how the focus on individual consciousness (through concepts like mindset and conduct) resonated with an older conceptual template in which labor and virtue were mutually constitutive—and in which the ability to define them was a large part of the basis of political authority.

As I have indicated above, the *chuanxiao* emphasis on the importance of self-improvement and proper morals to profit-generating activities echoed the state's position. In fact, many industry leaders, including some state intellectuals, saw *chuanxiao* as an answer to the very problem of how to channel entrepreneurial impulses into correct actions. From these people's perspective, *chuanxiao* could be used as a didactic tool for the raising of national quality, as a crucial aid to China's economic development. Consider the following excerpt from the state-run industry journal, *Direct Selling Review* (*Chuanxiao yanjiu*).

In reality, the majority of Chinese consumers are lacking in education, not only in consumption but in many other ways as well. For instance, as soon as they leave school they feel that education has nothing to do with them. . . . Therefore, the continuing adult education that has been so well established in other countries has met with great difficulties in China. . . . The *chuanxiao* industry has brought new changes. Its focus on education of all sorts such as consumers' consumption education, management skills education, and personal cultivation is a fresh approach for those participating in direct sales. It also broadens consumers' horizons. (Shang 1996)

The editors of the journal, which was published by a research institute under the auspices of the national-level Department of Industry and Commerce, often shared with me their excitement about the educational value of MLM. "Learn how to conduct yourself properly and you will have learned success," stated one front-page editorial ("Study: Another Value of MLM" 1997). *Chuanxiao* was the answer to the question: How can Chinese workers raise their quality, in order to enable the nation to develop more quickly? And yet despite its narratives of individual responsibility, morality, and social cohesion—which we might think the state would find attractive—*chuanxiao* was seen as problematic. It created hundreds of thousands of organized entrepreneurs whose sense of the moral significance of their work derived from the corporation rather than the Party.

Civilizing the Market

Chuanxiao taught participants how to become moral through marketing. Equally important, it sanitized the process of selling, promising an environment of virtuous commercial activity that protected its members from a hostile external commercial world. For many marketers, *chuanxiao* was an opportunity to escape the problems of what was commonly referred to as "traditional business" (*chuantong shengyi*). Many public testimonies began with the phrase, "I used to be in traditional business." In this popular narrative, *chuanxiao* was a kinder, gentler, more inclusive and egalitarian kind of entrepreneurial practice. It gave one the chance to succeed "on one's own," unlike traditional business, which excluded many people by being entirely dependent on social connections and access to start-up funds. (The irony, of course, is that success in *chuanxiao* was entirely dependent on social connections and access to start-up funds.) The appeal lay in the fact that supposedly anyone could succeed—even those without reserves of cultural or political capital. In one sense, *chuanxiao* appeared to offer a sanctuary for those who might otherwise have had trouble positioning themselves comfortably or honorably within the national rhetoric of civility and market success. While little about the industry was explicitly politically oppositional, it was no surprise that the prospect of an alternative authority on morality and labor was unacceptable to the CCP.

This chapter begins with a description of the 1998 state ban on the Chinese multilevel marketing industry, followed by a discussion of the ways that proletarian labor, revolutionary consciousness, and political virtue were configured under Mao. This conceptual model still shapes contemporary understandings of labor, self-cultivation, and virtue today. The notion that virtue produces and is produced by participation in certain categories of work is still visible in official narratives of the centrality of civility and quality in the national marketization project. Yet the state has not been able to clarify the political significance of morally correct entrepreneurship. *Chuanxiao*, more than any other social institution in the 1990s, presented a coherent alternative vision of morality and the market. As I have suggested above, central *chuanxiao* principles such as *xintai* and *zuoren* modeled the state's position on self-cultivation and work, recouping the older Maoist-era discourse on labor. But *chuanxiao* displaced the glories formerly associated with labor performed for wages from the state onto entrepreneurial work performed for commissions from a transnational company. Within the older discursive template, authorship of the discourse on virtue and labor was an inherently political move; therefore, *chuanxiao* narratives and practices were rightly perceived as a largely indirect challenge to state authority. The challenge, and the response, laid bare the thorny problem of what kinds of political participation can be expected or achieved in the transition from socialist proletariat to market socialist entrepreneur.

Notes

1. The industry's exemplar is the Amway corporation.
2. However, as we see in other countries as well, this type of operation could never have existed without a considerable amount of official support at the provincial level or higher.
3. These manuals offered such culturally specific hints as, "Genghis Khan was able to conquer Europe because he firmly believed 'I am the best'" (*Nanfang zhoumo*, 1/16/98).
4. These estimates are provided by researchers Li Shaohua and Yang Qian, deputy editor and chief editor respectively of the Beijing Commercial Management Cadre Institute's now-defunct journal, *Chuanxiao yanjiu* (Direct Selling Review).
5. In 1997 most urbanites had at least heard of *chuanxiao*, and many had friends or family who had tried it if they had not themselves. Very few who had tried it felt that it was immoral, only that they were not suited for it. More often it was those who had never been tempted who felt most indignant.

6. The actual distribution of products relied heavily on distributor labor. The company would ship the product out to higher-ranking network members who would take it upon themselves to deliver it to their downlines or downlines would travel, often for many hours, to pick up products. If distributors were fortunate enough to live in a major city, they might also be able to get the product at branch offices.

7. This was a major blow to several of China's largest direct marketing companies, all American: Mary Kay, Avon, Tupperware, and Amway. The ban's effect on these giants had previously been protested by American officials. The negotiating team of U.S. Trade Representative Charlene Barshefsky, herself due to arrive in Beijing the day after the ban was announced, spent much of the day before her arrival pressing Chinese officials to find a solution that would not harm the American companies.

8. In the end, a total of sixty-four foreign direct sales businesses were allowed to "change their working patterns" from direct sales to retailing, and were granted licenses to operate in January 1999 ("Foreign Direct Sales Firms" 1999). Amway, for one, has been allowed to "restructure" its marketing system, but conversations with distributors suggest that their business operates much as it did before the ban. It doubled its sales in the 1999–2000 year, generating US$241.5 million ("Amway China 1999–2000"). To my knowledge, restructuring was not an option for domestic firms. While I have been unable to follow up on the fates of many of the companies and marketers with whom I worked, a December 1999 article in the *China Economic Times* reported that MLM firms in Hebei continued to operate "covertly" ("Pyramid Sales in Langfang City" 1999). The article warned that the state ban had resulted in such companies going underground, which made it even more difficult for the state to monitor or regulate them. Several other companies once active on the mainland are now selling their products to American audiences.

9. Another term for this might be "political citizenship" as used by Wen-hsin Yeh 1997: 71.

10. The relationships between the concepts of quality (*suzhi*), civilization (*wenming*), and culture (*wenhua*) are far too complex to address in this paper. For pertinent discussion, see Rofel (1998), Anagnost (1997), and Hoffman (2001). See also Rofel (1999: 451-474) on the notion of quality in the cultural construction of urban Chinese male homosexuality.

11. Originally: "*Women maide shi renge, er bu shi chanpin.*"

12. See Jeffery (2001b) for further discussion of training seminars.

13. As with the concept of self-cultivation and rectification, the idea of a superior serving as a moral example has been central in Confucian ethics for more than 2,000 years. The Confucian way of governance included the "ideal that it is a nobleman's privileged responsibility to set the world in order by assuming a position of leadership and rendering public service to society" (Chang 1996: 73). In a more recent and perhaps more relevant historical instance, Yeh notes that the Bank of China in 1930s Shanghai was managed with a neo-Confucian "philosophy [that] placed heavy emphasis on the character and behavior of individual employees," and "top leaders were not merely executive administrators . . . but also moral leaders and professional teachers whose conduct and standards were to set an example for the average employee" (Yeh 1997: 65).

14. Such references to Buddhism were fairly common in written and oral narratives, but were by no means central to the mainland MLM identity. I would guess that reworked "Buddhist" philosophies play a much larger role in Taiwan and Hong Kong,

where Buddhism is more a part of everyday life for many people. While there is a resurgence of Buddhist belief and interest in mainland China, it remains, I would argue, an important though still peripheral factor in the cultural construction of the market.

Bibliography

"Amway China 1999–00. Turnover Seen at $241.5 Million." 2000. Asia Pulse Pte Limited. November 3.

Anagnost, Ann. 1997. *National Past-times: Narrative, Representation and Power in Modern China.* Durham, NC: Duke University Press.

Butterfield, Stephen. 1985. *Amway: The Cult of Free Enterprise.* Boston: South End Press.

Chang Hao. 1996. "The Intellectual Heritage of the Confucian Ideal of *Ching-shih.*" In Tu Wei-ming, ed., *Confucian Traditions in East Asian Modernity.* Cambridge: Harvard University Press, pp. 72–91.

Fewsmith, Joseph. 1995. "Neoconservatism and the End of the Dengist Era." *Asian Survey* 35 (7): 635–651.

"Foreign Direct Sales Firms Get License for Salesman." 1999. *China Business Information Network.* January 13. www.getfacts.com.amyway.in_the_news/china_must_retail.

Hershatter, Gail. 1993. "The Subaltern Speaks Back: Reflections on Subaltern Theory and Chinese History." *positions: East Asia cultures critique* 1 (1): 103–130.

Hinton, William. 1966. *Fanshen: A Documentary of Revolution in a Chinese Village.* New York: Vintage Books.

Hoffman, Lisa. 2001. " 'Desire-Ability' and Discipline in Dalian: Social Constructions of Labor Markets for College Graduate." In Chen et al., *Ethnographies of the Urban in 1900s China.* Durham, NC: Duke University Press.

Jeffery, Lyn. 2001a. "Selling Selves: Meanings of the Market in the People's Republic." Doctoral dissertation, University of California, Santa Cruz.

———. 2001b. "Place and Transnational Marketing Networks in the PRC." In Chen et al., *Ethnographies of the Urban in 1900s China.* Durham, NC: Duke University Press.

Kelly, David. 1991. "Chinese Marxism Since Tiananmen: Between Evaporation and Dismemberment." In David Goodman and Gerald Segal, eds., *China in the Nineties.* Oxford: Clarendon Press.

Meisner, Maurice. 1982. *Marxism, Maoism and Utopianism.* Madison: University of Wisconsin Press.

Misra, Kalpana. 1998. *From Post-Maoism to Post-Marxism: The Erosion of Official Ideology in Deng's China.* New York: Routledge.

Perry, Elizabeth. 1997. "From Native Place to Workplace: Labor Origins and Outcomes of China's *Danwei* System." In Xiaobo Lu and Elizabeth Perry, eds., *Danwei: The Changing Chinese Workplace in Historical and Comparative Perspective.* Armonk, NY: M.E. Sharpe, pp. 42–59.

"Pyramid Sales in Langfang City Flourish Again." 1999. *China Economic Times,* December 11, p. 1.

Rickett, Allyn and Adele. 1957. *Prisoners of Liberation.* New York: Cameron Associates.

Rofel, Lisa. 1998. *Other Modernities: Gendered Yearnings in China After Socialism.* Berkeley: University of California Press.

————. 1999. "Qualities of Desire: Imagining Gay Identity in China." *GLQ* 5 (4): 451–474.

Shang Yan. 1996. "Cleaning Up MLM Corporate Classrooms." *Chuanxiao Yanjiu* (Direct Selling Review) 1 (January): 29–30.

Sun Baoluo and Guo Guo song, "Yige Peiyang pianzi de tiantang (A Con Artist Training Heaven). Nanyang Zhouno (Southern Weekend). January 16, 1998.

"Study: Another Value of MLM." 1998. *Chuanxiao Yanjiu* (Direct Selling Review). 3 (March): 1.

Wuhan Xintian Baojianpin, Inc. n.d. *Jingxiaoshang NDO xunlian jiangyi* (Distributor NDO Training Teaching Materials). Wuhan: China.

Yeh, Wen-hsin. 1997. "The Republican Origins of the *Danwei*: The Case of Shanghai's Bank of China." In Xiaobo Lu and Elizabeth Perry, eds. *Danwei: The Changing Chinese Workplace in Historical and Comparative Perspective*. Armonk, NY: M.E. Sharpe, pp. 60–88.

Zhao, Shilong. 1998. "Six Hostages Taken in Demand for Refund and Expenses: Pingtang MLM Guests Wander Back to Their Villages with Broken Dreams." *Nanfang Zhoumo* May 1.

Zhongguo huagongbao zhoukan (China Chemical Industry Weekly). 1998. May 8.

Index

Abbott, Andrew, 107
Acs, Zoltan, 40
Administrative inspections, transaction costs of, 196–197
Adris protection company, 95
Age, self employment and, 7, 13, 16, 18, 24, 31
Aleks-Zapad private security company, 88
Amihud, Y., 162
Anagnost, Ann, 334, 335
Andreyev, N., 204
Anheier, Helmut K., 258, 259
Anli village, Henan, China, 74
Anthropological ethnographic methods, 280–281
Apartment privatization, 14, 17
Arbitration courts, in Russia, 202–203, 211
Argus private security company, 88, 95
Arum, Richard, 6, 7, 10
Árvay, János, 40
Aslund, Anders, 4, 11
Asset restructuring, 233–234
Auditing services, transaction cost of, 206– 207
Audretsch, David B., 40
Azudová, L'ubica, 42

Bakatin, Vadim, 84
Bakhtin, Mikhail, 279, 317n.3
Baltik-Escort protection company, 99
Banasiński, Cesary, 105

Banka Bohemia, 227, 229
Banks
    cashing operations of, 298–299
    conciliation process in, 237–238, 241–242
    restructuring, 227, 229
Barley, Stephen R., 105, 107
Barnard, Chester, 163
Barrs Protection company, 95
Barter exchanges and offsets, 194
Bartlett, David L., 50
Baum, Joel A.C., 106
Becker, David G., 140
Begly, T.N., 162
Benáček, Vladimir, 40, 48
Benson, Elżbieta W., xviii, 104–129, 108
Beveridge, Andrew A., 258, 261
Bian, Yanjie, 9
Biernat, Stanislaw, 105
Birch, David L., 4
Blasi, Joseph R., 4
Bobkov, Philip, 87
Bohatá, Marie, 47
Bonnell, Victoria E., xiii-xxii
Bourdieu, Pierre, 258, 259
Bowman, N., 162, 163
Boycko, Maxim, 4
Boyd, D.P., 162
Brainerd, Elizabeth, 3
Brazil, democratization in, 145
Brecher, Richard, 135
Bribes, as transaction cost, 195–199